Global Politics of Regionalism

GLOBAL POLITICS OF REGIONALISM

Theory and Practice

Edited by
Mary Farrell, Björn Hettne,
and Luk Van Langenhove

Pluto Press

LONDON • ANN ARBOR, MI

First published 2005 by Pluto Press
345 Archway Road, London N6 5AA
and 839 Greene Street, Ann Arbor, MI 48106

www.plutobooks.com

British Library Cataloguing in Publication Data
A catalogue record for this book is available from the British Library

ISBN   978 0 7453 2262 9 paperback

Library of Congress Cataloging-in-Publication Data

Global politics of regionalism : an introduction / edited by Mary Farrell, Björn Hettne, and Luk Van Langenhove.
     p. cm.
   Includes bibliographical references.
   ISBN 0–7453–2263–8 (hardback) — ISBN 0–7453–2262–X (pbk.)
   1. Regionalism (International organization) I. Farrell, Mary, 1956– II. Hettne, Björn, 1939– III. Langenhove, Luk Van.
   JZ5330.G56 2005
   327.1—dc22

                                                                                  2005006046

10   9   8   7   6   5   4   3   2   1

Designed and produced for Pluto Press by
Chase Publishing Services Ltd, Fortescue, Sidmouth, EX10 9QG, England
Typeset from disk by Stanford DTP Services, Northampton, England
Printed on demand in the EU by
CPI Antony Rowe, Chippenham and Eastbourne, England

Contents

PART THREE   MAPPING REGIONAL APPROACHES

PART FOUR   CONCLUSION

Preface

In the contemporary world where so much academic literature, political debate, popular discourse and even media attention is devoted to the topic of globalisation, it seems almost essential to swim against the tide and call attention to other phenomena taking place all around the world. Despite the seeming inevitability of the forces of globalisation, it is wise to take a critical look at such processes and to reflect upon alternative movements and tendencies that are emerging, or strengthening, below the global level. That is what this book aims to do.

The decade of the 1990s witnessed a resurgence of interest in regionalism, and the momentum generated by regional integration processes in Asia, Africa and the Americas suggested that the phenomenon was not confined to the European Union. Of course, some cases suggest the increased level of regional activity and cooperation represents a defence or reaction to globalisation, and an attempt by governments to collectively claw back some autonomy over decision-making and to manage both the positive and negative aspects of greater international independence. However, increased interdependence has been around for a while, and certainly since the 1970s, so it is reasonable to take a detailed look at developments in the respective regions and to examine the nature of these developments and the rationale behind them.

With the benefit of a group of leading specialists in the field of regionalism, and using a number of disciplinary perspectives to elaborate on the theoretical perspectives that have guided the research community towards a deeper understanding of the subject matter, this volume provides an insight into the rich experience of regionalism and its different forms across the globe. The concern is to draw out the nuances of distinctive approaches to regional cooperation, and to highlight both what is particular and the generalising tendencies. Taking this approach, we find out why regionalism in Africa has not made the same progress as in other parts of the world, so far at any rate; and we find out that in the North American experience integration processes are constructing a *de facto* region, even though nobody calls it a region.

In the Middle East, where regional cooperation might be expected to foster positive welfare effects, endemic problems hinder progress on cooperation; while in South Asia, the contradictory conditions in the region leave an indelible mark on cooperative processes. Taking a different approach, some issue areas naturally lend themselves to regional cooperation, and have formed the basis for enhanced regionalism. Other issue areas almost demand a regional response, and security is one such case. The book looks both at cases of regionalism, and at a selected number of issue areas typical of contemporary regionalism.

This book is the result of a project that was initiated by the United Nations University (UNU) and forms part of a long tradition of interest in the field of regional integration. In 1996, the UNU World Institute for Development Economics Research (UNU-WIDER) commissioned a large research project on the topic of regionalism, the outcome of which was the five-volume series Studies in the New Regionalism under the leadership of Björn Hettne at the Department of Peace and Development Research at Göteborg University. The new regionalism approach is based upon the assumption that the multi-dimensionality of contemporary processes warrants a new type of analysis, which transcends the dominant theories of regional integration. Under the new regionalism approach, integration is conceptualised as a multi-dimensional and socially constructed phenomenon, where cooperation occurs across economic, political, security, environment and development areas.

In 2001, a new UNU research and training centre (UNU-CRIS) was set up in Bruges, Belgium, focused upon comparative regional integration studies. The goal of UNU-CRIS is to promote policy-relevant knowledge about new and evolving forms of regional governance and cooperation. Research at UNU-CRIS is directed at (i) monitoring regional integration; (ii) exploring relations between regional integration and such issues as security, trade, governance, and development, and (iii) advancing capacity development for regional integration initiatives.

At the start of the twenty-first century, the world is witness to new influences on the nation-state and contemporary challenges have prompted many analysts to suggest that we may be witnessing a transition from the classical Westphalian order to a world order where regional organisations will play an important role in global governance. This volume is the result of a UNU-CRIS/PADRIGU project to explore some of the contemporary developments in regionalism and to identify key questions for international relations arising out of the phenomena and observable processes in different parts of the world, and the implications for the nature of an evolving world order. Nine scholars affiliated to UNU-CRIS and/or PADRIGU together with thirteen other leading scholars in the field, embracing a variety of disciplinary perspectives, have contributed to this volume and to a workshop held in Bruges in 2004 where first drafts of the chapters were presented and discussed.

The editors would very much like to extend their gratitude to the contributors, all of whom were exemplary in their commitment to this project, and good-naturedly responded to the various editorial requests while keeping to the respective deadlines. We would also like to thank most sincerely the staff at Pluto Press for accepting the proposal and guiding the project throughout. Colleagues at both UNU-CRIS and PADRIGU provided a springboard for much thought-provoking discussion and new ideas. Finally, warm thanks to Kim Reynvoet, Sabrina Vanstechelman, and Pascale Vantorre for typing and administrative support given with customary cheerful efficiency.

Mary Farrell
Björn Hettne
Luk Van Langenhove

List of Abbreviations

ABF	Asian Bond Fund
ACP	Countries of Africa, Caribbean and the Pacific
AEC	African Economic Community
AFTA	ASEAN Free Trade Area
AMF	Asian Monetary Fund
AMU	Arab Maghreb Union
APEC	Asia-Pacific Economic Cooperation
ARF	ASEAN Regional Forum
ASA	ASEAN Swap Arrangement; Association of Southeast Asia
ASEAN	Association of Southeast Asian Nations
ASEAN+1	ASEAN, with India
ASEAN+3	ASEAN, with China, Japan and South Korea
ASEAN+5	ASEAN, with Indonesia, Malaysia, the Philippines, Singapore and Thailand
ASEM	Asia–Europe Meeting
AU	African Union
AWC	Augmented Washington Consensus
BCEAO	Banque centrale des Etats de l'Afrique de l'ouest
BEAC	Banque des Etats d'Afrique Centrale
BECC	Border Environment Cooperation Commission
BENELUX	Belgium–Netherlands–Luxembourg
BIMSTEC	Bangladesh, India, Myanmar, Sri Lanka and Thailand Economic Cooperation
BLSN	Botswana, Lesotho, Swaziland, Namibia
BSA	bilateral swap agreements
CACM	Central American Common Market
CAFTA	China–ASEAN Free Trade Area
CAN	Comunidad Andina
CARICOM	Caribbean Common Market
CEAO	Communauté Economique de l'Afrique de l'ouest
CEMAC	Communauté Economique et Monétaire d'Afrique Centrale
CEN-SAD	Community of Sahelian-Saharan States

CFA	Communauté Financière Africaine
CICIR	China Institute of Contemporary International Relations
CIS	Commonwealth of Independent States
CM	common market
CMI	Chiang Mai Initiative
COMECON	Council for Mutual Economic Cooperation
COMESA	Common Market for East and Southern Africa
CoR	Committee of the Regions
CRIS	Comparative Regional Integration Studies
CSCE	Conference on Security and Cooperation in Europe
CU	customs union
DBSA	Development Bank of Southern Africa
DC	development corridor
DRC	Democratic Republic of Congo
DSB	dispute settlement body
EAC	East African Community
EC	European Commission
ECB	European Central Bank
ECAS	European Citizens Action Service
ECCAS	Economic Community of Central African States
ECCB	Eastern Caribbean Central Bank
ECJ	European Court of Justice
ECO	Economic Cooperation Organisation
ECOMOG	ECOWAS Monitoring Group
ECOWAS	Economic Community of West African States
ECSC	European Coal and Steel Community
EEA	European Economic Area
EEC	European Economic Community
EMS	European monetary system
EMU	European monetary union; economic and monetary union
ERM	Exchange Rate Mechanism
ESCB	European System of Central Banks
EU	European Union
FDI	foreign direct investment
FTA	free trade area
FTAA	Free Trade Area of the Americas
GATT	General Agreement on Tariffs and Trade

GCC   Gulf Cooperation Council
GDP   gross domestic product
GMS   Greater Mekong Sub-region

HDR   Human Development Report

IDB   Inter-American Development Bank
IGAD   Intergovernmental Authority on Development
IGADD   Intergovernmental Authority on Drought and
               Development
IGO   intergovernmental organisation
IIT   intra-industry trade
ILO   International Labour Organisation
IMF   International Monetary Fund
IOC-ARC   Indian Ocean Rim Association for Regional
               Cooperation

MDC   Maputo Development Corridor
MEDB   Middle East Development Bank
MENA   Middle East and North Africa
MEP   Member of European Parliament
MEPI   Middle East Partnership Initiative
Mercosur   Mercado Común Del Sur/Southern Cone Common
               Market
MFN   most-favoured nation
MGC   Mekong–Gange Cooperation
MNC   multinational corporation
MNE   multinational enterprise
MU   monetary union

NADBank   BankNorth American Development Bank
NAFTA   North American Free Trade Agreement
NATO   North Atlantic Treaty Organisation
NEPAD   New Partnership for Africa's Development
NGO   non-governmental organisation
NIPEO   new international political and economic order

OAS   Organisation of American States
OAU   Organisation of African Unity
OCA   optimum currency area
OECD   Organisation for Economic Cooperation and
               Development
OECS   Organisation of East Caribbean States

OIC	Organisation of Islamic Conferences
OPEC	Organisation of Petroleum Exporting Countries
OSCE	Organisation for Security and Cooperation in Europe
PADRIGU	Peace and Development Research Institute Göteborg University
PLO	Palestine Liberation Organisation
PSC	Peace and Security Council
REC	Regional Economic Community
SAARC	South Asian Association for Regional Cooperation
SACU	South African Customs Union
SADC	Southern African Development Coordination
SADCC	Southern African Development Coordination Conference
SAFTA	South Asian Free Trade Agreement
SAGQ	South Asian Growth Quadrangle
SAPTA	South Asian Preferential Trading Agreement
SAR	Special Administrative Region
SCO	Shanghai Cooperation Organisation; Security Cooperation Organisation
SDI	spatial development initiative
SEATO	Southeast Asian Treaty Organisation
SIJORI	Singapore, the Jahore province of Malaysia, and Riau province of Indonesia (or, Southern Growth Triangle)
SMC	Standing Mediation Committee
TRIPS	trade-related intellectual property rights
UEMOA	Union Economique et Monétaire de l'Ouest africain
UN	United Nations
UNDP	United Nations Development Programme
UPA	United Progressive Alliance
UNU	United Nations University
UNU-WIDER	UNU World Institute for Development Economics Research
WAEMU	West African Economic and Monetary Union
WC	Washington Consensus
WTO	World Trade Organisation
ZOFPAN	Zone of Freedom, Peace and Neutrality

1
The Global Politics of Regionalism: An Introduction

Mary Farrell

The early years of the twenty-first century have witnessed an intensification in regionalism across the globe. Just over a decade after one of the late twentieth century's defining moments, the collapse of the Soviet Union and the end of the Cold War, the contemporary world is characterised by a dual movement of integration and fragmentation. With the end of the former Soviet empire and the collapse of one of the post-war superpowers, in its wake came new states moving towards democracy, some by accession to the European Union (EU).

Elsewhere, renewed interest in regionalism has seen even reluctant actors move towards deeper cooperative arrangements and enhanced integration with neighbouring countries through either formal or informal institutional frameworks. One example of a region that overcame its historical reticence towards cooperative decision-making and shared sovereignty is that of the ASEAN region (Association of Southeast Asian Nations) – motivated in part by economic difficulties that many of the member countries experienced in the wake of the 1997 financial crisis. In Africa, similar moves were underway across a continent that had flirted with regional cooperation for over three decades and during this time had seen the overlapping membership of many countries in several regional organisations fail to achieve economic development in what remained the world's most impoverished region.

In the face of growing poverty, the spread of diseases such as AIDS and malaria, and almost total marginalisation in the world economy, donor aid fatigue and the general endorsement of neoliberal economic policies on the part of the international institutions, a number of African leaders began to recognise the virtue of regional and sub-regional cooperation as a possible route out of the malaise that affected the entire continent. Thus, the idea of pan-African unity put forward by Kwame Nkrumah, Ghana's first post-independence leader, was re-endorsed once more in the vision of an African Union with the Treaty signed in 2001. Almost simultaneously, the announcement of the New Partnership for Africa's Development (NEPAD) suggested a rush towards cooperation among the African countries that was far removed from the leisurely pace of political and economic interaction in the wake of independence. Suddenly, the continent was hit by a spate of new initiatives, and the revival of dormant agreements as the African countries awoke to the realisation that globalisation had not brought any discernible benefits to either individual countries or the continent at large. The best option available seemed to lie with collective action in the form of enhanced regional integration, to foster formal, institutionalised cooperation alongside the informal cross-border initiatives emerging through public and/or private activity under micro-regionalism.

This volume starts from two premises. The first one is that regionalism is a response to globalisation and a reaction to the diverse aspects of global processes in their entirety. As indicated in much of the literature, globalisation is a many-faceted phenomenon, eliciting both positive and negative impacts for countries, and the latter have the opportunity to respond through regionalism as both a defensive and an offensive strategy.

The second premise is based upon the recognition that regionalism emerges from the internal dynamics of the region, and the motivations and strategies of regional actors. Just as there are many models of regionalism around the world, with no dominant paradigm to which all countries and regions subscribe, so too we can find a degree of diversity in how regionalist processes are understood and conceptualised in the literature. As Louise Fawcett has suggested, 'there is no commonly accepted view of the "the new regionalism" nor indeed of its place in any evolving international order. The debate on regionalism remains very much an open one' (Fawcett and Hurrell, 1995, 36).

Yet the regionalism processes so clearly evident in Europe, Asia and Africa did not suggest the generalisation of any particular model, least of all the European model which is often regarded as a benchmark for regional integration. As the chapters in Part Three of this volume clearly show, distinct patterns and forms of regionalism have emerged and continue to develop their own particular rhythm across the world. Shaped in part by the internal regional dynamics on the one hand, and on the other by external pressures such as globalisation, instability, security threats (both external and internal) and increased competition which affected the behaviour and strategies of both economic and political actors, regional actors sought solutions to common problems through collective actions and decision-making to foster enhanced regionalism.

One broad feature of regionalism discernible in the studies presented here is the diversity of practice that is evident in different parts of the world. A second consideration is the mixed record of success apparent in different regional groupings. An interesting and indeed intriguing question is why some countries fail to engage in successful cooperation, why some cases of regionalism make little progress beyond the initial stage of signing the treaty that is intended to form the basis of future interactions between the political and economic actors of the signatory states.

Related to the question of success or failure of regionalism are the attitudes towards cooperation by individual states, and the motivation to go ahead with this kind of policy or to reject it outright. Economic and political motivations certainly play their part in the actions of actors; however, the importance of identity and self-perception should also be recognised and this is underscored in several of the chapters in this volume (including those by Pastor, Slocum, and Zhang).

GLOBAL FORCES

Globalisation has become one of the most-talked about phenomena of the second half of the twentieth century. The theme has spawned almost an entire industry in itself as the academic community latched on to this phenomenon, catching the attention of such disciplines as economics, political economy, sociology, cultural theory, and a host of multidisciplinary analyses.

What were the causal forces, and the actual and potential effects of globalisation? These two key questions have been earnestly examined in the large (and still growing) volume of literature on globalisation. While the causes of globalisation are many and varied, there is a general consensus on the role that new technologies, the strategies of multinational corporations, and state policies and preferences for liberalisation have played as combined driving forces. The international institutions have also been instrumental in promoting globalisation, not least the programmes and policies of the International Monetary Fund and its sister organisation, the World Bank, together with the General Agreement on Tarrifs and Trade and its successor, the World Trade Organisation.

A third question, and ultimately the most important consideration, is how can governments and societies respond to globalisation? What are the options available to governments in a world where national boundaries are criss-crossed by mobile (and volatile) capital flows, by an increasing volume of trade (and the competition that comes with it), and by a growing influx of people from third countries, some in search of economic opportunities and others in flight from persecution, war or famine?

These flows of capital, trade and people characterise the contemporary phase of globalisation. For some countries, and some groups, the interconnectedness that results from international trade, global capital mobility, and the movement of people in search of new opportunities constitutes a positive outcome that is broadly welfare enhancing. However, there is another side to globalisation with less welcome effects – international activities (and the interconnectedness that we have referred to above) can be found in the less salubrious areas of transnational criminal activities, the drugs trade, people-trafficking, terrorism and illegal arms trafficking. The latter activities have been frequently associated with the weakening of national borders in general, and the limitations on the capacity of weak states in particular. In many of the latter, internal conflict and ethnic rivalry have added to national instability, while economic and political crises offered emigration as the only viable option for survival.

Although we can broadly identify the driving forces, and the architects of globalisation, it has become very clear that the processes of globalisation, once unleashed, have generated mixed results for countries at all levels of development. Not all groups and societies regard globalisation as the unmixed blessing its supporters would suggest. Recent years have seen critical opposition to globalisation growing, with voices being raised among social and consumer groups, environmentalists, certain business interests, and trade unions. Even states have come to regard globalisation with a degree of wariness, mindful of domestic interests clamouring for protection on the one hand, and of the actual or perceived threat to the state's autonomy on the other hand.

Since the world has been unable to construct a truly global governance system, one that is comprehensive in scope and with the capacity to manage and regulate (including the possession of a legal enforcement capability underpinned by political legitimacy), the states have turned to other forms of cooperation at the regional level in order to deal with common problems and shared interests.

In a world where the Westphalian state system faces a barrage of attacks to its sovereignty and authority, governments have come to view cooperative decision-making as a crucial means to strengthen that sovereignty and to exercise shared authority in the framework of regional cooperation. Almost simultaneously, non-state actors have also engaged in an extensive network of cross-border relations – in such diverse fields as economy, environment, society, education, and even healthcare. Mention has already been made of the non-legal interactions and criminal activities that operate on an increasingly international level, constructing international and global networks that are therefore beyond the jurisdiction of national legal systems and outside the reach of national law enforcement agencies.

Substantial cooperation has emerged among democratic countries, partly out of necessity and partly driven by the political strategies of the countries involved (Slaughter, 2004; Solingen, 1998). In the contemporary world, much of this cooperation is prompted by concerns over such issues as crime, terrorism and counter-terrorist policies. There is of course the risk that these issues come to dominate the international agenda to the exclusion of broader concerns related to human welfare.

Long before the events of 11 September 2001 provided the opportunity for the launch of an international agenda based upon one overriding concern, the fight against international terrorism (however ill-defined), governments, public officials and non-governmental actors were coming together across borders to solve common problems – in trade, financial regulation, peace settlement, security management, and economic development.

The building blocks for both formal and informal cooperation have been in place for some time, in most of the regions across the globe. Of course, there are differences in terms of how these building blocks of cooperation have been put together, and what sort of regional community is emerging. The next sections elaborate on the conceptual diversity of regionalism, and highlight the range of approaches used in this volume.

FROM TRADE TO MONEY

The very nature of regionalism is one of great diversity, as the examples presented in this volume indicate. Perhaps not surprisingly, the theoretical literature is also characterised by the diversity of perspectives, with disciplines such as economics, political science, international relations (and their sub-branches) all contributing their respective analytical frameworks to explain how and why state and non-state actors cooperate across the traditional nation-state boundaries.

Even less surprising than the wide range of multidisciplinary perspectives is the reality that accompanies it, in the often-limited communication between the disciplines. While it is undeniable that true interdisciplinarity can be extremely difficult to attain, there is no reason why separate disciplines cannot undertake a discourse or the practitioners engage in cross-disciplinary discussion of processes that each is individually interested in describing and studying.

For economists, the point of departure is the set of economic linkages formed through trade in an integrated area, where the removal of tariffs and non-tariff barriers is expected to produce significant increases in overall economic welfare for the countries involved, even if the gains are unevenly spread across economic sectors and societal groups. The seminal work in the early 1960s by Bela Balassa encouraged economists to engage in further explanations of the different forms (or levels) of economic integration, and the likely impact of tariff liberalisation in such areas as competition, structural change, scale economies and levels of investment. Economic integration produces a shift in trading patterns, with the participating countries (and their industrial firms) switching from prior trading partners to new partners within the integration area.

As Gavin and De Lombaerde point out in Chapter 5, contemporary forms of regional economic integration have become more complex than the Balassa model originally suggested, since effective trade liberalisation will require even more regulatory reforms by the participating governments, extending beyond the narrow area of trade/commercial policy to include harmonisation of standards, redistribution policies, and greater consideration of how to manage the tendency for concentration of economic resources (especially finance, labour, and production facilities).

The theory of regional economic integration focused on trade or money, often indeed dealing with one or the other separately. More recently, economic and political economy perspectives have begun to consider the combined effects and issues arising from economic and monetary integration. Implicit in economic (i.e. trade) integration is the movement towards an integrated market whose spatial dimensions extend across several national boundaries. For many analysts, the creation of a single market calls forth the need for a single monetary unit, to reduce the transaction costs of using competing currencies in a unified trading area.

Initially, the theoretical work on monetary integration concentrated upon the question of the optimum size of the monetary union. The puzzle was a real issue of concern for theorists and policy-makers, the latter in particular since the exchange rate had been the traditional instrument of policy available to governments for use when the economy suffered an economic disturbance out of line with the economic trends in the trading partners (economies).

In cases where capital and labour were not so mobile as to effect an adjustment to counteract the effects of economic crisis, then an adjustment of the exchange rate would serve to retain competitiveness. Monetary integration among a group of countries means that any individual country loses the possibility to use the exchange rate as an instrument of economic (monetary) policy. Problems arise when economic conditions are diverse across the integrated area, and a one-size-fits-all monetary policy may be unsuited to the particular conditions in a given country. Chapter 5 outlines the complications arising from monetary integration, and the different implications for policy-makers.

Interestingly, the traditional approach of trade integration followed after some time by monetary integration (as happened with the European experience) is not being adopted in other parts of the world. The question of whether trade integration should precede monetary integration is one that has been raised, but not answered conclusively or definitively. In Chapter 8, Cuyvers et al. portray the diversity of positions on exchange rate policies taken by governments across the world, against the background of a global capital market.

Many regions have sought to counter the uncertainties that a volatile global capital market can produce by cooperating in exchange rate arrangements and, as Chapter 8 clearly indicates, there remains a great diversity of arrangements that operate with varying degrees of success. Above all, however, these diverse arrangements can be categorised in two broad approaches: at one end of the spectrum, governments decide on flexible exchange rates while, at the opposite end, the decision rests on a choice of linking the currency to a hard peg – an extreme case being the use of an external currency (most often the dollar) as the currency of choice in the domestic economy.

POLITICAL SCIENCE MEETS INTERNATIONAL RELATIONS

In the literature it is common to find academic studies categorised according to two waves of regionalism occurring over the period since the Second World War (Breslin et al., 2002). The first wave of studies emerged in the 1950s, coinciding with the appearance of the European Coal and Steel Community (ECSC) and the European Community. An influential body of scholars, including Ernst Haas and Leon Lindberg, drew upon earlier work by the functionalist writers such as David Mitrany, to develop the neo-functionalist theory of integration (Rosamond, 2000). After a period of doubt over the predictive capability in the mid-1970s and the slow progress towards integration in a Europe that was suffering an unprecedented economic crisis accompanied by stagflation, neo-functionalism returned to popularity in the 1980s with the resurgence of integration under the Single Market Programme, and European monetary union.

Neo-functionalism explained the process of integration as a set of functional (i.e. economic) spillovers, leading to economic and political integration, with actors transferring their expectations, and loyalties to a supranational central authority. Important elements in the theory included the role of political actors (national and supranational), and the transfer of expectations to a supranational institution that would be expected to meet the demands of actors and economic agents (replacing the role formerly taken by national authorities).

Critics considered neo-functionalism relied too much on the concept of spillover, and particularly criticised the automaticity of the process, as well as highlighting the teleological nature of the theory, something which did not appear to be borne out by the evidence to date. Other critics considered that integration (in this case, the European experience) was driven by states themselves, and how far the integration process would go depended upon the strategies and decisions of key states. In essence, integration was an intergovernmental phenomenon.

By the end of the 1980s, integration theory was dominated by the debate between the intergovernmentalists and the supranationalists, mirroring the neo-realist versus neoliberalist debates in international relations theory. As theoretical work on (European) integration continued to be refined during the 1990s, regional integration schemes and regional free trade agreements were beginning to appear in other parts of the world, attracting the interest of scholars not primarily working on the European integration case. This allowed new perspectives to emerge, most notably the work on new regionalism (Hettne et al., 1999).

REGIONALISM (RE)DEFINED

In the new regionalism approach, regions were regarded not simply as formal organisations (as was the case in studies of the EU), nor as a 'given' but rather understood as constructed and re-constructed in the process of global transformation. Thus, the region is not a static form, but dynamic in its development and open to change and adaptation.

Taking a broader view than the theories mentioned in the preceding section, regionalism was regarded as a multidimensional form of integration embracing economic, cultural, political and social aspects, thereby extending the understanding of regional activities beyond the creation of free trade agreements or security regimes. Regionalism is also considered to have a strategic goal of region-building, of establishing regional coherence and identity.

Regionalism is therefore seen as a more diverse form of integration than that suggested by other theories, although there are also some similarities. Contemporary regionalism is really made up of many different regionalisms, reflecting different conditions, values and even ideological positions across the global arena – it is a product of the historical, social and political conditions, the strengths and weaknesses of any particular region. Processes of regionalisation emerge from 'below' and 'within' the region, with communities and societies responding to a variety of push and pull factors to engage in cooperation within diverse types of regionalist frameworks. As a consequence of this, the actors engaged in regionalism include states, non-state actors, organisations and social groupings.

This volume is concerned to examine regionalist projects in different parts of the world, using the approaches described above. In each of the specific cases examined in Part Three, the region is understood within the framework of a territorial entity that is continually changing and adapting through regionalisation processes. Further, it is recognised that regionalism is prone to integration and potential disintegration, that the pace of change is uneven, and that regionalism is often a contested project, subject to reversal or to greater coherence as the level of 'regionness' changes.

In Part Two, we focus upon some of the issues given prominence in the literature on regionalism – with chapters on the linkage between macro- and micro-regionalism, regional security, and the role of identity in region-building. The regionalism approach encompasses a normative element more explicitly than other approaches to regional cooperation. Hence, regionalism is understood as both a general and observable phenomenon and as an ideological project – the project being the construction of a regionalist order in a specified 'region' or as a type of world order. In the concluding chapter, Björn Hettne discusses the case for and the challenges to the construction of a regionalised and multilateral world order.

WHY STUDY REGIONALISM?

It may be pertinent at this point to consider the question, why this volume? And what is its significance among the existing literature on regionalism? What does this study offer by way of an enhanced understanding of contemporary regionalism? The volume brings together a group of scholars with expertise in the subject matter of regionalism, with area studies expertise and specific disciplinary skills that are applied in a comprehensive manner to produce a multidisciplinary examination of such issues as the position of regionalism in international relations theory, the role of law and emerging constitutionalism in shaping regional projects, economic theories underlying regional economic and financial cooperation, and the significance and possibilities of constructing regional identities. The volume complements existing literature on comparative regionalism, but also offers value-added in the blend of the theoretical and the empirical dimensions, as well as the attention given to specific issues such as law, security and identity.

Similarly, the 'area' authors have detailed knowledge of the particular region that they write about in this volume, and they succeed in elaborating the complexities and issues from a position of competence and an intimate understanding of the region. Taking account of regionalism's normative dimension, it is a timely opportunity to reassess the state of regionalism in a world currently preoccupied by the behaviour of the sole superpower, concerned by its all-embracing strategy around an international fight against terrorism, and anxious over an all-embracing unilateralism and its attendant risks for world order, regional security and the very multilateral system which America helped to design after the Second World War. One of the side-effects of this unipolar moment is to take attention away from the rest of the world, so that the developments and progress towards cooperation as well as the difficulties are subsumed by the dominance of American interests in the international agenda. Yet we should recognise that elsewhere in the world regionalism is an emerging force, and it is worthwhile to address the possible implications for global order.

THE COMPARATIVE PERSPECTIVE

This volume sets out the experience of regionalism in a number of different parts of the world, without aiming to offer a comprehensive overview of all existing forms and typologies. Part Three sets out seven distinctive cases, where the authors provide a critical insight into the contemporary processes actually operating in each region, the successes and failures of the regionalist project, the internal dynamics as well as the external forces that combine to shape the nature and form of regionalism.

Many academic contributions to the field of regionalism have sought to offer an examination of particular regional experiments (Breslin et al., 2002; Fawcett and Hurrell, 1995; Laursen, 2003). The importance of the empirical analyses is undeniable, and particularly so in the context of recognising the individuality of each specific case. There is no reason to accept the view that a particular model of regionalism offers a paradigm for others to follow, any more than it is reasonable to accept that a particular developmental model used with success in one state can be simply applied without any adaptation by all other states that seek to emulate the success of the former. It is imperative to look at the conditions (political, economic and social) and the historical context in each case in order to understand the nature of regionalism and to explain the processes, as well as appreciate the diversity of models.

A brief review of our cases will clarify this need to avoid a tendency towards generalisation. In Chapter 10, Helen E.S. Nesadurai elaborates on the economic regionalism that characterises the Asia-Pacific, embracing the different regional projects such as APEC (Asia-Pacific Economic Cooperation), ASEAN and the ASEAN+3 groupings – where economic liberalisation is pursued as a way to counter marginalisation in the global economy, and at the same time to meet individual countries' concerns over regional security, financial stability, and the containment of China.

Daniel Bach takes a critical perspective on African regionalism, to consider why there is a continued gap between the rhetoric of African (and international) leaders concerning regionalism and the reality of inadequate institution-building, weak policy implementation, and an unwillingness on the part of state leaders to instrumentalise the regional organisations they had collectively agreed to establish, instead leaving these regional organisations moribund, weak in terms of authority and unclear of their functional capacity.

In Chapter 12, Helena Lindholm Schulz and Michael Schulz examine the record of regional cooperation in the Middle East – paradoxically, regarded by the outside world as a region, which 'outsiders' have constructed on the basis of ideological lines and a memory of pan-Arabism drawn from recent history. This external vision of the Middle East 'region' is not entirely commensurate with the actual degree of cooperation among the countries, and the authors find that economic regionalism and other political initiatives have been hindered or obstructed by the continued tensions and a failure among the countries to construct common visions or recognise shared interests.

The reverse appears to be the case for the Americas, and in Chapter 13 Robert Pastor presents us with the intriguing puzzle – why is North America not seen as a region, when in fact the area encompassing the United States, Canada and Mexico has achieved within a decade a level of (economic) integration on par with that of the EU?

Pastor's study elaborates on the importance of geography, and the significance of history in establishing the necessary conditions that would subsequently define a favourable and receptive environment for a particular form of regionalism – in the North American area. With the continental drift that separated North America from Latin America, the former could forge strong economic, political and cultural ties among the three participating countries, surprising enough in view of the asymmetry among the countries and the dominant position of the United States. Pastor suggests that a key factor in making regionalism a reality, in the face of such strong differences among the participants, was the leadership role taken by the two smaller countries in the grouping, Canada and Mexico. Historically, both countries had a history of defensive nationalism towards the much larger and more powerful neighbour, and any proposal from the United States for regional cooperation would surely be considered by the two smaller neighbours with suspicion as to the true motives, and accompanied by the fear of being dominated by America.

While Pastor argues that region-building was in this case based upon growing interaction at the economic, social and cultural levels, he attributes less significance to the role of institutions in the process. Instead, the chapter makes a strong case for the construction of a regional identity based upon similar values and a positive shift in attitudes towards the neighbouring country, an attitudinal change that Pastor suggests can be found in all three countries.

However, a note of caution is suggested in the observation that whatever people might say in surveys on identity and attitudes to their neighbours, individuals in this region are pragmatic and motivated by economic considerations. Whenever they consider their culture to be at risk, positive attitudinal stances will give way to resistance to integration.

By way of contrast, Brigid Gavin's chapter on Europe reveals a much more institutionalised regionalism than was ever intended or even desired by the architects of the North American regionalist project. The European project has long been the subject of study from a variety of theoretical perspectives spanning functionalism, neo-functionalism, intergovernmentalism, and social-constructivists (Rosamond, 2000). The EU has evolved into a mature regional community, combining a form of regional governance that is both complex and comprehensive with a legal order that is distinguishable by its rejection of national sovereignty, the founding principle that is at the heart of international law.

Regionalism is of course well-established in Europe, with two waves in the second half of the twentieth century that produced a dense network of regional organisations to address security, economic and political concerns – including the North Atlantic Treaty Organisation, the Western European Union, the Council of Europe, the ECSC, Euratom, the European Economic Community, the Council for Mutual Economic Cooperation, and the Warsaw Treaty Organisation. A critical and comprehensive analysis of European regionalism would demand a more lengthy account than is possible within the space limitations of this volume. Consequently, we confine ourselves to the EU as a case of European regionalism, without however implying any judgement on the other forms of regionalism. Several features of this case are worthy of note in any comparative study of regionalism. One feature is the delicate balance between law and politics, a combination that serves to both promote and manage the processes of regional integration – sometimes EU law has pushed integration in areas not previously intended by European governments while, at other times, the political actors (national governments or supranational institutions) have manipulated politico-legal processes to manage or limit the forward march of regional integration.

A second feature of the European case is the degree to which integration took place with the involvement of political elites, and the limited involvement and widespread disinterest of the European public. An issue is the degree to which a European identity has developed, or indeed the extent to which a regional identity is necessary in the process of region-building. So far, it appears not to have been an essential prerequisite for regionalism, nor a condition for moving forward towards deeper integration. The discussion suggests that Europe may reach a limit to regional integration, without some formal recognition of popular sovereignty even as it also acknowledges the challenge to construct a solid regional identity in a community of 25 or more states.

Tie Jun Zhang's chapter on China picks up on the issue of the dominant actor in regionalism that Robert Pastor has identified in the North American case, and the issue of identity hinted at in Brigid Gavin's contribution, and elaborated in more depth in the chapter by Nikki Slocum and Luk Van Langenhove. The case of China is interesting to students of regionalism for a number of reasons, even though some would not immediately regard it as relevant in a study of this nature. Zhang discusses the dual identity of a country with the real potential to become a regional hegemon and a serious player in the contemporary and future regionalist project in Asia. In this case, identity is less the product of shared historical, social and cultural experiences (although these are important) and much more a construction by the Chinese leadership and its intellectual followers.

Zhang's chapter is of particular interest for the insight into the approach of the Chinese authorities as the country sets out on the path towards regionalism. It provides also an interesting and somewhat intriguing case of the role of identity – not as part of region-building processes, but rather as the precondition for acceptance into the regional community.

In Chapter 16, S.D. Muni examines the particular case of regionalism in the Indian Ocean, pointing to one of the questions raised by scholars, namely what constitutes a Region. In this case, it is a geographic space marked out by the countries located on the rim of the ocean. Muni contrasts the regionalism in this part of the world with the European experience, and situates the Indian Ocean Region within the evolution of regionalism in the wider Asia – in particular, with the wave of economic liberalisation and open regionalism that is characterised in the form of APEC, ASEAN and South Asian Association for Regional Cooperation.

The Indian Ocean Region is of course very large, and embraces a number of regional groupings and regionalist projects within it. South Asia has particular interest for international relations scholars and regionalism analysts, since it is an area that has failed to develop a strong regional cooperative dynamic, while it reflects internal dynamics, tensions and rivalries between the two countries, India and Pakistan. The area offers a perfect case for the construction of a regional security community, yet the ongoing tensions between these two powerful countries and their history of discord and conflict have power to be obstacles against the emergence of regional cooperation.

There is a tendency, and indeed a danger in comparative regionalism of being tempted to use 'the European model' as a benchmark against which all other forms of regionalism are judged, and as a consequence found wanting in terms of legal, institutional, political or social arrangements. Of course, this results in a less than adequate understanding of what is actually going on in a particular regional grouping, what processes are in fact evolving, and what actors are involved in the construction of a regional community. Who are the region-builders and what form of regionalist project is under construction? What are the processes, and how are these processes shaping a regional community. These questions should form the starting point for the analysis of each case. It is then up to the reader to make his/her own individual interpretation and comparative analysis.

Among the enormous growth in regional projects over the last two decades of the twentieth century, a trend which appears set to continue and to strengthen in the coming decades, it is an almost impossible task to include all the developments in a volume of this nature. With the limitations of space, decisions must be considered and selections made to illustrate broad trends, particular approaches, individual limitations in regionalism, or other features. Of necessity, this means leaving out some cases or covering other cases in greater or lesser detail than the reader might wish for. Similarly, in attempting to present a range of disciplinary perspectives the challenge is to balance appropriate viewpoints while maintaining a coherent focus through the choice of regional cases and the discussion of relevant, generic issues that play an important part in contemporary regionalism, including issues such as identity, security, and financial stability.

ORGANISATION OF THE BOOK

The volume is divided into four parts – the first part deals with the historical and different theoretical perspectives; the second part examines some concrete issues related to regionalism, looking at security, identity, and monetary cooperation; Part Three examines some cases of regionalism in different parts of the world; Part Four offers a conclusion with a review of regionalism in world order. In Chapter 2, Louise Fawcett places the subject of regionalism in an historical context. She begins by clarifying the definitions of regionalism, and points to the prospects and possibilities in the regional phenomenon, thus identifying some of the critical success factors behind the forms of regionalism discussed in Part Three.

In Chapter 3, Andrew Hurrell draws upon international relations theory to reflect upon the complexity of regionalism in different parts of the world. He establishes the importance of globalisation in shaping and driving the regionalist project, and shares with Foqué and Steenbergen the view that the regional level is the most appropriate and viable level for action to manage the pressures and demands of global capitalism. In reviewing the intra-regional theorising, Hurrell suggests that the differences between theories may be overstated, and that the real question is how regions get to the stage in which cooperation can emerge in the first place. This is indeed a fundamental question, one that is especially crucial in areas such as Africa where continuing conflicts hinder the development of regional economic and political cooperation. Hurrell also reintroduces the role of power-political factors in regionalism, a reality that is central to many of the regions examined in Part Three.

In Chapter 4, René Foqué and Jacques Steenbergen address the vitally important issue of how and whether regionalism can address or correct the excesses arising from globalisation through law and in particular an enhanced constitutional framework. The chapter reviews the case for a constitutional order, arguing persuasively the need to apply a legal-regulatory order based upon the principle of subsidiarity.

In Chapter 5, Brigid Gavin and Philippe De Lombaerde throw light on the nature of contemporary economic regionalism, and suggest how economic regionalism can produce winners and losers. This is an outcome that is often given little attention in the political negotiations – but the reality of this inequity can become a future problem and even a limit to regionalism. Similarly, economic theory has established a precise set of conditions that are required for regional financial cooperation. In view of the constraints imposed upon governments and monetary authorities, the theory on optimum currency areas provides a blueprint for how and when countries might pursue successful monetary union.

Part Two addresses several key issues in contemporary regionalism. In Chapter 6, Fredrik Söderbaum explores the links between micro-regionalism and macro-regionalism. Macro-regions exist between the state and the global level, while micro-regions exist between the national and the local (sub-national) level. Söderbaum is concerned to address the theoretical limitations that fail to take account of the complexities and linkages between different scales of regionalisms. The chapter distinguishes between different types of micro-regions, and presents a comparative examination of the micro–macro linkages in different parts of the world, concluding with some reflections on the future linkages between micro- and macro-regionalism.

In Chapter 7, Elzbieta Stadtmüller examines the mutual connections between regional cooperation in its new form and new challenges for security. She reviews the obstacles for regional cooperation in respect of different types of security problems, and argues that the effective involvement of regional organisations in conflict management depends on the commitment of member states, shared values and interests, the institutional/financial/material capacity, and the legitimacy of involvement. These requirements prove to be vital, yet are often missing in some of the world's trouble spots, most recently in Africa, and in Iraq. Her conclusion that the regional dimension of security cannot be separated from the global order raises questions that are taken up in the concluding chapter.

In Chapter 8, Ludo Cuyvers et al. address a number of interesting issues related to one aspect of contemporary regionalism, that of monetary cooperation. As the chapter shows, forms of monetary cooperation exist or are under construction in many regions of the world and, true to the conceptual understanding of regionalism discussed earlier, there is a diversity of models with no dominant paradigm. Clearly, the global financial market generates a degree of volatility that makes governments more willing to consider alternatives to free-floating exchange rates, even when cooperative arrangements erode or impinge upon national monetary sovereignty.

In Chapter 9, Nikki Slocum and Luk Van Langenhove examine the nature of regional identity and discuss the significance of identity in structures of governance. The chapter addresses some of the important implications in creating identities, particularly where identity conflicts are a source of insecurity, terrorism and even war, and suggests that the development of a 'regional' identity can expand cultural freedoms and avoid the conflicts associated with national rivalries.

Part Three (Chapters 10–16) examines a number of regionalist projects in different parts of the world. In totality the cases suggest the diversity of regionalism, and indicate there is, at least so far, no dominant model of regionalism. As these cases have been discussed in the preceding section, we will not elaborate on the detail of each case here. Instead, it is useful to consider some of the connecting features and cross-cutting themes in the volume.

The suggestion that regionalism could help the participating countries to remain engaged with the global economy is borne out by the case of Asian regionalism, a model which also in part further reinforces the neoliberal norms, ideas and practices of global governance. Yet regionalism in Africa has singularly failed to address the continent's marginalisation in the world economy, despite the many regional initiatives that have been attempted. In this case, the rhetoric of cooperation has not translated into substantive cooperation with the possibility of generating economic development and political change. Regional instability, internal conflicts and ethnic divisions remain significant obstacles towards the achievement of integration.

Both the North American and the European cases described in this volume can be seen as reflecting offensive and defensive regionalist strategies – in the former, economic integration offered the chance to compete against the EU, while Canada and Mexico had limited options by going it alone in a global economy. The EU strategy of enlargement is consistent with the region-building project, while it also supports the notion of regionalism as an ever-changing reconstruction of reality.

However, certain critical success factors need to be in place within any region – including political stability, the absence of conflict, and a general political commitment among potential states. The Middle East example shows that pan-Arabism has proved inadequate to achieve the necessary coherence required to foster regional cooperation, while in the case of South Asia the rivalry between the two large powers, India and Pakistan, presents severe limitations for building regional cooperation, even when the smaller, neighbouring countries are in favour.

The chapters presented in Part Three offer a range of insights into specific cases of regionalism. While taken together these cases offer a basis for comparative study of regional processes, it should also be noted that each constitutes a stand-alone examination of the regionalist experience in the individual cases, highlighting particular forms and processes, local challenges or political priorities, the successes and failures that shape each form of regionalism.

It has been suggested that 'the proliferation of regionalist arrangements raises complex and difficult questions concerning the character and maintenance of international order .... in both the politico-security and politico-economic spheres questions of stability and order are closely bound up with the relationship between regionalist institutions and arrangements on the one hand and global or multilateral bodies on the other' (Fawcett and Hurrell, 1995, 4). A decade later, this statement continues to hold true, to an even greater extent than was envisaged when it was first written. In the concluding chapter of this volume, Björn Hettne shows just how pertinent the issue of international order has become for any regional grouping concerned about stability.

Part One

Theoretical Approaches to Regionalism

2
Regionalism from an Historical Perspective[1]

Louise Fawcett

This chapter sets out some elements for a comparative history and analysis of regionalism. It does not engage in a detailed discussion of any particular region or regionalism, but offers a broad perspective and a framework for discussion for contemporary theory and practice. Regionalism and regionalisation – terms which invite confusion and require careful defining – do not take place in a vacuum. While their progress is necessarily informed by geographical, political, economic, strategic, and cultural concerns that are region specific, they also take place in an environment that is in turn informed by norms, trends, values and practices that relate to different regional and global settings. Hence a comparative survey is particularly helpful in understanding current patterns and the development of regionalism.

This chapter regards regionalism in broadly positive terms, as a 'good' that states and non-state actors desire and encourage, and one that merits promotion by regional and international communities. The United Nations Security Council has certainly supported such a view, encouraging in 2004, for example, renewed discussion on the further strengthening of regional organisations. For those concerned with international order, regionalism has many identifiable qualities. Aside from promoting economic, political and security cooperation and community, it can consolidate state building and democratisation, check heavy-handed behaviour by strong states and global institutions, generate and lock in norms and values, increase transparency, and make states and international institutions more accountable. Like democratisation, it also has a 'contagion' effect (Whitehead, 1996, 5–8). Regional actors draw on, copy and link up with other experiences, and here the phenomenon of inter-regionalism is important. Recent examples from Europe in particular, but also the Americas, Africa and Asia support these claims.

This is not to deny its negative aspects, some of which I develop below. Here, the discussion is about voluntary as opposed to coercive regionalism of the Co-Prosperity or Warsaw Pact type, though that distinction can be a subtle one. Regions might be 'enclaves of reaction' (Falk, 2002, 177) or the source of disorder, of terrorism and other crimes. Not all actors are interested in promoting the order-inducing properties of regionalism. But regional problems invite regional solutions. Terrorism, for example, cannot only be addressed at the global or state level. There are many instances where the region may be the most appropriate level of action, and regional institutions have responded, though not in uniform fashion. In a world of complex and diverse threats and challenges, where state power is inadequate and existing multilateral institutions face severe overload or whose agendas are heavily skewed to favour key states, regionalism is both desirable and necessary. Geographically, ideationally and functionally it is well suited to address questions of regional governance.

Not all share this view. In certain circles, there persists a belief in the principle of universality, of the primacy of the United Nations (UN) and other multilateral institutions, particularly in matters of peace, security and development. The founding fathers of the League of Nations, the UN and Bretton Woods institutions initially opposed the dilution of global goals – as do contemporary advocates of cosmopolitan governance – and in current approaches to international problem solving, the global level remains the first port of call. Regional actors and states might support universalism, or a UN-first approach, as a check on unreliable partners or the misuse of hegemonic power. Another side of this coin is provided by realist approaches to cooperation, which discredit the belief that institutions – regional or not – can mitigate international anarchy. And from the perspective of certain parts of the world today, this view remains salient. In some regions, state power acts as a continuing brake on regional initiatives; for some states, including the United States in its current foreign policy phase, regionalism is seen as a useful, but disposable source of legitimacy.

This chapter stands back from current debates about US unilateralism, and the evolution of a set of policies, that at least since the events of 11 September 2001, have been regarded as unfriendly to institutions in general and regionalism in particular. Simplistically, we can agree that both as regards behaviour towards organisations of which it is a member, like the UN or North Atlantic Treaty Organisation (NATO), and even towards region building, say in Latin America – through the North American Free Trade Agreement (NAFTA) or Free Trade Area of the Americas processes – there has been something of a break with previous policy. But this pattern of regional and institutional engagement and disengagement has always fluctuated and shifted, reflective of internal debate and outside threat. It is unlikely to be permanent. In this respect the analysis by Joseph Nye, on the enduring need for allies and institutions, remains relevant (Nye, 2002). The same is also true, though to a lesser extent, of other regional great powers, whose interest in regionalism may similarly wax and wane – consider the early European experience. Further, regionalism may find spaces to grow and develop alongside, or in response to unilateralism. More useful for our purposes is a longer view, mapping the development of regionalism over time, which suggests that the steady expansion of interdependence since the Second World War, together with a growing awareness of the *possibilities* of regionalism, has generated a momentum that started in the Americas, the Arab world and Europe, but has taken hold in a generalised, if highly unequal way such that there is no part of the world where it has failed to make an impression on state behaviour at some level.

This regional momentum has proved unstoppable, extending into ever new and diverse domains. Whether in promoting growth triangles or free trade areas, encouraging democratic practice, providing post-conflict services in war and disaster zones, or shaping responses to terrorism, regional initiatives – from civil society networks and non-governmental actors at one level, to trade alliances and formal state-based institutions at another – play out roles that daily impact upon peoples and states, softening the contours of globalisation and state power.

Thus conceived, regionalism has large, if untapped potential. It is best seen not as an alternative, but a significant complementary layer of governance. Some tasks can be performed better by states, multilateral institutions or non-governmental organisations. What has emerged is a *de facto* division of labour, sometimes consensual, sometimes contested, where regional actors take on increasingly important roles, contributing to what have been called 'multilayered' or 'hybrid' forms of governance (Scholte, 2000).

Although the definitional issues arising from a discussion of regionalism are dealt with elsewhere (see Chapter 1), I start with a brief elaboration of terms, emphasising the need for an expansive and flexible understanding of regions and regionalism. The chapter then moves to an historical and comparative analysis of regional processes, before offering a broad balance sheet of the challenges and opportunities facing contemporary regionalism. While that balance sheet will necessarily look different depending upon the region in question, it is none the less useful to reflect on the current state of the art, since there are many lessons for both established regions and regionalisms, as well as for those whose experiences are more recent or patchy. There are also important lessons to be drawn in respect of regionalism's place within the structures of global governance.

DEFINING REGIONS, REGIONALISM AND REGIONALISATION

Definitions of regions, regionalism and regionalisation have long presented difficulties to scholars. The terms are not fixed, and have been subject to multiple interpretations. History is useful here, not only in charting a course for regional projects but in showing how the vocabulary, along with the practice of regionalism has changed and evolved. Older ideas of geographically defined regions and state-based regionalisms have given way to more fluid and expansive understandings, which aim to capture the new nature and extent of regional domains – in which states compete with a host of other actors for command of regional spaces and policies. Understanding regions and regionalism today demands a degree of definitional flexibility, and here I propose a multilevel and multipurpose definition, one that moves beyond geography, and beyond states. While this may appear outlandish in regions where state building itself remains incomplete, moving beyond narrow definitions is important since they tend to be self-limiting, and exclude the newer reaches of regional action.

In regard to *regions*, we find that a simple territorial definition may not take us very far – we need to refine regions to incorporate commonality, interaction and hence the possibility of cooperation. One perspective could be to see regions as units or 'zones' based on groups, states or territories, whose members share some identifiable traits: the Organisation for Economic Cooperation and Development or the Islamic countries, the G-22 or the 'South' for example. A central character of such zones is that they are smaller than the international system of states, but larger than any individual state or non-state unit; they may be permanent or temporary, institutionalised or not.

Our understanding of regions naturally flows into a concept of *regionalism* as a policy and project whereby states and non-state actors cooperate and coordinate strategy within a given region. Here aspects of regime theory are helpful in identifying norms, rules and procedures around which the expectations of different actors converge (Krasner, 1983, 2). The aim of regionalism is to pursue and promote common goals in one or more issue areas. Understood thus, it ranges from promoting a sense of regional awareness or community – *soft* regionalism, through consolidating regional groups and networks to pan- or sub-regional groups formalised by inter-state arrangements and organisation – *hard* regionalism. The relationship between the two is complex. Hard regionalism can precede or flow from soft regionalism – contrast the experience of Europe with that of the Arab world.

Regionalism thus conceived – as policy and project – evidently can operate both above and below the state level. And sub- or supra-state regional activity can inform state-level activity and so on. The state is no longer regionalism's only gatekeeper – recall the role of civil society in the NAFTA process. Indeed, a truly successful regionalist project today presupposes eventual linkages between state and non-state actors, but also cooperation across regions creating an interlocking network of regional governance structures, such as those already found in Europe, and parts of the Americas. All this might form part of a networked governance model, a 'New World Order' as sketched out by Anne-Marie Slaughter, very different from the order proposed by US President George Bush in the wake of the Gulf War of 1991 (Slaughter, 2004).

Finally, as regards regionalisation, a term that is sometimes confused or used interchangeably with regionalism, and I would merely draw out a few distinctions here. If regionalism is a policy or project, regionalisation is first and foremost a process. Like globalisation, it may take place as the result of spontaneous or autonomous forces. At its most basic it means no more than a concentration of activity – of trade, peoples, ideas, even conflict – at a regional level. This interaction may give rise to the formation of regions, and in turn to the emergence of regional actors, networks and organisations. It may thus both precede and flow from regionalism. The regionalisation of trade, markets and investment, and its consequences is familiar territory for students of international political economy and regional integration. Such regionalisation has yielded trade alliances, blocs and formal institutions.

In the security domain, *regionalisation* has come to aquire a somewhat different meaning. It is used to refer to regional, as opposed to global, responses to conflicts that have themselves often become regionalised: where inter- and intra-state wars spill over borders and affect and draw in neighbouring countries and actors, attracting the attention of the international community. These region-level conflicts do not only involve local actors and institutions, as in the case of the Economic Community of West African States (ECOWAS) intervention in Sierra Leone. In regions whose own institutions are weak or non-existent, we have seen a growing trend towards the involvement of 'out of area' regional institutions: two recent examples are the engagement of NATO in Afghanistan, or the European Union (EU) in the Congo.

The importance of regionalisation is made daily apparent by the attention it receives in diverse multilateral fora, in the UN, international financial institutions and related circles about the appropriate division of labour in the promotion of international peace and security, or in reference to aid, trade and development policy. In this context it is about developing, devolving power and responsibility to the appropriate regional level. If major financial crises have typically been dealt with at the global, rather than regional level (Russia, Argentina) post-Cold War international conflicts, and this includes other examples from Africa (Liberia), Asia (East Timor), Europe (Yugoslavia) and the former USSR (Georgia) have been the scene for diverse experiments in regionalising peace and security. Indeed measuring the success or failure of regionalism at the security level has become increasingly linked to the ability of regional groups to act as security providers inside and outside their respective areas, to contribute to what has been called an 'evolving architecture of regionalisation' (Fawcett, 2003, 11–30).

Revisiting terms and hence the parameters of regional action is important. Still one should not be confined by them, nor indeed to throw up one's hands in despair at their diverse nature and use. Ultimately regions and regionalism *are* what states and other actors make of them. To make sense of the idea of regionalism, a certain amount of both definitional and theoretical elasticity is required: there is no 'ideal' region, or any single agenda to which all regions aspire. Regions, like states, are of varying compositions, capabilities and aspirations. They may also be fluid and changing in their make up. Regionness, like identity is 'not given once and for all: it is built up and changes' (Maalouf, 2003, 23). At a practical level, the UN Charter, in its definition of regional agencies is imprecise and inclusive.

Aside from the above difficulties attached to discussions of regionalism, a related problem lies in its Eurocentrism. While regionalism and regionalisation are clearly global phenomena, as reflected in the title of this volume, a cursory review of the literature reveals an enormous, and often unhelpful bias in terms of analysing and explaining their progress and prospects in terms of the European experience. If some early models were intended for export, the disappointments of extra-European regionalism led to few sustained studies of its nature and progress. Europe's capture of the regional paradigm has been hard to shift, and persists in the newer literature on 'inter-regionalism', epitomised by the Asia–Europe Meeting process, though there is now more evidence of alternative approaches. Here I move beyond Europe, and the variety of models it offers. In thinking comparatively and theoretically about regionalism, it is important to offer a broader analytical and comparative focus, pulling together evidence from different regions and practices. The African, Latin American or Southeast Asian, Middle Eastern, or more recently the Central Asian cases offer different empirical and theoretical insights – about shared identities and values, self-sufficiency, containment and the management of unequal power.

Certainly in contemplating the regional phenomena, we must recognise that the make up of the region under discussion is vital to understanding its prospects and possibilities. In particular, the nature and capacity of states and regimes are central to any discussion of regionalism, though it would be unwise to discount regions because of regime type or state instability. Regionalism may thrive better in a democratic environment where civil society is relatively advanced, but it is not only the preserve of democracies, as examples from Southeast Asia also show. Democracy and trade proved a strong combination in the creation of a Southern Cone Common Market (Mercosur); their absence has helped prevent the development of an Arab one, moves to promote an Arab Free Trade Area by 2008 notwithstanding. Similarly security regionalism has worked better for some areas, (contrast ECOWAS to the Gulf Cooperation Council (GCC)) and so on. The point here is to discover and develop those functions which particular regional groups are most adept at performing at a given time. It is also appropriate to think of different ways to improve regional capacity; and there is a role for the international community in this regard.

The next part of the chapter reviews the history of regionalism from a comparative perspective, an exercise which helps to illuminate the present state of the art. It is also salutary to remind ourselves that while for some parts of the world regionalism is a very recent and rather shallow phenomenon, there are important antecedents in terms of revealing the limitations and prospects of current practice. To a large extent present experience and understanding of regionalism remains grounded in its past.

REGIONALISM IN HISTORICAL PERSPECTIVE

Broadly speaking, regionalism has always been with us. Regions as empires, spheres of influence, or just powerful states and their allies have dominated in different international systems. Regions – like Europe in the nineteenth century – were world leaders. In a more modern sense however, since regionalism and regionalisation are distinguished from universal others, thus representing activity that is less than global, we might profitably start with looking at the international system that emerged after the First World War. The 1920s provide an arena for considering the place of regional groups in the context of a League of Nations system which accorded them legitimacy (in Article 21 of the Covenant); they are also important for mirroring the still important debates about universalism versus regionalism, sovereignty and collective security. A lesson of the League, and one reaffirmed today in the UN, was that the organisation could not act as a key security provider when the great powers reserved enforcement for themselves.

Outside the League, beyond functional cooperation, reflected in the growth of international agencies, formal institutions were few (one exception was the Inter-American System); non-state based organisations fewer – the Comintern was one example. That any institution could deliver peace and security, provide a vehicle for economic cooperation and integration, or promote a common ideology, was a novel idea, and one that failed the test of the 1930s. Security was sought unilaterally through ententes and alliances of either permanent or ad hoc nature. Economic interdependencies were deep in many instances, but there was not sovereignty pooling in any sense. States called the tune. But the League, like the UN later, encouraged states and peoples to think differently about peace, security, equality and development, contributing to a new definition of international relations, and a changed normative architecture. Similarly, the experience of the 1930s informed cooperative efforts in the early European institutions post-Second World War.

Once embedded, such ideas persisted, to be refurbished in the UN era, which in turn came to embrace regionalism more squarely. Following lobbying from different states, notably Arab and Latin American, the UN legitimised regional agencies, offering them, in Chapter VIII, Art. 52, for example, a formal if undefined role in conflict resolution. Regional economic and social commissions were also an early and integral part of UN activity, drawing in a wide range of actors and setting up new agendas – consider the influential Economic Commission for Latin America. In short, the principle of regional action and cooperation was firmly established. And the Charter link is important here for the endorsement and legitimacy it supplied and the accountability it demanded.

At one level, the possibility of regional action, or of meaningful relations evolving with the UN and regional agency, was curtailed by the Cold War and the composition of the Security Council. But the region as unit of analysis was elevated by the East–West divide, which created an exemplary regional system. With the evident constraints on the UN, peace and security were delivered unilaterally or regionally, through the Warsaw Pact, NATO and related institutions. At another level, the European Community project, built around the idea of economic community, but with security and democratic consolidation as key priorities, became a powerful model.

This empowerment of regional actors, despite their superpower dependence, and the relative quiescence of the UN, created a powerful precedent. Regional organisations proliferated in the post-war period, notably the Organisation of African Unity, Organisation of American States (OAS), the League of Arab States, as well as the NATO-inspired security pacts such as the Southeast Asian Treaty Organisation and the Central Treaty Organisation. Some spawned, like the UN, a set of related organisations: regional development banks and the like – huge bureaucracies drawing on regional as well as external funds and expertise. A network of inter-regional relationships developed alongside the business of states and multilateral institutions. The record of all this activity was necessarily mixed: some institutions reached an early plateau and failed to thrive, others expanded and survived, in the fashion once described by Karl Deutsch (1978, 226). The dual challenges of decolonisation and the Cold War made coherence difficult or enabled institutions to be captured by powerful members or outside actors. But these were key years for regionalism with lessons, not only in economic integration and institutional development, but balancing power, non-alignment, and the development of security communities. Transnational and non-governmental actors, multinational corporations, aid agencies and the like, many also with regional focus, also start to encroach on the international scene, shifting the normative frame of regional operations.

For developing countries in particular, regionalism had the added appeal of a 'southern' movement, of reformist Third Worldism, as expressed by groups like the Non-Aligned Movement and the Group of 77. As was also the case with the Arab states in the Organisation of Petroleum Exporting Countries, who raised oil prices in response to the Arab–Israel War of 1973, regionalism was a 'southern' issue. Such parallels continue today, with the continuing representation of developing country interests in diverse multilateral and regional fora, where 'contesting globalisation' has become a recurring regional or trans-regional theme. The World Social Forum is one example.

Interesting also, from a contemporary perspective, was the growth of sub-regional cooperation which took place in the late Cold War period, demonstrating the refocusing of regional concerns from economics to security (Buzan and Waever, 2003). This saw diverse regional actors in more assertive, post-independence mode, seeking new roles for themselves in shaping the local economic and security environment. Changing economic orthodoxy, the example of Europe, and a more narrowly defined set of security concerns pushed states into new cooperative projects. Some examples are the Association of Southeast Asian Nations, the Caribbean Common Market, ECOWAS, South African Development Coordination, the South Asian Association for Regional Cooperation, the GCC and the Economic Cooperation Organisation. Somewhat different in their geographical reach and orientation were the Conference on Security and Cooperation in Europe (CSCE, now the Organisation of Security and Cooperation in Europe, or OSCE) and the Organisation of Islamic Conferences (OIC): the OSCE demonstrating the application of the lowest common security denominator to a still diverse political and ideological regional framework, the OIC representing a statist attempt to appeal to a trans-regional identity: Islam.

All of the above groups whether aspiring to pan-regional or sub-regional status were products of the Cold War era, yet have survived into the present, showing how earlier reasons for cooperation may not have changed. Many have adapted their agendas and even charters to fit the new economic and security architecture that has since evolved. As we now witness ever newer impulses to regionalism, which at times complement and at times contradict older patterns and trends, the lessons of the past remain relevant.

THE NEW REGIONAL CLIMATE

If the Cold War proved to be an arena for selective, but cumulative regional growth and projects, the post-Cold War period offered new scope and opportunities. Although in retrospect it might appear that many of the older limitations and constraints on regional behaviour had hardly been removed, expectations soared that the end of the Cold War would indeed offer new incentives to international organisations. Despite, or partly because of the parallel process of globalisation, regionalisation has grown in salience. Both the number and membership of regional organisations, as well as interest in what was dubbed the 'new regionalism', has grown exponentially. The process appears irreversible, no longer to be dismissed by critics as a mere fad. The regionalism of the 1990s was promoted by the decentralisation of the international system and the removal of superpower overlay; growth or regional identities. Changing regional power balances found expression in new institutional forms and practices. There was also a trickle down effect from the UN and also the EU (like in the 1960s) as far as the empowerment and perceived capability of international institutions was concerned, reminiscent, in the latter case, of the 1960s. The Single European Act generated competitive region-building in both the Asia-Pacific region and the Americas. Economic regionalism was spurred on generally by doubts and fears about globalisation, and the nature of the multilateral trading order. Despite ongoing reforms to the Bretton Woods and GATT (General Agreement on Tariffs and Trade) institutions, these still remain inhospitable to all but the more robust developing economies.

As regards security, the spiralling of intra-state wars and growing pressure on the United Nations promoted in turn further task sharing with regional organisations, with terms like regionalisation and sub-contracting creeping into the vocabulary of cooperation. Different UN Secretary Generals, notably Boutros Boutros-Ghali, have called for a greater role in this regard. He spoke of the new regionalism, not as 'resurgent spheres of influence but as a complement to healthy internationalism' (Boutros-Ghali, 2000, 110–13). Nor was regional action limited to state-directed activity – non-governmental organisations (NGOs) were also empowered. So in many ways the post-Cold War environment demanded a greater regional awareness and involvement, and was actively promoted by a range of international actors. The larger space that has thus been opened for regionalism is important both to the more competent regional groups, but also to those regions which lack viable structures, or whose own institutions are weak.

If regionalism has expanded to meet new demands and needs, it has also prospered in a more permissive international environment where regions have been relatively freer to assert their own identity and purpose. There is little doubt that most regional actors and groups welcome this development and the opportunity it has brought to increase their say and representation. Regionalism has, for weaker states, provided a point of entry into a Western-dominated order, in which their interests are often perceived as marginalised, and also a forum where interaction and agenda-setting were possible. It may guarantee a seat at the negotiating table. These impulses are necessarily poorly developed in regions of the 'periphery' where organisations are weak or new. But there is growing awareness of the possibility of regional groups influencing developments within their own area and contributing to norm creation over time, and there are quite robust examples from Europe, but also the Americas, Southeast Asia and Africa to show this. A lesson here for emerging states that may yet have only poorly developed institutions, or those who have traditionally relied on the politics of power, is that they cannot afford to ignore the potential of regionalism.

non-state-based regionalisms: whose weight has increased significantly, as their presence at population, environment and trade fora demonstrate. Just as important is their security role in post-conflict peacebuilding as deliverers of aid, relief and related services.

Theoretically, as discussed in this volume and elsewhere, there are almost as many ways of explaining regionalism as there are types of regionalism themselves. Much depends upon the vantage point of the observer. Both from an historical and contemporary perspective, as suggested here, aspects of realism retain crucial explanatory value when applied to the regional initiatives of many emerging as well as established states. Regionalism remains tightly constrained by the exigencies of state security and power, and the resultant balancing and bandwagoning behaviour. Structuralist notions of core and periphery regions are also useful: core regions set the dominant economic, political, and security agendas; peripheral regions have more limited choices. Yet more liberal theories of interdependence, neo-functionalism and institutionalism also have particular value in examining patterns in regions like Europe where economic integration and security community is well established. Some have started to have more purchase elsewhere as regions pass from the early to the later, more mature, stages of regionalism.

The politics of identity, captured by theories of social constructivism, which prioritise shared experience, learning and reality – as against crude measurement of state power – also offer some interesting clues. Alone, it does not explain the success or failure of a given regional project: shared identity is not a sufficient condition of regionalism. Yet identity invariably kicks in at some stage of the regional process. For the case of the Middle East, identity – as Arabism or Islam – explains important aspects of alliance behaviour, but there remains a striking disjuncture between shared ideas and institutions (Barnett, 1996, 400–47). In East and Southeast Asia, the notion of an Asian way appears to have some salience in framing regional options in both trade and security matters, the more so since the Asian financial crises and 11 September. In the European case, construction of a shared identity has gone hand in hand with institutional development and deepening integration.

PROBLEMS AND PROSPECTS

Such considerations serve as a backdrop to considering the present state of the debate, a discussion of some of the difficulties most commonly associated with regionalism, as well as to revisiting some of the arguments in its favour before offering some tentative conclusions. Three related issues, drawn from historical experience and present reality, remain particularly pertinent to discussing contemporary regionalism: capacity, sovereignty, and hegemony.

First, the ability of any group to impact on any given regional space depends on the capacity of its members. The mere creation of a regional grouping, usually the result of the signing of multilateral treaties and agreements, may have no more than rhetorical consequence if members are unable or unwilling to proceed to further stages of cooperation. Will, for example, the Caspian Sea Cooperation Organisation advance from a 'concept' to a fully fledged organisation (Herzig, 2004)? The limited capacity and resources of many groups, especially outside the advanced industrialised countries, are obstacles to action, whether in the military, economic, diplomatic or institutional sphere. Such limitations are augmented by Charter constraints, which place high priority on principles like sovereignty and non-interference. Where suspicion, rivalry and competition are persistent, the prospects for cooperation are further reduced. It is perhaps not an unfair critique of a number of institutions that they have never gone beyond the debate and discussion stage, and can thus be dismissed as mere talking shops. Such was the case with a number of attempts to ape the early EC-style institutions in developing countries. Not all the newer institutions will endure or produce significant results, but some will, and the reasons for this will relate to state capacity, regime type, domestic as well as external pressures and influences, levels of interdependence and the growth and development of shared interests. Since none of these conditions are fixed, groups whose roles are currently limited could assume new functions. Mercosur is an example of a grouping which built on the experience of the 1960s to reemerge more forcefully as an organisation with a viable economic, but also political and security dimension, which its members are anxious to see preserved.

The bigger point to stress here is that the capacity of states is an impediment to cooperation, and will, along with the nature of the regional and international environment, crucially affect the success or failure of any regional project, as many examples from the sphere of peacekeeping demonstrate (Lepgold, 2003). Hence the relative newness or fragility of states may be an important factor; in an unstable system cooperation is likely to be sporadic and superficial, limited to one or two functions, and driven by powerful insiders and outsiders. However from such unpromising beginnings a stable system can emerge showing how an appreciation of the time frame is important in judging regionalism's prospects: conditions change and with them the prospects for further cooperation. Perhaps a good analogy, again, is that of the early experience of developing countries whose initial attempts at cooperation took place in conditions that are not so dissimilar to those of the Soviet successor states.

The ability of states to cooperate is linked to their willingness to do so, and here the constraints that sovereignty imposes plays a central role. While for some, regionalism sets the stage for a decline in the salience of states, for others it can be seen as a means for their individual or collective advancement – an enduring fear of early functionalist writers. States cooperate in regions as they do in alliances, in self-regarding fashion, and in furtherance of their security interests. It is sovereignty that still matters for states and its resilience will always check and balance any cooperative project, particularly where sovereignty is fragile, having only recently been obtained. Hence, new states are particularly sensitive to such encroachment.

Though much cited, the sovereignty argument does not constitute a convincing case against regionalism. Former UN Secretary General Boutros-Ghali has famously observed that 'the time of absolute and exclusive sovereignty ... has passed' (Boutros-Ghali, 1992, 17). And this comment is relevant to the work of international institutions. Certainly the principle has become more porous in respect of the UN Charter where new norms in respect of intervention for humanitarian and other purposes are emerging. The same could be said for NATO and other European institutions. Similar changes may be observed in the Charters of the AU and OAS – note the Inter-American Democratic Charter of 2001 – and smaller groups like ECOWAS and Mercosur. Others adhere strictly to the principle. Respecting sovereignty may constrain, but does not preclude regional-level activity, and the Southeast Asia states have some lessons here. ASEAN may have failed to act over East Timor (though ultimately contributing forces to the Australian-led mission in 1999), yet in their proactive response to the earlier Cambodian crisis, confidence-building measures and the politics of consensus and cooperation, all helped contribute to a more secure regional environment. A third, and related problem, for regional groups is that of dominant states or hegemons. The relationship between regionalism and hegemony poses an interesting challenge. While state sovereignty reduces the capacity of regionalism, strong states are also likely to abuse it. Critics argue that regional groups merely serve the interests of different states, usually powerful ones. It is often the case that one major actor sets the agenda in any regional organisation. That actor may have been instrumental in its creation and maintenance, or at times the dominant role may pass from one state to another. All regional activity in the Americas is predicated on the dominant role of the United States, whether bandwagoning in NAFTA or balancing in Mercosur. In that respect the Monroe Doctrine, as an early statement of hemispheric regionalism, lives on. Elsewhere we can see how the achievements of ECOWAS have depended on Nigerian muscle, or how the Saudis have regarded the OIC as their own project. In an emerging region like Central Asia, institution building has much to do with balancing or bandwagoning with the local strong power, often Russia (Allison, 2004). Seen at its most negative, regionalism can be viewed as an instrument for the assertion of hegemonic control (Mittelman and Falk, 1999, 175). One might further argue that hegemons by their very nature eschew deep commitment to institutions which will limit their freedom of action (and some recent parallels are pertinent here: the sidestepping of NATO by the US for example).

Hegemony is a poor reason for decrying regional action: it is an argument for setting standards and guidelines; for promoting institutional democratisation. Strong powers play a vital role in promoting regional peace and security – acting where others are unable or unwilling. In this regard parallel cooperation with UN structures and guidelines can help modify behaviour, mitigating hegemony and increasing accountability. Institutions can promote greater transparency, but importantly also supply legitimacy that may be lacking from unilateral efforts. States may choose to ignore international law and institutions, but such actions have costs, both at the domestic and international level.

Hegemons may be reined in by regional organisations (Germany in Europe is the obvious early example), even those they have been instrumental in creating. For Latin American states, the OAS has at times acted as a vehicle for containment, albeit a limited one, of their powerful northern neighbour.

CONCLUSION

The above note is an appropriate one on which to end a review of the history and prospects of regionalism, at a time when those prospects appear to have been seriously compromised by the behaviour of the world's leading hegemon. For some, the events of 11 September 2001, and the subsequent development of strong unilateralism on the part of the US, and the corresponding pull of bilateral as opposed to multilateral or regional understandings between the US and its allies, suggest the disposability of regionalism: indeed the death of any emerging liberal global or regional order. This view is both simplistic and shortsighted, and reflective of too rosy a view of the processes of regionalisation and globalisation. There is rarely a clear divide between unilateral and multilateral choices, more often than not cooperating with others is a necessity rather than an option. Selective unilateralism can reduce, but also enhance regional autonomy and options.

We have, of course, been reminded of the limits of regionalism, and recent events provide a useful cautionary lesson. But if a review of the history of regionalism shows precisely how bumpy its progress has been, it also demonstrates its relative robustness and progressive, if uneven development. First we have witnessed a variety of experiments with different regional types, from those, which have a broad reach to narrower sub-regional projects. The range of activity has been similarly diverse, from economics and politics, to security and culture. Charter pronouncements, which profess an economic agenda, may overlie political or security intentions. Or institutions can evolve to acquire new functions. Some of the regionalisms discussed here have already done so. All this does not, in itself, necessarily indicate deep cooperation or integration, in the sense of uniting previously disparate parts to form some identifiable whole. What it does show is that regionalism has an importance that transcends the agenda of individual states and actors, and hence can modify patterns of behaviour. In this respect regionalism retains an important, if complex relationship to international order.

It is no longer possible or appropriate to engage in a starry-eyed exercise about regionalism's prospects, or to present regionalism as an alternative paradigm to any global or state-led order. In exploring its history and different domains, this chapter has highlighted its many limitations at different levels. Still regionalism, both as a demonstration of shared identity, and collective action, is now well established globally. Sustained high-level cooperation remains unlikely outside core regions: this would require more stable and durable regional systems to emerge, ones in which state power is consolidated, where regional rivalries are mitigated, where shared interests can be identified and fostered. A stable regional system is not a sufficient condition for regionalism, but it helps. International cooperation and support is also important, states can learn from the aid and experience of others. In these and other areas outlined here, the lessons of the past continue to prove instructive.

NOTE

1. This chapter draws on L. Fawcett, 'Exploring Regional Domains: A Comparative History of Regionalism', *International Affairs* 80/3 (2004) 429–46.

3
The Regional Dimension in International Relations Theory

Andrew Hurrell

This chapter is not concerned with the trajectory of particular examples of regionalism. Its purpose is rather to clarify the main sets of theoretical ideas that have been used to explain and understand regionalism in different parts of the world. The study of regionalism is complex and contested. Given the enormous range of potentially relevant writing, it is far from clear what should be included under the heading 'The Regional Dimension in International Relations Theory', especially within the compass of one short chapter. In the first section I will reflect on this complexity and consider some of the issues that arise. The second section examines some of the principal ways in which the changing character and dynamics of the global system feed into explanations of regionalism. The third section examines the traditional heartland of theories of regionalism – the links between increasing cross-border exchange, patterns of institutionalisation and the character of the regional polity. Here my purpose is not to try and cover in any detail the wide-ranging and well-known debates that dominate the analysis of regionalism within Europe. It is rather to stress the degree to which the divergent schools of European integration theory share the same conceptual space, and to draw out those elements in the regional equation that an over-concentration on Europe can lead us to neglect, but that are nevertheless central to the global politics of regionalism.

THEORIES, DEFINITIONS AND QUESTIONS

What is meant by the 'regional dimension' to International Relations theory? It may be the case, for example, the regional level of analysis in global politics has been sorely neglected within mainstream writing on International Relations. Perhaps this was always true; or perhaps it was simply that the end of the Cold War and the dynamics of globalisation made it ever more important to unpack regional-level dynamics and factors. But, whichever is the case, all this might mean is that we should take the standard range of general theories of International Relations and deploy them at the regional level. The international politics of regional spaces, then, are not necessarily different in kind or in their essential character from the international politics of other spaces or domains. There is, in other words, no specifically 'regional dimension' to IR theory.

In favour of such a view is the extent to which the study of comparative regionalism has been hindered by so-called theories of regionalism which turn out to be little more than the translation of a particular set of European experiences into a more abstract theoretical language. Indeed it is worth noting that the strongly comparative element in 1960s regionalist writing (for example Nye, 1971) has generally not been emulated by more recent integration theorists (for an important exception see Mattli, 1999). Rather than try and understand other regions through the distorting mirror of Europe, it is better to think in general theoretical terms and in ways that draw both on traditional International Relations and on other areas of social thought. Hence we should consider foundational sets of ideas (how do institutions emerge? what are the causes of conflict? how might we think about the relationship between economic interaction and political identity?) before they have become too encrusted by their application to a particular region or case.

In related vein, it might also be the case that many regionalist developments are substantively very important, but theoretically of little interest. Thus changes in the salience of intra-regional relations, in the density and scope of regional interaction, and in patterns of enmity and amity within a region – all of these will no doubt matter hugely for those interested in a particular region and in the foreign policies of major states within that region. But there is no reason why they necessarily lead to any theoretically interesting puzzles. They may be politically very important; but theoretically they are rather easily explicable, and explicable with a rather traditional theoretical toolkit.

What would change this picture? Potentially three things. First, the character of developments within a particular region might have shifted in ways that challenge or undermine orthodox IR accounts which typically concentrate on constellations of power and interest among states. For example, the traditional toolkit may be singularly inappropriate for analysing regions of the world in which state capacity has eroded, inter-state norms and institutions have disappeared, and new patterns of (usually highly conflictual) politics have emerged. Africa is the most obvious example (see Lemke, 2003, 114–38). Alternatively, others suggest that regionalism has already involved the emergence of new kinds of complex regional polities, characterised by high and rising levels of social, political and economic interdependence and by multilevel and polycentric systems of governance (Ruggie, 1993, 139–74). Here too regional politics seem to be impossible to understand within the old IR world of states, power and interest. It is far too limiting to see regionalism solely in terms of a coalition, an alliance, or even an elaborate set of inter-state institutions. Europe is obviously in most people's minds when they think in this way. But Europe is both a stimulus and a snare. On the one hand, it is a constant stimulus to think out of the box and to push theory in new directions. On the other, it is a snare given the degree to which the search for the novel and the transformative can easily lead to the neglect of the old and the familiar and given the tremendous differences that continue to distinguish the European case from regionalism in all other parts of the world. After all, the most important 'lesson' of Europe is that there are so few good grounds for believing that Europe is the future of other regions.

Second, there might be categories of explanation, which although intrinsically general and universal, serve to highlight differences across regions. Most important is the enormous variety of entities which are placed under the heading of 'the state' and the way in which the process of state formation in different regions of the world has produced different kinds of regional international societies. IR theory has too often assumed that 'a state is a state is a state'; or else has adopted extreme and unhelpful dichotomies between 'strong' states and 'failed' states. States may not necessarily have failed; but they often bear rather little resemblance to Weberian idealisations and this can have important implications for regional politics. Equally, the history of regional state formation has produced regional international societies which may have elective affinities with the allegedly universal Westphalian original but which also have important distinctive features – not necessarily because of cultural difference but because of radically different historical trajectories, patterns of regional interaction, and geopolitical and economic contexts.

Third, regional distinctiveness might itself become part of the explanatory picture. Here we would place those who insist that culture makes a difference, with culture understood not necessarily in terms of a particular civilisation but rather in terms of the lasting legacy of attitudes and beliefs in society derived from authoritative teachings and recurrent, large-scale socialisation processes and embedded in complex and elaborate systems of discourse. A good example is the argument that the success of the Association of Southeast Asian Nations (ASEAN) and the absence of European-style regional institutions reflects an 'ASEAN way' based on a particular set of norms and a particular kind of diplomatic culture (Acharya, 2000).

A further general point concerns the varied purposes to which theories of regionalism can be put. The study of the new regionalism has underlined the degree to which, even if its form and dominant rhetoric are economic, regionalism is an extremely complex and dynamic process made up of not one but a series of interacting and often competing logics – logics of economic and technological transformation and societal integration, logics of power-political competition; logics of security (both inter-state and societal); and logics of identity and community. Regionalism is best viewed as an unstable and indeterminate process of multiple and competing logics with no overriding teleology or single end point. Dynamic regions are inherently unstable with little possibility of freezing the status quo. Given this complexity, it is very unlikely that any single theory will be able to explain complex regionalism, let alone predict its future. This is especially true of Europe where rival theories are able to capture important explanatory logics and can often muster significant evidence in their support – but only at the cost of ignoring or downplaying countervailing trends and equally powerful developments. This complexity also makes it important for the analyst to stand back from the assumption of so many regional enthusiasts that regionalism is necessarily a good thing or, at least, to see normative commitment to region-building as part of the explanation of regionalism (see this chapter's Conclusion, below).

How one approaches these complex and varied logics will depend very heavily on the purpose of the enquiry, and on how theory is being used. For those interested in a particular region, theory is often a way of thinking about potentially relevant explanatory logics and of placing a particular case within a set of broader conceptual categories. Hence we ask rather traditional questions: of what more general category is this regionalist development, event or phenomenon an instance? What hypotheses would theory x or y suggest about the character or dynamics of regionalism in this case? What would be observable implications of such a hypothesis? What evidence would help shed light on its validity? Especially for those interested in particular regions, theory is often an important means of making explicit and bringing out into the open what is taken for granted or simply assumed. To the politician involved or to the regional specialist, something may be such an obvious feature of the regional landscape that its explanatory importance is neglected. On the other hand, those who are interested in the development of theory will tend to look at regions in rather different ways. Their purpose is not to provide a full or complete account of a particular example of regionalism but rather to use cases to develop or test a particular theory. So what may often come across to the regional specialist as a crude simplification is a deliberate way of trying to clarify a particular explanatory logic or to sharpen our understanding of how different sorts of logics may relate to each other.

Third, and perhaps most important, 'regionalism' is a blanket term that covers a wide range of very different developments and processes. It is vital to be clear about what is being explained – processes of social or economic regionalisation; the growth of regional awareness or identity; the formation of inter-state regional institutions or state-promoted economic integration; or the emergence of politically cohesive regional blocs. Specific definitions vary. The precise terms are not in themselves important. But the underlying distinctions matter greatly and much regionalist analysis is muddled precisely because commentators are seeking to explain very different phenomena or are insufficiently clear about the relationship amongst the varied processes described under the banner of 'regionalism'.

REGIONALISM AND THE GLOBAL SYSTEM

In discussions of the new regionalism in the 1990s, it was common, first, to see globalisation as the most important feature of a fast-changing global system, and, second, to stress the close links that existed between globalisation and regionalism (see Gamble and Payne, 1996; Hettne, 1999). Pushed to their extreme, arguments of this kind again undercut the notion of a specifically regional dimension to IR theory. As Hettne explains: 'In a globalised world, regionalism as such is not the appropriate object for theorising. Rather, the focus ... should be on the regional factor or dimension in global transformation' (Hettne, 1999, 23). Two themes recur.

In the first place, the same kinds of complexity that characterise globalisation will be reflected in developments at the regional level and this should press analysts to look beyond conventional approaches to regional integration. On this view, then, the new regionalism needs to be understood as a multidimensional and multilevel process, which is not based solely on or around states, but reflects the activities of states, firms and social groups and networks. Regionalism needs to be viewed as taking place within a range of arenas, involving a heterogeneous set of actors, acting both 'from above' and 'from below' and tying together material factors and ideas and identities. On this account, many of the common themes of globalisation (greater pluralism of actors, new range of issues, multilevel or hybrid forms of governance) will naturally play out also at the regional level.

Second, and more important, regionalism is seen as a critical part of the political economy of globalisation and of the strategies that states (and other actors) have adopted in the face of globalisation. For some, regionalism is seen as one amongst a range of contending world order projects and, in particular, as a conscious attempt to reassert political control over increased economic liberalisation and globalisation. For others, regionalism takes on a more specifically political economy focus – either reproducing dominant forms of neoliberal economic governance at the regional level, or serving as a form of resistance to globalisation and as a platform where alternative norms and practices can be developed. But, from this perspective, the crucial point is that it needs to be understood within the global restructuring of power and production. A number of related arguments can be listed here, in very bald summary:

- that the region is the most appropriate and viable level to reconcile the changing and intensifying pressures of global capitalist competition on the one hand with the need for political regulation and management on the other;

- that it is easier to negotiate 'deep integration' and the sorts of deeply intrusive rules needed to manage globalisation at the regional level given that value and societal consensus is likely to be higher and that the political problems of governance beyond the state are likely to be more manageable;

- that, for many developing countries, regionalism can be part of a process of controlled or negotiated integration into the global economy;

- that, especially for developed countries, it offers a favourable level at which to recast the post-1945 bargain between market liberalisation on the one hand and social protection on the other.

- Finally, both the idea that regions matter and specific regionalist models come to be diffused across the world – through institutional competition (especially between the European Union (EU) and North American Free Trade Agreement (NAFTA) models of regional economic integration); through teaching and support (as with EU support for Latin American regionalism); and through conditionality (as with the process of EU enlargement).

Depending on exactly what one puts in the 'globalisation basket', it is evident that the links between globalisation and regionalism have been, and remain, very important. Nevertheless it has also been true that much writing and analysis in the 1990s overemphasised the importance of globalisation – both its alleged transformationist character and its links to regionalism; and underplayed the continued importance of the international political system and of the power-political logics which have dominated that system. Indeed the distribution of power in the international system has been one of the most consistently important factors explaining patterns of regionalist activity across different periods (see Mansfield and Milner, 1999, 602–8). Two arguments need to be distinguished.

The first runs in support of realism, or at least classical realism, namely that unequal power (especially in social settings characterised by weak institutions and deep value conflict) tends to create its own autonomous logic which cannot be subsumed within the operation of capitalist markets (Marx's great blindspot), nor easily tamed by the functioning of civil society (as so many liberals have hoped). But second, and this time against realism, there is the crucial need to understand the way in which changing economic and social conditions (including the impact of globalisation), shifts the character, scope and arenas of power competition. Following from this logic, many regionalist arrangements have been centrally concerned with maximising bargaining power in a globalised world. Even if it is dressed up in other terms, a great deal of regionalist activity does have the character of an outwardly directed alliance or coalition. The strategic rationale of Mercosur for Brazil (vis-à-vis the United States in the Free Trade Area of the Americas (FTAA), the EU, and within the World Trade Organisation (WTO)) has been the most enduring factor in explaining its importance to Brazil.

Globalisation, however, has shifted the context and character of this rather traditional and theoretically rather obvious pattern of behaviour. Thus, deregulation and a changed role of the state domestically have been accompanied by massive re-regulation at the supra-state level and the emergence of an increasingly dense layer of administrative governance. Who wins and who loses in the political economy of globalisation is significantly determined by the power to shape these increasingly dense, far-reaching and deeply intrusive sets of rules, norms and institutions. In some areas these rules and norms have been embedded within and built around inter-state agreements and institutions (as in the WTO); in others it has involved different forms of transnational regulation, both public and private; in still others, the central political battle is about how far markets should be subject to political management and regulation (most notably in terms of global finance). But in all of the cases, the idea has grown up that regionalism is a central and critical part of increasing bargaining power and political capacity. One form of potential power is directly focused on bargaining and coalitional strategies: but behind this lurks the critical issue (certainly in terms of trade) of market size which, in turn, shapes the capacity to negotiate effectively; to retaliate within the structures of the WTO; and, to engage in 'regulatory mercantilism' – the way in which norms and practices that develop within large economic areas become internationally established.

The increasing assertiveness and unilateralist policies of the Bush administration have served to increase the salience of this aspect of regionalism, as in recent debates over Europe's role. Some stress the notion of Europe as a pole or a counterweight to the United States. Whatever new forms of governance, statehood and sovereignty may have been developed within Europe, its impact outside will be through the creation of a power in a classic sense. For others, Europe's role is very different. Here Europe serves not as a counterweight but as a counterpoint. Power is not bringing projected, or at least not power in its traditional, hard, form. Instead Europe's influence rests on its provision of a model – a model of social order and of a particular brand of advanced capitalism; but, above all, as a model of governance beyond the state. For many it is this kind of soft power that Europe should seek to project. Europe, in other words, should seek to externalise its internal political project and social and political values associated with it. And it is these values and this model that other countries and regions can invoke or appeal to.

Problems, however, affect both of these options. There is no consensus on the power-political projection model; the weaknesses of Europe as a power-political player are well known, especially in the military field; and the severity of the current challenges must make one doubt whether Kissingerian questions as to the seriousness of Europe as 'real' political player have been overcome. The soft power route is far more plausible. And yet many of these same issues affect the notion of Europe as the projector of an alternative model of global governance. In part the difficulties follow from the uncomfortable gap between what Europe practises and preaches internally and its external actions. But in part the European paradox remains. Europe's tremendous success lay in overcoming the old Hobbesian world of wars and conflict by creating a set of political arrangements that simply could not function according to the old-style power-political logic of traditional nation-states. But this very success has bedevilled subsequent attempts to project its power, whether of a hard or soft variety.

A further crucial power-political factor at the systemic level concerns security. For many analysts the end of the Cold War removed the global security overlay that had either dominated, or at least, strongly influenced, patterns of regional security in many parts of the world. Regions were 'set free'; and regional logics came to predominate in the production of insecurity – both traditional, but especially non-traditional (often related to the negative externalities produced by increasing levels of regional exchange and interdependence); and in terms of the management of insecurity, with increased incentives for regional states to deal with their own problems and a decreased incentive for outside powers to intervene or become involved.

This changing security context has had a profound impact on regionalism in many parts of the world (Buzan and Waever, 2003): it has forced greater recognition of the underlying politico-security bargains that actually underpin regionalism even when the public face of regionalism is purely economic (as with Asia-Pacific). The character of regionalist projects and the nature of the challenges facing them have been decisively influenced by security and geopolitical imperatives. Thus geopolitics and security have been far more important in explaining the process of enlargement than the sorts of interest-driven, exchange-related processes stressed by integration theorists. In both Europe and other parts of the world (including NAFTA and Mercosur), we have also seen the generation of insecurities as a result of problematic and destabilising proximity to strongly integrating regional cores, and we have witnessed attempts to manage insecure peripheries by the manipulation and management of the terms for inclusion and membership of regional groupings. The links between increasing patterns of interdependence and different forms of insecurity were already a significant feature of regionalism well before 11 September 2001. But the post-11 September security climate has made this aspect of regionalism ever more salient.

A central question (and one to which we cannot yet know the answer) concerns the extent to which we are witnessing the re-emergence of global and globalising security logic. The so-called war on terror is understood as global by many, particularly in the US; and the notion of this being a new 'world war' has been argued by a number of analysts. Whether it is in any real sense 'global' or whether it is 'only global' because the leading power in the world is treating it as such (compare with the perception of a global communist threat and the way in which this created its own reality), it is nevertheless the security issue that has come to complicate and influence regional security in many parts of the world. Outside of the Middle East, the major political impact is twofold: first, the extent to which it leads to conflict over the nature of the security agenda and over the relative priority to be attached to terrorism and proliferation issues; and second, the extent to which often fragile regionalist arrangements may be unable to withstand the strains imposed by

- direct conflicts over security issues;
- conflicts over the securitisation of many issues that were hitherto either outside of the security realm (for example money laundering) or had security implications but which were not viewed by the US as core security concerns by the US (as with migration or the links between drugs, crime and terrorism).

INTRA-REGIONAL THEORISING

The heartland of the theory of regionalism focuses on the impact of rising levels of regional exchange and the links between economic integration, institutions and identify. (For overviews of European integration theory see Rosamond, 2000 amongst the most important perspectives see Moravcsik, 1998; Schmitter 2003; and Sandholtz and Stone Sweet, 1998.) As is well known, it grew out of the European experience. It tended to take as its starting point the desire to create a common market and to intentionally privilege transnational economic interests – in order to avoid the recurrence of war and conflict, to promote economic welfare, and to protect a particular kind of economic model. The most important division is between those who see regionalism principally in terms of state interests and inter-state arrangements and those who see integration as producing more complex regional polities. Conventionally, and again within the European context, this distinction is usually cast as a debate between intergovernmentalism and neo-functionalism. However, it is more useful for comparative regionalism to try and capture the distinction in more general terms.

For the statist, the proliferation of international and regional institutions is commonly associated with increased levels of transnational exchange and communication. Institutions are needed to deal with the ever more complex dilemmas of collective action that emerge as regions become increasingly integrated and interdependent. It is around this basic insight that mainstream institutionalism is constructed and developed. Institutions are viewed as purposively generated solutions to different kinds of collective action problems that are created by increasing density and depth of interaction and interdependence. This agency-centred institutionalism views institutions as affecting decision-making by altering cost-benefit calculations: reducing transaction costs, providing information and transparency, and facilitating enforcement. On the rationalist institutionalist account institutions affect state behaviour by making it rational to cooperate and by altering incentives. Institutions affect actor strategies (but not their underlying preferences) by reducing transaction costs, by identifying focal points for coordinated behaviour, and by providing frameworks for productive issue-linkage. In the context of Europe, this view sees states as in control of the process of integration and institution-building; it concentrates on the grand bargains that have shaped integration; and it sees the move towards supranationalism in terms of controlled and limited delegation (hence the popularity of principal-agent approaches to regional institutions).

One variation of this dominant theme seeks to add a theory of preference formation (hence liberal intergovernmentalism), but to restrict this preference formation to domestic rather than international or transnational forces and factors (which would effectively push it towards neo-functionalism). The second variation moves in a more cognitive or constructivist direction, in which ongoing interaction can shift actors' understandings and identities and in which institutions are strong to the extent that they shift actors' understandings of problems and of the existence and character of cooperative outcomes (via increased technical knowledge) or they create processes of socialisation by which norms and values are diffused. Actors come to internalise external norms via institutionalised interaction leading to changes in both interest and identity.

Those who look beyond states see the possibility of far-more complex regional systems and structures of transnational governance. This account stresses the pluralism of the norm-creating processes; the role of private market actors and civil society groups in articulating values which are then assimilated in inter-state institutions; and the increased range of informal, yet norm-governed, governance mechanisms often built around complex regional networks, both transnational and trans-governmental. Tied closely to processes of social and economic regionalisation this view sees traditional inter-state law as increasingly subsumed within a broader process in which old distinctions between public and private international law and between municipal and international law are being steadily eroded. The state loses its place as the privileged sovereign institution and instead becomes one of many actors and one participant in a broader and more complex social and legal process. In its European embodiment, this view stresses ongoing process and interaction, rather than one-off bargains; the role of supranational institutions; the internal expansionist logic of complex legal arrangements; the importance of transnational pluralist politics; and the tendency of dynamic integration to create new policy challenges and new arenas for policy-relevant behaviour.

There is obviously more that could be said about these kinds of regionalist theory. Moreover, the insights and the issues arising from this way of thinking emerge whenever we see high and rising levels of regional exchange, integration and inter-penetration. But what is most striking is the extent to which these sorts of theories share so many features and occupy the same conceptual space. Of course the differences between them matter. But the intensity of the theoretical debates has obscured the very important similarities and provides a good example of the narcissism of small difference. When we place this genre of theorising within a broader, global and comparative context, different sets of empirical questions and theoretical puzzles emerge. Four points need to be emphasised.

First, we need constantly to think about how regions get to the stage in which the issue of cooperation and economic integration can emerge in the first place. Remember that most European integration writing is not very interested in the founding of the EU or in the initial 'move to institutions'. It is primarily concerned with what happens thereafter. Moreover, institutionalism is most powerful in those cases where there is both an objective common interest that can be captured by the right institutional design and a subjective sense of the value of cooperative behaviour. The analyst assumes that the players view each other as legitimate and that there is a common language for bargaining; a shared perception of potential gains; and some mechanism for at least potentially securing contracting. But in many regions, it is the move from conflict to potential cooperation that is theoretically most challenging, as well as those factors that affect the domestic preconditions (democratic politics, a stable and reasonably effective state and so on). A great deal of regionalist activity outside Europe seems to be driven by conscious political efforts to create the conditions that much integration theory takes as necessary for successful regionalism but which are so clearly weak or absent in so many parts of the world. What is often so striking is the political drive to build or re-build regional exchange or interaction, often from very low levels.

Second, integration theory in Europe tended to separate out the particular interests that arose from increasing regional exchange from the broader foreign policies within which state interests were embedded. Integration did not just reflect some interest-driven logic. It also fitted very closely with a very particular set of convergent but historically contingent national foreign policies and national foreign policy ideologies. Within Europe, Germany provides the clearest and most important example. This suggests, for example, that the real challenge of enlargement is that it brings into the Union countries with very different traditions of thought about the world and about their place within the world. In other regions, it suggests that we cannot avoid the obvious need to understand the role that regions play in the foreign policies of the major regional states and the extent to which they have a perceived interest in developing regions and regional cooperation.

Third, there are important cases where we find complex and growing patterns of regionalisation but where this neither leads to higher levels of institutionalisation, nor does it necessarily challenge or affect dominant patterns of inter-state relations. It is far from clear that European-influenced regional theory gives us much of a handle on these sorts of cases. In North America, many of the interest-based logics of integration theory do apply but they need to be set against other, equally powerful, power-based logics (see below). The Asia-Pacific region is also particularly important, in questioning exactly how, why and for whom increased regionalisation actually matters.

Fourth, and perhaps most important, has been the relative neglect of power and of power-political factors within regions. Power has, of course, not been wholly absent from European theories of integration, but it has been secondary to questions of interest, and, more recently, of identity. For example, much of the dominant story of Europe focuses on the struggle between the nation-state and supranational institutions; it is a battle between principals and agents; and a conflict over competences. This is certainly an important element of the story; but so too are the distributional conflicts that take place amongst states (and more complex coalitions of interest) over the 'institutionalisation of partiality' – over whose interests will be embodied in particular policy solutions. Equally, some of the most important power-related aspects of European integration only emerge when they are challenged – for example the crucial bargain that ensures that the voice and rights of smaller states are respected as part of the legitimacy of the overall institutional arrangement – something that is now under challenge from the move towards more hierarchically-structured forms of regional governance in Europe.

But when we look at really existing regionalism outside Europe, power becomes very central indeed. As against those who understand regionalism in and around ASEAN in terms of regional norms and regional identity, others have seen a prior balance of power as the essential precondition for effective regionalism and have stressed the continued central role of US power. And nowhere does unequal power matter more than in two of the most deep-rooted regionalist arrangements outside Europe: NAFTA and Mercosur. In both cases (and in the FTAA) hegemony is a central defining feature.

Moreover if we think about regionalism in and around the Commonwealth of Independent States or about the role of Chinese power within Asian regionalism, the power-related aspects of regionalism are clearly crucial. To make progress we need to press further the analytic distinction between issue-specific interests and power-related interests (Hurrell, forthcoming). Power-related interests emerge when there are significant cross-linkages between an institutional arrangement concerned with the management of one or more substantive issues on the one hand and the broader character and dynamic of a power relationship on the other. These cross-linkages may derive from the distribution of the costs and benefits of cooperation, or from the structure of the institution itself, or from the particular role played by an institution within the broader structures of hegemonic power.

What sorts of power-related interests do weaker states have in the creation and maintenance of regional institutions? In the first place, institutions provide important platforms for influence for emerging states by constraining the freedom of the most powerful through established rules and procedures. The most fundamental goal is to tie down Gulliver in as many ways as possible, however thin the individual institutional threads may be. The move towards institutions often follows, or is closely connected, with the broader foreign policy strategy of bandwagoning – active alignment with the locally dominant state in the hope of receiving benefits, protection, or special treatment. Second, institutions open up 'voice opportunities' that allow relatively weak states to make known their interests and to bid for political support in the broader marketplace of ideas. Third, and related, institutions provide opportunities for influence via what might be called 'insider-activism'. Fourth, institutions provide political space to build new coalitions in order to try and affect emerging norms in ways that are congruent with their interests and to counter-balance or at least deflect the preferences and policies of the most powerful.

Liberals are keen to argue that hegemony cannot account adequately either for the creation or the sustainability of institutions. One important part of this argument stresses the role of overt efforts by the hegemon to compel or induce compliance with the rules of an institution or regime. This is what hegemony is all about. If such efforts cannot be identified, then we should conclude that hegemony plays no role and that other (liberal) explanations must be sought. Yet hegemony can play crucial roles in the functioning of institutions without overt efforts or specific policies. The existence of hegemonic power itself creates a powerful logic of hegemonic deference. Weaker states have such an important stake in institutions and in keeping the hegemon at least partially integrated within those institutions that they are willing to accord deference to the hegemon, to tolerate displays of unilateralism, and to acquiesce in actions that place the hegemon on (or beyond) the borders of legality. The persistence of an institution in such cases does not need to flow from the power of its formal rules, nor directly from the actions of the hegemon, but from this logic of hegemonic deference. The problem for weaker states is how to capture the joint gains stressed by the institutionalists, but in such a way as to keep the powerful both engaged and, hopefully, constrained.

What of the powerful state? Again a number of interests and logics emerge. First, there is the notion of strategic restraint and the role of regional institutions in signalling that strategic restraint. If the dominant power wishes to maintain its predominant position, then it should act with strategic restraint so as to prevent the emergence of potential rivals. A rational hegemon will engage in a degree of self-restraint and institutional self-binding in order to undercut others' perceptions of threat. Second, hegemonic states use institutions to project, cement and stabilise their power. This may involve the use of institutions to promote so-called milieu goals or engage in 'agenda setting'. But 'agenda setting' misses out the ways in which institutionalised and legalised integration locks states into a particular sets of norms and rules. Power is not simply about interactions between specific actors with one state seeking to change or shape the actions of another. It cannot be reduced to the interactions of pre-given actors. It is also about the constitution of action and of the material and discursive conditions for action. Even if institutions are about effective and efficient means of dealing with the impact of regionalisation and integration, we need to ask which institutions are chosen and why. Power, not effectiveness or efficiency, is often the central determinant of that choice. For powerful states the choice is often not between institutions and no institutions, but rather which institutions offer the best trade-off between effectiveness on the one hand and the maximisation of the control and self-insulation on the other. Finally, hegemonic states use institutions in order to legitimate their power. Power is, after all, a social attribute. To understand power in international relations we must place it side by side with other quintessentially social concepts such as prestige, authority and legitimacy. A great deal of the struggle for political power is the quest for authoritative control that avoids costly and dangerous reliance on brute force and coercion.

CONCLUSION: THE NECESSITY OF THE NORMATIVE?

In previous rounds of regionalism, the regionalist wave rose but then broke and receded. Predictions that regionalism was here to stay proved unfounded. Outside Europe by the early 1970s various regions were littered with failed and discredited regionalist schemes, whether of economic integration or of political cooperation, and whether at the macro, micro or meso level. This time around it is striking that, in many parts of the world, politicians and analysts seem convinced that regional cooperation has to move forward and has to be made to work – despite the very limited results that have been achieved outside of the EU and NAFTA and the real problems within both of these; despite the severe challenges facing South American regionalism; and despite the extremely limited results elsewhere.

How should we account for the apparently very strongly embedded idea that regionalism does form an important element of international order? This chapter has considered the way in which global economic and politico-security factors work to reinforce the attractions of regionalism; it has also surveyed some of the most important intra-regionalist logics and the theoretical ideas with which they are associated. But can they account for the continued power of the regionalist idea? It is not possible to make sense of the global politics of regionalism without noting both the normative pull of the regionalist idea and the relative place of regionalism within broader debates on international order.

Here it is important to underscore the more defensive imperatives that have come to characterise many examples of regionalism over the past few years. Hence we can see a continued emphasis on regionalism as a response to economic crisis and failure and to the shared regional perception of needing one's neighbours as partners in a politically and economically nasty and threatening world. The political imperative to keep trying to 'relaunch' Mercosur with a strong emphasis on its character as a 'political project' provides one example. Asian regionalism provides a further example, whether in the face of the financial crisis or, in the case of ASEAN, the diversion of foreign direct investment to China. Whatever the actual limits to purely Asian responses to the financial crises of the late 1990s, there has been a significant sense that the region needs to develop a greater sense of its own identity and of its own capacity to deal with economic vulnerability (especially in the financial and monetary field). The African case provides an even more striking example of regionalism launched on the back of crisis, human disasters, and widespread political and economic failure.

These sorts of developments place centre-stage the old regionalist problem: how likely is it that regionalist arrangements can be sustained by political will and in the absence of compelling and concrete economic rationales and results? But they also underscore the importance of distinguishing between regionalism as description and regionalism as prescription – regionalism as a normative position, as a political programme, or as a doctrine as to how international relations ought to be organised. As with the more general idea of interdependence, there is often a strong sense that the states of a given region are all in the same 'regional boat', ecologically, strategically, economically; that they are not pulling together; but that, either explicitly stated or implicitly implied, they should put aside national egoisms and devise new forms of cooperation. Clearly when regionalist rhetoric or exhortations fly too strongly in the face of hard material realities and brute political, military or economic facts, then there is little reason to expect success. But, as constructivists remind us, brute facts are not as straightforward as they are sometimes made to appear. It is how political actors perceive and interpret the idea of a region that is critical: all regions are socially constructed but region-building is politically programmatic. Political agency and normative commitment are central to the practice of politics and need also to be reflected in the analysis of politics.

Finally, we cannot consider the strengths and weakness of regionalism without setting regionalism against other conceptions of political organisation and world order. Here it may be useful to look back on the sorts of intuitions and understandings that fuelled writing on regionalism in the early post-1945 period. At that time many writers (from Carr to Kojève) believed that the day of the nation-state was over in an age of total war, advanced capitalism and atavistic nationalism. If this were true, they argued, surely regionalism must emerge as either the most viable or the most attractive of the plausible alternative frameworks for social, political and economic organisation. Given the Cold War, effective universal or global governance was impossible. Empire (which is, after all, by far the most historically powerful alternative to the nation-state) was widely viewed by the 1950s as both normatively unattractive and decreasingly viable.

To what extent does this pattern of thinking still hold true? Although debates on global order in the 1990s sought to avoid the stark dichotomy between globalism and regionalism and to stress the potential synergies between multilateral and regional organisation, strong notions of global governance are not looking very plausible. Well before the arrival of the Bush administration, the (allegedly liberal) multilateralism of the post-Cold War world had, for many states and social groups, already been heavily contaminated by the power and special interests of the rich and powerful. Moreover, despite the best efforts of liberal imperialists and the surge of neo-conservative apologists for imperialism, there is very little to suggest that neo-hegemonic or neo-imperial forms of global order are either normatively acceptable or indeed remotely practical.

So we are therefore perhaps condemned to think in regional terms because of the limits of the state as the basis for social order in a complex, integrated and globalised world, and because of the difficulties of finding other alternatives. Regionalism is unlikely to emerge as the dominant organising principle of world order. But it has some particular advantages. It can certainly serve as an organising framework for the capturing of regional common interests. But it can also contribute to the two other tasks that any minimally acceptable international order must address: the management of unequal power, and the mediation of deep and abiding cultural differences and value conflict.

4
Regionalism: A Constitutional Framework for Global Challenges?

René Foqué and Jacques Steenbergen

As societies feel primarily challenged by globalisation, a constitutional framework for regionalism will strengthen the legitimacy of regional initiatives most effectively if it is seen as a contribution to the management of globalisation. Two key examples of initiatives aiming at a structured environment for the management of such challenges are the World Trade Organisation (WTO) and the European Union (EU). The EU is the regional initiative that probably went the furthest in exploring the frontiers of regionalism. Moreover, the question whether further progress requires a constitutional model is now the key issue in the debate on its future.

In this chapter, the EU is seen as a laboratory to study the relations between the processes of regionalisation and constitutionalisation. Two models for regional organisations can be distinguished. Technical organisations designed to deal with technical regional issues can adopt governance and control structures similar to the rules on governance that apply to private organisations and traditional intergovernmental organisations. Organisations designed to deal with issues that require decisions with a political dimension need a structure in which such decisions are either made by a politically legitimated body or by consensus between politically legitimated bodies.

This chapter is based on the following assumptions:

- Societies risk disintegration by multiple forms of destructive behaviour when they feel at the mercy of developments that they can no longer hope to control.
- Structured societies feel primarily challenged by globalisation: under conditions of globalisation, states lose the ability to govern their domestic market, and ultimately to preserve and shape their identity, because of international market developments (Beck, 1997, 28; Poiares Maduro, 2003, 268).
- Isolationism, protectionism and militant nationalism are logical defence strategies in societies that hope to restore or preserve what little control they can retain over their cultural, socio-economic and political environment. In the absence of rational solutions, reasonable people can be tempted by populism and by extremist views at either end of the political spectrum (Taguieff, 2002).

54

- The principle of subsidiarity requires that problems be addressed at the level at which they can be solved most effectively, and that decision-making power is allocated accordingly (MacCormick, 1999; Craig and de Burca, 2003). The subsidiarity principle is probably the most appropriate key to a rational management of global challenges.

It follows that one needs not only to see how regional organisations can contribute to the organisation of relations between states,[1] since the management of globalisation and its impact requires more than an interface between existing entities. It requires a platform for the common management of challenges that transgress the national dimension – such as can be seen in the two examples of the WTO as a global, and the EU as a regional organisation.

The EU is at a crossroads, hesitating more than ever between (almost) becoming a state and remaining a regional (and in its political dimension often intergovernmental) organisation. The creation of a structured entity with international legal personality, its own currency, and a common foreign and defence policy clearly moves the EU closer to the traditional model of a state. Together with the European Economic Area (EEA),[2] the EU is the most articulated example of a regional organisation that systematically uses the rule of law for the governance of its own structure and to achieve its goals within the community of its members.

The Andean Community, the Association of Southeast Asian Nations, Mercosur and the North American Free Trade Agreement are examples of regional market organisations at different stages in the development from a preferential trade agreement to a free trade zone and customs union, with varying characteristics of a common market if not the ambition to grow towards an economic union. The EU is the regional initiative that probably went the furthest in exploring the frontiers of regionalism. This chapter will therefore draw primarily on the experience of the EU. Moreover, the question whether further progress requires a constitutional model is now the key issue in the debate on its future.

It also follows that a constitutional framework for regionalism will strengthen the legitimacy of regional initiatives most effectively if it is seen as a contribution to the management of globalisation. We therefore consider that a theoretical framework for regionalism needs to build on an analysis of globalisation and of the prerequisites for the management of its impact.

GLOBAL CHALLENGES

The globalisation of markets is a virtually unavoidable consequence of technological development. Disposable income and cost of consumption are dependent on the ability to sell goods and services beyond the borders of our domestic markets. Thanks to half a century of efforts in GATT (General Agreement on Tariffs and Trade) to liberalise world markets on a basis of reciprocity, the emergence of new markets continued to benefit the old industrial powers (Steenbergen, De Clercq and Foqué, 1983).[3] Globalisation is mostly perceived as a threat to employment by imports and dislocation, but access to markets abroad is also a condition for preserving employment in all sectors that can only justify present levels of activity by access to foreign markets.

We therefore face the choice between a protected market with a significant contraction of the economy, and the degree of free trade necessary for the preservation of export-dependent employment. And while parts of our societies find it increasingly difficult to handle the pressure, others risk to go elsewhere if they become convinced that they are fighting a lost battle at home. Brain drain is among the worst that can happen when a society needs to rethink itself.

Loss of employment is the most visible damage caused by globalisation. But other types of damage caused by globalisation can be more significant than the loss of employment itself. The confrontation with successive rationalisation and restructuring schemes in enterprises, repeated changes in management and management objectives, the fear for the unknown in multicultural societies, all contribute to insecurities among people and a feeling that they are losing their benchmarks. They lose the confidence that problems can be solved by rational interaction in existing frameworks. This process gradually erodes the ability to respond constructively to challenges, and to cope with change as well as loss.

A trade or industrial policy approach, and especially a defensive trade policy, is often seen as the conceptually most obvious response to the pressures of globalisation. However, for the above-mentioned reasons both protectionism and an excessive pursuit of competitiveness by relentless rationalisation can be net destroyers of employment. It is therefore surprising that relatively less (or less focused) attention goes to other approaches, addressing various preconditions or consequences of globalisation.

Low cost and ease of transport are prerequisites for globalisation. Environmental disasters caused by antiquated ships under the control of non-trained staff and transporting hazardous cargo, massive road accidents that are caused by overloaded trucks driven by sleepy, underpaid truckers, total reliance on the internet while its management and sustainability remain opaque, are all examples of a globalisation that may partly be based on questionable premises. The elimination of unacceptable risks and a realistic costing of all necessary interfaces will not eliminate the threats of globalisation, but it may reduce the pressure to more manageable proportions.

The same holds true for improved and better-enforced international environmental and labour standards. Loss of employment by foreign competition is perceived as more threatening if a society is exposed to competition that is deemed to be unfair. It is increasingly held that competitive pressure should not be allowed to endanger our social model if the exporters derive their competitive advantage from a blatant disregard for minimal labour standards. There are therefore good reasons to complement existing product standards increasingly with environmental and/or labour standards relating to their production process (Sacerdoti, 1997). The International Labour Organisation has worked for decades towards globally acceptable minimum labour standards (Canela-Cacho, 1997).

An approach based on labour or environmental standards addresses the problems of globalisation at the roots because such standards have an impact on the conditions and cost of production in the countries of origin. They try to eliminate the 'unfairness' in competition as is illustrated by the use of the term 'social dumping'. But there lies also the major disadvantage or limitation: like rules on domestic subsidies in international trade, labour protection and environmental standards aim at regulating domestic policies of foreign countries. They can therefore not be imposed without their agreement, if not active involvement.

The capacity of societies for effective policy-making and policy implementation requires a well-structured public domain in which citizens can develop their significant autonomy. This is in turn a condition for their effective participation in public affairs and their capability to deal with change. A strong public domain implies a strong civil society with stable institutions and common procedures (Ingram, 1994; Sen, 1993). It is by definition transparent. The combination of transparency and predictable procedures in open institutions creates both the conditions for innovative action and for the security needed by individuals and communities to foster the necessary self-confidence and to allow for mutual recognition (Taylor, 1994; Habermas, 1994). A constitutional model needs to structure the public domain and the interaction between state, civil society, and individuals.

For the public domain to function effectively, it is necessary that:

- problems can be addressed at the level at which they can be solved most effectively, and that decision-making power is therefore allocated to the most appropriate level, or that, failing an adequate institutional structure, decision makers cooperate horizontally, and that
- political control can be exercised at the level at which decisions are taken, and that
- the rule of law organises the formality of the public domain by organising transparent and predictable procedures allowing for the effective enforcement of rights in open institutions (Foqué, 1992).

Scope for a more integrated approach (1): industrial and trade policy

The trade policy and other approaches converge when market access is restricted to goods and services that are produced with due regard to the environment in social conditions deemed acceptable in the countries of importation (Trebilcock, 1997; Vandaele, 2003). They further converge when settlement of dispute mechanisms of the WTO are used to improve the enforceability of fairness standards that impact on the working and living environment of citizens, thus fostering their capacity for significant autonomy.

Ever since the emphasis in trade policy switched from tariffs to non-tariff trade barriers (i.e. since the Tokyo Round) trade policy became increasingly concerned with the compatibility and adjustment of domestic policies. This involvement has two dimensions:

- free trade objectives can only be achieved if national measures that constitute trade barriers are neutralised by mutual recognition, or if such measures are either harmonised or abolished. The European Commission approach to the completion of the single market by 1992 was a case in point, and the White Paper reflected these various options (Com (85) 310 June 15, 1985) (Meyers and Steenbergen, 1987);
- trade policy instruments and institutions can be effective tools to enforce international standards and agreements. This is well illustrated by the history of the TRIPS (trade-related intellectual property rights) agreement: the risk of trade sanctions is an effective incentive to implement agreed minimum levels of intellectual property protection.

The WTO illustrates that such efforts can be 'hosted' efficiently by a trade policy organisation.

Scope for a more integrated approach (2): education

The trade policy and other approaches also converge when education policies help to prepare people to participate in a changing world and to manage change. First-class education and a favourable environment for research and development are key factors to attract and retain investments. They are equally important too for the development of the above-mentioned capacity for significant autonomy.

Already in the Greek concept of *paideia*, education aimed equally at the development of the capacity of citizens for personal autonomy and the development of the political community as a democracy. The discovery of the world order (the cosmopolitan perspective) requires the ability to reflect in the practice of technical skills, as well as the ability to reflect *ex post* on past practice (Jaeger, 1967; Nussbaum, 1997).

There is therefore not only a need, but also scope for a more integrated management of globalisation. A theoretical framework for constitutional thinking must offer a framework to structure relations between actors and institutions in a strong civil society of autonomous citizens (Foqué, 1996). It requires more than a rule-book reflecting existing arrangements, and more than the ability to enact *ad hoc* solutions. As the reflection on the structuring of structures, it needs to guide the use of the rule of law for guaranteeing such relations. The relational concept of law goes back to Montesquieu. Principles such as subsidiarity and proportionality are key tools for the organisation of constitutional relations and help to make such relations more explicit if not transparent (Gerven, 1991; Ellis, 1999). A constitutional framework should be supported by a well-focused education system and it should foster an integrated use of industrial, trade, and other policies in a balanced approach to societal challenges (Dworkin, 1986; Riley, 2001).

REGIONALISM AND THE MANAGEMENT OF GLOBALISATION

Not all markets are global. The scope of proactive industrial, trade and competition policies that aim at fostering the competitiveness of domestic operators on global markets can be limited to parts of society that are effectively exposed to global pressures.

Markets are not global (but local, national or regional[4]) once there is no significant risk that customers will turn to imports from outside the region, and no significant risk that domestic producers will be tempted to dislocate to low-cost production countries outside the region. By this definition, we can establish a list of goods and services with a local market, such as aspects of distribution, restaurants and hotels, and many (but certainly not all) medical services. The list may, however, prove to be frustratingly short.

But local, national, regional and global levels are not only relevant in respect of globalisation in order to determine the level of vulnerability to loss of employment. Even though intra-region dislocation of production may not be seen as less threatening to local employment than global dislocation (as is illustrated by the reactions to the enlargement of the EU), regionalism can help to create areas in which globalisation can more easily be managed.

In the light of the above, there are therefore at least two types of justification for regional initiatives and structures: some issues are regional and require a regional approach; some issues are global, but can, for the time being, only be addressed at a regional level. And issues may be easier to be addressed at a regional level because the region is more homogeneous, or it has stronger institutions with a better capacity to manage conflicting interests. Both aspects are illustrated by the development from GATT to the WTO and by the development of the EU.

Notwithstanding the progress in trade liberalisation at WTO level, it is inevitably easier to create free trade zones within a more homogeneous social and regulatory environment. Because non-tariff barriers often result from valid non-trade policy related concerns, the abolition of measures that constitute non-tariff trade barriers is seldom an option. Mutual recognition is the least painful option but it requires significant confidence in the rules and enforcement mechanisms of trade partners.[5] Mutual recognition and effective harmonisation mostly require an already relatively homogeneous environment.

The EU was initially an example of a region that was sufficiently homogeneous to allow for the development from a customs union to a common market. It would be interesting to know better to what extent the policies for the completion of the internal market stimulated the impressive development of Ireland, Portugal and Spain (and more recently also Greece). It looks as if its progress towards a single market facilitated the convergence between the initial member states and countries that had at accession a significantly lower economic performance. It would also be a useful indication for other regions if we could demonstrate that the completion of the European internal market helped to maintain (if not to re-create) the conditions for its durable success.

Notwithstanding the success of the internal market, the establishment of a (partial) monetary union and the introduction of the euro fundamentally changed the need for cohesion: no monetary union is sustainable without sufficient economic convergence, and no economic convergence is sustainable without political consensus. Few predicted that by 2002 most member states would meet the criteria. But not all member states did succeed in meeting the conditions while some met the criteria but were not willing to accept the discipline. The common project thus proved to generate a remarkable willingness to pay the price for the right to play at centre court. But the project also generates centrifugal tendencies that increasingly characterise the Union. In the accession of ten new member states on 1 May 2004 with 75 million inhabitants (and a combined economic weight comparable to the Netherlands), the EU faced an even more difficult challenge. The new member states offer an attractive (low-cost) destination for investment previously targeted at countries in the western reach of the community, and the challenge now is for the Union to justify itself by its capacity to manage a heterogeneous region and by its ability to eliminate unfair disadvantages. It will, more than ever, have to achieve its stated goal of promoting *'throughout the Community a harmonious, balanced and sustainable development'*.

REGIONALISM, SUBSIDIARITY AND EFFICIENCY

In the light of the above, a constitutional framework for regionalism should at least impose a *subsidiarity test*. If a regional approach ignores the global nature of issues, initiatives are bound to fail. And their failure will destroy confidence in a regional approach. When regional initiatives address issues that are indeed regional, or if they are part of an integrated effort to manage globalisation, they are more likely to be successful. And if they fail, their failure is less likely to affect the legitimacy of regionalism.

In the Maastricht Treaty, the subsidiarity principle was formally written into the EU Treaty. However, it aims at limiting the transfer of power from the member states (national level) to the Union (regional level). Increasingly, there is a need to think of a similar approach to constitutionalise relations between the regional level and the global level (Walker, 2003).[6] The more developed regional organisations can be relatively reluctant to accommodate global structures. This is illustrated by the case law of the EU Court of Justice on the legal effect of GATT or WTO law in the EU legal order (Peers, 2003). WTO law is more willing to accept regional differentiation, and to modulate the most-favoured nation principle when issues that have a global dimension can, for the time being, only be addressed at a regional level (von Bogdandy and Makatsch, 2003).[7]

A well-balanced implementation of the general principle of subsidiarity implies an *efficiency test*. Structures are generally held to be efficient if they allow for effective management and ensure continuity. In a world of global and regional challenges, a theoretical framework for constitutional thinking needs to distinguish between at least two types of institutions of which the efficiency may be judged differently. One type of institution structures society, inspiring a sense of 'belonging', and satisfying aspirations to participate in the organisation and government of the public domain.[8] The archetype of such institution is the constitutional state. These institutions may need to be flexible but should offer stability. It is important that they are perceived as being effective, but inefficiency should normally lead to reform rather than to dissolution.

The second type of institution would reflect a more limited scope in order to deal with issues that cannot be handled efficiently at the level of states. If the handling of such issues requires the stability of an organisation, such organisations will be judged primarily on the efficiency of their policies and their problem-solving capability. They may need to stabilise solutions but also to be flexible – they should not outlast the problems they are supposed to solve. These organisations are not meant to structure society. They are not the political *agora* where policies are agreed and where the public domain is governed. They are primarily technical organisations.

It is important to distinguish both types of institutions, and to manage expectations accordingly. But both types coexist in a multilayered continuum. It is most important that the relations between both types are carefully articulated. If citizens cannot clearly see the distinction, and the need for both types, they will distrust technical organisations handling significant issues because these institutions do not structure the participation of citizens in policy-making. They will also lose confidence in the state because its relevance erodes as it loses control over issues delegated to technical organisations. It is therefore also important that policy-making remains concentrated in institutions that meet the requirements of the first type. Policy implementation can be delegated to the institutions of the second type.

The EU can in this context be assimilated with a state, or seen as a reaction by states in an attempt to regain control over their destiny, or as an instrument by which states formalise the transfer of power to the market. Initially, it was mostly seen as a market organisation, and it was (still is?) judged accordingly when the economic environment deteriorated. The active involvement of its institutions in the management of an economic crisis tends to be highly technical, and too difficult to assess by the non-initiated to be an effective response to the expectations that have been created (Mertens de Wilmars and Steenbergen, 1984). One of the key problems of the EU remains that, notwithstanding significant efforts, it is not yet perceived or structured as an institution of the first type where citizens feel that they participate in policy-making. But the member states' autonomy has already been reduced in many areas to policy-implementing bodies. The fact that the democratic participation is mostly indirect (citizens elect national governments who make EU policy in the Council of Ministers) is no longer sufficient to avoid the so-called democratic deficit, when the direct impact of the national government on EU policy-making is both limited and often not transparent. It is to be feared that this problem will significantly increase after enlargement. Even when we accept the transfer of policy-making powers required for the proper management of a common currency, enlargement and the increased need for majority voting almost compel the Union to transform itself to a state-type institution – or to regress into a free trade arrangement.

However, in the context of regionalism and globalisation, it is unavoidable that major issues are discussed and decided in forums that cannot be expected to meet the requirements for the first type of institutions. This may for example apply to aspects that need to be integrated in a coherent policy, including issues in industrial trade policy and even the arena of education.

Regional organisations are often of the second type. When significant policies are made in an intergovernmental (or contractual) framework, the input of the parties should have political legitimacy and the impact of each of the participants should remain sufficiently strong and visible. This explains and justifies the reluctance to abandon the requirement of consensus or unanimity in intergovernmental organisations.

THE USE OF THE RULE OF LAW

The scope for decision-making in each of the above-mentioned types of organisations can be broader when clear rules and principles limit discretionary powers by allowing for an effective review of decisions (Dworkin, 1977). Discretionary powers can be limited in at least two different ways by clearly formulating the mission of the organisation; or, when organisational rules can develop in a coherent legal order. The formulation of a mission in the basic instruments of an organisation may initially help to empower organisations, as has been the case for the EU since its inception in the Treaty of Rome. But there is also the risk of being identified with a simple policy when the consensus on the mission erodes. This jeopardises the development of a genuine political debate and may compromise legitimacy of an institution as the forum to structure the political domain.

The need for political legitimation (by political decision-making or by agreement between politically legitimated bodies) can be limited to a smaller number of generic decisions if implementing decisions are subject to effective legal review. The EU, and in particular the Court of Justice, consistently positioned EU law (and earlier EEC or EC law) as a specific legal order in which the courts can develop a set of general principles. By reviewing acts of Community institutions and member states the Court helped to define a political *agora*. Thus, the development of a legal order can precede the development of a political order (Mertens de Wilmars, 1983).

Preconditions for such development are a sufficiently articulated set of initial rules and a (judicial) body that can review decisions with accepted authority. However, there are limits to what a rule-enforcing body can do if the politically competent authorities fail to offer the proper direction (Steenbergen, 1986). It follows from the nature of judicial review that it can contribute more effectively (and sometimes even creatively) to the progress of negative integration and the management of 'disciplinary' mechanisms (i.e. agreements that say what members should not do), than to positive integration requiring decisions on policy rather than the review of decisions. The development from a power-oriented to a rule-oriented model may therefore create the adequate framework for the handling of issues that require few political decisions.

But a rule-oriented model (such as the WTO framework) will never be stronger than the legitimacy of its rules. The acceptance of a rule defines the scope for a rule- oriented approach. Rules may derive their legitimacy from an agreement to which the relevant parties adhered explicitly (as in international treaties), or from the decision-making by a legitimated body.

It is not clear whether or when rules and principles can also derive legitimacy from general acceptance as part of a 'cosmopolitan legal order'. Some core human rights have acquired such legitimacy, partly through the consistent use of treaty instruments and the mechanisms of the United Nations. Notwithstanding the efforts of the UN, the WTO (and GATT) and various regional organisations, we do not have the impression that socio-economic or cultural rights and general trade law principles have already acquired a similar standing (Petersmann, 2003). And as long as a significant percentage of citizens still identifies a rule with a policy they oppose, reference to such rules is unlikely to contribute to the acceptance of a constitutional framework that helps to face global challenges. The institutions upholding such rights are more likely to be rejected in conjunction with the policies to which they are linked and identified. The admission that policies result from a balance of power is, in the absence of an underlying consensus on substantive rules, more likely to strengthen the acceptance of institutions.

Regional institutions and rules can therefore only make a significant contribution if they are supported by or structured in politically legitimated structures (such as states). Technical organisations can be in charge of the implementation of policies. When technical organisations are perceived to erode the effectiveness of politically legitimated bodies because states lose the ability to manage significant parts of the public domain, they jeopardise the confidence in the democratic processes without creating the conditions for their own effectiveness. When technical organisations and their rules are disconnected from an environment that is supported by the inner morality of law, they fall victim to naive instrumentalism (Summers, 1977). Technical organisations need the acceptance of an autonomous citizenship in a deliberative democracy: politics should be left to political institutions, either by giving adequate political structures to the relevant organisations or by dealing with the relevant issues in agreements between legitimated bodies on a consensual basis (Habermas, 1996).

Political legitimacy implies more than an agreement on broad principles. Structures need to provide for the enforceable implementation of such rules in effective dispute resolution. An effective review requires the acceptance of the rule of law, expressed in a coherent set of general principles and concretised in specific constitutional structures and procedures. While negotiated rules may often not inspire the cohesion required in order to counteract effectively the consequential damage of globalisation, the criticism that they remain ineffective because of lack of enforcement is largely unjustified. Even prior to the establishment of the WTO and its vastly improved dispute-resolution mechanisms, the much-maligned GATT system performed much better than its reputation suggested. In the WTO, complaints are brought before panels of independent experts (Cameron and Campbell, 1998). Their reports are accepted unless rejected by consensus. Decisions accepting a panel report can be appealed on questions of law before the Appelate Body. In case a party does not conform with a ruling within a reasonable period of time, the injured party is automatically authorised to take retaliatory measures. Retaliation consists in restrictions on imports from the party that has infringed its obligations that are equivalent to the loss in export opportunities for the injured party. Thus, the WTO dispute-resolution mechanisms can effectively help to maintain the balance between the benefits the WTO members derive from the agreements and the pressures on their socio-economic systems, provided the party that has infringed its obligations has exports to the injured party.

In respect of enforcement, regionalism can facilitate the enforcement of global rules. This is illustrated by the extent to which EU law can help to give effect to international public law (Wouters and van Eeckhoutte, 2002), and by the fact that in the WTO dispute-resolution mechanisms regionalism can make it easier to design effective sanctions. Bundling trade relations in regional entities helps to increase the efficiency of sanctions because it makes it more likely that retaliation can be targeted at economically or politically sensitive exports.

CONCLUSION

In the light of the above, we can use the following (constitutional) typology for regional organisations designed to deal with regional issues. First, when regional issues are technical (i.e. without a significant impact on the socio-economic equilibrium), or if the implementation of political agreements does not require political decisions, the management of such issues can be delegated to technical organisations. Their governance and control structures can be similar to the rules on governance that apply to private organisations.

Second, the management of such issues can also be delegated to traditional intergovernmental organisations with a well-defined mandate but without the need for consensus in implementing decisions.

Third, it follows from the above that matters are more complicated when more is needed than the implementation of an existing agreement, and if the management of the relevant issues requires frequent decisions with a political dimension. Such decisions should either be made by a politically legitimated body or by consensus between politically legitimated bodies (this is in international organisations in which decisions are taken by consensus by politically legitimated governments).

The key question is whether regionalism can contribute to a constitutional framework that helps to face global challenges. Globalisation has fundamentally changed the regional agenda so that the real issues that are not local are mostly global, but the tools to best manage these issues tend to be at the level we still tend to see as regional. Regionalism can also be part of a strategy to improve the management of globalisation. This requires, however, a framework that makes the relationships between various levels (local, national, regional and global) conceptually transparent, and that carefully articulates the institutionalisation of decision-making. A balanced and stable development of regionalism needs to be embedded in an operational constitutional order that translates a workable reflective equilibrium between shared political values and their effective implementation (Rawls, 1971).

If regional organisations are called upon to participate in the management of global issues, we can use the same typology as used for purely regional organisations. But to the extent that the political legitimacy of agreements such as trade agreements is more vulnerable, the global structure will need to rely more on the legitimacy of its members. Few regional technical organisations can then be an adequate interface between the local and the global level. This is particularly challenging to the EU and the WTO; to the WTO because it can only make significant progress in the management of non-tariff trade barriers by the gradual development of its legal system while depending on the legitimacy of its members for the acceptance of its rules; to the EU because the EU has not yet succeeded in creating a credible alternative structure for the governance of the public domain in areas where even larger member states already risk their credibility. The EU tends moreover to make progress by differentiating the extent to which its member states need to commit to key policies such as the common currency.

This contribution leaves us therefore with at least two questions. First, how can we structure decision-making so as to give everybody the assurance that they have a reasonable degree of control over their destiny or at least the comfort that forces they can identify are in control? Can we only achieve this goal by reconstructing the state at the least regional level (such as in the EU), or will it be sufficient to continue with pragmatic improvements to more *ad hoc* structures such as the WTO, provided their place in the constitutional continuum is well defined and transparent?

Second, how far can the EU proceed as a component in the constitutional continuum between the local and the global level with pragmatic (technocratic) solutions *à géométrie variable*, without being part of the problem instead of being the key element in the regional response to global challenges? From a European regional perspective, the two questions and the challenges to the WTO and the EU are much related. Both are concerned with the limits to constitutional pluralism.

This is in line with our conclusion in respect of the need for a constitutional articulation of various levels of decision-making: the WTO can be more pragmatic in its structures and policies if its rules are legitimised by the intra-regional legitimacy of the Union's rules and policies. But this also means that the EU risks exporting any legitimacy deficit it has to the WTO. Seen from a small EU member state, there are not many options: Either the EU develops into a member of the world order with genuine internal legitimacy, i.e. the EU evolves into the key platform structuring a significant segment of the public domain and we can then envisage the world as a league of majors and feel involved; or, small member states resign to micro-state status and their citizens abdicate from any ambitions to have a collective structured impact on global developments. Few seem psychologically equipped to make this work, with possible exceptions (in the case of Europe) in Denmark and Switzerland.

The situation of larger EU member states is more difficult. For a large member state such as the UK, notions of state autonomy and independence are still strong. But what would be the position of the UK in the WTO if the hardcore of the EU evolves into the civil equivalent of a superpower with member states on its periphery who neither adopt the common currency nor several of its key policies? The common market may be all the UK wants from the European construction. But even if the EU continues to participate in the WTO as common market as it has done since the Kennedy Round, is it reasonable to expect that its agenda and policies will be determined by its periphery, any more than the EU's agenda is defined in the EEA? And what will be the position of France and Germany if they are no less but also no more powerful in the Union than such states as California, New York or Texas are in the US?

The position of countries in other parts of the world is somewhat different. The smaller ones have even less hope than EU member states of making a difference on the world stage unless they group their efforts. But the larger countries in the Americas and Asia are so large that they probably can do without an international regional interface. Instead, they need to structure along sub-national regionalism the interface between the local and the national level.

It is difficult to (re)construct legitimacy at a regional level. But ambitions, if not the existential need to be involved, are no less difficult to curb. Some hope that the internet culture will give a constitutional dimension to flexible, non-structured networks that will make most of our present problems obsolete. Technology certainly facilitates the participation in a knowledge society. It can also broaden the scope for pluralism by facilitating transparency. It is, however, questionable whether technology will help citizens participate in the scheme of principles and institutional values structuring society such as the rule of law. We will need to strike a careful balance between effective individual survival strategies and structured and democratically legitimised governance.

NOTES

1. Regions can be smaller or larger than the territory of one state. In this chapter we will focus on regional initiatives of states, involving regions covering the territory of more than one state.

2. Consisting of the EU, Iceland, Liechtenstein and Norway. It can roughly be described as an internal market organisation with the market regulations of the EU and its legal order but without the EU's more political dimension.

3. It has been estimated that tariffs were reduced on average by 38 per cent, with a reduction of the average tariff between industrialised countries from 6.3 to 3.9 per cent. 43 per cent of trade between industrialised countries is no longer subject to tariffs, as compared to 20 per cent before the closing of the Uruguay Round.

4. In competition law, relevant geographic markets can be global, regional (for example European), national or local. However, in competition law, relevant markets are more defined in the light of customer behaviour than supply-side developments.

5. One of the best and most influential examples is the 'Cassis de Dijon' judgment of the Court of Justice of the European Communities in 1979, which insisted that under certain specified conditions member states should accept in their own markets products approved for sale by other member states.

6. Walker (2003) distinguishes clearly the need to constitutionalise the relations between the EU and the WTO from the debate on the constitutionalisation of the WTO.

7. See for example article XXIV GATT, article 4 TRIPS and especially articles V and Vbis GATS.

8. In our opinion, closer to the 'invisible touch of statehood' than required for the structuring of a 'polity' as used by Walker (2003, 33 et seq).

5

Economic Theories of Regional Integration

Brigid Gavin and Philippe De Lombaerde

INTRODUCTION

Regional integration has long attracted the attention of economists, and there is a well-developed body of theory to explain both trade and monetary integration. Trade integration distinguishes between free trade areas (FTAs), customs unions (CUs) and common markets (CMs). An FTA is the simplest form of economic integration whereby countries agree to liberalise their internal trade but each country maintains autonomy in its external level of protection. A CU takes integration one step further by establishing not only internal free trade but also a common external tariff. This implies that members agree to give up their national sovereignty over trade policy towards non-members and to transfer it to a central community authority. A CM entails the free movement of factors of production – capital and labour – which implies 'deep integration', that is liberalisation of behind-the-border regulatory barriers to trade (Balassa, 1961).

Monetary integration leads to the adoption of a common currency, the acceptance of a common monetary policy and the establishment of a regional monetary authority with responsibility for the conduct of this policy. Economic and monetary union (EMU) goes further and establishes complete unification of fiscal and monetary policies under a regional authority so that the members then become regions of one nation.

This chapter outlines the economic perspectives on regional integration, and identifies the evolution in theoretical explanations of increasingly complex cooperative processes among the countries involved in integration arrangements. The following sections distinguish between integration in the areas of trade and the monetary arena, highlighting theoretical issues behind some of today's more pressing problems and the questions facing many policy-makers as they consider how to negotiate the next phase of integration, or why some policy-makers decide not to move ahead with deeper integration. Ultimately, the decision to integrate trade policy or to establish some form of cooperative monetary arrangement is a political one, and the chapter concludes by considering whether political integration should precede or follow monetary integration.

TRADE INTEGRATION – THE TRADITIONAL VIEW

Traditionally, CUs were considered as synonymous with free trade and so they were treated within the classical free-trade paradigm. Prominent examples from the nineteenth century were the United States CU, between the agricultural south and the nascent industrial north, and the German *Zollverein*. Almost a century later, the view of the CU as a move towards free trade was modified by Jacob Viner's work, when he identified the paradox of regional trade integration, which does not necessarily increase economic welfare (Viner, 1950). All forms of regional trade integration take place between a limited number of countries and they involve discrimination against the rest of the world.[1]

Following Viner's contributions to regional integration theory, this field of knowledge emerged as an important sub-discipline of international trade theory, even challenging some of its most revered tenets. Viner's seminal work was followed by major new developments in 'the theory of the second best'[2] by Meade (1955) and Lipsey (1957). Since the 1960s, regional trade integration in practice has provided one of the most fruitful 'laboratories' for advancing international trade theory. The early experience of European integration in the 1960s would eventually bring about a shift of trade patterns and greater 'intra-industry' trade,[3] stimulating new thinking about international trade under conditions of imperfect competition. Trade theory shifted away from emphasis on country-specific 'comparative advantage' towards industry-specific factors such as increasing returns and external economies as the drivers of international trade. This, in turn, provided a new impetus for 'regional economics' leading to new conceptualisation about specialisation and 'economic geography' (Krugman, 1991, 483–99).

Static analysis (short-term)

Countries engage in trade for the benefits which the larger international market can bring. Specific trading arrangements such as CUs contribute particular advantages, while also effecting a shift in the pre-existing structure of trade.

CU theory is derived from a partial equilibrium analysis of the welfare effects of tariff elimination under conditions of perfect competition. Trade creation will occur when there is a shift from a high cost source outside the CU to a low cost internal source, which implies an overall increase in productive efficiency in the world. If the opposite occurs following the formation of a CU, there will be trade diversion, which, by implication, means a decrease in productive efficiency in the world. For example, if the home country in the CU, which is a major industrial country, replaces food imports from a low cost producer by imports from its higher cost producer inside the union following the formation of the union, world economic welfare will be adversely affected. Trade diversion is all the more negative the greater the difference between the price prevailing within the CU and the price prevailing on the world market.

Viner's model refers to the supply side of the economy and neglects the effects on demand following the elimination of tariffs. The removal of tariffs will lead to lower prices for consumers and the quantity demanded is likely to rise. In response to increased demand in the partner country, the home country will increase production. This 'trade expansion' in the words of Meade can occur simultaneously with trade creation and trade diversion.

The desirability of CUs will depend on the extent of trade creation and trade expansion, with their positive welfare effects, against the negative effects of trade diversion. Therefore it is important to identify the conditions under which CUs will be beneficial to the world. If trade expansion goes with trade creation, then welfare will always increase. But if trade expansion goes with trade diversion, then welfare may decrease as the negative welfare effects of the latter may outweigh the positive welfare effect of the former. In this context there has been much debate about whether the partner economies in the union are 'competitive' or 'complementary'.

[The static analysis of CU theory focuses on the once-and-for-all effects of lower prices resulting from the elimination of tariffs and the increased competition between countries.]As such it only captures the short-term effects and fails to capture the dynamic effects of industrial restructuring which the trade liberalisation will unleash. Many economists believe that it is those longer-term dynamic effects, which are the most important and will have the most long-lasting effects.

Dynamic analysis (long-term?.)

Among the most important dynamic effects are economies of scale, enhanced competition and increased incentives for investment. However, the process of industrial restructuring may be inhibited by different national standards and regulations that effectively fragment markets and distort competition.

Governments frequently justify regional integration for the purpose of exploiting the gains from economies of scale more fully. Internal economies refer to the economies of scale that are internal to the firm or the industry to which the firm belongs and which result in lower production costs. Those economies of scale usually derive from more efficient use of technology and more efficient management techniques. Thus the formation of an enlarged regional market will lead to a dynamic restructuring as firms aim for optimal scale of production and lower production costs through economies of scale. Major rationalisation of business operations will lead to significant economies of scale, previously inhibited by national trade barriers.

External economies include all the inter- and intra-industrial linkages that result in cost reductions. External economies may be both pecuniary and non-pecuniary. Pecuniary external effects occur when the price of intermediate goods used in the production of final goods becomes lower as a result of internal economies of scale. Non-pecuniary external effects are typically derived from intensification of technological progress especially when technological spillovers occur. This acceleration of both the rate and diffusion of technological progress is frequently the outcome of a more intensive integration process.

In summary, economies of scale include all cost-cutting rationalisation measures taken by firms, the building of new plants and concentrating production in the most efficient plants. The dynamic growth effects of economies of scale are based on the assumption that the gains made are re-invested which extends the scope of endogenous (internal) growth.

Equally important is the stimulus to competition and investment that the enlarged regional market will bring. Large firms in small countries previously protected by national tariff walls will lose their monopolistic 'quiet life' as border protection is dismantled and they are faced with tough new competition in the larger market. The investment stimulus will include inflows of foreign direct investment (FDI), which brings additional competition in the form of new technology and managerial know-how. And, once the first multinational enterprises (MNEs) have jumped over the tariff wall of the CU, others will 'follow the leader' and switch from trade to investment too for fear of missing out on lucrative new markets. This situation could lead to investment diversion, a phenomenon that reflects the fact that third country MNEs will favour the CU over other countries to have better access to the enlarged market.

Despite the much touted positive benefits of economies of scale and enhanced competition, there is need for scepticism. Economies of scale, as some economists contend, can only be achieved at the cost of a reduction in the number of competitors in the market and a reduction of product variety. Industrial restructuring is usually associated with a rising wave of mergers leading to greater concentration. There is, therefore, the risk of recreating an oligopolistic structure at the regional level to replace what existed at the national level. And, since oligopolistic structures serve to reduce pressure for cost cutting and inhibit price-cutting, the effects on competition will not be benign. Enhanced competition in the enlarged regional market will inevitably depend upon the existence of competition policy and measures to control cartels and other anti-competitive practices.

The harmonisation of standards

The elimination of barriers to trade in goods and services will not always ensure guaranteed access to the enlarged regional market which firms expect. As trade barriers at the border are removed, different national standards and regulations may continue to fragment markets. National regulations are not intended as barriers *per se* but they may act as *de facto* barriers and serve to distort competition.

Regulation is designed to redress the problem of market failure but the question arises of how to decide whether this regulation should be at the national or regional level. The principle of subsidiarity is the answer. The principle is based on the premise that regulation should be made closest to the source of the problem, unless there is some compelling reason to have regional regulation.

Competition between national regulatory standards may allow some members to set the lowest possible standards because the adverse effects will be felt by consumers in other countries. Such a cooperative regional strategy would provide incentives for a 'race to the bottom' concerning standard quality. Harmonisation based on legislation would provide a stronger outcome in terms of quality and it would also have greater credibility. Of course, this scenario depends on the assumption that the regulators have not been captured by special interests.

THE NEW REGIONAL INTEGRATION

The new regionalism of the 1990s differed from the old regionalism of the 1960s in a number of important ways (Ethier, 2001). Contemporary integration typically involves a number of small countries that are willing to link up with a large neighbouring country which plays the role of regional hegemon. The small countries are involved in a process of unilateral liberalisation and they want to consolidate it by linking up with a large anchor country. Current regional integration processes rest upon deep integration; agreements go beyond liberalisation of tariffs to include the removal of regulatory barriers relating to liberalisation of services and investment issues. Small countries consider regional integration as a means to strengthen their bargaining position in international trade negotiations.

Contemporary economic integration theory emphasises the dynamic effects of economic integration, the interaction between trade and investment and the role of institutional arrangements as incentives for regional integration. As a result of the structural changes in the global economy in the 1990s brought about by globalisation, FDI has become increasingly important in the global economy. Firms have an incentive to switch from trade to FDI when trading costs, for example, transport costs, are relatively higher than investment costs.

Since the size of the market influences FDI inflows, the enlarged regional market will attract investment inflows. Small countries compete to attract foreign investment by regionalising their market and they may be willing to pay a premium for this by undertaking considerable economic reforms. By linking up with a large country, small countries gain credibility in the eyes of foreign investors based on the belief that the large country will play the role of hegemon in the club and enforce the rules.

Political economy considerations also play a determining role in new regionalism. Trade liberalisation, in practice, is a mercantilist exercise in which governments weigh up the 'benefits' of foreign market access for their exporters against the 'costs' of increased import competition for their home industries. The larger the reduction in multilateral trade barriers, the greater the cost in terms of adverse effects on special interests at home – a fact that has to be reckoned with in national elections. Governments prefer regional trade liberalisation because by negotiating with a smaller number of countries, they can reduce the number of special interests affected. So the trade-off is between regional trade liberalisation with a limited number of countries, leading to deep integration and global trade liberalisation that remains at the level of shallow integration. Multilateral trade liberalisation fosters global trade, which increases transport costs relative to regional trade. Regional integration will favour FDI at the expense of trade because investment costs are falling relatively more rapidly than transport costs.

Although trade creation leads to economic growth, there may well be uneven distribution of the gains, in other words, there will be losers as well as winners. The 'cost of adjustment' following trade liberalisation becomes a public policy issue because it requires occupational or geographic mobility of the work force. It may also lead to increasing divergence between rich and poor countries in a CU and growing regional inequalities, with adverse affects on the social and political cohesion of the union.

If regional trade integration leads to more intra-industry trade (IIT), the adjustment process will be smoother and the European Union (EU) has provided a good case study to support this view. When the Community carried out its first round of trade integration in the 1960s, it coincided with an increase in IIT. However, industrial adjustment needs to be analysed as a dynamic process and a high incidence in one period is not necessarily an indication that this will continue to occur in the future.

Increasing attention has been focused on the adjustment process under conditions of imperfect competition. The new theories of 'economic geography' predict that economic integration will promote concentration of industry closest to their largest markets. These models have drawn attention to the fact that regional disparities may increase due to agglomeration effects. Agglomeration economies, which refer to the external economies associated with the concentration of resources and industry in a particular location, play a key role in regional inequalities. And the theory suggests that there are systematic processes at work that are beyond the powers of the region, and that contribute to regional decline.

Firms may be drawn to relocate in core regions where external economies and spillovers between concentrations of industries producing intermediate and final products are available to a greater extent than in the peripheral regions. Location at the centre may provide advantages from technological spillovers as well as proximity to other firms. This trend, if left unchecked, could produce increasing divergence between core and peripheral regions. A process of cumulative causation could reinforce inequalities between regions.

To a greater or lesser extent, regional integration schemes have their 'periphery countries', which are far away from the large markets at the core, and where per capita national income is much lower than in core countries. Since economic disparities can have a negative impact on social and political cohesion, the EU in particular has responded by providing 'structural funds' to invest in infrastructures, road and communications networks and other public investments to promote development. Although the case for structural funds is based on sound theory, the recent experience has shown that regional inequality may not be such a great problem as in the past. First of all, manufacturing industry has become more decentralised and spread out. This trend has been reinforced by falling transport costs and firms are not clustering in one region to the same extent.

Moreover, trade liberalisation is only one fact in creating divergence between rich and poor countries in the region. The experience of the EU shows that poor macroeconomic policy management has also caused divergence in economic performance between countries. Lax monetary policy and expansionary fiscal policy will stunt economic growth and lack of wage discipline in labour markets will adversely affect unemployment (Barry, 2003). Trade integration produces an additional set of dynamics for the countries involved, and making it work effectively may require a move to even deeper integration, extending to the coordination of macroeconomic policies and, ultimately, monetary integration.

REGIONAL MONETARY INTEGRATION

In different parts of the world, regional monetary integration is being considered by economists and politicians as a means to further deepen or reinforce sometimes stagnating trade-based integration schemes, to reap the benefits of stable exchange rates and credible regional monetary institutions, and/or to find answers to the volatility of global capital markets and the absence of an adequate global monetary infrastructure.

Although in some cases (like the EMU or the Communauté Financière Africaine zone) regional monetary integration is seen as a 'political' rather than an 'economic' decision, there is no doubt that an understanding of cost and benefits of regional monetary integration is crucial for arguing in favour or against such policies or to understand the achievements or failures of certain arrangements. [Optimum currency area (OCA) theory is the mainstream theoretical framework for analysing these costs and benefits.]

OCA theory poses the problem of the relevance and the choice of the policy domain for monetary policy, and presents a number of criteria, both microeconomic and macroeconomic, to determine the optimal size of monetary unions (MUs). Recent developments have focused on the choice of the OCA criteria, empirical methods to test these criteria, the relationship between monetary and fiscal policies at the regional level and the entry decision for new members to existing MUs. In the following paragraphs we will first briefly present Robert Mundell's original proposals and then the more recent developments.

Optimum currency area theory

Mundell's 1961 article is a radical departure from the understanding of (national) exchange rate policies; it laid the foundations for what would become an economic theory of regional integration, and the obligatory reference point for modern economic analysis of the desirability of monetary integration. The exchange rate debate had until then, taken the policy level for granted and concentrated on the choice between fixed and flexible rates. The modern case for floating exchange rates was made by Friedman, arguing that floating rates allowed for monetary independence, protection against real shocks and a smooth macroeconomic adjustment mechanism (Friedman, 1953).

Mundell (1961) showed – with the help of a series of examples – that the debate about fixed and flexible rates can be a sterile and irrelevant debate from the point of view of macroeconomic adjustment, if the issue of the extension of the area subject to the exchange rate policy is not contemplated.

Consider, for example, two countries (the US and Canada), each of which contain two regions (east and west) within their borders. These regions are characterised by dominant economic activities, cars in the west and timber in the east. An asymmetric shock that alters the relative demand for the two goods in both countries, with downward rigidity of prices and wages, produces unemployment and inflationary pressures in the respective regions and leaves the central banks with a dilemma: inflating or disinflating the economy? What is certain in this case is that exchange rate policies do not offer a way out. [The situation in both countries could be resolved with inter-regional mobility of production factors.] This would diminish the inflationary pressures in one region and resolve the unemployment problem in the other.

In another example where both countries are specialising in the production of only one product, and thus without (inter-industry) factor mobility, the argument in favour of flexible exchange rates would be valid, to the extent that the adjustment of the exchange rate can reduce the macroeconomic adjustment cost and absorb the asymmetric shock, devaluating the currency of the country negatively affected by the shock in the form of a reduction in the relative demand for its good. However, as Mundell points out, a restrictive monetary policy in the surplus country with the inflationary pressures, would oblige the deficit country to carry the whole adjustment cost. There is a clear case, he argued, in favour of the coordination of international monetary policies in order to avoid the deflationary effect of restrictive policies in the surplus countries.

With these examples, Mundell showed that a conceptual distinction between a 'country' and an (economic) 'region' should be made. The region is thereby defined as an area characterised by (internal) factor mobility. For Mundell, the region is theoretically the adequate level for the definition of exchange rate policy. Countries in the real world may coincide with a region, may consist of various regions or may be smaller than a region. If they are smaller than a region, monetary integration would be (economically) justified.

The lesson which is generally retained from Mundell's exposition is that exchange rates should be fixed within areas (regions) characterised by perfect intra-regional factor mobility, whereas they should be flexible between regions in the absence of inter-regional factor mobility. However, in the same article, Mundell accepts that the exclusive use of this criterion would imply an unrealistic proliferation of currency areas possessing a dominating economic activity (homogeneous regions), because only such regions do not face the lack of inter-industry factor mobility (especially labour). The efficiency costs (transaction and valuation costs) would obviously be too high.

In Mundell's view, the choice of the exchange rate and the delimitation of the currency zones is thus not only a problem of macroeconomic stability, it should be the result of a cost-benefit analysis. The loss of the exchange rate instrument for macroeconomic stabilisation is considered as a cost of monetary integration, which has to be weighed against the efficiency gains (minimisation of transaction and valorisation costs) of having a common currency.

Over time, emphasis has shifted from the Mundellian structural criteria to more policy-related criteria. Rather than focusing on factor mobility, economists turned their attention to the question of whether converging policies and/or the flexibilisation of labour markets and prices create the conditions for MU and whether a political commitment exists from the side of the authorities.

Recent discussions on monetary integration have been influenced by the evolution of international macroeconomics and the further sophistication of the economic models.[4] New features and variables have been added to the models; these include: the formation of expectations by the economic agents, the credibility of the monetary authorities, a more detailed typology of price and wage rigidities and shocks, the role of labour market institutions, and so on. The new views in macroeconomics tend to incline towards predicting lower costs of abandoning national monetary policies, compared to the original views. This has obvious implications for the cost-benefit calculus proposed by Mundell and strengthens the case for monetary integration.

Finally, given the fact that Mundell's work proposes measurable tools for the evaluation of the convenience of monetary integration, it has inspired a substantial amount of empirical work. This work deals with trade integration and factor markets and mobility, although most recent work concentrates on the measurement of the degree of symmetry of the external shocks and the synchronicity of economic cycles. In the next sections we will focus on several of the critiques and further developments of OCA theory.

Openness and diversification

According to McKinnon (1963) and Kenen (1969), the OCA, rather than being defined in terms of labour mobility, should be defined as the area that permits three policy objectives: a stable price level, full employment and a balanced external account. In their early contributions to OCA theory, these authors proposed two new OCA criteria: openness and diversification.

McKinnon (1963) explores the consequences of different degrees of openness for the optimality of the exchange rate regime. He argues that in relatively open economies – economies with a high import ratio (M/GDP) or a high tradables/non-tradables ratio – with flexible exchange rates, the domestic currency loses 'utility' as a value deposit, because its purchasing power becomes unstable. In addition, the exchange rate volatility is directly reflected in domestic prices. A depreciation leads automatically to inflation and a loss of competitiveness if exports have a high import content. Therefore, McKinnon recommends fixed exchange rates for small open economies and flexible rates for large closed economies. In closed economies, the flexible exchange rates facilitate balance-of-payments adjustment without causing inflation.

McKinnon's analysis assumes that shocks are internal to the economy. Yet this is not self-evident; the source of volatility could be external, which would invalidate his proposition. According to McKinnon, it makes sense to fix the exchange rate in a country vis-à-vis a trade partner when the former country is more sensitive to shocks than the latter. This happens when the economy is smaller, more open and less diversified, and the other bigger, less open and more diversified. However, in a binational or regional context, McKinnon's logic leads to an impossibility: with monetary integration it is impossible that all member countries succeed in fixing their currency vis-à-vis a more stable partner. Leadership and political commitment are therefore important factors in the formation of a MU. However, if the external price level is less stable than the internal price level (contrary to McKinnon's assumption), more open economies might need more flexible exchange rates, reversing by this the original argument.

Later on, McKinnon's widely accepted thesis was questioned by Gros and Steinherr (1997) to show that the cost of fixing exchange rates actually rises with the degree of openness in the presence of external shocks, because the cost of inadequate exchange rates is higher with a larger external sector. In the presence of an internal shock, trade liberalisation reduces its impact on domestic demand and production, so that the cost of fixing the exchange rate diminishes with openness. As far as policy formulation is concerned, this implies that in order to evaluate the cost of abandoning a flexible exchange rate, it is not sufficient to analyse the degree of openness of the economy but also the importance of external shocks should be assessed. In other words, the cost of abandoning the exchange rate as an adjustment instrument is greater for an economy with a high degree of openness and an industrial structure and export pattern that are very different from those of the region than for a country that also displays a different export structure but which is relatively closed.

Kenen proposes also an alternative criterion to identify OCAs. He maintains that the diversification of the productive structure – the number of regions of homogeneous production within a country – is more relevant than the Mundellian criterion of factor mobility. According to Kenen, (i) very diversified national economies, with therefore a diversified export supply, do not need as frequent adjustments of the terms of trade compared to a non-diversified economy, and (ii) when confronting specific negative shocks, their effect on employment levels is not so drastic. Kenen maintains that exchange rates should be fixed in very diversified economies, and adds that this should be complemented with nominal wage controls and regional fiscal policies.

McKinnon (1969) pointed out that Kenen's conclusions are not compatible with his own. Whereas he recommended fixed exchange rates for small open economies, Kenen's logic implies a recommendation of fixed exchange rates for large and relatively closed economies because larger economies tend to be more diversified and imply less dependence on foreign markets.

Monetary and fiscal policies

Once the optimal extension of a MU is established, the question rises whether monetary integration should be complemented by a fiscal policy with the same dominion. This question has been considered mainly in the context of European monetary cooperation. Economics offers different approaches to tackle the thorny question of whether to coordinate fiscal policy.

From the perspective of macroeconomics, the starting point for analysing the needs for and the benefits of international coordination of macroeconomic policies is the open economy. The model shows that a case for coordination can be built when national macroeconomic policies become ineffective in an open economy context. The model analyses the effectiveness of fiscal policies (fiscal expansion) and monetary policies (monetary expansion) under different exchange rate regimes (fixed and flexible) and with different degrees of international capital mobility (high or low). If regional integration implies more capital mobility and the fixing of exchange rates (in order to minimise transaction costs related to increasing interconnectedness), the model shows that national monetary policies become ineffective, whereas fiscal policies remain effective.[5] This general result is, broadly speaking, confirmed and even strengthened in the 'new classical' models, although these present radical departures from the assumptions in the Mundell model. This suggests that (regional) coordination of monetary policies should be advocated, leaving fiscal policies a matter for national governments.

Another perspective is suggested by fiscal federalism, where multilevel government is the preferred framework through which policies are implemented, in accordance with some agreed arrangements for the distribution of public decision-making. To the extent that monetary integration contributes to the mobilisation of production factors, generation of more cross-border spillovers, and so on, the spending capacity at the macro-regional level should be strengthened. However, fiscal federalism is not primarily interested in macroeconomic adjustment and a preference for lower (here: national and sub-national) government levels is usually expressed, for both economic and political reasons.

From within the OCA framework, Kenen (1969) argued however that the dominion of fiscal policy should preferably coincide with the dominion of monetary policy if an optimal policy combination is being sought. He adds that these jurisdictions should not be too small because of efficiency reasons (transaction costs linked to the use of different currencies) and economies of scale (especially relevant for fiscal policy). In Kenen's view, currency areas will necessarily include various homogeneous production regions and should be accompanied by a fiscal federalism capable of playing a stabilising role when member countries or sub-regions are affected by adverse (asymmetric) shocks.

In spite of conflicting views over the impact of MU and decentralised fiscal policy (the risk of inflationary public spending), the case remains strong that monetary integration contributes to lower inflation through a more independent central bank and increased transparency and price competition.

The discussions on European cohesion policy shifted the focus of fiscal policy from short term macroeconomic adjustment to medium and longer term real convergence. This is understandable from a policy perspective because in many regional integration initiatives, convergence is either explicitly stated as an objective of integration, or is at least an implied outcome of it (Meeusen and Villaverde, 2002).

Contrary to neo-classical growth models, the more recent endogenous growth models (Lucas, 1988; Romer, 1990) do not predict macroeconomic convergence between integrating countries, because of initial differences in human capital and institutions, combined with increasing returns. Regional convergence, provided that it is a policy objective, would thus require redistributive policies (cohesion policies) at the regional level. As Barry and Begg (2003) observe, there is however no consensus in the literature on how monetary integration will affect convergence among member states.

SEQUENCING MONETARY AND POLITICAL INTEGRATION

Different views exist on the optimal sequencing of monetary and political integration decisions. Kenen's views on the need for a supranational fiscal transfer system able to target asymmetric shocks, as discussed before, suggest that a workable MU is only feasible if a considerable degree of political integration has been reached first. Political integration generates convergence of policy preferences and political will. Current views still see political integration (previous to or simultaneous with monetary integration) as a possible strategy to reduce national idiosyncrasies which generate asymmetric shocks that have a political or institutional origin, if markets cannot be made more flexible.

The question of political and monetary integration has been much debated in the context of the EU (Theurl, 1995; Eichengreen, 1996). Theurl argues that when monetary integration among a group of countries does not coincide with an OCA, the inevitable and persistent economic imbalances may be conducive to an acceleration of the process of political integration. An apolitical MU is only feasible (conceivable) with the fiction of an OCA, converging economies, the absence of asymmetric shocks, a monetary policy strictly geared towards stabilisation, and disciplined national economic policies. According to Theurl, this is neither realistic nor desirable; political integration is necessary for reaching higher levels of intra-regional solidarity. The adequate sequence of monetary and political integration is also treated in Pivetti (1998), who criticises the conception adopted in the Delors report and the Maastricht Treaty according to which monetary integration precedes political integration. Pivetti argues that as long as certain political and social objectives continue to be national objectives, the national state should not be prevented to use policy instruments like controls on capital flows. In other words, monetary integration should be accompanied by political integration in order to elevate the objectives related to unemployment, income distribution, living standards, and so on, to the supranational level.

An alternative view is offered by Alesina and Spolaore who show that whereas openness (interdependence) increases the need for international economic policy coordination, requiring some kind of supranational (regional) institutional arrangement, openness does not necessarily have the same effect on the need for political integration (Alesina and Spolaore, 2003).

As we mentioned before, it has been argued that monetary integration should be seen as driven by political rather than economic determinants. Therefore, before concluding, a few words should be said about the capacity of economic theories and variables to explain and predict real-world exchange rate policies.

The relevance of economic theories of exchange rate policies and monetary integration depends on the capacity of these theories to explain the choice and performance of alternative sets of policies. Reviewing the empirical literature, it seems that economic theories alone do not explain the choice of exchange rate regimes, nor that there is any universally dominant set of determinants (Papaioannou, 2003). There is evidence, however, that many of the variables suggested by OCA theory significantly contribute to the determination of exchange rate regime choice, especially in the long run and alongside historical, political and institutional determinants.

Bayoumi and Eichengreen (1998) also tested the predictive power of OCA theory. Using cross-section data for 21 countries, they showed first that the factors included in OCA theory explain well the volatility of exchange rates. They also showed that this correlation can be consistently explained by the same theory. The benefits of flexible exchange rates are higher with more outspoken asymmetric shocks and more need for relative price adjustments. The costs of such a regime are higher in small open economies where the liquidity of the currency deteriorates more with exchange rate variability. They also developed a model that shows that asymmetric shocks increase the pressures on the exchange markets, requiring more frequent adjustments, and that trade liberalisation causes more intervention by the monetary authorities.

CONCLUSION

This chapter has shown how the development of regional trade and monetary integration has fostered new theoretical thinking in both fields. Regional trade integration has contributed to new fields of enquiry about economies of scale, intra-industry trade, economic geography and harmonisation of standards. Innovative thinking has challenged some of the major tenets of neo-classical trade theory and has also led to innovative policy proposals enabling deeper integration between countries.

The theory of monetary integration contrasts the (mostly microeconomic) gains from currency union with the (mostly macroeconomic) losses of abandoning an autonomous monetary policy. OCA theory lacks operational precision and reflects a degree of ambiguity for consideration as a scientific instrument to clearly and unequivocally identify the optimal size of currency areas. However, OCA theory does offer the necessary elements for a structured evaluation of concrete policy options related to regional monetary cooperation and integration (De Lombaerde, 2002).

In relation to the debate on the role of macro-regions in future global governance, economic theories of regional integration predict a more important role for this policy level, or, in other words, net benefits of greater (deeper) regional integration. The reason is that if the trends of more intense trade in goods and services, international capital flows and migration continue, there will be a growing need for regional policies and regulatory frameworks, although in a functional relationship with other (lower or higher) policy levels. These predictable shifts in optimal policy levels will have important (and often problematic) consequences for politics and institutions.

NOTES

1. To clarify the terminology, we distinguish regional integration among a group of neighbouring countries from bilateral free trade agreements.
2. The theory of the second best asserts that domestic market failure justifies government intervention in free trade. It argues that a laissez-faire approach is desirable in any one market only if all other markets are working properly. If they are not, government intervention that appears to distort incentives in one market may actually increase welfare by offsetting the consequences of market failure elsewhere.
3. Intra-industry trade, which involves exports and imports of similar products, is distinguished from inter-industry trade, which is based on the comparative advantage of countries.
4. For an overview, see Horvath (2003).
5. The view according to which open capital markets, monetary policy autonomy and fixed exchange rates are not compatible and one of these policy objectives should be given up, is known in the literature as the 'impossibility trinity', or the 'trilemma'.

Part Two

Key Issues in Regional Cooperation

6
Exploring the Links between
Micro-Regionalism and Macro-Regionalism

Fredrik Söderbaum

Today's regionalism is a multidimensional and pluralistic phenomenon, involving many different actors, appearing in different guises and also emerging on different scales or 'levels' (for example macro-, sub- and micro-regionalism). But even if the pluralism of contemporary regionalism is often accepted, there is a tendency to deal mainly with one of the scales of regionalism at a time instead of exploring to what extent and how they are related and interconnected. There is in particular a great divide between the discourse of macro-regionalism (the main concern in this book) and the discourse of micro-regionalism (regional and urban studies). This gap is unfortunate and constitutes in my view one of the missing links in the study of regionalism as conducted so far. This is one of the reasons for the under-emphasis of the heterogeneity and pluralism of regionalism as well as micro-issues 'on the ground'. In response this chapter explores the much neglected links between micro-regionalism and macro-regionalism.

Macro-regions ('world regions') are here seen as large territorial units or subsystems, between the 'state' and the 'global' level (for example Europe or the European Union (EU)), whereas micro-regions exist between the 'national' and the 'local' (municipal) level, and are either sub-national or cross-border (for example Flanders or Øresund region). In the past there have been overly sharp distinctions between these two types of regions, and they have been treated as two very different phenomena and with few linkages between them. The view of this chapter is that learning more about their linkages (and similarities) will enhance our understanding of the 'regional phenomenon' in a more comprehensive sense.

In bridging the gap it is not sufficient to dichotomise them as either 'from above' (macro) or 'from below' (micro), which has often been the case in the past.

Globalisation has not spawned such ideal types but, rather, a mix of contested [...] regional projects: in various degrees spontaneous or deliberate, home-grown or emulated. These include different generations or iterations of the NIC [Newly Industrialised Countries] model, growth triangles and polygons often encompassing

EPZs [Export Processing Zones] and development corridors, and transfrontier growth areas. (Mittelman, 2000, 158)

Thus, all regions can be created both from 'above' and from 'below'; sometimes the state has more autonomy with regard to social forces and at other times the global market penetrates more deeply.

The links between micro-regionalism and macro-regionalism are not simply under-explored from an 'empirical' point of view. The neglect is also a theoretical and conceptual problem. The coexistence of micro-regionalism and macro-regionalism and above all their intriguing relationships are poorly explained by the traditional theories that dominate the research field, especially realism, liberalism, liberal intergovernmentalism and regional economic integration. In response, this chapter is both theoretical and empirical.

The chapter is structured as follows. The next two sections elaborate how theories and analytical perspectives need to be adjusted in order to better account for the complexities and linkages between different scales of regionalisms. The first section argues that we need to transcend the state as the main spatial category in our analysis and insert it into a more multiscalar political landscape. Once such a multiscalar perspective is accepted we will automatically start to pay more attention to other spaces, particularly macro-regions and micro-regions. In the second section it is then emphasised that we should also nuance and adjust the way we theorise and conceptualise regional space and scales of regionalism. As an inroad to further analysis, the third section distinguishes between different types of micro-regions: physical-geographic, cultural, economic, administrative/planning and finally political micro-regions. Thereafter follows a comparative exploration of the micro–macro linkages in some illuminating cases around the world: Europe, Southeast Asia and Southern Africa. The concluding section draws the pieces together and also makes some reflections on the future linkages between micro-regionalism and macro-regionalism.

NUANCING SPACE: A MULTISCALAR PERSPECTIVE

Mainstream and rationalist international relations theory is characterised by an inability to problematise space. Niemann is correct in that there has been a systematic exclusion of spatial analysis from the debate of global politics and there is a deep-seated theoretical inability in the dominant frameworks in international relations to come to grips with social phenomena which cannot be represented solely through national scale (Niemann, 2000, 4–5).

Two closely related assumptions about state and space have plagued the debate, which both help to explain why the national scale has been able to feature so prominently. The first notion is that much of the international relations discussion has been dominated by an analogy where '*states are treated as if they are the ontological and moral equivalents to individual persons*'. This assumption privileges the territorial scale of the state by associating it with the character and moral agency of the individual person, an intellectually powerful feature of Western political theory (Agnew, 1998, 3, emphasis in original). The second and often associated metaphor is that of 'states as home'. These two metaphors have deep implications for the understanding of space: 'In fact, it is difficult to think and talk of international relations without using these metaphors. By the same token, they limit our vision' (Jönsson et al., 2000, 15). These metaphors carry with them specific and often misleading understandings of who and what is 'inside' and 'outside'.

Elsewhere, I have argued for a 'global social theory', which refers to a social science that is no longer constructed so heavily around the nation-state (Hettne and Söderbaum, 1999, 358–68). Such global social theory departs from the fact that we need to transcend orthodox notions about the Westphalian nation-state. The problems and challenges facing the nation-state and the Westphalian order are many, complex and interrelated. Some are external, coming from the global system or the macro-region, some are internal, coming from various movements that question the territorial integrity, sovereignty, and legitimacy, for example the constitutive elements of the nation-state. In fact, the external and internal processes are intimately linked, which at the same time explains why micro-regionalism and macro-regionalism often hang together.

Jessop (2003) shows that the overwhelming dominance of the national scale is associated with the 'thirty glorious years' of economic expansion after the end of the Second World War. However, since then the process of globalisation has further intensified and can now be seen to have reached a qualitatively new stage, with deep implications for space and scale. Globalism implies as its ideological core the growth of a world market, increasingly penetrating and dominating 'national' economies, which in the process are bound to lose some of their 'nationness' (Hettne and Söderbaum, 1999, 358–68). This historical retreat from its Westphalian functions also implies a dramatically changed relationship between the state and civil society, and in particular a tendency for the state to become increasingly alienated from civil society. In this process of change, legitimacy, loyalty, identity, function and even sovereignty are transferred up or down in the system, to other political entities than the nation-state or central government – for example to macro-polities or micro-polities. This makes it necessary to transcend the conventional obsession with the nation-state as the dominant political unit in the global system and instead think in terms of a more complex, multilevel political structure, in which the state assumes different functions.

When the 'taken for granted' national scale is problematised, then other scales/spaces automatically receive more recognition. A richer and more nuanced conception of context and space sees the state's territory as only one of a number of different geographical scales (Agnew, 1998, 2). In Jessop's (2003, 182) language 'there is a proliferation of discursively constituted and institutionally materialised and embedded spatial scales ... that are related in increasingly complex tangled hierarchies rather than being simply nested one with the other, with different temporalities as well as spatialities'.

From such a perspective, there is no pre-given set of spaces and scales; instead new spaces emerge or existing ones gain in 'thickness'. Different scales of action are linked in a variety of complex ways. This is rather similar to the perspective of 'multilevel governance', which has started to challenge conventional theories about EU. Multilevel governance, according to Hooghe and Marks (2001), conceptualises the EU as a polity where decision-making authority is dispersed across multiple territorial levels (for example the European, the national and the micro-regional). Just like the multiscalar perspective advanced here, the proponents of multilevel governance correctly draw attention to not only the tiers of governance as such, but also the fluidity and links between them. This implies that there is a complex set of actors (state and non-state) who are nested into different policy scales, which in turn blurs the distinction between the international and the domestic.

NUANCING REGIONAL SPACE

The concept of 'region' stems from the Latin word for *regio*, which means 'direction' (Jönsson et al., 2000, 15). It is also derived from the Latin verb *rego*: 'to steer' or 'to rule'. Subsequently, the concept of region has frequently been used to denote 'border' or a delimited space, often a 'province'. Many mainstream disciplines and discourses have maintained a strong emphasis on 'territory', 'function' and 'rule' in the study and definition of regions. Regardless of whether the focus has been on macro-regions or micro-regions, a considerable degree of research capacity has been devoted to determine what 'types' of regions are the most functional, instrumental and efficient (to rule). Furthermore, too often, especially in political science and economics, regions have been taken as pre-given, defined in advance of research, and seen as particular policy-led and institutional/administrative frameworks.

It is of course possible to explore links between micro-regionalism and macro-regionalism through analytical perspectives and concepts that take regions as pre-given. There are, for instance, many interesting studies on the linkages between the European Commission and the myriad micro-regional administrative-political entities in Europe. Constructivist and reflectivist perspectives emphasise that 'regional space' is increasingly becoming much more elusive and multifaceted both conceptually and concretely, at least compared to what was the case during the era of old regionalism which featured the dominance of national space. Scholars in the constructivist and reflectivist camp fruitfully emphasise that regions must not be taken for granted; that they are neither 'natural', objective, essential nor simply material objects. Regions are processes; they are in the making (or un-making), their boundaries are shifting, and as Hettne (2003, 27) points out, 'in the constructivist approach regions come to life as we talk and think about them'. Seen from this perspective, regions are seldom unitary, homogeneous or discrete units. There are no 'natural' or given regions, but these are constructed, deconstructed and reconstructed – intentionally or unintentionally – from the outside or from within, by collective human action and identity formation. These types of theoretical perspectives also draw attention to the pluralism, overlap, and at times even competition between different region-builders and regionalisation strategies at different scales.

Nuancing scales of regionalism

It is more or less generally accepted that we can distinguish between at least three general scales or levels of regionalism (Hettne et al., 1999; cf. Breslin and Hook, 2002). Macro-regions ('world regions' or 'international regions') are large territorial units or subsystems, between the 'state' and the 'global' level. Below macro-regions are sub-regions (or meso-regions) and their 'sub' prefix indicates that they only make sense and must be understood in relation to macro-regions (for example there can be no sub-regions without reference to a larger macro-region). Sub-regions are similar to macro-regions in that they also exist between the global and the national level, but on a lower 'level' than the higher level macro-regions (for example also referring to regional territories of whole groups of countries). The Nordic region within Western Europe is one example. The Mano River Union in West Africa is another. Hitherto, these two levels of regions have been the foci in the field of international relations.

Micro-regions as defined in this chapter exist between the 'national' and the 'local' level, because they consist of 'sub-national' territories and not whole countries. Historically, micro-regions have been seen as sub-national regions within the territorial boundaries of particular nation-states (or before that empires). This is one of the main explanations why the discourse of micro-regions has been sharply separated from the discourse of macro-regionalism. Another reason why the linkages have been overlooked is that scholars have made overly sharp distinctions between the different scales of regionalism. This is at least partly explained by the rigidity of disciplinary boundaries, whereby international relations scholars have been concerned first and foremost with macro- and sub-regions whereas those in regional and urban studies have focused on micro-regions, and until recently often on purely sub-national ones.

In the history of mankind, borders have only rarely been hermetically sealed, so cross-border interaction is no novelty as such. What is new is that the construction of micro-regions has become an explicit strategic objective pursued by a range of public and private forces within and beyond their national borders. This is revealed both in that purely sub-national micro-regions increasingly take on a transnational disposition and in the strong tendency to form cross-border regions (which can be defined as territorial units that comprise contiguous sub-national units from two or more nation-states).

In recent decades micro-regionalism in Europe and Southeast Asia have been referred to in the debate (Breslin and Hook, 2002; Perkmann and Sum, 2002). It is important to recognise the emergence of the same phenomenon in other parts of the world as well. These micro-regions may or may not fall within the borders of a particular nation-state. Increasingly, micro-regions are constituted by a network of transactions and collaboration across national boundaries, which may very well emerge as an alternative or in opposition to the challenged state, and sometimes also in competition with states-led regionalism (Jessop, 2003). However, as illustrated by the concepts of growth polygons, growth triangles, development corridors (DCs) and spatial development initiatives (SDIs), micro-regionalism is often created by networks of state and non-state actors, and even interpersonal transnational networks (ethnic or family networks, religious ties, etc.) (Mittelman, 2000; Perkmann and Sum, 2002). Thus, conventional distinctions between international and domestic as well as between state and non-state actors are being diluted.

In this context, it needs saying that not all micro-regions will necessarily be 'micro' or small in character. Some micro-regions are not very large while others certainly are. The size of micro-regions depends often on the size of the higher levels of regions as well as the size of the countries involved. As an example, given the comprehensive size of North America as a macro-region and its constituent countries, it is also to be expected that some micro-regions in North America can be very large. There is in fact a functional unity to the entire US–Mexican *maquiladora* cross-border zone, which can be understood as a rather comprehensive 'Cal-Mex' or 'Tex-Mex' cross-border micro-region. This explains why it is more appropriate to talk about a hierarchical set of scales of regionalism and not necessarily different qualities and sizes of regionalism.

Still, it is evident that micro-level forms of regionalism may sometimes be less formal/inter-state than the formal macro-regions; they may be more reflective of private sector interests than those of either states or civil societies, as in many corridors or growth triangles. However, at the same time there is increasing evidence that also macro- and sub-regions are increasingly influenced by non-state actors. So, if regions are made up by actors other than states alone, and if state boundaries are becoming more fluid, then it also becomes more difficult to uphold old distinctions between micro- and macro-regionalism.

The argument put forward here is that our understanding of the links between scales of regionalism will be limited by static, pre-given regional delimitations, or by the view that macro-regions and micro-regionalisms necessarily are different phenomena (although they sometimes are). Of particular interest for the purposes of this chapter is that constructivist and reflectivist perspectives enable us to overcome old dichotomies and recognise that various regional spaces tend to be connected to an increasing extent: one regional scale can trigger reactions and responses at another scale and vice versa.

VARIETIES OF MICRO-REGIONS

Micro-regions appear in various guises and shapes. It is possible to differentiate between at least five general types, which are of relevance for sub-national as well as cross-border regions: (i) physical-geographic regions; (ii) cultural regions; (iii) economic regions; (iv) administrative/planning regions; and (v) political regions (cf. Keating, 1997, 2–5; Jönsson et al., 2000, 139).

Especially in earlier periods but to some extent also in the present context, micro-regions are determined by physical geography. Throughout history, societies and areas have been united by lakes, rivers and roads, whereas they have often been separated by mountains and forests. Transportation facilities often influenced earlier settlements and societies, and created systems that over the centuries have shaped patterns of interaction, which in turn has lead to the construction of micro-regions. The Norwegian fjord valleys, river basins such as the Zambezi, Mekong, lakes such as the Black Sea, the Great Lakes in Africa and North America, and ecological zones such as the Amazonas all count as physical-geographic regions.

Cultural regions may have their origins in physical-geographic regions. However, they endure because of their association with culture and identity. As Jönsson et al. (2000, 139) point out, 'identity is a dual concept. It connotes remoteness and delimitation as well as commonality and community – external remoteness and internal community.' Cultural regions often include a shared history and religion as well as linguistic and cultural similarities. French-speaking Quebec in Canada, Flanders in Belgium, the Lozi region in Southern Africa, Kurdistan in the Middle East are all examples of cultural regions, and under different historical circumstances these could actually have become nation-states. Often there is a complicated and at times even hostile relationship between the cultural micro-region and national government(s). Sometimes the agents of cultural micro-regions espouse separatism and old-style nationalism. This can be witnessed around the world, but as Keating (1997, 3) underlines, 'many contemporary minority nationalist movements have recognised the limitations of sovereignty and traditional statehood and are seeking new forms of recognition and autonomy within a more interdependent world and continental order ... Movements of cultural defence thus link up with ideas of endogenous development theory.'

Economic regions come in many varieties. They should be understood with regard to economic characteristics and criteria, such as industrialised/deindustrialised, urban/rural, tourist-oriented, steel producing (Keating, 1997, 2). An economic region is often functional and demarcated from the outside world in terms of transportation, contacts and other dependencies and flows that connect peoples and structures (Jönsson et al., 2000, 139). These types of micro-regions may also refer to regional production systems and territories/zones for economic development. More recently, theorists have placed emphasis on new economic micro-regions marked by local and endogenous development but which are related to economic globalisation, technological changes and shifts in the factors of economic production (Ohmae, 1995; Keating, 1997, 2).

The administrative/planning region is essentially a functional region as well, but of a different type than the previous one. It is made up for purposes of decision-making, policy-making or simply for the collection and publication of statistics. The Italian regions, the Swedish counties, and many provinces in the South are administrative/planning regions. Many of these regions tend to have little dynamism in their own right; they are not related to geography, culture, economics and they have no political function and also lack directly elected bodies. On the other hand, their importance and dynamism seem to increase as a result of the fact that many functions that were previously state prerogatives are today often transferred or decentralised to these micro-regions.

Political regions differ from administrative/planning regions in that they have democratically elected assemblies or councils as well as accountable executive bodies. In essence, they are fully-fledged regional governments. But there are many different political and constitutional situations with regard to such regional governments, ranging from the powerful German and Austrian Länder, the Belgian political regions, the States in the US and the Provinces in Canada, which have replaced the central government in many of its functions, to political regions in other federal states such as India, Nigeria, Ethiopia, Somalia and Russia, and to the rather weak French regions and the South African provinces (cf. Keating, 1997, 4).

These different types of micro-regions form literally a patchwork. It is possible that one type dominates within a given area, while at other times they compete, overlap or proceed in parallel. Generalisations can of course be misleading, but it seems that economic and political/administrative motives are often the spur of today's micro-regionalism. As Keating (1998, 72–3) points out, 'new regionalism is modernising and forward looking, in contrast to an older provincialism, which represented resistance to change and defence of tradition'. We may still be witnessing quests for separatism and increased political autonomy, but sometimes this may rather be a post-Westphalian instrument in a new political landscape and context rather than the ultimate goal.

As indicated earlier in the chapter, a distinction should be made between sub-national and cross-border micro-regions. The conventional form of micro-regionalism is purely sub-national and takes place within the parameters of a nation-state. This type of micro-regionalism is often emerging for political/administrative/planning, democratic or economic/distributional motives and often it is shaped by the relationship between central government and micro-regional administrative or political forces. It can therefore be described as vertical (Jönsson et al., 2000, 149).

In contrast, cross-border micro-regionalism is often horizontal and networked. It takes place along the external boundaries of the state and often the motives are economic rather than political and security oriented as during the Cold War, although political and cultural motives may enter into the process as well. Cross-border micro-regions often involve a wide range of different public and private forces and other local/regional actors grouped in more horizontal networks.

COMPARATIVE EXPLORATIONS OF THE MICRO–MACRO PROBLEM

Micro-regionalism and macro-regionalism can be linked in a number of different ways. Examples in the literature suggest that macro-regionalism can require micro-regionalism; that macro-regionalism is opening up space for or giving rise to micro-regionalism; that macro-regionalism is creating 'trust' or institutions that can be used by micro-regionalism; that macro-regionalism is proceeding through micro-regionalism; that macro-regionalism and micro-regionalism are complementary; that micro-regionalism is competing with macro-regionalism; that micro-regionalism is giving rise to macro-regionalism; and that the two forms of regionalism are not related or proceed in parallel (Breslin and Higgott, 2003, 167–82; Breslin and Hook, 2002; Hettne and Söderbaum, 2000, 457–74; Jessop, 2003; Mittelman, 2000; Perkmann and Sum, 2002). Rather than trying to illustrate each and every one of the possible linkages, I will explore how the 'micro–macro problem' is played out in three strategically selected macro-regions, namely Europe, Southeast Asia and Southern Africa.

Europe

From the 1960s and onwards micro-regions have become an increasingly important component of the political landscape in Western Europe. Before that only a few European states, such as Germany, Austria and Switzerland, had strong micro-regions. Some centralised states, such as the United Kingdom, Ireland and Greece, have regionalised through setting up administrative/planning regions, whereas for instance Belgium has become a fully-fledged federal state, with overlapping political, cultural and economic regions (Keating, 1997, 9).

Perhaps the most important explanatory variable behind the rise of micro-regionalism in Europe is the nation-state itself, which has decentralised and supported micro-regions as part of restructuring. However, it is important to acknowledge that the rise of micro-regionalism is at the same time causally related to European integration. This process started several decades ago. A micro-regional policy was stipulated already in the Rome Treaty, but we must look to the EU's re-launch in the mid-1980s for the decisive phase that brought micro-regionalism and macro-regionalism closer together, both in theory and practice (Bourne, 2003, 278). The Single European Act and then the Maastricht Treaty made the EU take micro-regional development more seriously, and also prompted a significant increase in the structural funds and community funds for poorer regions in the EU. This made the EU more friendly towards micro-regions at the same time as it turned micro-regional actors into both lobbyists and stakeholders in the EU decision-making process.

The EU's micro-regional policy aims to reduce economic disparities within the Union. It has several explanations. Firstly, it is generally accepted that European integration and the single market exacerbates economic disparities between the centre and the periphery, and the regional policy should distribute resources and enhance competitiveness of the poorer micro-regions. Secondly, the deepening of EU restricts the policy instruments that individual member states can make use of in order to deal with domestic economic disparities and support micro-regional development. Thirdly, it has also been argued that EU regional funds have served as side-payments or compensation to persuade the consent of poorer states and in order to facilitate bargains over non-regional issues.

The EU's structural funds are comprehensive. Between 2000 and 2006 a total of about €257 billion was allocated to all structural instruments, of which €213 billion was earmarked for the 15 member states, and the rest to accession states and to the Cohesion Fund. This represents approximately 37 per cent of the EU budget for the period up to 2006 (European Commission, 2004). Such large funds necessarily create a logic of their own, and there is evidence that some countries have 'regionalised' their policy-making and administrative systems 'simply to gain a position of competitive advantage with regard to access to European structural funds' (Keating, 1997, 9).

Micro-regional actors have become more important in EU politics during the last two decades. Micro-regions seek to gather information, take part in decision-making and lobby EU politics in a variety of different ways, as seen for instance in that more than 170 micro-regions have set information and representation offices in Brussels and also formed international micro-regional associations for managing matters of mutual concern, such as the Assembly of European Regions (Bourne, 2003, 280; see <www.blbe.irisnet. be/europe/repres_en.htm>). The Maastricht Treaty provided for setting up a Committee of the Regions (CoR), which began operating in 1994, and before the enlargement in 2004 it had 222 representatives of local and regional authorities in the EU member states. The CoR has the right to initiate and make recommendations on the EU's regional policy. Although it is an advisory body with weak formal powers, there is evidence that the Commission is taking its opinions seriously. As Bourne points out:

the very creation of such a body in the EU was a significant breakthrough. It recognised regional authorities as legitimate participants in EU decision making and represented an important departure from the hitherto prevalent idea that only central governments ought to represent their state in the EU. (Bourne, 2003, 281)

According to Jönsson et al. (2000, 147) border regions in state peripheries are most likely to undergo change and then try to take advantage of new circumstances of the changed European political landscape. Breslin and Higgott expand further on this point:

Cross-border micro-regionalism in Europe (for example between France and Spain) can be seen as a consequence of higher levels of formal regionalism in the EU. The authority and efficacy of national governments in dealing with trans-boundary issues has been transformed, some would say undermined, by a dual movement: both 'upwards' and 'downwards' that results in the transfer of national sovereignty to the EU in some issue areas. Institutional changes at the EU level, as well as new communication technologies and the development of transportation, have encouraged the formation of regional networks based on common developmental interests. (Breslin and Higgott, 2003, 180)

Sometimes micro-regionalism is a key strategy to 'by-pass' central government or the inefficiencies inherent in national space, at other times micro-regionalism can be pushed, used and assisted by central governments to develop micro-regional spaces, especially for political/administrative/ planning and/or economic purposes.

Summing up, there is, undoubtedly, a micro-regional dimension in the European integration process. But this must not, as Bourne (2003, 290–1) correctly points out, be interpreted as the emergence of the idea of EU as 'Europe of the Regions', whereby micro-regions rather than states constitute the principal units in the policy process. States will continue to be important actors in EU politics. However, as emphasised by the model of multilevel governance, it is hard to deny that the state no longer has monopoly over European-level policy-making, and that decision-making authority is dispersed between actors from multiple levels of governance, including micro-regional actors.

Southeast Asia

The 'growth triangle' is one of the most important forms of micro-regionalism in Southeast Asia. Since the 1990s growth triangles are often considered as a driving force for economic growth in the Southeast Asian economies. Growth triangles utilise the different endowments of the various countries, exploiting cooperative trade for production and development opportunities. These initiatives are constructed around partnerships between the private sector and the state, which explains why they have been referred to as a form of 'trans-state development'. In this partnership the private sector provides capital for investment whereas the public sector provides infrastructure, fiscal incentives, and the administrative framework to attract industry and investment.

The Southern Growth Triangle – also known as SIJORI (Singapore, the Johore province of Malaysia, and Riau province of Indonesia) – is both the most well-known and most successful of the growth triangles in Southeast Asia. Other examples include southern Thailand–northern Sumatra–northern Malaysia and the ASEAN (Association of Southeast Asian Nations) Growth Triangle covering the Sarawak–Brunei–Sabah area.

SIJORI was formed in 1989 and covers a population of about 6 million people. It is built on a vertical division of labour, whereby Singapore serves as the supplier of advanced electronic infrastructure, technology, financial and insurance services, a comfortable international entrance port, and international know-how. The Batam island (in Riau, Indonesia) is supplying low cost labour and land, whereas Johore (Malaysia) provides semi-skilled labour, industrial sites and competence. The functioning of the SIJORI is not without frictions, particularly related to the fact that Singapore is seen as the main beneficiary and that it is received as cementing a vertical division of labour.

The growth triangles are particularly interesting from the perspective of the micro–macro relationship, not the least since there exists a series of interpretations of the nature of these linkages. The growth triangle strategy has been described in a multitude of ways in the literature, for instance, as a response to global political transformation; as a complement to macro-regional economic integration; as paving the way for macro-regionalism; and as a way to achieve regional integration while avoiding time-consuming macro-regional political bureaucracy.

The linkages between the macro-framework (ASEAN) and micro-regionalism (growth triangles) are not straightforward or easily defined. It should however be recognised that ASEAN does not consider lower-level micro-regionalism as competition. On the contrary, ASEAN has tried to capitalise upon and internalise the momentum around the growth triangles, claiming that these form part of the 'ASEAN way'. This is seen in that, for instance, in 1992 ASEAN formally adopted the idea of growth triangles, outlined a legal and economic framework for them and also stated that they should be seen as complementary to broader macro-regional economic integration and the proposed ASEAN Free Trade Area. It has even been suggested that the growth triangles will spur a Southeast Asian identity and enhance the role of ASEAN in the larger East Asian region. Although the relevance of the latter claims can be discussed, it seems that the two forms of regionalism are complementary rather than competitive, and that growth triangles have enjoyed some stability from the more politically oriented ASEAN framework.

Southern Africa

The SDIs and DCs in Southern Africa constitute the most important form of policy-driven micro-regionalism in Southern Africa. These initiatives are especially frequent in South Africa (where the SDI concept was first developed) and in Mozambique, but there are also real and potential SDIs/DCs in several other countries in Southern Africa and further afield in Africa (see <www.africansdi.com>).

The SDIs/DCs purport to be short-term and targeted attempts to stimulate economic 'growth' by creating globally competitive spatial entities through new investment, infrastructural development and job creation. Many but not all of the SDIs and DCs are cross-border in nature. The strategy is to implement one or several industrial 'mega-projects' such as the Mozambique Aluminium Smelter in the economic micro-region, which are then supposed to enhance different types of spread effects and linkages in the economy. The SDIs/DCs are governed by a limited group of experts and policy-makers who come together with private investors in small, flexible and rather introverted policy networks, in order to fast-track implementation of bankable investment projects in the micro-region. These networks work rather well for those on the 'inside' and for the purposes of big business, but have few links to people and stakeholders on the 'outside' (Söderbaum and Taylor, 2003).

It is evident that both South Africa's and Mozambique's SDI/DC strategies are consistent and an integral part of their respective national (neoliberal) economic reform programmes. Furthermore, especially South African leaders and ministers, including both Thabo Mbeki and Nelson Mandela, have repeatedly emphasised that SDIs/DCs contribute to the 'African renaissance' and what is today known as the New Partnership for Africa's Development (DBSA, 2001).

Officially the SDIs/DCs are stated to contribute to macro-regional economic integration in the Southern African Development Coordination (SADC) region. It is also evident that SADC tries to capitalise on the momentum around the SDIs/DCs. Similarly to ASEAN in the case of growth triangles, SADC officials claim that development corridors are part of 'SADC's way of doing things'.[1] It is certainly correct that during apartheid SADC's predecessor, the Southern African Development Coordination Conference (SADCC), tried to keep transport corridors functional, especially the Beira corridor in Mozambique, in spite of attacks from the apartheid state and Renamo. However, a recent volume on the 'flagship' of the SDIs/DCs, the Maputo Development Corridor (MDC), shows that there is a rather uneasy relationship between micro-regionalism and macro-regionalism in Southern Africa. In fact, the two may contradict one another, or certainly stimulate processes that undermine aspects of one or the other.

The case of the MDC demonstrates that micro-regionalism at least partly emerges as an alternative construction to the formal SADC project. Divergent processes stimulated by the MDC have been shown to create asymmetrical relations at a whole host of levels, deepening uneven development and sparking what may in some ways be regarded as a crisis in governance. Particularly important is that the promoters of the MDC in South Africa are trying to prevent the micro-regional project from being associated, or in their language 'hijacked' by the ineffectiveness and 'politics' of SADC.[2] Even if the Mozambican actors involved in micro-regionalism are not as polemic towards SADC regionalism, there is no compelling evidence that linkages extend beyond mere rhetoric.

Furthermore, the type of 'on the ground' process found in the MDC micro-region and driven by a series of micro-regional actors – customs evasion, smuggling, the evasion of an effective form of state surveillance, the elevation of capital over and beyond the national administration – calls into question the compatibility of the MDC micro-regional project with the wider SADC vision of a developmentally-oriented Southern Africa moving ahead as one.

Hence, the case of the MDC suggests that micro-regions and broader macro-regions are uneasy bedfellows, which may hold within them both powerful contradictions and the potential for destabilisation of any wider macro-regional 'vision'. With this said, however, it is reasonable to argue that seen in an historical perspective the process of macro-regionalism within SADCC/SADC has created a fertile ground for SDIs/DCs in Southern Africa.

CONCLUSION

Our understanding of the different dimensions, actors and issues of today's regionalism is rapidly increasing. The point of departure of this chapter is that the links between macro-regionalism and micro-regionalism have often been overlooked, and this chapter has tried to bridge the gap between the two discourses – theoretically as well as through some comparative reflections on Europe, Southeast Asia and Southern Africa.

There is consensus in the debate that global and world order transformation processes, particularly globalisation, influence and give rise to micro-regionalism. Security motives used to be more prominent during the Cold War, whereas today it is widely held that cooperation and integration across borders can create opportunities for economic growth and reaping the benefits of globalisation, although in some areas of the world more than others. According to some observers, especially 'hyperglobalists' such as Kenichi Ohmae (1995), the nation-state is no longer considered an adequate unit for economic activity: it is too small for global aspects and too large for the (micro-)regional dimensions. In a hyperglobalist manner, Ohmae (falsely) argues that we are witnessing the end of the nation-state, or at least considers it to be a passive actor and a victim of cross-border processes, resulting in what he refers to as a 'region-state'. However, the hyperglobalists misunderstand the role of national scale and central government actors, as well as the political economy of space and scale. We should not do away with the state and national space, but insert not only the state but also the macro-region into a multiscalar framework.

Nowhere in the world is the relationship between micro-regionalism and macro-regionalism more evident (and perhaps also more dynamic) than in Europe. The deepening of EU since the mid-1980s has undoubtedly enhanced micro-regionalism. The EU has become more region-friendly in a variety of ways and at the same time micro-regional actors have become both lobbyists and stakeholders in EU politics. European micro-regions may be pushed by states, mainly for political/administrative and economic reasons, but gradually micro-regions have also gained more autonomy and in a sense become actors in their own right. Especially peripheral micro-regions seek to bypass central governments or transcend the inefficiencies of national space and instead directly link into macro-regional or global economic spaces. Thus, at least in certain regards the multilevel governance model makes increasing sense of the European political landscape, thus challenging conventional theories of EU politics.

The growth triangles in Southeast Asia and SDIs/DCs in Southern Africa are first and foremost economic instruments designed to tie a given micro-region into wider macro-regional and global economies. The increased adoption of neoliberal and export-growth policies in the South is a crucial explanatory variable for understanding the emergence of these types of economic micro-regions. Central governments are often crucial actors, especially by their forging of partnerships with big business. But since the micro-regions are often created to foster cross-border integration they may also – by design or by default – contribute to the disaggregation of domestic national economies (Breslin and Higgott, 2003, 178). An important difference between Southeast Asia and Southern Africa is that the relationship between micro-regionalism and macro-regionalism is largely complementary or even enhanced in the former, whereas it is more competitive in the latter.

By way of conclusion, I will reflect on the future linkages between micro-regionalism and macro-regionalism. Perhaps somewhat simplisticly, I see three broad scenarios for the future. The first and perhaps also the least likely scenario, 'fading away', suggests that the different scales of regionalism are slowly being overtaken and replaced by other processes such as neo-Westphalianism or non-territorial processes, especially globalisation.

The second scenario, 'the expansion/dilution syndrome', implies that continuing enlargement and expansion of macro-regionalism affects its functioning and reinforces lower-level regional dynamics, leaving state and non-state actors alike to concentrate their energies at a more meso- or micro-level.[3] This scenario should not be ruled out in the European context, and in a sense it has already started to emerge. By the same token, the unwieldy enlargement of SADC to include the problematic state of the Democratic Republic of Congo has already reinforced processes of 'variable geometry' and 'multispeedism' within that macro-region, and renewed concentration of energy on other regionalist projects as well as novel development corridors and cross-border micro-regions.

A third alternative can be conceptualised as 'increasing regionness' (Hettne and Söderbaum, 2000, 457–74). In this scenario micro-regions of various sorts will flourish and become a permanent feature of the larger macro-region, thus contributing to the diversity and increasing level of cross-border relations within the macro-region. Increasing regionness implies that the pattern of micro-regions will not have different visions than the larger macro-region, but relate to it in a mutually reinforcing manner. This implies in turn that authority, power and decision-making are not centralised but layered, dispersed across multiple scales of governance. This does not suggest repetitions of a European path, simply that the centralised Westphalian nation-state project will allow for a multilevel governance structure, where the macro-regional as well as the micro-regional level for historical and pragmatic reasons will be more important.

NOTES

1. Government official, Division of Multilateral Economic Relations, SADC Affairs, Maputo, Mozambique (interview 5 March 1999), and Alfredo Namitete, Chairman of Committee of Senior Officials, Southern African Transport and Communications Commission, Mozambique (interview 6 April 2000).
2. Interview with Jennifer Smith, Regional SDI Support Unit, Development Bank of Southern Africa, Midrand, 2 September 2003.
3. I am grateful to Tim Shaw for pinpointing this scenario.

7
Regional Dimensions of Security[1]

Elzbieta Stadtmüller

During the 1990s major changes in the international environment also led to a major re-evaluation of security. On the one hand, instability, disintegration, globalisation, unipolarity brought critical challenges. Peace and security began to be understood multidimensionally, not only with regard to the protection or enhancement of the state but also to the protection of other communities and individuals. I shall develop such meanings in this chapter as especially useful in the context of regionalism. On the other hand, an extraordinarily broader cooperation, built on mutual trust and formal regional arrangements, has emerged.

This chapter considers mutual connections between regional cooperation in its new form and new challenges for security. The first section shows the contemporary meaning of security; the second section considers the prospects and obstacles for regional cooperation in respect of five types of security problems; the third section links regional security to the global level. These aspects have to be seen, however, in the broader contexts of contemporary trends such as globalisation, governance and a quest for a new world order.

One of the key words in contemporary analyses is globalisation. Its contemporary form results in deeper and faster changes to our lives than ever before and seriously influences the security environment. Strategic globality, as Rasmussen noticed after 11 September 2001, has taken on a new quality because 'the development of a civilian global infrastructure allows civilians to project power on a global scale'; and '... it is no longer just First World conflicts that are exported to the Third World. Now the Third World is able to bring its conflicts to the First World as well' (2002, 326). We can easily add many examples of such a reverse export, apart from 11 September and other terrorist actions. They are connected first of all with non-military security: the questions of immigrants, refugees, and growing poverty. The process of globalisation though opens up new prospects; it has turned out to be exclusive rather than inclusive, and has widened the inequalities between countries, regions and social groups within them. Globalisation is also associated very often with Americanisation or Westernisation, which leads to vivid protests and anti-global movements, and stores up conflicts for the future. We live in an age of transition – from what is clear (at least so far as security is concerned), but to what? I agree with those analyses which point to the end of an era which was characterised by 'ontological security', a term used by Anthony Giddens (1991, 35) for the certainty which could be expected in this area during the Cold War period. The present time is better described by the term 'reflexive security' (Rasmussen 2001, 285–309) because in our world we are unsure about where dangers can come from, how to interpret their roots, and how to react to them. The security policy of each state and at the global level is a subject for reflection and discussion, not simply acceptance.

This new 'ontological insecurity' can be easily adapted to all areas of our contemporary life, and fits perfectly the multidimensional definition of security. In fact, we are overwhelmed by the challenges involved in making our environment more secure in every field. However, this process mirrors chaos rather than order. Our ideas of security vary from the active creation of a transcendent, closer, united, cooperative world to finding peace (in its cold form, however) in isolation and the strengthening of our own identities in preparation for the battle against 'others'. Hence the current discourse on security in the contemporary world is concerned with the ways and means of governing it.

The concept of 'governance', very often combined with the qualifier 'good', is another key problem in the present analysis. Its meaning is very broad, refers also to principles and procedures like regimes, but differs from them because it exists not only in well-defined areas, is not confined to a single sphere of endeavour, and is connected with whole global order (Rosenau and Czempiel, 1992, 5–9). Different actors, governmental and non-governmental, participate in the process of governance, acting on many levels, creating flexible networks, using non-standardised mechanisms. However, an idea of efficient 'global governance' or 'international governance' still does not exist in reality and at present it is an intellectual and moral choice to envisage the future of the world in this way. At a normative level, it requires a 'cosmopolitan society' (Held, 1995), an 'international version' of the strong civil society, where democracy prevails to uphold dialogue, goodwill and shared values.

Although we are uncertain how our world will look in the future we do not need to predict it – if we understand the present era as a transitional stage, the main characteristics are clear enough: uncertainty, many kinds of conflicts, unsolved global problems, pervasive poverty and deepening inequality, and human insecurity. Therefore the contemporary security challenge is how to bring some degree of stability and predictability during the period of transition while the new structure of governance emerges. Regional institutions can have a critical role to play. This is because of the need to accumulate resources (intelligence, logistics, capabilities); the serious importance of local crises usually connected with the region (especially in

Africa); the fierce inter-state rivalries in some regions, with the potential to develop into new conflicts (South Asia, East Asia, Middle East). Regional institutions in this latter case are valuable for confidence building, and the shift from antagonism to coexistence.

A 'NEW SECURITY' ENVIRONMENT

The suppression of violence (negative peace) has been gradually replaced by a far more ambitious idea, that of the creation of a lasting (positive) peace – a development that is critical in an era of transition. Positive peace has also been defined in terms of post-conflict peacebuilding, which includes democracy and economic development (Shaw, 1996). However, these values can also be seen as the best way to prevent possible conflicts. The West presented the Third World and the post-communist countries with these desiderata, demanding economic reform, good governance, democratisation, and respect for human rights as a condition of their assistance programmes. This seemed a very reasonable way to a stable peace. However, we can now recognise some unforeseen destabilising effects of such conditionality. The cases of Burundi or Rwanda (1993–94) show that pressure for democratisation can result in ethnic violence. So, on the one hand, the process of transformation to a democratic system and a free market is a necessary condition of a stable peace but, on the other hand, it can lead to the multidimensional insecurity of societies. It seems that one possible remedy is to combine this pressure for reforms with an organised system of support, and the monitoring of possible tensions. And regional institutions seem irreplaceable in such a role. Europe with its relatively strong and stable institutions offers an obvious example. Although no other region has as many institutions, there are attempts in some other regions to follow this pattern. In what ways, then, can regional institutions assist in the establishment of a positive peace?

The best way to manage conflict, it is widely agreed, is to prevent it. As the evidence in the international environment suggests, the record on successful implementation methods is poor. Usually 'conflict management' means 'conflict containment', that is preventing escalation, limiting violence and stopping the aggressor. This stage, though most dramatic and visible to the broad public, is in fact less crucial for long-term peace and security than another aspect of conflict management, namely the termination of the conflict by means of resolution and settlement. This is fundamental because reaching agreements, which stop violence can have only temporary success if the sources of the conflict remain. In all these aspects of conflict management the activity of regional institutions may be critical. However, their success will also depend on the type of conflict and changes in the legitimisation of such activity. For example, in case of conflicts within states, the rule of non-intervention (at least without the invitation of member states) which was built into regional systems – such as the Organisation of American States, the Association of Southeast Asian Nations (ASEAN), Organisation of African Unity (OAU), African Union, the Economic Community of West African States, and the Organisation of Security and Cooperation in Europe – blocked the legal possibility of preventing violence. Currently this rule has become increasingly controversial since there are two basic rights in conflict. On the one hand, the right of the international community to intervene on humanitarian grounds, and on the other the right of state sovereignty. Sometimes, upholding the status quo means supporting oppressive governments, even deliberately in the case of the OAU or the Gulf Cooperation Council (Alagappa, 1997, 432).

The effective involvement of regional organisations in conflict management depends on several factors such as the range of commitment of member states, shared values and interests, the institutional, financial, and material capacity, and the legitimacy of that involvement. The events in the Balkans showed that even quite strong, stable, and well-organised institutions like the European Union (EU) were far from efficient. The question of Iraq divided members of the EU and the North Atlantic Treaty Organisation (NATO), while the contemporary enlargement of both these organisations raises new question about their ability to make decisions. Also, the mutual relations between them can be a subject of concern, as lack of coordination and, still worse, competitive behaviour may undermine legitimacy and credibility, and lead to inefficiency. During the 1990s there was a serious increase in the demand for peace operations, starting with the successful military intervention in 1991 in Iraq. On the one hand, supporting democracy and human rights came to be seen as 'politically correct' and the number of states ready to participate in the peace operations increased (to over 60). On the other hand, the Western powers which were expected to bear this burden became less inclined to intervene outside their own spheres of influence because they were are not ready to accept the material and human costs (US in Somalia, 1992–93). As Jakobsen noted: 'Western leaders increasingly became prisoners of their own rhetoric and were pressed to do something about conflicts they would have preferred to ignore' (2002, 274). On the other hand, the number of wars and armed conflicts is decreasing, and in 2003 was at its lowest level since 1965. The highest number of wars, 50, was reached at the beginning of the 1990s, at a time when the Soviet Union and Yugoslavia were disintegrating. By 2003 this figure had fallen to 25, with a further 16 'armed conflicts', most of them in the so-called Third World.

But military security is only one dimension of general security. Bloody conflicts are more visible and dramatic at first sight, but in fact they cause fewer casualties, deaths, and everyday tragedy in the world than other dimensions of insecurity such as poverty, health, and the environment. Apart from this, efficient and long-lasting prevention of violent conflicts very often demands a new approach to development. The latter is connected with the concept of human security, because it includes security against poverty, a guarantee of fundamental human rights, and emancipation from oppressive power structures (Thomas, 2000). As the UNDP's Human Development Report in 1994 stated:

> For too long, the concept of security has been shaped by the potential conflict between states. For too long, security has been equated with threats to a country's borders. For too long, nations have sought arms to protect their security. For most people today, a feeling of insecurity arises more from worries about daily life than from the dread of a cataclysmic world event. Job security, income security, health security, environmental security, security from crime, these are the emerging concerns of human security all over the world. (UNDP, 1994, 3)

Obviously the new military dangers, which have emerged or increased lately show that we cannot forget about these kinds of threats. But, on the other hand, these new threats and conflicts hurt civilians first and foremost since they are the ones who pay the highest price for terrorist acts and for anti-terrorist wars. Numbers are even more persuasive: each year 15 million people die from hunger-related causes compared with the 30 million killed in the battles of two world wars of the twentieth century. Over 800 million people are starving, 1 billion live on less than US$1 per day, and lack access to health services and sources of pure drinking water. The direct aid for the poorest states is US$55 billion yearly (only one quarter of the military budget of the US alone), which means that the Millennium project to reduce by half the number of the poorest people by 2015 seems unrealistic without an increase in aid or, more importantly, structural changes in global economics and the social order (UNDP, 2003). Here again it seems that regional arrangements can play a crucial role, perhaps the most important role, in this type of security above all.

Changing this human security environment is a necessary element in building the 'positive' peace I mentioned at the outset. Miller (2000) placed regional peace on three levels: cold, normal and warm. There are three strategies for regional conflict resolution. The first is international and is based on a concert of great powers or a stabilising hegemon, and it can bring only a cold peace. The other two levels interestingly use regional mechanisms, enhancing regional legitimacy (resulting in a neutral peace) and liberalisation (leading to a warm peace). The latter produces a situation '... in which regional war is unthinkable in any scenario of international or regional change. Even if some issues are still in dispute among the regional states, the use of force is completely out of the question as an option for addressing them' (Miller, 2000, 159). Such a situation is achievable only if states are able to develop effective regional institutions, collective security, economic ties, common concerns about the environment and cultural exchanges, and they share the same, democratic liberal system. This latter is crucial for exclusion of war. Mutual trust is then both a condition and a result of this situation, encouraging more advanced forms of regionalism and the further spread of regionalisation. Hence, many contemporary debates on security and peace focus inevitably on regional arrangements (Fortmann et al., 1997).

REGIONAL ARRANGEMENTS AND AGENCIES FOR SECURITY: PROSPECTS AND OBSTACLES

The search for international security by means of regional solutions arises from the recognition that universal organisations are as yet unable to create a system that would be really effective in ending current conflicts and, at the same time, acceptable to the whole global community. In this situation, a region could be an intermediate stage between interests at the state and global level. We can assume that political, economic, and cultural ties are much stronger than geographical ones alone, and therefore these links could reinforce peace and order in particular regions of the world. If unified regions existed, it would be much easier for the members of universal organisations to negotiate global interests and to resolve problems that are common to all the members of the international community. The question of national security here is important since in its multidimensional form it often demands regional cooperation (Hettne, 2001, 1–53). In practice, this may operate on two tracks – the quest for security in the face of external threats leads to regional arrangements, but also membership of such structures helps strengthen security in a region in a number of ways. Economic, technological, political, and cultural linkages stabilise relations, and the exchange of people and information builds common trust. Regional cooperation offers a platform for interactions at the global level, and the reduction of partners (from national states to regional groups) sets limits to possible conflicts. However, the reduction of partners is dangerous for the global international regime if regional arrangements become exclusive and culturally monistic. But it seems that such a prognosis has no place in contemporary forms of regional cooperation. This is because they are constructed not on cultural foundations but on the basis of geographical, economic and other ties (Teló, 2001, 14–16). Some regional arrangements have a strong multicultural membership (ASEAN or Asia-Pacific Economic Cooperation), others have signed association agreements with regions from another culture (for example the EU and Africa, or the EU and Pacific countries).

So, rather, the new regionalism serves cross-cultural convergence, though it is easy to imagine also that the question of a common identity can begin to play an important role and work against such an open approach. For example, some of the Asian countries prefer to create Asian regional cooperation such as ASEAN, with China, Japan and South Korea (ASEAN+3) rather than cooperation across the whole of the Pacific area. Sometimes also within the EU, the debate on exclusion of the Balkans or Turkey is built on cultural differentiation. Another danger stems from the fact that regional organisations without a global, well-functioning system can be seen as threatening each other. In this way we could 'achieve' a new version of the security dilemma, defined as the risk of reducing one's security by acts intended to increase it (Buzan, 1991), and regional institutions rather than states become the source of new tensions.

It is possible to analyse the relations between security and regionalism from various angles (see Buzan and Waever, 2003). We can focus on different dimensions of security implemented by regional arrangements, be they societal, military, economic, or environmental. Or we can consider the specific situation in different regions and describe the activity of each regional institution (Buzan and Waever, 2003). Finally, we can enumerate several security problems and look at different regional responses to them. This chapter cannot deal in depth with all of these issues so it will focus mainly on the last approach. How far, then, can regional institutions respond to different types of security problems such as, for example, inter-state conflicts, the case of failing states, intra-state conflicts, peacebuilding, and establishing multidimensional security in stable regions.

Considering *inter-state tensions* first, though 'traditional' tensions of this type still exist, they are less frequent than during the Cold War period. Global attention has focused on, for example, the Asia region: India–Pakistan relations, China–Taiwan, and the Middle East. In some cases, for example North Korea, regionalism has had little success in solving the problem. But a meeting of the South Asian Association for Regional Cooperation in January 2004 on the question of the free trade area served also to re-start the dialogue between India and Pakistan over Kashmir, after deep crises in 2002. Across the region, the states share similar problems, ranging from domestic conflicts, ethnic and religious tensions, political instability and human insecurity. This is not a promising prospect for successful regional cooperation. On the other hand, India has one of the most rapidly growing economies and Pakistan has not much choice if does not want partnership with isolated or turbulent states like Iraq, Iran or Afghanistan. Moreover, East Asia is developing rapidly and this may lead to the marginalisation of South Asian states, making the case for stronger regional arrangements more pressing in order to counter the risks associated with existing regional dynamics.

There is no simple solution to the China–Taiwan issue. But the growing economic development and strength of China can paradoxically help in the peaceful management of potential conflict. East Asia seems to offer an increasingly successful story of regionalisation. China has already engaged in economic cooperation with ASEAN, Japan and South Korea, but also in security matters. A 'strategic partnership' was signed between ASEAN and China in October 2003 on Bali. China's ambition is to build a free trade area in the whole of East Asia before 2010. The region would have its own Monetary Fund and aim to promote the organisation of cooperation and development, and would also seek to balance the unilateral influence of the US in this region's security. China's agreement to participate in the negotiations of six states on the nuclear programme of North Korea also indicates that a multilateral structure of security can emerge in the region. It is possible that these new factors will diminish the diverse tensions and conflicts (in Taiwan, Myanmar, North Korea), stabilise the region and have a positive influence also on South Asia. This part of Asia may be the next region after Europe to create a security region and open the way to cooperation with other regions. On the other hand, it may initiate a process of inter-regional rivalry.

Latin America is a good example of regionalism (Mercosur, Andean Community) softening tensions between states of the region. Arguably this became possible only when there was a growth of democracy in the individual states. This democratic trend helped to shift this region in the direction of 'warm peace' from its 'neutral form' characteristic of the twentieth century (Miller, 2000, 172–4; also Hurrell, 1998), with the promise of serving the needs of human security in the process although progress on the latter has been somewhat mixed. One could imagine that regionalism could also be an efficient solution to Middle East problems, finding a place and role for Israel in the region, creating a future for a Palestinian state, and helping in the development of the Arab states. Unfortunately the imagination required is of a high order because until now achievements have been limited to either a cold peace kept by force or resulted from the military and diplomatic power of the US.

As well as examples of integration, the 1990s also saw signs of disintegration, including the phenomena of fragmented or *failed states*. The international community took its stand on the imperative of non-intervention in domestic turbulence and reacted helplessly to these developments. But can sovereignty be respected if state structures do not exist, if the state's territory is constantly changed during running battles for control, if crime, mass rape, and even genocide are constant features? Intervention in such cases came to be widely accepted. However, the legal basis for such intervention is still unclear; who is allowed to intervene, and how much disintegration should take place before external action can be justified? The response of one neighbouring state, or even a group of them, will always raise doubts about their intentions. It seems, therefore, that the future will belong more to regional organisations than to global ones because it is the region that is directly hurt by an emerging 'black hole' in its geographical area, and by the consequential destabilisation and the flood of refugees. The absence of a regional reaction was demonstrated in the Horn of Africa where national states failed. The process of fragmentation was also a tragic reality in the Balkans. Can we believe that states such as Indonesia, with its divided territory and its many ethnic and religious groups, will avoid this fate? Each of these cases relates closely to the question of regional responses to security problems.

Most armed conflicts and wars today have an *intra-state* character. With the exception of Colombia, they are concentrated in Africa and Asia. Struggles for territory, ideological and political divisions, and conflicts over power, religion and ethnicity sometimes leading to ethnic cleansing have been the cause of wars, sometimes long-lasting, around the world. The most tragic aspect of these conflicts is the increasing violence against civilians and the abuse of human rights in every respect.

The problem of the right to intervene, as I indicated in the case of failing states, returns yet again and presents itself as even more controversial in the case of strong states. The reason is clear: states do exist in these cases, sometimes powerful states in the form of dictatorships, so it is impossible to question their sovereignty from the standpoint of states' rights rather than human rights. In Kosovo in 1999 the first intervention was for the defence of human rights, but this highlighted many dilemmas (Stadtmüller, 2002, 62).

Differentiating between 'good' and 'bad' dictators on the basis of the position they occupy in the international war against terrorism is another controversial question. New examples of this can be found in the Central Asia region with the leading role of Uzbekistan. It is questionable also whether, after a military operation and the removal of a dictator, it is possible to build a stable peace (Afghanistan and Iraq offer important lessons here). The answer will depend on the level of development and the strength of regional arrangements (here the Balkans can provide another kind of 'lesson').

It is doubtful whether one universal solution is possible; the response has to vary depending on the particular case. It is important that we take the first step towards the rejection of ethnic cleansing to provide a warning to dictators that their impunity is limited. The idea of humanitarian intervention begins to compete with the 'free hand of the state' within its border. But which method is more fruitful? One approach is to apply pressure to dictators but without intervention, in the hope that they will choose 'a carrot' not 'a stick' one day (Libya could be an interesting example) or as alternative, liberate people by military actions. If the latter course of action is taken, the legal basis for such action is unclear. Nor is it clear who is legally entitled to carry it out. Similarly if we accept regimes, it is not obvious who has the right to say that they move 'one step too far' in violation of human rights.

Equally unclear is how the domestic wars of powerful states should be dealt with, states which are important actors in the international regime and may be involved in mutual cooperation across the world, in many respects very fruitfully (China and Tibet, Russia and Chechnya).

Arguably, regionalism in its new form is one of the most promising solutions to the above-mentioned issues provided that certain conditions are met: strong regional institutions with a consistency of views and policy, an ability to act coherently, a willingness to pay the costs, a basis of economic power which would be attractive for other states of the region, and a strong military capability. Obviously successful regionalism will also depend on the internal processes in other states, which are 'a subject' of pressure; such regional institutions have to offer an alternative, a partnership for other societies and regimes at some point. Under such conditions they can play an efficient role in helping to prevent domestic tensions spilling over into violence, in peacebuilding (post-war reconstruction), or assisting the processes of transition.

It seems that in the 1990s Europe illustrated very well both the weaknesses and the power of regional institutions in *building a 'democratic peace'*. The Conference on Security and Cooperation in Europe meeting in Paris (1990) can be interpreted as a revolutionary moment for the new Europe because they accepted democracy as the only legitimate form of governance and, as a result, changed the rules on the external sovereignty of states, established under the Westphalian Peace agreement, and gave the international community the right to scrutinise the ability of states to provide a democratic internal order. Europe developed a 'security regionalism' which, according to Hettne's definition, means 'attempts by the states and other actors in a particular geographical area – a region in the making – to transform a security complex with conflict-generating inter-state and intra-state relations towards a security community with cooperative external relations and domestic peace' (2001, 13). An example of Franco-German reconciliation was followed in the 1990s by a similarly successful German–Polish attempt, and by progress in removing hostility and fears in Polish–Ukrainian and Polish–Lithuanian relations.

Peace was also served by the ability of regionalism, especially in the countries of East Central Europe, to either stop the processes of ethnic disintegration of states or to make such processes less painful through the practice of a new supranational framework which embraced ethnic groups or newly established states. But regionalism will only work if there is a willingness on the part of nations/societies to meet the responsibilities as well as the rights of inclusion. We can assume that recognition of the special role of institutions (especially effective ones like NATO and the EU) was dominant in all East Central Europe states' political thinking. Can we anticipate that other regions will be able to follow such a pattern (East Asia cooperation built on the basis of China–Japan reconciliation, South Asia on India–Pakistan, both these regions on India–China cooperation, Middle East on Israel–Arab states' common interests)?

The EU has the chance to show its ability in its own neighbourhood, before moving towards a more active role in global governance. Undoubtedly the Union showed in the 1990s that such governance brings positive results. Candidate countries quickly and easily adopted democratic rules and norms, and modernised in an attempt to achieve membership of the EU and NATO. However this was mostly containment, not real governance (Pridham et al., 1997; Whitehead, 1996). Now the EU has to develop a comprehensive, cohesive economic-political strategy towards all the European states which have not been accepted in the present wave of enlargement, and also towards Russia which has to be treated separately but inclusively. In the context of rapid change, exclusiveness in regional arrangements cannot serve cooperation and security well. In this sense in March 2003 the EU proposed a new framework for relations with its eastern and southern neighbours (Wider Europe, 2003).

Despite some still unresolved problems in parts of Europe, a major part of this continent is fully stabilised and without even a remote possibility of military conflicts, with regional arrangements linking most of the countries in various forms and on different levels. But this is only the first step towards *establishing a multidimensional security community*, a so-called 'warm peace'. Though Europe is on the whole relatively rich and developed, it is still far from united. Regional cooperation for development is necessary if we want the prevention of inter-state and intra-state wars to succeed. Hence, on the one hand the EU has to find a way of stabilising its own internal development and on the other it has to respond to regional security problems. It will have to play an active role in building a security system embracing the whole of Europe and all dimensions of peace. The possibility of such a prospect is a subject of debate between idealistic and realistic approaches (Seidelmann, 1998, 41–50). In addition, Europe cannot escape the security threats emanating from other parts of world. But the same situation applies to every region, which has been able to solve intra- and inter-state conflicts. In the last resort, regional institutions cannot respond efficiently to all security problems unless they are part of a global framework.

GLOBAL AND REGIONAL SECURITY

The regional dimension of security cannot be separated from the global order. At this level we have to consider both multilateralism, the role of the United Nations (UN), and unilateralism, the special position of the US. The literature on the new regionalism is replete with considerations about the positive or negative impact of this process on the global level of governance, that is to say, on the present multilateral system. One view is that regionalism offers an alternative to multilateralism, leading traditionally to the separation of regions and competition between them. Apart from this, the new regional structures develop in a parallel way to the global intergovernmental system. If we keep our mind on the old track of the Westphalian system and the multilateralism created after the Second World War in the shape of the UN, it seems obvious. However, we can think about another sort of 'new multilateralism' established not on the ground of single states but on their regional arrangements. For example, the new regionalism is driven rather by global and private forces than by governmental or national pressures. Moreover, as intra-regional structures are created, a complementary development is the supra-regional groups, which embrace them, and regional arrangements are also open for association with non-members. Furthermore, the area of regional activity is broader than the economic alone, since it concerns development and security, which may lead to cooperation with other regions. We can add that even very big, continental countries are abandoning their autarkic approaches, while there is no evidence that trade between regions has been damaged by the rapid growth of interaction within regions.

It seems equally important that at the beginning of the new century, in the light of increasing conflicts, multilateralism in the present form of the UN and other global institutions began to be seen as inefficient (Knight, 2000, 158–225). The search for security led to the UN's activity being supplemented by regional cooperation. The end of the Cold War had raised hopes of efficient management of a number of conflicts by the UN. It is possible to point to some successes on this route, such as the first Gulf War, Cambodia, and Haiti, but also dramatic failures in the Balkans, Rwanda, and Somalia. This situation led to a consideration by the UN of the role of regional arrangements and agencies (intergovernmental and non-governmental), not as competitors at the universal level but as effective promoters of international security. Arguments for their involvements are obvious: they are more familiar with the regional situation, and they are deeply interested in establishing peace so are more ready to act.

However, they also suffer several limitations, including the lack of a mandate and limited resources if the major powers are not included in such a group. Hence, effective task-sharing between the UN and regional institutions requires not only this new approach but also changes in the present Charter to develop the rules and procedures governing such cooperation. Taking into account that the position, strength, and capacity of regional/sub-regional arrangements, as well as the intensity and form of conflicts in different regions vary widely, this task will not be easy. On the other hand, keeping the present system of *ad hoc* initiated cooperation may lead to controversies. These controversies stem from both political and legal considerations because authorisation or delegation by the UN for such military actions (under Articles 53(1), 42, 48(2)) do not cover all new challenges. Problems are also connected with the ambiguous status of some organisations such as NATO, evolving from a collective self-defence organisation to a participant in regional or even global enforcement actions (Wet, 2002, 1–37).

The important question in relations between the UN and regional organisations is to clarify the responsibility of each level, the flow of information, and the rules of accountability. According to Alagappa 'regional institutions ... should take the lead in conflict prevention, while the UN or other actors may be better able to take the lead in the other stages of conflict management. This functional division of labour, however, is an abstract one that should be modified for specific cases' (1997, 437). I would agree with this last sentence because it seems that the role of regional arrangements is increasing also in the other stages of conflict management, especially when the major powers of the region are included in these agencies and are ready to act. The UN has to play its role of coordinator but also has to share its burdens with more appropriate regional institutions. This seems to be one of the most important radical reforms currently under consideration by the UN.

Any discussion of stability and security on the global level must of necessity take into account the political changes connected with the so-called Atlantic World Order upon which Western security was based for many years after the Second World War. Today, relations between Europe and the United States are in disrepair. And this situation results not only from the last clash over the Iraqi question but from the chain of earlier events and also concerns the 'philosophy' of the new world order, the rules and norms of global governance, the right to use power, international law and society, generally a paradigm of international relations. On the other hand the deep split between Americans and Europeans may be diminished by continuing strong ties, the sharing of the general values of a democratic system, human rights, and the maintenance of physical security, which was achieved after the Second World War. Moreover Europe as a whole, and even the EU, is divided over transatlantic cooperation; however, it seems that Europe divides along the lines of methods rather than values; that sees different ways of dealing with the United States' role and unilateralism, rather than accepting this new situation.

One of the results of the attacks on 11 September 2001 was to show the global nature of security, while an important effect was the influence on the Americans' view of their own security. Until then they could safely assume that wars took place on 'foreign soil', but 'no longer' as Paul Wolfowitz, Deputy Secretary of Defense, told Congress (Wolfowitz, 2001). This shock led to a quite simple idea: American security is equal to global security; everything which serves American security makes the world secure. It follows that the US has the moral right to act as a guardian of global interests as well as its own. Problems begin when we try to define these 'global interests'. As Rasmussen noticed correctly, the European governments have a reflexive security dilemma: '... if they needed the United States for their security, how could they reject the American strategy? On the other hand, most of them believed that the American strategy actually would not solve the security problems, and perhaps even create new ones' (2002, 342). Yet it seems also that the US, even ruled by the Bush administration, is aware that its incomparable power can only become acceptable to the rest of the world when it is an element in a regional and global network of arrangements and institutions.

So, the question is how to share responsibility for regional and global security between not only the UN and regional agencies but also regional agencies and the US. The Americans are involved in regional cooperation and security agreements in different parts of the world, including their strongest link with Europe. This therefore raises the question of relations with the EU (Lindstrom, 2003). For example, can the EU assume only non-security responsibilities leaving NATO (US) in the role of guarantor of military security? Clearly the answer to such a question depends on each particular case, but in general it would be necessary to have consistent, general, common ideas of when, how, and under what conditions the EU is ready as a whole to be involved. Its lack of state power, the multilateral internal system, and the primacy of economic instruments leads to understandable weakness in coping with the traditional challenges to a nation-state. But on the other hand the EU is quite well prepared and well suited to cope with the postmodern era of interdependence, multiculturalism, networks of structures and multidimensional and multilevel bargaining. Declaring its readiness for better democratic governance itself, it is able to undertake a democratising role in global governance. It can do this through its involvement in inter-regional cooperation and dialogue with governmental and non-governmental actors. But, there is a large gap between aspiration and performance. The role of other regional arrangements in global governance is even more uncertain.

CONCLUSIONS

Regionalism, integration, globalisation, multilateralism are each portrayed as threatening to many states, their national governments and societies and especially in countries at early stages of development. They are associated with dilution or even loss of sovereignty, while also stimulating global competition that inevitably generates painful adjustments on the part of states and groups within them. But isolation from these processes is unrealistic for any state. In the long term, regional cooperation can be helpful in providing economic stabilisation and multidimensional security.

Approaches to international security in the post-Cold War world have to comprise several arrangements and actors, as a matter of sufficiency. Regional institutions as well as global ones can play an invaluable role in the broad security area; each of them has clear limitations but also strength. They can provide diplomatic and economic, if not military, power. The EU role in relation to Eastern Europe in the post-1989 period is one such positive example. Also, the expansion of ASEAN to Indochina and cooperation with China, South Korea and Japan can bring greater stabilisation for the whole region. Regional institutions are able to respond to different types of security problems such as inter-state and intra-state conflicts, including the case of failing states; they can participate effectively in peace reconstruction; and finally they have a potential opportunity to establish multidimensional security communities. How realistic is such a belief? If it stemmed only from trust in the goodwill of international actors – not too much, but it seems that contemporary trends in the world economy and politics have created quite fertile ground for close, actually inevitable, regional cooperation. And this view is shared by both idealists and those who favour cooperation on the basis of rational interests.

The new regionalism can also provide a new version of multilateralism, helping to reshape the UN system and global governance. The new regionalism does not seem exclusive and protectionist, it is created from below and responds to the contemporary trends in the economy, in technological development, and in human expectations. These trends cut across regions and push them to bargain, cooperate with, and accommodate, one another. Present tendencies show too that even small states can play important roles at the regional level, which definitely means more real equality than in traditional multilateralist arrangements that guaranteed 'one vote for one state'. In fact, however, only the big powers ruled these institutions. Regional structures representing their particular members, even weak ones, will be more equal partners each to another, as well towards singular powers like the US, Japan, China. There is also a realistic chance that these later examples of 'superpowers' will be members or part-members of regional structures, which will establish interconnected networks of global cooperation and governance. Moreover, the main and long-lasting problems of the contemporary world do not seem connected with the traditional, narrow interpretation of security, the military one (despite the present 'antiterrorism war', and even in this case a network is necessary for achieving success) and the real challenges continue to be linked to the question of how to create new mechanisms that will better serve human security and development.

NOTE

1. I would like to thank particularly warmly my friend and colleague from Bradford University, Thomas Lane, for his numerous helpful suggestions and correction of English.

8
Regional Monetary
Cooperation and Integration

Ludo Cuyvers, Philippe De Lombaerde,
Eric De Souza and David Fielding

The second half of the twentieth century witnessed an unprecedented growth in the global capital market, driven by the liberalisation of national capital markets and the technological revolution. Under the Bretton Woods agreement in 1944, the International Monetary Fund (IMF) was given the responsibility for the management of the international monetary system under a system of managed exchange rates. When this system eventually collapsed in 1971, the IMF continued to manage the international financial system, but in drastically different circumstances and indeed with a different interpretation of its remit. Growing financial instability at the global level, combined with the perception of inadequate management and leadership on the part of the international financial authorities, led some countries to cooperate in setting up their own regional exchange rate systems, to move towards deeper forms of monetary cooperation and, as in the case of the European Union (EU), to full currency union. The Asian financial crisis of 1997 acted also as a catalyst for the development of new ideas about the potential role of regional monetary arrangements.

Situating regional monetary integration in the context of post-Bretton Woods exchange rate policies, this chapter will chart different regional approaches to monetary cooperation and integration taken in Europe, Sub-Saharan Africa, Latin America and the Caribbean, and East and Southeast Asia, and will consider why a diversity of positions has emerged. The chapter also evaluates the longer-term prospects for monetary integration, against the background of global financial uncertainty and a lack of consensus over best-practice monetary and exchange rate arrangements.

THE BIPOLAR VIEW ON EXCHANGE RATE POLICY

According to the bipolar view, since the 1990s, there has been a trend towards the two extremes of the policy spectrum, and thus towards the abandonment of intermediary exchange rate systems. In a world of more mobile capital, these intermediary systems are seen as being difficult to implement and sustain credibly. The bipolar view should thus be understood as being both a policy prescription for exchange rate policy in the context of the world economy at the turn of the millennium and an empirical interpretation of recent monetary history.

On the basis of declared (*de jure*) exchange rate regimes, the bipolar view seems obvious. Recent figures on the decade of the 1990s show that both hard pegs (from 16 per cent to 24 per cent of notifications) and floating regimes (from 23 per cent to 42 per cent) have regained importance at the cost of the intermediate exchange rate arrangements.

In the different regions outside Europe, the same pattern of bipolarity can be observed to a greater or lesser extent. The 1980s and 1990s saw an abandonment of fixed (but adjustable) exchange rates across most of Sub-Saharan Africa. The exchange rate peg was replaced either by a free float, or, in some cases, by an intermediate system. The outstanding exception to the move towards floating exchange rates was the Communauté Financière Africaine (CFA) Franc Zone with its hard peg.

Current exchange rate policies in the Americas illustrate perhaps better the bipolar view; since the 1990s there is a clear tendency towards either flexible rates or hard pegs (including dollarisation where a country opts for the use of the dollar as the currency of exchange, either officially or *de facto*). Several countries, such as Chile, Brazil, Mexico and Venezuela, abandoned their intermediate regimes and successfully opted for flexible rates, often pressured by circumstances. The financial crisis in Argentina in 2002 also resulted in the adoption of a floating regime, displacing the currency board system which had been in place since the early 1990s. A few smaller countries opted for the dollarisation of their economies. The Asian crisis led several countries of the East and Southeast Asian regions to ultimately abandon intermediate regimes, moving mainly in the direction of flexible rates.

Although the bipolar view is shared by many analysts, there is no consensus about the generality of the policy device. Bordo (2003), for example, defends the case for intermediate systems for transition countries that lack financial and institutional maturity to float freely. Neither there is a consensus on the empirical facts and their interpretation. On the basis of alternative classifications of *de facto* exchange rates, the bipolar view seems less evident. In the rest of the chapter, we will concentrate on the hard peg policy option (monetary integration).

REGIONAL MONETARY INTEGRATION IN THE WORLD

Western Europe

Although the European Economic Community (EEC) initially considered the idea of a monetary union (MU) in the Werner Report of 1970, its member states finally opted for the much less ambitious goal of fixed but adjustable intra-regional exchange rates after the collapse of the Bretton Woods system. The move to a MU was decided at the meeting of the Heads of State or Government of the EEC at the Hague in December 1969.[1] It requested that a plan by stages be drawn up by the Council of Ministers with a view to the creation of an economic and monetary union (EMU) through a gradual series of stages the result being the Werner Report, quickly relegated to history as economic crises erupted.

Following a period of floating exchange rates, the European Monetary System (EMS) came into existence in March 1979, and it lasted until the third stage of EMU, starting on 1 January 1999 (Treaty of Maastricht), when national currencies were replaced by a single currency, the euro; a single monetary authority, the European System of Central Banks (ESCB), was established; and a single monetary policy was introduced. The ESCB is composed of the European Central Bank (ECB) and the National Central Banks of the participating member states.

Sub-Saharan Africa

The CFA zone evolved from the monetary institutions of the last phase of French colonial Africa.[2] In 1955, five years before independence, the Metropolitan French authorities devolved the right to issue currency onto two newly created institutions: the Banque des Etats d'Afrique Centrale and Cameroon, later renamed the Bank of Central African States (BEAC), and the Central Bank of West African States (BCEAO). These banks issued their own notes for use in French Equatorial Africa (including Cameroon) and French West Africa (including Togo).

After political independence (1960–62), the central banks in the Franc Zone retained their function and their currencies, and the French Treasury continued to guarantee convertibility. All of the newly independent Central African states, notably Cameroon, the Central African Republic, the Congo Republic, Gabon and Chad adhered to this MU under the auspices of the BEAC.[3] Côte d'Ivoire, Dahomey (later Bénin), Upper Volta (later Burkina Faso), Mali, Mauritania, Niger and Senegal formed the independent and separate West African Economic and Monetary Union (WAEMU) under the auspices of the BCEAO.

Outside of the Franc Zone, most of the newly independent African states chose to create their own national currencies and central banks.

In the first years of independence in the mid-1960s, many former British colonies appeared to be following the same route as the Franc Zone countries. There were three separate MUs issuing currency tied to the pound sterling: the West African Currency Board composed of The Gambia, Sierra Leone; the East African Currency Board, with Kenya, Tanzania, Uganda; and the Central African Pound area, embracing Malawi, Zambia and the then Southern Rhodesia. In some respects, the monetary links between these countries and the former colonial power were less extensive than in the case of the Franc Zone. The constitutions of the anglophone monetary areas did not specify a large proactive role for the British Treasury.

However, between 1964 and 1971 all three of these currency arrangements gradually dissolved. The British government was forced to devalue the pound against the US dollar in the late 1960s, and with relatively little British interest in the sterling zone, there was not much incentive for the newly independent states to pursue a link with the pound. Moreover, political tensions between the different African states created pressure to set up national central banks issuing a national currency.

The Lomé meeting of ECOWAS (Economic Community of West African States) heads of state in 1999 set out detailed plans for regional monetary integration among both francophone and anglophone states in West Africa (Bawumia, 2002). The ultimate aim envisaged in these plans was a merging of the WAEMU with a yet to be created anglophone MU among The Gambia, Ghana, Guinea-Conakry, Nigeria, Sierra Leone and Liberia.

In Southern Africa, monetary integration has been attempted with some degree of success. Many of the frontline states bordering South Africa retained close economic links with the country, even when independence from Britain led to greater political divergence from the apartheid government. Substantial labour flows across the South African border made economic independence impossible. The rand circulated freely in Botswana, Lesotho and Swaziland, and also in Namibia, which remained under South African control until the 1990s. Over time these countries created their own central banks which issued their own notes. But these new currencies circulated alongside the rand, precluding any substantial degree of monetary independence. The national currencies have remained pegged against the rand under a currency board system and there is a substantial amount of cooperation with the South African Reserve Bank.

The end of the apartheid system in South Africa in the 1990s opened the way for regional economic cooperation to become politically feasible. The Southern African Development Community (SADC) now incorporates the rand area plus Angola, Democratic Republic of Congo, Malawi, Mauritius, Mozambique, the Seychelles, Tanzania, Zambia and Zimbabwe. However, these countries now have independent flexible exchange rate regimes,[4] and wider monetary cooperation is as yet entirely hypothetical.

In March 2004 Kenya, Tanzania and Uganda ratified the treaty creating the East African Community (EAC) Customs Union. The treaty established a common external tariff as a first step towards wider economic integration. The EAC treaty states that the customs union will be followed at some future date by a common market, and then by a MU but the plan for a single currency is as yet less detailed than in West Africa.

Latin America and the Caribbean

The only example of a sustained currency union in this region is the Eastern Caribbean currency zone, installed by the UK in the 1950s. In a few cases, small countries opted for the official dollarisation of their economies. Ecuador dollarised its economy in 2000; El Salvador followed in 2001. These countries joined Panama, where the dollar has been legal tender since 1904.

The Organisation of East Caribbean States (OECS) was created in 1981. It includes the independent states: Antigua and Barbuda, Dominica, Grenada, Santa-Lucia, Saint Kitts and Nevis, Saint Vincent and the Grenadines, and the two British territories of Anguilla and Montserrat. Since the 1950s a currency board was installed by the UK and stayed in place until the 1970s. As a consequence of the devaluations of the pound and the uncertainty in the international monetary system, the Eastern Caribbean dollar was fixed in terms of the US dollar in 1976. The Eastern Caribbean Central Bank (ECCB) was created in 1983. The regime has been characterised as a quasi-currency board.[5] The ECCB illustrates the possibility of reaping technical economies of scale in regional monetary institutions among small countries (Goto, 2001, 160).

Although ideas for common currencies have been launched on different occasions for the North American Free Trade Agreement (NAFTA), Caribbean Common Market (CARICOM), Central America, Comunidad Andina (CAN) and Mercosur, these ideas have not yet achieved momentum. However, since 1966, a reciprocal payments system has existed in the Latin American Integration Association. The agreement on the creation of the Andean Reserve Fund was signed in 1976. In 1988 it was decided to 'open' the Fund to other Latin American countries and re-name it as the Latin American Reserve Fund. Its mission is to provide financial resources to member countries to contribute to the stabilisation of their balance of payments (Zahler, 1997).[6]

East and Southeast Asia

In East and Southeast Asia weaker forms of regional monetary cooperation have emerged until now, falling far short of currency union in all the cases. This reflects the generally lower levels of economic integration in the region. In 1977, the central banks and monetary authorities of the Association of Southeast Asian Nations, with Indonesia, Malaysia, the Philippines, Singapore and Thailand (ASEAN+5) established the ASEAN Swap Arrangement (ASA). The aim of the ASA was to provide the member countries with sufficient international liquidity in case of balance of payments problems. In 1997, the Lao PDR and Myanmar acceded to the ASA. This was the monetary cooperation framework that operated at the outbreak of the Asian financial crisis in 1997.

At the end of September 1997, and for most observers unexpectedly, Japan proposed the creation of an Asian Monetary Fund (AMF). The largest part of the national contributions to the AMF would come from Japan, but Hong Kong, Taiwan and Singapore were also prepared to contribute. In spite of enthusiastic reactions from the Asian countries, the Japanese proposal was blocked by the adverse reactions from major Western countries and from the IMF (Lipsey, 2003). A compromise was sought in the Manila Framework, with a financing agreement that would supplement the IMF financing, involving 14 Asia-Pacific nations.

On 6 May 2000, on the occasion of a meeting of Finance Ministers, it was agreed to extend the ASA to all ASEAN member countries and to include China, Japan and South Korea, with a significant increase in the initial financial provision. This agreement is labelled the Chiang Mai Initiative. It consists of a network of bilateral swap agreements (BSA) between the 13 countries, with the same purpose as the ASA.

In order not to get the same adverse reaction from the US and the IMF, the BSA is complementary to the IMF, as it was agreed that at most 10 per cent of a bilateral swap could be done without any link to the IMF, which evidently severely limits the efficiency of the BSA both in terms of timing and conditions attached to support.

In June 2003, the central banks of Australia, China, Hong Kong, Indonesia, Japan, South Korea, Malaysia, New Zealand, the Philippines, Singapore and Thailand announced the establishment of the Asian Bond Fund (ABF). It aims at managing a fund, which will come from Asian and Pacific countries, and investing this fund in a basket of liquid dollar-denominated Asian government bonds (Yam, 2003). The ABF will facilitate the re-investment of a small portion of Asia's international reserves back into the region while at the same time aiding the development of regional capital markets.

At the ASEAN Summit on 15–16 December 1998 in Hanoi, one of the proposals endorsed a study into the feasibility of establishing a common currency. This was followed, in August 2003 at the Manila Summit, by the adoption of a 'roadmap' for establishing by 2020 a level of integration similar to the EU, and for an ASEAN common currency. Many observers and policy-makers are, however, sceptical whether it will be possible to reach a common currency by then.

REGIONAL MONETARY INTEGRATION: A TYPOLOGICAL APPROACH

Conceptual and theoretical models of regional economic integration, in general, and of monetary integration, in particular, are very much a reflection of European integration history. The well-known Balassa stages model (Balassa, 1961) has become the standard reference for conceptualising the phenomenon of regional economic integration (see Chapter 5). However, the study of integration outside Europe and comparative approaches require a richer and more flexible conceptual framework. This is true for trade integration (where such diverse arrangements as the hub and spoke model, open regionalism, growth circles, all represent the complex and varied concepts that emerged outside Europe) and also for monetary integration. In many cases, asymmetric forms of monetary integration have been set up.

The asymmetries in the arrangements reflect economic and/or political regional hegemonies (US in the Americas and Asia, France (EU) in Africa, UK in Africa and the Caribbean, ...). An extreme case is official dollarisation, when a country or a group of countries decide to consider the dollar (or some other foreign currency) as the legal tender. Intermediate arrangements (CFA and rand zones) imply certain responsibilities for the monetary authorities of the hegemonic power (France, South Africa) in the form of shared seigniorage and guaranteed convertibility. Looking at the Franc Zone constitutions, for example, the obligations for the partners fall into two categories. First, there are the constitutional principles designed to achieve the goal of complete financial integration between member states. Under this heading fall the guarantees of convertibility between CFA and French francs (euros), and the fixed exchange rate. Maintenance of the principles implies a heavy obligation on the part of France, with some obligations on the part of the CFA. Secondly, there are the administrative structures to which member states bind themselves, and which prevent (or at least, which are designed to prevent) African states free-riding on French guarantees, and on each other. These entail considerable loss of economic sovereignty on the part of the African states.

Dollarisation is a unilateral asymmetrical alternative to classical monetary integration where the issuing monetary authority remains passive or, at most, collaborates informally. Its adoption has been seriously considered in various countries on the American continent and in the Caribbean. This is related to the fact that many countries are relatively dependent on the US economy and to the relatively high levels of *de facto* dollarisation of their economies. Whereas Panama has used the US dollar as official means of payment since 1904, Ecuador and El Salvador decided to dollarise their economies only recently.

A number of issues that have been raised in the recent literature on monetary integration in a Latin American context are related to the differences between 'classical' monetary integration (between neighbouring interdependent economies of more or less comparable development levels) and dollarisation. For many countries in the region these are two clearly distinct options; however, the relative costs and benefits of both options are not easily established *ex ante*.[7]

Dollarisation permits the countries that opt for this policy to acquire monetary stability and policy credibility in the short run, thus bringing down interest rates and/or reducing volatility, without the cost of (regional) institution building. Dollarisation also reduces transaction costs related to economic relations with the US (and other dollarised economies) so that a positive impulse might be expected on trade and investment flows. The price of dollarisation is related to the loss of an autonomous monetary policy instrument and the loss of seigniorage.

GRADUALISM AND SEQUENCING

As we mentioned in the previous section, dollarisation can and has been pushed through in times of crisis and high inflation and has proved to be potentially effective in the short run. Its merit in the long run should still be evaluated and is likely to depend crucially on the level of interdependence vis-à-vis the US economy, as the Argentine case shows.

A completely different story is told in the European case, which shows the importance of gradualism in setting up a symmetrical (classical) currency union. Indeed, the implementation of the EMU was preceded by four decades of institutional linkage building and converging policy preferences. For authors like Cohen (2003, 275–92), this is an essential feature of European monetary integration. He predicts that other regions like Mercosur, CARICOM, CAN, ASEAN will also need such a long transition period to reach sufficient levels of political commitment.

When the move to a European MU was first considered at the Hague Summit of the EEC in December 1969, immediately two opposing views of how to proceed emerged: the so-called 'economist' view and the 'monetarist' view. The former held that a high degree of convergence both in economic fundamentals and in economic policies was a prerequisite for the creation of a MU. The latter promoted a rapid introduction of a MU with economic convergence as a consequence. The Werner Report viewed MU as the total and irreversible convertibility of currencies, the elimination of margins of fluctuation in exchange rates, the irrevocable fixing of exchange rate parities, and the complete liberalisation of capital movements. It was agnostic on whether national currencies should be replaced by a single currency. It proposed that MU be achieved in three steps over a period of ten years. The experience of the 1970s and 1980s revealed quite clearly that fixed but irrevocable exchange rates and the maintenance of national currencies (and national monetary authorities) cannot be considered equivalent to the replacement of national currencies by a single currency and a single monetary authority.

The Smithsonian Agreement of December 1971 attempted to rescue the Bretton Woods system by increasing the fluctuation margins of other currencies with regard to the US dollar from plus or minus 1 per cent to plus or minus 2.25 per cent, but the arrangement failed and was finally abandoned in 1973. Several EEC countries considered these margins to be too wide. Several attempts were undertaken to reduce these margins on a voluntary participation basis for the member states. These attempts were known as the establishment of a 'snake' of European exchange rates, at first within 'the tunnel' defined by the Smithsonian Agreement, and on its own after March 1973 when the tunnel ceased to exist. The currency composition of the snake was extremely volatile and changes in parities frequent. It lasted until 13 March 1979 when it was replaced by the European Monetary System (EMS). The centerpiece of the EMS was the Exchange Rate Mechanism (ERM) which defined a system of fixed exchange rates between participating countries.

The EMS was in operation from 1979 to 1998. We can further distinguish three sub-periods: *March 1979 to January 1987*: During the first sub-period, the member states participating in the ERM did not at first take into account the constraints imposed on economic policies by a fixed exchange rate regime. Only from 1983 onwards was the lesson learnt, and economic policies were adjusted accordingly. The result was that there were eleven realignments in this period. During this time, the EMS truly functioned as a fixed but adjustable exchange rate regime, a regime in which extended periods of stable nominal exchange rates were punctuated with realignments.

February 1987 to September 1992: The second sub-period is known as the period of the 'hard EMS'. The only realignment that occurred was a technical realignment when Italy reduced its exchange rate fluctuations bands to the normal ones. Speculation against currencies belonging to the ERM had practically ceased because of renewed interest in a MU between EEC countries which resulted in markets being convinced that MU was not too far away. The period ended when hopes were dashed by the negative results of a referendum on the Maastricht Treaty in Denmark in June 1992 and an expected negative result in France in September.

October 1992 to December 1998: On 2 August 1993, the fluctuation margins of the ERM were 'temporarily' widened to plus or minus 15 per cent. The EMS continued to subsist in limbo with the addition of a few countries (and currencies) while awaiting the arrival of MU. This sub-period was dominated by preparations for the start of a MU between qualifying countries according to rules laid down in the Maastricht Treaty on the EU which entered into force on 1 November 1993.

The European Council meeting at Hannover in June 1988 had given a new impetus to monetary integration. The commissioned Delors Report on EMU, was published in April 1989. It envisaged an evolution towards MU in three stages. The first stage came into force on 1 July 1990 and led to the complete liberalisation of capital movements between member states. The second and third stages were incorporated into the Maastricht Treaty. The second stage began on 1 January 1994 and involved the creation of the European Monetary Institute, precursor to the ECB, with the task of preparing for the third and final stage of EMU.

The third stage of EMU started on 1 January 1999, a deadline imposed by the Treaty. It was the final and definitive step towards monetary integration between the member states of the EU. Only member states that satisfied the 'convergence criteria' could qualify for MU, and were obliged to participate except for the UK and Denmark, which had obtained an 'opt-out' in the Treaty. These convergence criteria concerned (a) price stability: for the preceding year the average inflation rate must not exceed that of the best three states by more than 1.5 per cent; (b) interest rate convergence: for the preceding year the average long-term interest rate must not exceed that of the best three states (in term of inflation) by more than 2 per cent; (c) budget discipline: government budget deficit must be less than 3 per cent of GDP, and the government debt cannot exceed 60 per cent of GDP; (d) exchange rate stability: for the preceding two years no exchange rate realignments. All member states (prior to enlargement of the EU on 1 May 2004), except Sweden, Denmark and the UK, belong to EMU.

OPTIMAL CURRENCY AREAS

The key question is why would countries wish to cooperate in monetary arrangements that impinge upon national sovereignty in the area of monetary policy, the freedom to choose the most appropriate interest rates and/or exchange rates to suit the economic conditions at any given moment? Optimum currency area (OCA) theory is the mainstream theoretical framework for analysing the structural economic factors that determine the net (positive or negative) effect of forming a currency area among countries. Whereas in the short run, political considerations and events, alongside other economic circumstances, might well condition or even impose exchange rate choices, OCA theory is particularly relevant in the medium and long run (see Chapter 5). Therefore, a look at the results of the empirical tests of the OCA conditions for different regions is likely to shed light on the future world map of currency zones.

The economists' view according to which the formation of currency unions is fundamentally explained by variables suggested by OCA theory has been challenged by Cohen (1998) and others. According to Cohen, a combination of the presence of a regional hegemon committed to monetary integration, as suggested by traditional realism, and the presence of a network of linkages and commitments that make the cost of a dependent monetary policy acceptable to all members, as suggested by the institutional approach, are sufficient conditions for successful monetary integration, each of these being separately necessary conditions. According to Cohen, historical analysis shows that economic linkages are insufficient to sustain the necessary commitment beyond the short run.

Euro-zone

The *ex ante* tests of the OCA criteria for the euro-zone were not unanimously favourable to the formation of the EMU. The empirical analyses based on (macroeconomic) shock symmetry, taken as a 'meta' property of OCAs and following the methodology developed by Blanchard and Quah (1989, 655–73) and Bayoumi and Eichengreen (1992), usually identify an OCA around Germany, with a smaller size than EMU, including Germany, the BENELUX and, but not always, France and Denmark, as core countries (Mongelli, 2002). In addition, the various studies do not predict consistent patterns of widening the initial union around the core. Other empirically supported arguments against EMU included the low levels of labour mobility, the low levels of price and wage flexibility, the structural differences between the core countries and the periphery, and the absence of a strong fiscal federalism to accompany MU.

The discrepancy between the actual extension of the EMU and the economically optimal size of it is often interpreted as a demonstration of the dominance of political variables over economic variables (Verdun, 1996). Although the decision to create the EMU is obviously the result of a complex interplay between both types of variables, Mundell defended the MU since 1965, and explained why the economic case for a currency union might be stronger than the empirical tests might suggest. His position can be summarised in six points: (i) it is not realistic to think that wage earners in open economies will exhibit monetary illusion for a long time; (ii) internal capital mobility is able to substitute for labour mobility to facilitate adjustment; (iii) a too strict application of Mundell's criteria would reveal that national economies are not optimal; additional and more flexible criteria should be used anyway; (iv) the OCA criteria are endogenous to an important degree – this means, for example, that trade interdependence is not only a condition for monetary integration but also a consequence of it; (v) the benefits of currency union and the integrating effect on financial markets are systematically underestimated; and (vi) the euro can serve as a counterweight for the dollar in a more stable global financial system (Mundell, 1998).

Sub-Saharan Africa

Several papers focus on the extent to which macroeconomic shocks differ between the Franc Zone economies and their neighbours, and among the Franc Zone countries themselves. Hoffmaister et al. (1998, 132–60) conclude that the Franc Zone countries are relatively less susceptible to shocks that originate within the domestic economy, and relatively more susceptible to external shocks impacting on the price of imports and exports. *If* these asymmetries persisted with the creation of a wider ECOWAS MU, then there would be a cause for concern. Two papers that apply a similar methodology to individual Franc Zone countries are Fielding and Shields (2001, 199–223) and Coleman (2004). To a certain extent these papers' findings are consistent with those of Hoffmaister et al.: for example, in terms of the relative importance of domestic shocks in countries outside the Franc Zone. In terms of the degree of homogeneity within the Franc Zone, however, the results are mixed and sensitive to the assumptions used to derive information about the size, timing and nature of the shocks.

Research on West African macroeconomic convergence from a more general perspective, including a view of indicators of fiscal convergence, suggests the results are mixed, with differing degrees of homogeneity within and beyond the Franc Zone (Bénassy-Quéré and Coupet, 2003; Bamba, 2004). Bénassy-Quéré and Coupet suggest that there is an economic rationale for an alternative partitioning of the Franc Zone on economic grounds. The suggested five groups of countries they look at are Bénin, Burkina Faso, Mali and Togo; Côte d'Ivoire, Senegal and Gambia; Cameroon, Central African Republic and Chad; Congo, Gabon and Nigeria; Guinea-Bissau, Niger, Ghana and Sierra Leone.

There is a similar group of papers reviewing the degree of macroeconomic homogeneity within the SADC region. Agbeyegbe (2002), Grandes (2003) and Khamfula and Huizinga (2004, 699–714) all look at the degree of asymmetry of macroeconomic shocks in Southern Africa. There is a broad consensus that the rand zone countries face very similar shocks, which is not surprising, given the degree of labour mobility between them. There is also some evidence that the macroeconomic shocks of a further group of countries (Malawi, Mauritius, Zimbabwe) are quite similar to the rand zone core. However, across the whole of the SADC region there is a great deal of heterogeneity, which suggests that a MU encompassing the whole area would lead to substantial costs.

Less has been written about the potential for MU in East Africa. A number of early studies sought to determine whether Africa's existing MUs in the Franc Zone could promote economic growth (Devarajan and de Melo, 1987). When CFA members are compared with a large sample of less developed countries, their growth is significantly lower than the aggregate for the rest of the sample. When CFA members are compared with just the rest of Sub-Saharan Africa, statistically significantly better performance by CFA members appears.

This approach is open to the criticism that its treatment of the factors determining economic growth is rather crude, allowing for no quantification of the effects of natural resources and geography on growth. Plane (1988) tries to avoid this criticism by beginning with a general model of economic growth for a large sample of less developed countries. Plane then tests whether the cross-country residual is dependent on Franc Zone membership. Although the weighted average of residuals for the Franc Zone is positive, and the residual for Africa outside the Franc Zone negative, the difference is not significant.

The evidence for a link between long-term growth and Franc Zone membership is therefore rather weak. However, another aspect of MU in Africa is the degree of central bank independence that it entails. Here, there is much stronger evidence. A number of papers have consistently found Franc Zone membership to be associated with lower average rates of inflation, *ceteris paribus* (Bleaney and Fielding, 2002, 233–45).

Recent work by Fielding and Shields (2004) tests the endogeneity of OCA criteria for the Franc Zone. It is a good case because the creation of the CFA institutions is a consequence of French colonial history, and exogenous to the contemporary economic characteristics of the countries. Their paper concludes that there is strong evidence that the stability of the Franc Zone monetary system has encouraged higher trade and that membership has a significant impact on the degree of shock correlation between country pairs.

In the light of this evidence, one should perhaps reinterpret the results on the costs of MU membership in the SADC region and in East Africa. It is true that countries in these regions at present exhibit a great deal of macroeconomic heterogeneity. However, the magnitude of this heterogeneity is likely to fall on the formation of a currency union. As noted by Khamfula and Huizinga (2004), the fall is unlikely to be enough as yet to make it sensible to form a MU between countries as diverse as South Africa and the Democratic Republic of Congo. Nevertheless, it is not necessary to wait for complete convergence before forming a currency union.

Latin America and the Caribbean

Most empirical work on the prospects of monetary integration in the Americas, using an OCA framework, has been concentrated on NAFTA and Mercosur.

As far as NAFTA is concerned, Bayoumi and Eichengreen (1994, 125–65) found that the Mexican economy is characterised by significant supply shocks that are negatively correlated with the supply shocks in the industrial regions of the US. The authors concluded that fixing the Mexican currency in terms of the US dollar would imply a high cost for Mexico. With a somewhat more sophisticated methodology, Lalonde and St-Amant (1995, 431–59) also reached the conclusion that the shocks observed in the Mexican economy are very different from those in the US and Canada, whereas the regions within the US undergo generally common shocks. With both internal and external shocks, the MU would imply an important cost for Mexico in terms of the stabilisation of its economy.

With respect to CARICOM, Manioc and Montauban (2002) analysed trade and specialisation patterns, estimated gravity models to assess the potential of intra-regional trade and calculated correlations of GDP growth and inflation rates. Their general conclusion is that on the basis of OCA criteria, there is no firm ground for creating a MU, especially if it would imply abandoning exchange rate stability vis-à-vis the dollar.

Goto's assessment of monetary integration of the OECS countries compares the growth rates and other macroeconomic indicators of OECS economies with those of a 'control group', consisting of Barbados, Jamaica, Trinidad and Tobago (Goto, 2001, 157–74). The general conclusions are that the OECS economies show stronger economic growth records than the reference group, more stable prices and exchange rates, and that they attract relatively more Foreign Direct Investment.

In general, the case for regional monetary integration in the Americas is not very strong. For one thing, insufficient levels of trust and low levels of political integration constitute obstacles to progress towards monetary integration in the near future (Cohen, 2003). This conclusion is in time with the views held by the Inter-American Development Bank and the IMF (Berg, 2003). Independently of political and institutional conditions, economic evaluations do not point in this direction yet. Higher intra-regional trade intensities would be required. The larger countries are still relatively closed. Only Mexico and a few small Central American or Caribbean countries have a dominant trade partner, the US. Macroeconomic correlations are usually lower than in Western Europe. The degree of co-movement of financial variables does not permit the recognition by the financial markets of Latin America as a bloc. In doing so, the region would be subject to common shocks, justifying common monetary policy action.

For the Central American countries and the Caribbean, growing interdependence, combined with the potential gains from policy credibility and economies of scale, might shift the balance in favour of monetary integration or dollarisation in the future. Likewise, the case for dollarising the Mexican economy might become stronger with increasing interdependence. The evidence suggests that the Central American Common Market (CACM) is closest to meeting the conditions for MU, especially if they adopt a hard peg in relation to the dollar.

East and Southeast Asia

The issue whether groups and sub-groups of Asian countries could establish a common currency, is much debated in the academic literature, especially since the 1997 crisis, but in spite of some initiatives within ASEAN, hardly of relevance in actual regional politics. The academic discussion is intimately related to the question of which, if any, countries in Asia can be considered as a group as an OCA.

A number of studies analyse a relatively wide set of countries comprising both East Asian countries and ASEAN member countries. Eichengreen and Bayoumi (1996), for example, conclude that East Asia satisfies the standard OCA criteria as well as the EU countries. As arguments against monetary integration, they see the lack of development of the domestic financial systems, and the lack of institutions and political will at the regional level. Similar methodologies but different variables and data sets are used by Yuen (2000), Trivisvanet (2001), Zhang et al. (2002) and Saxena (2003). Starting from a set of countries including ASEAN+5, Japan, Korea, Taiwan, Hong-Kong, China, Australia and New Zealand, Yuen proposes a multispeed strategy towards monetary integration. Three sub-regional MUs could be formed in an initial phase: Singapore and Malaysia, Japan and Korea, Taiwan and Hong-Kong. Other countries could then join one of these unions, which could finally be integrated in a wider East Asian MU. Trivisvavet considers a slightly reduced set with ASEAN+5, Japan, Korea and Hong-Kong. It is found that the group has characteristics of an OCA. An optimal scenario with gradualism would imply that the Southeast Asian countries, with the exception of Indonesia but possibly including Korea, form a MU, after which the other countries could join later. Zhang et al. find that the structural shocks affecting ASEAN+5, the US, Japan, Korea, Taiwan, Hong-Kong and China are less symmetric and have a larger size on average, compared to the EU, although the adjustment speed is faster. No sufficient evidence is found that East Asia forms an OCA. It is not excluded however that smaller subsets of countries might engage in processes of monetary integration. Saxena (2003) finds that most of the countries comprised by ASEAN, along with Japan, Korea, China and India, show positive correlations for supply disturbances and high labour mobility. The countries concerned could form a currency union around the yen, on the condition that the yen–dollar exchange rate can be stabilised.

Goto (2003) uses principal component analysis of seven macroeconomic variables for Indonesia, Korea, the Philippines, Singapore, Thailand and Japan. A relatively high degree of synchronisation with Japanese variables is observed, which has dramatically increased since the 1990s. The five countries might consider forming a MU around Japan.

Bayoumi and Mauro (1999) and Ng (2002, 113–34) confined the analysis of shock symmetry to ASEAN. According to the first authors, ASEAN members are less suited than those of the EU, a few years before the Maastricht Treaty, for forming a currency union. Deeper economic integration and a firm political commitment in the region are necessary pre-conditions. According to Ng, shocks in Southeast Asia are more strongly correlated than in EU and external shocks are more strongly correlated than in NAFTA. Indonesia, Singapore and Malaysia show a relatively high degree of correlation of shocks. According to Cohen (2003), the lack of political integration and solidarity, necessary to sustain the needed degree of commitment, is the main obstacle to monetary integration.

Sterner and Skoog (2003) analyse the degrees of openness, the degrees of product diversification, similarities of industrial structure, similarities of inflation rates, degrees of correlation of macroeconomic variables for ASEAN. ASEAN does not appear to constitute an OCA. The three countries of Malaysia, Singapore and Thailand could form the core of a monetary union, as could a group of five countries (Malaysia, Singapore, Thailand, Philippines and Indonesia), gradually expanding according to pre-set entrance criteria.

CONCLUSIONS

After the collapse of the Bretton Woods system, countries experimented with different exchange rate policies. According to the bipolar view, in a world of free capital movements, only flexible rates or hard pegs are feasible policy options.

This chapter charted moves towards regional monetary integration and cooperation in different regions in the world. Although most of the regional initiatives can be characterised as weak forms of monetary cooperation (reserve pooling, exchange rate bands, ...), a number of MUs have emerged in Europe, Sub-Saharan Africa, Latin America and the Caribbean. These have taken different forms, from classical (symmetric) currency unions to (asymmetrical) dollarisation. The drivers of the processes also differ from case to case. Often, political motivations seem to have dominated the economic motivations and forces at the time of the decision. In some cases, specific circumstances of economic and/or political crisis changed the course of monetary policies abruptly, in other cases, the constitution of MUs has taken decades of gradualism.

Although *ex post* analyses are still scarce, there are theoretical and empirical reasons to believe that currency unions have the potential to generate net positive effects on the effectiveness of monetary policy (credibility, technical economies of scale, volumes of pooled reserves, ...), positive microeconomic effects (lower transaction costs), and positive macroeconomic effects (inflation, growth). However, the politically desirable or acceptable distribution of these effects among currency union members is not an automatic outcome of the process of monetary integration.

Empirical evaluations of the conditions for monetary integration, following the lines traced by OCA theory, do not provide us with clear-cut policy prescriptions. Few regions would qualify for an OCA if strict criteria would be followed. The benefits of forming a currency union should not be underestimated, however, and they are – at least partly – endogenous. MUs in Central America and Southern Africa and the widening of the CFA zone and the Eastern Caribbean currency union should not be excluded in the future. The role and policies of the regional hegemonic powers (US on the American continent, EU/EMU vis-à-vis Eastern Europe and Africa, Japan in Eastern Asia, South Africa vis-à-vis its neighbours) will be a critical factor for tracing the future of monetary integration.

NOTES

1. Belgium and Luxembourg created the Belgium-Luxembourg Economic Union (BLEU) as early as 1921. The treaty provided for the establishment of a customs union, an economic union and a monetary union.
2. The CFA is known as Communauté Financière Africaine in the BCEAO area and Cooperation Financière en Afrique Centrale in the BEAC area.
3. These were joined in 1985 by the former Spanish colony of Equatorial Guinea.
4. Except the Seychelles, which maintains a basket peg.
5. On the ECCB, see <www.eccb-centralbank.org>.
6. On FLAR, see <www.flar.net>.
7. Kenen (2002, 100–3) grouped the differences between unilateral arrangements and fully-fledged MU under two rubrics: (i) governance and accountability, and (ii) optimality and the policy domain.

9

Identity and Regional Integration

Nikki Slocum and Luk Van Langenhove

Processes of regional integration are driven by people with a national background and affect people that are citizens from existing nations. So why is it that let's say some Belgians are promoting a European project? Is it because they feel more European than Belgian? Or because they identify themselves not enough with Belgians? Chopra, Frank and Schroder discuss in their book *National Identity and Regional Cooperation* a number of related questions such as 'what is "regional" identity made up of? How does it come into existence? Is it singular or plural? How does it interrelate with so-called "national" identities? Does it produce a regional identity, or are we waiting for a regional identity to produce a regional integration?' (1999, 6). This set of questions is interesting because it starts from the assumption that regional identity exists and that it is 'something' that needs to be linked to regions and nations on the one hand (as geographical and political entities) and to people (as citizens) on the other hand.

This chapter will explore these assumptions and deal with the relationships between two phenomena: (i) the processes of regional integration and (ii) the way people use references to regions and regional integration in talking about themselves and others.

WHAT IS IDENTITY?

Identity is a concept used both by social scientists and by people in ordinary language in different ways. One cluster of meanings refers to what constitutes the individuality of something, that is what makes a single individual entity distinct from another one. A second cluster of meanings is focused upon what kind of common characteristics a class of entities might have, that is to what extent there are similarities between members of a group. Speaking about identity can be done when talking about people, but also when referring to groups of people, to societies, objects, geographical regions and so on. For our purposes it is important to stress that for instance 'Europe' can be talked about as a source of identity to *people*, but equally so one can talk about European identity when referring to a certain geographical region.

In a chapter on 'Identity and Regional Integration', it is appropriate to tackle the question as to what 'identity' is. With the emergence of sovereign states, also emerged the ideological belief that people born and living within the boundaries of a sovereign state have a 'shared identity' that is the basis for a collective interest and that transcends the differences that there might be within that country (differences in class for instance or differences between regions within the country). It was the 'nationbuilding' exercises of the twentieth century that have pushed most states into promoting a sense of homogeneity and a feeling of a singular identity. This shared identity is the basis for *nationalism* and *national identity*. Ethic, national or religious identities are based upon myths and worldviews that define who is a group member (often including also who are the group's enemies) and that are based upon a certain interpretation of history (Smith, 1986). Such mythological representations can be used by political leaders to gain support for a certain 'cause'. This can lead people to experience their identity in a competition-game for esteem and status within their group, where the other group's gain is automatically perceived as their own loss. There are no win-win situations possible and threats are experienced as threats to the existence of the group as a whole (Horowitz, 1985). In today's established nations a whole set of habits in everyday life constantly 'flag' the nation in the lives of people. This appears in political discourses, but also in cultural products and even in banal things such as the structuring of newspapers. Consequently, an identity is to be found in the embodied habits of social life. To 'have' a national or political identity is to possess ways of talking about nationhood.

Some authors have addressed that question, 'What is identity' more directly. Cerutti and Enno, for instance, has defined political identity as the

> set of images of the world, of values and principles that we recognise to be ours: in as much as we share them we feel like 'we'. It is not something that can be established from outside the group ... it must be felt as such in a more or less clear manner by the group's members, who engage in private exchange and public debate about how to determinate those values and to modify them when circumstances have changed and require a change of consciousness. (2001, 4)

In Cerutti and Enno's view, identity has two main moments: *mirror-identity* and *wall-identity*. In the former people look at themselves in an internal mirror and find in the shared ideas, values and principles something that gives a meaning to their communal as well as to their individual life, which are to an extent interconnected. As a *wall*, identity is marked by the ambivalence of having two faces: the wall is a boundary, but it is also load-bearing. As a structural wall it gives the group (nation, local, community, party) consistency and individuality.

Von Busekist (2004, 81–98) takes a different approach, emphasising the non-essential nature of identity. The author writes:

An analysis of 'collective identity' must be attentive to the following six traits:

- It is dynamic and consequently dependent on the context and on the individuals that compose it.
- It is constructed and consequently dependent upon entrepreneurs (individuals or institutions).
- It rests on a tradition or a collective, acceptable and legitimate statement of this tradition (which can nonetheless be questioned, critiqued and finally give rise to a new tradition), and as a result it maintains a particular relation to history.
- It maintains a close relation to the system of (political) values in which it moves, whether that is a relation of approbation or rejection, in an internal or international system ...
- It draws borders, and consequently has an interior and an exterior of common recognition, an in-group and an out-group, friends and adversaries ...
- Finally, it possesses a centre, a central motif as in music or a pertinent common denominator that permits individuals to recognise and articulate their attachment when it is conscious. (p. 82)

While Von Busekist proposes a less essentialist description of 'identity' than does Cerutti and Enno, she still reifies the concept. In our view, 'identity' cannot 'draw borders', 'maintain a close relation' or 'possess' anything. Being a concept, 'identity' – like other concepts – is used by actors toward various ends (Austin, 1961). Its meaning is dependent upon the way it is used in a particular context and is thus situation specific. To understand identity, a researcher must examine the ways in which the concept is used and to what ends.

WHAT DOES IDENTITY HAVE TO DO WITH REGIONAL INTEGRATION?

Since the establishment of the Westphalian world order (1648), which parcelled the world into discrete national territories that are 'sovereign' nation-states, people have commonly referred to themselves and others with respect to which of these national parcels they are citizens of. Some have argued that the 'national identities' that emerged are 'natural' forms of identity. Others point out that, as a product of the Westphalian system, they are relatively new creations; yet to say, 'I'm Belgian', 'He's Spanish' or 'They're American' quickly became *second* nature. As Billig (1996, 186) writes, '... ordinary ways of speaking and experiencing the world – or the habitus, to use Bourdieu's term – will be suffused with nationalist meanings, creating an environment in which it seems "natural" to possess national identities'.

But, with the processes of regional integration, other territorial identities – such as Europe – have gained importance. Regional integration in Europe affects an ever-larger share of the activities of national governments and thus also of the life of European citizens. The so-called 'democratic deficit' refers to a gap between Europe and its citizens. In this type of discourse, the remedy to bridge the gap is more involvement of the citizens in the Europeanisation. And in order to have more involvement, people need to identify themselves with Europe. The next step seems then to be a promotion of a sense of European identity. Today, the development of a sense of European identity is widely seen as an important prerequisite for the success of the European project.

But what exactly is European identity and European citizenship, and how does it relate to other forms of identity such as national identity? And how does a sense of European identity relate to supporting the process of European integration?

Concomitant to globalisation, regional integration has been seen as a process that challenges the concept of the sovereign nation-state and, along with it, these corresponding 'national identities'. There are three important assumptions in this Westphalian paradigm that are being challenged in the processes of globalisation and regional integration: state sovereignty, citizenship, and territorialism/geographical boundedness. These assumptions regarding nation-states have also often been underlying in studies of (national) identities. Let us now look at each of these assumptions and how they are being challenged.

The concepts '(nation-)state' and 'sovereignty' are inextricably interlinked in that sovereignty denotes the international legal personality of a state. Sovereignty means 'completely independent' and refers to the concept of the state as the only legitimate authority to govern and to enforce laws in a given territory. Indeed, the enforcement of laws, and its monopoly over the use of (violent) force to do so, and to protect itself from threats against this exclusive 'right', is considered the distinguishing characteristic of the state. Giddens (1990) describes nation-states as 'territorially bounded ... administrative units' that act as 'power containers'. In this Westphalian system, the citizens of the state are bound in a set of reciprocal duties and rights, and states are accorded the exclusive right to represent the interests of 'their' citizens toward the international community. It is now taken for granted that almost every person has a nationality, but this is not an inherent attribute of humans; it is a social construction, created and reproduced in discourse. The fact that nationality is taken for granted, that the system appears natural and its assumptions are rarely questioned, evidences the observation that nationalism has become 'the most successful political ideology in human history'. In the words of Billig (1996, 183), nationalism is not an extremist phenomenon but refers to '... those beliefs and assumptions by which it appears "natural" for the world to be divided into separate nation-states, and, thus, for the world of nations to be reproduced as today's "natural" social environment'.

With the spread of advanced communications technologies, one of the drivers of globalisation, the notion that a state – or anything else – can be independent has been severely put into question. Small countries and especially developing countries have long perceived their economic and political dependence upon larger and more powerful countries, such as the US, and now interdependency in the areas of environment, health and security is becoming increasingly evident. This growing awareness of the intrinsic interdependency of states has shattered traditional notions of state sovereignty, as have challenges to state-centred conceptions of security and the right to use (violent) force. Billig (1996) points out that the state has been treated as more sacred than persons, as many wars have been fought in the name of protecting states while thousands of people have been sacrificed in the process. Referring to the 1990 Gulf War, he criticises the fact that 'the gassing of Kurdish women and children failed to provoke the sort of global reaction which followed the annexation of Kuwait, an established nation with United Nations (UN) membership and its own postage stamps' (Billig, 1996, 182), and similar can be said of the second War on Iraq and of the Second World War. Efforts to put persons, rather than states, at the centre of security have led to the development of the 'human security' concept. In turn, a focus on the security of humans has broadened the understanding of security to encompass health, environment, democracy and other aspects of governance. Consequently, human sovereignty (and rights) is gaining headway on the notion of state sovereignty.

While states have been accepted under the Westphalian system as having the exclusive right to represent their interests to the international community, processes of globalisation and regional integration have introduced new actors and systems of governance. It can also be argued that citizenship can no longer be exclusively attributed to nation-states. Other actors such as sub-national entities or supranational regimes also deliver different kinds of rights and duties to people. Actors such as multinational corporations, supra- and international bodies like the United Nations (UN), the European Union (EU), the African Union, Flanders, Catalonia and other micro- and macro-regional organisations as well as international political parties, cultural/religious movements and even terrorist organisations have emerged to address interests and issues that are not delimited by national political or geographical borders. The burgeoning of these multifarious new actors reflects that states are no longer necessarily (the most) efficacious institutions through which people can address and represent their interests. As a result, the state's monopoly on people's citizenship (and identification) is beginning to be eroded.

As a further consequence of the emergence of these new actors, the coincidence of governance and territoriality is being questioned. While some of the new actors can simply be identified with a different geographical scale, others defy geographical borders or are completely non-territorial. Immediately following the 11 September 2001 attacks, the US became steeped in discussion over how to retaliate, because the terrorists were members of a network with global reach, not an enemy state that could be attacked in the traditional manner. The Bilderberg conference, created in 1954, is a not-so-secretive 'secretive gathering of global power brokers', attended by 'tycoons, politicians and diplomats from Europe and the US' by invitation only, described collectively as 'the high priests of globalisation' (Cowell and Halbfinger, 2004, 3). According to Cowell and Halbfinger (2004, 3), 'critics of the Bilderberg conference argue that, while it may not make formal decisions, it creates a consensus that spreads among business and political elites, molding a global agenda'. Does this informal nature mean that the conference has less power and influence on governance issues than more formalised institutions?

In 1918, the Austrian Karl Renner (1918, 1964, 16) theorised a dissociation between territory and population in a system in which national identity 'does not repose upon a geographical inscription, but rather upon a deliberate choice of the individuals who freely proclaim that they belong to a given nation, that is, a cultural community' and the responsibilities of the state are limited to the administration of the common affairs of these 'nations'. This system was applied in Lithuania and Estonia in the 1920s and is currently employed in Hungary (Von Busekist, 2004, 81–98).

Most fundamentally, the nature of the state as an actor has been queried. (Nation-)states are concepts, not real things, and as all concepts, they are created and reproduced by persons in discourse. Certain individuals then position themselves as acting on behalf of the state and in the interest of 'its' citizens. With the use of positioning theory, Slocum and Van Langenhove (2003; 2004) have illuminated the process by which persons position themselves as acting on the behalf of a state – or on the behalf of a region or global organisation, as has become more frequent with the prevalence of regional integration and globalisation. For example, Osama bin Laden positioned himself as acting on behalf of the 'Islamic nation' in calling for *jihad* (holy war) in the following passage:

Our Islamic nation has been tasting [horror] for more [than] 80 years, of humiliation and disgrace, its sons killed and their blood spilled, its sanctities desecrated. Gold has blessed a group of vanguard Muslims, the forefront of Islam, to destroy America. Those [Muslims] have stood in defense of their weak children, their brothers and sisters in Palestine and other Muslim nations .... I tell them that these events have divided the world into two camps, the camp of the faithful and the camp of infidels. Every Muslim must rise to defend his religion. The wind of faith is blowing and the wind of change is blowing to remove evil from the Peninsula of Muhammad, peace is upon him.[1]

Important to note is that in the same speech, bin Laden not only positions himself with the right to act on behalf of this purported group, the Islamic nation, but also contributes to (re-)creating it by giving the concept currency and hence legitimacy. This is true of all concepts: it is in employing them that we give them meaning, whether or not we are aware of this. So in this view, national identity is an outcome of discursive processes. As especially in Europe such discourses have been going on for more than two centuries now, the national identities are deeply rooted in daily life. There is a whole set of symbols that can be used when 'expressing' one's identity: a common history, a language, cultural monuments, historic sites, national dishes and of course national sport teams. Such symbols are organised in myths that are usually based partly upon truth and partly upon selective or exaggerated issues.

The reification of national and regional identity

The ideology of nationalism is also frequently (and often unwittingly) assumed, spread and reproduced by social scientists studying and analysing the very same phenomenon, as Beck (1998, 50–1) points out:

> The organisational scheme [of the nation-state] is not only externally valid, but also internally. The internal space, as distinguishable from external individual communities, is subdivided into inner totalities. On the one hand, these are thought about and analysed as *collective identities* (classes, estates, religious and ethnic groups, distinct ways of life for men and women). On the other hand, they are theoretically conceived and differentiated according to the organism-metaphor of *social systems*, separated and ordered into the individual worlds of economics, politics, law, science, family and so forth, with their 'logics' ('codes'). The internal homogeneity is essentially a creation of state control. All sorts of social practices – production, culture, language, job market, capital, education – are normed, influenced limited, rationalised, and at the very least, labeled according to a nation-state scheme. The state pre-determines a territorial unit as a 'container', in which statistics of economic and social processes and situations are systematically collected. In this manner, the categories of the state's self-observation become categories of the empirical social sciences, such that the social sciences confirm the bureaucratic definitions of reality. (Translation by first author; emphasis in original)

Just as Beck criticises social scientists for reifying the nation-state, the same can be said of much of the literature on national (and other 'forms' of) identity, and how it is affected by regional integration. In so doing, the authors of this literature (unwittingly) promulgate nationalism (Hopkins and Reicher, 1996).

Hopkins and Reicher (1996, 91) warn that 'when researching people's perceptions of their social world, any methodology which assumes particular categories necessarily forces our participants to respond in terms that may not be their own' and that this can encourage the view that particular categories are non-problematic and inevitable, or natural. Many authors of studies have done precisely this. Torregrosa (1996, 111–21) asked participants to rate on a scale from one (not at all) to ten (very much) how much they liked the following peoples and presented a list of nationalities: Italians, Mexicans, Argentinians, Japanese, Germans, Russians, Chinese ... and so forth (p. 115, table 7.3). In so doing, the authors imply that national categories are relevant (and even important) to the issue of affability, or whether or not one likes a given person. Barrett (1996, 349–70) does the same with a regional, rather than national, category when asking child participants, 'Do you think the European people are clever or not clever (dirty or clean; hardworking or lazy; good or bad; aggressive or peaceful; friendly or unfriendly; happy or unhappy; nice or not nice) or what?' (p. 355, table 21.1: The questions contained in the interview schedule). In their study of 'Dimensions of Social Identity in Northern Ireland', Trew and Benson (1996) contribute to the reification of the categories entrenched in social conflict when they ask participants to 'please choose from the list below the term that you feel best describes how you feel' and offer the following list: 'A Protestant, A Unionist, Irish, A Loyalist, A Nationalist, Northern Irish, A Catholic, Ulster, British' (p. 140, Appendix, Measure of most important identity).

Employing a similar methodology is the Eurobarometer, often accepted as the standard reference for assessing people's opinions regarding Europe. In its section on Regional Identity, various versions of the questionnaire have posed the following questions:

People may feel different degrees of attachment to their town or village, to their region, to their country, [Eurobarometer 36: to the European Community; Eurobarometer 43.1bis: to the European Union] or to Europe [as a whole]. Please tell me how attached you feel to ...?

1. very attached
2. fairly attached
3. not very attached
4. not at all attached

'To which of these areas do you feel you belong most strongly? And which next? ECS71: city/locality, department, region, country, Europe, other. Eurobarometer 50.1: city/town/village, region, country, Europe, whole world.'

'I would like you to tell me how close you feel to the following groups of people. 1. The inhabitants of the city or village where you live/have lived most of your life; 2. The inhabitants of the region where you life; 3. Fellow (Nationality); 4. European Union citizens; 5. Fellow Europeans; ... (very close – quite close – not very close – not at all close).'

Since the 1980s the Eurobarometer surveys inquire whether people in Europe feel themselves citizens not only of their country but also of Europe and their local regions. In the 1996 survey (with more than 65,000 respondents), the following question was asked: 'In the near future, do you see yourself above all as a citizen of the EU, a citizen of your country or a citizen of your region?' Respondents were asked for first, second and third choices. The table below summarises the answers.

Citizenship?	1st choice (%)	2nd choice (%)	3rd choice (%)
European	13.7	19.8	57.8
National	63.9	30.4	3.7
Regional	20.1	49	26.9

According to these data, the number of people who feel primarily or even secondarily European is a clear minority. But does this mean that European identity is low?

Not only do such questionnaires force participants to use a certain category, but they also de-contextualise the statements to which they ask participants to respond. Utterances only have a sense within a context and according to which people orient themselves in their interactions. When handed a questionnaire and asked to do ratings on a Likert scale (for example, see Horenczyk, 1996, 241–50), the actual context of the statements is a research project whereby the respondents are left to guess at the intentions of the researcher in order to give the statements meaning. Thus, when presented with utterances such as 'Are you a European person?' (Barrett, 1996, 349–70) or 'It is important for me to be a citizen of the European Union', each participant of the study is left to imagine some (unspecified) context in which the utterance makes sense.

A discursive approach to identity

Rather than reify regional, national or any other sort of 'identity' by treating them as given, it is possible to consider a discursive approach to understanding how these and other meanings are constructed and what they are used to accomplish in a specific context (Slocum and Van Langenhove, 2004, 227–52). Hopkins and Reicher (1996, 64) emphasise that 'because nations are not "natural" or "given" but are instead social constructions, produced and reproduced through a series of social practices, it follows that we cannot accept that "national" identity exists "apart from" or "beneath" its social representation, or outside the conditions of its making'. Similarly, Billig (1996, 186) concludes that in order to understand nationalist meanings, 'analysts should pay particular attention to the way that the social-psychological aspects of nationhood are constituted within familiar discourse'.

Billig (1996, 186) notes, 'The imagining of "our" nation is the most obvious aspect of nationalism. The nationalist imagination is constructed around the first person plural, for it is an imagining of who "we" are'. He examines how the first person plural and other techniques are used by politicians in rather ambiguous manners in order to generate a notion of nationhood, for example by implying group homogeneity and distinguishing, implicitly or explicitly, from those who are not part of the group. It is in this way that concepts, such as 'nation', are developed and become the filters through which people experience life; in other words, it is in this way that social reality is constructed.

Hopkins and Reicher (1996) examine how various politicians constructed different meanings of 'Scottish' and 'British' in order to legitimise voting for or against Scottish independence from Britain. One technique used by people on both sides of the debate was to put Scotland and Britain in a European context – but in different ways. For example, they cite a Scottish National Party MEP saying:

'In the community the view of the UK is that they are half-hearted. De Gaulle said years of the UK entry; "England has not yet joined the community". For once I don't mind the misuse of the term "England". Scotland on the other hand is a European nation in spirit and history. Bruce's first act was to join the Hanseatic League. Our students went regularly to Leiden, Paris, Bologna, Valladolid. We have a Euro system of law. We had an Alliance with France for 800 years, with joint citizenship – a forerunner of the EC itself. In 1707 we got England and lost Europe. It was not a good bargain (Ewing, speech, 25 September 1993).' (p. 68)

In this construction, to be 'Scottish' is to be European, and it is to be a different nation than England, which is not European. The positioning is used to differentiate between Scotland and England and promote its independence. In contrast, the authors also cite, in contrast, a Conservative who constructs 'Scottish' as a lower-order identity of British and European:

'Yes I'm Scottish, we're all Scottish. I'm as Scottish as anyone else but I stand for the party of Union ... [Independence] is not going to make me more Scottish, it's not going to make anybody more Scottish ... It's like Dundee is part of Scotland, Scotland is part of the UK, the UK is part of Europe and Europe is part of the international structure and I think that the nearer you come down to the bottom, you're just coming to what's sort of inbred and inherent and this sense of belonging. And I think everyone in Europe would have that but it doesn't mean to say they're any less European (Conservative candidate, interview).' (p. 69)

In this construction to be Scottish is to be British and to be European; the three identities are constructed as compatible with the purpose of encouraging people to vote to have Scotland remain within the UK. What it is to be 'Scottish' and 'English' is constructed in different ways toward different ends, and this is very context specific.

Elsewhere, one of the authors of this chapter conducted a similar analysis of meaning in an examination of how various constructions of 'Danish' identity and the 'EU'/'EMU' (European monetary union) were used to endorse voting for or against Denmark joining the EMU in their 2000 Euro Referendum. In an attempt to have a systematic and structured approach to the analysis of discourse, she employed an analytical tool called the Positioning Triad from Positioning Theory (Slocum and Van Langenhove, 2004). Positioning Theory proposes a functional explanation for how meaning is constructed in discourse. It holds that three elements constitute the building blocks of meaning: storylines, actors with positions, and illocutionary (or social) forces – the positioning triad – and elaborates upon the relationship between these. In applying Positioning Theory to discourse on the Danish Euro Referendum, it was possible to examine how different storylines and positions were engendered by proponents and dissidents of EMU membership. For example, Pia Kjaersgaard, the leader of the Danish People's Party combines three storylines to position Denmark in opposition to Europe:

> The essential issue is the preservation of our sovereignty. The euro will erode our national authority and identity at a time when Denmark is already becoming more and more multiethnic and globalised. Do we want to lose control of our lives with more and more decisions made by the European Central Bank in Frankfurt or in Brussels? Do we want this multiculturalism, this multiethnicity, about which the country was never consulted? I say we don't want either.[2]

In this passage, three storylines can be identified: 'The EU invasion and usurpation of Danish sovereignty', 'The obliteration of Danish national identity' and 'The cultural/ethnic takeover'. Each was employed to position the EU as a menacing threat and to position Denmark as the victim. The rationale, of course, is to vote 'no' to Denmark joining the EMU; otherwise Danish identity, and Denmark itself, would be overwhelmed and eventually lost. One of the storylines employed by those endorsing Danish membership of the EMU was that 'The purpose of the E(M)U and its members is to promote peace, democracy and human rights.' For example, passages from the Maastricht Treaty highlight this storyline:

> Recalling the historic importance of the ending of the division of the European continent and the need to create firm bases for the construction of the future Europe,

Confirming their attachment to the principles of liberty, democracy and respect for human rights and fundamental freedoms and the rule of law,
Desiring to deepen the solidarity between their peoples while respecting their history, their culture and their traditions ...
Resolved to implement a common foreign and security policy including the eventual framing of a common defense policy, which might in time lead to a common defense, thereby reinforcing the European identity and its independence in order to promote peace, security and progress in Europe and in the world ...
Resolved to continue the process of creating an ever closer union among the peoples of Europe, in which decisions are taken as closely as possible to the citizen in accordance with the principle of subsidiarity ...
[The members] have decided to establish a European Union ....

Similarly, when polled about how she would vote in the referendum, a Danish citizen said, 'We see a lot of racism and intolerance in Europe and think the best way of tackling that is to have greater integration.'[3] This storyline is used to position the EU/EMU as promoting peace, democracy and human rights and thus implies that a 'yes' vote for joining the monetary union would likewise be an endorsement of these values.

Talking about regions

Having discussed the concept of identity in some detail in the previous sections, we are now in a position to have a closer look at the interrelation between regional integration and identity. A lot of literature on regional identity focuses upon Europe – probably because as Cerutti and Enno (2001) noted there is a feeling that the build-up of a European identity has not been keeping pace with the institutional processes of deepening the European integration.

To what extent will processes of regional integration have an effect upon people's identity? However, the two processes – regional integration and identity construction – can be mutually influential. Changes in governance can lead to changes in how we think (and talk) about ourselves; similarly changes in our identity constructions can promote new conceptions of how we govern 'ourselves' and who 'us' is. The *Human Development Report 2004* has stated that it is a myth to believe that people's ethnic or regional identities compete with their attachment to the state and that hence there is a trade-off between recognising diversity and unifying the state. This is indeed a myth as identity is not some kind of zero-sum game: individuals can and do 'have' multiple identities that are complementary and subject to the discursive spaces that are being created. This not only holds for national and sub-national identities, but also for supranational regional identities.

To what extent do people's identities need to change, or do new identities need to be developed, in order to enable regional integration to advance?

In the study of the Danish referendum, it was demonstrated that certain constructions of Danish national identity and of Europe positioned Denmark and Europe in opposition, thus acting as a barrier to the advancement of regional integration. However, other constructions of Danish identity and Europe promoted integration into the EMU. Identity constructions – whether they are national or regional – are discursive tools used to accomplish various social tasks, such as promoting a particular vote in an election. It is perhaps better to ask a different question: How can regional integration, and what kinds of identity constructions, can best facilitate human security?

Do various identities (local, national, supranational) compete, or can they coexist? Various researchers studying identity in Europe have asked 'whether national and European identities are consonant, dissonant, or indifferent' (Cinnirella, 1996, 258; Hofman, 1988; Allen et al., 1983). As in the first question above, the question itself is based upon the false premise that national and European identities are fixed things that are either compatible or not. One should not think in terms of a *zero-sum* model where identification with one entity comes at the expense of identification with another entity. The best answer to this question is: it depends on how they are constructed. As we have seen above, national and European identities can be constructed to be harmonious or in opposition to each other. Neither is 'true', because there is no 'real' identity of either sort to which one could compare either construction. Rather, both constructions are ways of *doing* something, for example promoting or discouraging regional integration. In the former, it is the social context of interaction that allows one sort of identity to become salient. For instance, when the Belgian soccer team plays, one can feel more Belgian and when the Flemish tennis player Clijsters plays against her Walloon and Belgian fellow countrywomen Henin-Hardenne, some will feel Flemish or Walloon .... In the later model, the identities are also invoked in a context-dependent way, but they enmesh and flow into each other in such a way that one cannot clearly define boundaries between one's Flemishness, Belgianness and one's Europeanness ...

Why is regional integration in Europe 'working' without changes in identity, according to the Eurobarometer? Based upon the presumption that 'identity' is a thing that can be measured, the Eurobarometer asks people to rate, for example, on a four-point scale, how much they 'feel attached' to Europe, to their region, country, and so on. As mentioned above, the categories offered by the questionnaire may not be categories in which respondents would naturally think about their attachments. Even if the participants would make a statement of their own volition such as 'I feel very attached to European Union citizens', the meaning of this statement – that is, what the locution accomplishes – can only be determined within a specific context. The statements in the Eurobarometer are removed from any natural context and are thus entirely ambiguous. Each respondent is left to attempt to work out what the researchers are trying to accomplish in posing such a question. Their answers reflect their suppositions regarding what the researcher is looking for; they are not a reflection of a hidden internal reality.

Why do people so often answer locally when asked about their identity? The way in which people respond to questions concerning their 'identity' depends upon the context in which they are asked. When one Belgian asks another about his identity, or even when questioned by anyone within Belgium, (s)he will likely reply by referring to a (more local) place within Belgium. This is because the respondent will infer from the context – Belgium – what sort of information his or her interlocutor is requesting. In this context, the answer 'Belgium' would presumably provide no useful information, because it is taken for granted. In contrast, if the same Belgian were asked the same question during a visit to Africa, he would certainly not refer to 'Antwerp' or another local community, but rather to 'Belgium' or 'Europe'. Thus, what we can conclude about people's 'local responses' is that many studies are conducted at a local level.

CONCLUSION: IMPLICATIONS FOR THE FUTURE

The discourse of researchers is equally generative in nature as that of other people's. Thus, it is important that, when making authoritative statements about the nature of 'identity' or aspects of regional integration, researchers understand that these statements contribute to reality construction. Hopkins and Reicher's (1996, 91) caution that, 'If change is to be possible and alternative constructions of the world entertained, academics must be sensitive to their own role in the reproduction of such a potent category and ensure that their theories, and the practices upon which they are based, facilitate rather than inhibit change.' We would like to add that change is not necessarily desirable for the sake of change *per se*. Rather it is important to examine the consequences of various sorts of constructions. In constructing an identity for 'us', what criteria am I highlighting to define 'us' and thus to divide 'us' and 'them', and what implications does this have? How can we construct our identities to promote human security? To a large extent, this entails creating democratic 'discursive space' that allows for all voices to be heard. However, it also entails taking responsibility for one's own constructions and their consequences.

Identity conflicts are an important source of insecurity, violence, terrorism and wars in the world. Identity conflicts are conflicts where there are not really tangible interests of states at stake but nationalist ideologies. The Balkans is a geographical area with many such identity conflicts. The relationship between China and Taiwan is another example: China has agreed to live for decades without *de facto* control over Taiwan, but it also blocks any *de jure* Taiwanese independence to the point that Taiwan fears its larger neighbour could be ready to go to war in order to prevent that. International terrorism may in certain cases be motivated by identity issues.

The *Human Development Report 2004* stated that globalisation has the potential to expand cultural freedoms, but only if people worldwide develop multiple and complementary identities as 'citizens of the world as well as citizens of a state and members of a cultural group' (UNDP, 2004, 89). Identities related to regional integration processes can certainly have the same potential. But is important to realise that people can choose what kind of group memberships they want to put forward. Identity has an element of choice! Identity has an element of choice and as such a region does not 'produce' a clear-cut and well-defined identity. The only thing that a region produces as a social actor are meaningful texts (for example the Maastricht Treaty), symbols (for example the European flag), institutions (for example the European Parliament) and so on. All these things can be used by people in their positionings. When people choose to position themselves as for instance 'We Europeans', they are actually creating Europe.

NOTES

1. Transcript published by *The New York Times*, 8 October 2001.
2. *The New York Times*, 10 September 2000. 'A Danish Identity Crisis: Are We Europeans?' by Roger Cohen.
3. Dorte Dinesen, 52, local councillor. From CNN.com In-Depth Specials – Denmark Decides. Vox pop. <http://europe.cnn.com/specials/2000/Denmark>.

Part Three

Mapping Regional Approaches

10
The Global Politics of Regionalism: Asia and the Asia-Pacific

Helen E. S. Nesadurai

INTRODUCTION

Economic regionalism in the Asia-Pacific[1] only took off after 1989 when the Asia-Pacific Economic Cooperation (APEC) forum was established. Followed soon after in 1992 by the Association of Southeast Asian Nations (ASEAN)[2] Free Trade Area (AFTA), these two regional projects dominated the regional economic landscape for much of the 1990s. Fourteen years on, the situation has altered dramatically. In 2004, the Asia-Pacific is host to a bewildering array of regional economic arrangements, with all of them having emerged during and since the Asian financial crisis of 1997–98. Among them are the China–ASEAN Free Trade Area (FTA) and a growing plethora of bilateral FTAs negotiated not only between Asia-Pacific states but also between the latter and states in other parts of the world. ASEAN chose in 2003 to expand AFTA by adopting the ASEAN Economic Community project (AEC) that aims to create a 'seamless' integrated Southeast Asian market by 2020. Another notable project, and one that scholars suggest could herald a broader, *East Asian* as opposed to Asia-Pacific or Southeast Asian regionalism is the ASEAN, with China, Japan and South Korea (ASEAN+3) forum, which brings together the ten members of ASEAN with their Northeast Asian counterparts – China, Japan and South Korea.

What is truly interesting about economic regionalism in the Asia-Pacific is not only its diversity and overlapping nature, but the fact that these projects delineate at least three distinct configurations of region:

- an Asia-Pacific trans-regional project centred on APEC;
- a Southeast Asian regional configuration through the various economic regionalism projects of ASEAN (notably AFTA and the AEC); and
- an East Asian regional project centred on the ASEAN+3. While the ASEAN–China FTA potentially contributes to an East Asian configuration of region, it also helps reinforce an ASEAN-centred economic regionalism as do the FTAs negotiated by ASEAN as a group with third parties.

These trends in Asia-Pacific economic regionalism raise at least three questions that this chapter aims to answer. First, what accounts for the proliferation of these distinct regional arrangements? Second, how do these different projects relate to each other? Are they competing or complementary projects? Third, how do these various regional arrangements impact on global governance and on the present US-centred world order? Do these regional projects merely reproduce at the regional level patterns of global governance currently centred on neoliberal ideas, norms and practices, do they undermine contemporary global governance by their adherence to alternative norms and practices, or do they help overcome deficiencies that currently exist in global governance arrangements? In addressing these questions, this chapter takes a Southeast Asian or ASEAN perspective, given that the ASEAN states are involved in all these various regional projects, either initiating them or shaping the form taken by them. An ASEAN-centred approach also illustrates more clearly how *developing* states are using economic regionalism, defined as a states-led project of regional economic cooperation/coordination to navigate global developments in ways that also accommodate their respective domestic socio-political priorities.

Following this brief introduction, the chapter turns to a conceptual discussion on regionalism and global governance, which also focuses on the motivations behind governments' decision to participate in regionalism. The analysis locates these decisions at the nexus between globalisation and the domestic political economy. The following three sections after that analyse the three main regional projects found in the Asia-Pacific region, beginning with APEC in the first section, ASEAN economic regionalism in the second, and APT and East Asian regionalism in the third section. The discussion focuses briefly on the reasons why these projects were established, the interrelationship between these different projects, and their implications for global governance and the US-centred world order. The dynamics of the bilateral FTAs is also addressed in the concluding section, which draws together the chapter's main lines of argument.

REGIONALISM, GLOBAL GOVERNANCE AND WORLD ORDER: A CONCEPTUAL EXPLORATION

In discussing how regionalism relates to global governance, it is important to first specify what global governance is. Higgott (2003) defines global governance as 'those arrangements ... that various actors attempt to put in place to advance, manage, control, regulate or mitigate market globalisation'. While a neoliberal approach to global governance prevailed for much of the 1990s, encapsulated by the norms of the Washington Consensus (WC), this has since given way to what has been termed the 'Augmented' Washington Consensus (AWC) (Rodrik, 2002) or the Post-

Washington Consensus (Higgott, 2000a, 131–53). Under the WC, economic liberalisation, deregulation and privatisation were central to national economic management, and the collective adoption of these practices by various governments was expected to lead to the creation of a single global market. The reworked approach to global governance through the AWC made its appearance as a result of two developments:

- the series of financial crises that first began in Thailand in July 1997, and
- growing civil society criticism of, and resistance to, the market fundamentalism of the globalisation project. While global governance under the AWC continues to reflect a set of neoliberal ideas and norms centred on liberalisation, deregulation and privatisation, it also incorporates a set of socio-political norms to help legitimate globalisation by mitigating its worst excesses. The focus on social safety nets and poverty reduction reflects this new dimension of global governance. However, the neoliberal credentials of global governance have been further strengthened in the AWC through emphasising flexible labour markets, independent central banks and inflation targeting (Rodrik, 2002, Table 1).

The present approach to global governance under the AWC is best regarded as a quasi-embedded neoliberal project that continues to privilege global market integration in line with the interests of globalisation's key proponents (the US especially and other industrial states, global capital, and the international financial institutions).[3] Nevertheless, the goal of a *self-regulating* global market that predominated during the 1990s (McMichael, 2000, 100–13) has been somewhat tempered by recognition among key segments of the global policy-making community that economic liberalisation not only needs to be better regulated, it must also be governed in ways that consciously address socio-economic and distributive issues.[4] In sum, contemporary global governance continues to privilege the goal of instituting a global market as expeditiously and as efficiently as possible through liberalisation, deregulation and privatisation. Underwritten also by a strong competitiveness logic, its aim is to institutionalise market governance in as many areas as possible, notwithstanding its newly incorporated socio-economic component. Nevertheless, the dominant actor in the international system, the US, tends to be impatient of the idea of global governance that also incorporates normative agendas, including engaging with civil society groups. To American policy-makers, such an approach undermines the efficient management of global liberalisation. In the context of the post-11 September 2001 security environment, moreover, Washington tends to view many issues, economic and trade issues as well, through its national security lenses, and in ways that dovetail with US national security interests (Higgott, 2003).

Regionalism and global governance

There are three possibilities with regard to how regionalism theoretically relates to global governance. First, regionalism may be understood as reproducing global governance at the regional level. A second view sees regionalism as a form of resistance to globalisation and the site where alternate norms, ideas and practices to those that predominate in contemporary global governance are consolidated. In the third view, regional governance aims for additional goals, developmental objectives for one or to address present gaps in global governance, rather than the mere replication of the competitiveness logic.

The view that regional governance reproduces global governance is one that not only regards the two as mutually reinforcing, but as projects born of 'similar needs and logics ... with no real distinction between regional and global governance' except for the reduced number of participants involved in the former (Ba, 2005). In this view, regionalism functions as the means to help insert its participants into the global economy, with the regional level employed as an instrument to achieve international competitiveness, a platform through which to participate in global production networks and global trade, as well as to attract international capital. In such instances, regional governance is likely to subscribe to many of the central neoliberal norms, ideas and practices of global governance, and together work towards the creation of a single global market with the regional level acting as a mere building bloc to globalisation.

Resistance projects, on the other hand, are best regarded as projects that seek to preserve through regionalism particular national policy instruments or domestic social and economic arrangements that are difficult to sustain individually under conditions of globalisation. It is difficult, however, to find among *contemporary* regional projects a clear instance of a project that is aimed at resistance to globalisation and one that is governed by norms and practices markedly opposed to those that underpin global governance. Historically though, there were many such projects in the developing world following decolonisation that were organised on the basis of shared concerns with self-determination, autonomy and anti-colonialism (Ba, 2005). Many national governments in the developing world also took on board dependency thinking and sought to insulate their respective economies from the vagaries of the world economy through a closed or inward-focused form of regional cooperation (Fawcett, 1995, 14–15). Since the mid-1980s, however, virtually all contemporary regionalist projects are aimed at facilitating the engagement of their members with the global economy, although the precise contours of these various projects may differ.

The third category of regionalist projects aims at regional governance to address a slew of national and/or transnational issues and problems in ways that may depart from the prevailing norms, ideas and practices of global governance even though these projects do not primarily reject globalisation. Developmental regionalism, in which a variety of developmental goals are addressed within a broadly neoliberal framework of market governance, is one such example. In this instance, there is explicit utilisation of public power at the regional level in pursuit of developmental or other strategic goals that go beyond the logic of competitiveness and 'freeing the market' that remain at the heart of global governance. One variant of developmental regionalism could see development planning at the regional level through the adoption of regional industrial strategies (Hettne, 1999). Another theoretical model of developmental regionalism involves partial and temporary protection or privileges accorded to domestic-owned capital as a way to nurture indigenous firms in the region before complete openness to foreign-owned capital is allowed (Nesadurai, 2003, 41–3). Alternatively, regional governance projects could be adopted to address deficiencies in global governance.

Motivations: between fear of marginalisation and domination

Which of these types of regional projects is adopted will depend on the interests and motivations of key 'regionalisation actors', including policy-makers, business actors and even civil society groups, as they respond to the pressures of globalisation or economic restructuring (Boas et al., 1999, 1065). Although virtually all contemporary regionalist projects represent collective responses to globalisation, policy-makers who ultimately make the political decision to engage in regional cooperation also take into account their respective domestic social and political imperatives when responding to globalisation and with respect to the type of regional project adopted (Nesadurai, 2004, 49–50). For most developing countries, the twin concerns of 'marginalisation and domination', which have shaped their foreign economic policies since the Second World War and decolonisation, continue to drive decision-making in the contemporary world economic order (Ba, 2005). On the one hand is the concern with marginalisation, or the fear of being left out of global economic activities that bring wealth to national economies and societies. By the late 1980s, most, if not all, developing country policy-makers accepted that integration into the global market is key to wealth creation, a far cry from their sentiments just a decade earlier that emphasised withdrawal or insulation from the world economy.

On the other hand, the contemporary world economy brings with it much uncertainty, particularly given the heightened degree of volatility posed by global capitalism today (Zoellick, 1997/98, 42; Stiglitz, 2002). This implies 'an almost certain loss of political and economic autonomy' (Ba, 2005). Under conditions of globalisation, the interests and priorities of external actors (other states, global corporations, global financial players or the international financial institutions) tend to override national priorities and concerns, particularly those of small, developing states that are price- and rule-takers in the international system. Regionalism potentially offers one way to mitigate the loss of autonomy policy-makers experience under globalisation by providing states with a collective capacity over the forces of globalisation they may not have had individually.

These twin concerns with marginalisation and domination pose a dilemma for the Southeast Asian states, where the political legitimacy of incumbent governments and of governing regimes more broadly continues to be derived from performance (Stubbs, 2001, 37–54). Performance legitimacy is based on governments' ability to *both* deliver material economic well-being to society more generally *and* to ensure that economic benefits are also selectively distributed to politically important individuals, groups or economic sectors to help sustain elite coalitions. Thus, any loss of policy autonomy, which might have otherwise allowed policy-makers some leeway to traverse between these sometimes competing domestic priorities, assumes greater political significance in Southeast Asia than in polities where political legitimacy derives from representation and process. In such instances, governments may have to engage in difficult balancing acts when making choices as to whether they fully engage with global economic processes and governance, which could undermine their distributive role, or whether they opt to retain policy autonomy but at the price of reducing their external economic engagement. Moreover, participation in global economic processes does not always guarantee economic gains, given the propensity of contemporary global capitalism to financial crises. Individual governments increasingly turn to regional cooperation to help them address these external challenges collectively but in ways that do not seriously jeopardise their respective domestic socio-political priorities. As the rest of this chapter shows, economic regionalism in the Asia-Pacific reflects precisely these competing dynamics.

THE APEC FORUM

Currently grouping 21 members, APEC was formed in 1989 as a ministerial-level meeting of twelve member countries, its original aim to provide an informal regional dialogue mechanism on trade matters.[5] It is best regarded as an inter-regional institution, given its exceedingly vast geographical scope and the fact that it encompasses a number of regional groupings within its contours. The reasons behind APEC's establishment have been extensively discussed elsewhere and will not be repeated here (Ravenhill, 2002). Suffice it to say that despite initial reservations on the part of the Southeast Asian states that the US, in particular, would dominate APEC and use it to impose Washington's preferred liberalising agenda on them, these governments came on board the project in 1989 (Nesadurai, 1996, 31–57).[6] Southeast Asian concern that they would become marginalised from the all-important US market was sufficient to overcome their wariness of APEC. These governments were concerned that the US would turn away from East Asia given its growing trade frictions with regional states *and* its embrace of North American economic regionalism, particularly as the waning Cold War made Southeast Asia less vital to the security interests of Washington. Through APEC, the Southeast Asian governments hoped to ensure their continued access to the US market by embedding the US in a regional framework.

Ever mindful that Washington would pressure them to liberalise their economies through the APEC mechanism in ways or at a pace unacceptable to them, APEC's Southeast Asian members sought to reduce any potential for their domination in the forum by insisting on unilateralism and consensus as APEC's two guiding principles. This reinforces APEC's approach to regional cooperation self-styled as 'open regionalism'.[7] This particular modus operandi adopted in APEC helped Southeast Asian governments retain considerable policy autonomy within the grouping even as APEC rapidly adopted a distinctively neoliberal economic agenda after its first leaders' summit held in Seattle in 1993. Trade and investment liberalisation had always been Washington's preferred agenda for APEC, which also reflected the growing demands from American capital for access to Asian markets in return for Asian access to the US market. Other pro-liberalisation governments in APEC, namely Australia, New Zealand and Canada, were generally supportive of APEC's neoliberal turn, as were the city-state economies of Hong Kong and Singapore (Ravenhill, 2002, 234–8). Other members in APEC occasionally supported its free trade agenda. Although most of APEC's Southeast Asian members were relatively open economies since the late 1980s, they were nevertheless concerned that any hasty liberalisation would undermine their own industrialisation efforts as well as their ability to meet domestic socio-political priorities.

The emphasis on open regionalism in APEC, supported by the ASEAN states and by Japan, South Korea and China helped ensure that APEC's key programmes in trade and investment liberalisation as well as competition policy are based on non-binding, unilateral/non-negotiated commitments and flexible implementation. This approach, more recently termed 'concerted unilateralism', effectively allows each member government substantial discretion in determining the concessions it is willing to make and its liberalisation schedule (Plummer, 1998, 308). Concerted unilateralism has, therefore, helped Asian governments avoid being imposed upon in APEC.

Trade and security in a post-11 September world: reinforcing a US-centric world order

The insistence on concerted unilateralism meant, however, that the US lost interest in APEC, especially after the 1998 Kuala Lumpur Summit when negotiations over the liberalisation of the forestry, fisheries and agriculture sector between Japan and the US ended in stalemate (Ravenhill, 2002, 235). With its liberalisation agenda in tatters, APEC now focuses on economic and technical cooperation, issues that Washington does not care too much about. For many of its members, APEC has clearly 'taken a back seat' as an exercise in regional economic governance (Ravenhill, 2002, 241). It was probably because such a vacuum existed in APEC in the first place that the global security concerns of the US centred on terrorism could quite easily assume centre-stage at the 2003 APEC Leaders Summit in Bangkok.

Much to the disquiet of a number of APEC members and the business community,[8] considerable attention at this Summit was devoted to specific security measures to counter transnational terrorism.[9] If Washington's terrorism-based security agenda continues to dominate future APEC meetings and its work programme, then APEC will help reproduce a US-centric regional order premised on the intertwining of economics, trade and US national security interests (Higgott, 2003). Even though APEC may be marginal in terms of its contribution towards regional and global *economic* governance, its shift towards a security role in the post-11 September era provides an Asia-Pacific building block that reinforces a US-centric world order and one presently focused on the war against terrorism.

ASEAN AND SOUTHEAST ASIAN ECONOMIC REGIONALISM

In the case of ASEAN economic regionalism, the AFTA project adopted in 1992 was a major success for the organisation after almost two decades of limited progress on economic cooperation. Despite a number of setbacks and disputes over implementation, the first phase of this project is virtually completed with intra-regional tariffs on manufactured items down to the stipulated 0–5 per cent as scheduled, with the exception of tariffs on agricultural items and on Malaysian automobiles.[10] A second project of economic regionalism was adopted in October 2003, namely the AEC project. The AEC aims to go beyond tariff reduction to consolidate regional liberalisation in services and investment that began in the mid-1990s, further reduce non-tariff barriers, harmonise product standards, as well as aim for the limited movement of skilled and professional workers within Southeast Asia (ASEAN, 2003). Its ultimate aim is for a 'seamless', integrated Southeast Asian market.

Regionalism and the imperative of FDI: avoiding economic marginalisation

ASEAN economic regionalism is primarily a response by the Southeast Asian governments to a deep fear of marginalisation from crucial sources of wealth creation in the global economy, principally foreign direct investment (FDI). The ASEAN governments used AFTA as a carrot by which to retain and attract FDI that these governments feared was being attracted to competing investment sites, particularly China. By 1992, ASEAN leaders and policy-makers had become keenly aware that foreign investors were eyeing the large, regional markets that were being put in place at that time, principally the North American Free Trade Agreement and the Single European Market, as well as China. These sites were attractive to investors both as investment/production sites within which transnational production chains could be organised and as markets to which regionally produced products could be sold (Rodan, 1993, 234). These developments demonstrated quite forcefully to the ASEAN leaders the potential utility of a similar project in ASEAN, especially when it became apparent that FDI inflows into ASEAN were displaying a declining trend in the early years of the 1990s. By this time, the ASEAN countries had grown highly dependent on FDI to fuel economic growth, which had also helped overcome some of the domestic socio-political tensions that had emerged in these countries during the downturn of the mid-1980s. The Southeast Asian governments were, consequently, highly vulnerable to any slowdown in FDI.

The FDI imperative not only accounts for the adoption of the AFTA project, it also explains why it was sustained since its initial adoption, its pace accelerated and its agenda expanded despite growing domestic business opposition to it. AFTA also became a key tool by which the ASEAN governments attempted to retain and attract FDI to the region during the turmoil of the Asian financial crisis when huge amounts of portfolio capital left the region and domestic investments dried up.[11] By further accelerating AFTA during 1998–99 and initiating a zero-tariff AFTA by 2010, the ASEAN governments were signalling to foreign investors that the region remained an attractive investment location (Bowles, 2000, 444).

ASEAN's preoccupation with maintaining access to FDI is also revealed by the grouping's short-lived attempt at developmental regionalism. While many of the ASEAN countries were highly dependent on FDI, and thus interested in using regionalism to ensure continued access to global capital, they were also troubled by the impact of global competition on the future of domestic-owned capital. In countries like Malaysia and Indonesia especially, domestic capital was often a key partner in governing elite coalitions while it was also important in fulfilling wider socio-economic and ultimately political goals, particularly in the context of ethnic politics. These governments were especially worried by the prospect that new multilateral rules on investment that emphasised national treatment and market access for all investors would soon become incorporated in the WTO, which would effectively allow multinational corporations maximum freedom of operation worldwide. Their response, supported by the other ASEAN states, was to use regional cooperation to help nurture domestic-owned firms before global investment rules that mandated complete liberalisation of investment regimes were put in place. By offering ASEAN domestic investors national treatment and market access privileges ahead of foreign investors in ASEAN's 1998 investment liberalisation programme, regional policy-makers intended these temporary investment preferences to stimulate the growth through regional expansion of domestic firms into larger enterprises able to compete with MNCs, including through forming ASEAN multinationals. It was ASEAN's attempt at developmental regionalism (Nesadurai, 2003, 99–127).

Despite these concerns over domestic capital, the FDI imperative became overwhelming by the middle of 2001 in the face of an expected slowdown in the global economy and the decline in FDI flows to regional economies. Member governments, consequently, gave up their attempt at developmental regionalism as they once again devoted their full attention to the FDI imperative in an effort to secure their primary source of growth and wealth creation, or face the domestic political consequences of another downturn. Although the differential treatment of foreign investors was not the main reason for the slowdown in FDI to ASEAN, member governments were nevertheless concerned that it could send the wrong signals to foreign investors at a time when ASEAN was facing a sharp fall in FDI inflows, particularly in competition with China. It is clear that concern over ASEAN's marginalisation from global investment and production networks took priority over domestic distributive priorities that had initially warranted the push towards developmental regionalism.

ASEAN economic regionalism: reinforcing global governance?

To the extent that ASEAN economic regionalism is aimed at, and results in, the creation of an integrated regional market with reduced or no barriers to the free flow of goods, services, and capital, then regionalism potentially contributes to global market integration. The quick decision to halt the developmental regionalism project and the embrace of the AEC project reveal that ASEAN's primary concern remains the region's full integration with the world economy, notably with global investment and production networks. Even the technical assistance programmes and the expanding social development agenda in ASEAN are largely aimed at facilitating the participation of ASEAN's less-developed new members in regional trade and investment liberalisation. Although internal differences over the pace and extent of liberalisation continue to challenge ASEAN economic integration, they are unlikely to result in the regional project taking on a form that will undermine global governance processes. Departures from strict neoliberal norms, ideas and practices do not always imply resistance to globalisation. Ultimately, ASEAN economic regionalism is all about ensuring that the Southeast Asian countries become full participants in the global economy, and often that path involves developmental objectives in regional governance.

The China–ASEAN FTA

Given ASEAN's deep concerns over competition from China not only for FDI but from low-priced Chinese products, it is unsurprising that ASEAN responded cautiously to China's proposal in late 2000 for a free trade area between ASEAN and China.[12] Despite the ambivalence of a number of member governments, the project was, nevertheless, formally endorsed by ASEAN in November 2001. It would have been difficult to reject the Chinese proposal, given the ASEAN countries' desire to engage with China on political and security issues. A fully operational China–ASEAN FTA was, however, scheduled for 2010 at the earliest in order to help ASEAN consolidate itself as a regional site for production and for domestic industries to make the transition to competing first in ASEAN.[13] All the ASEAN leaders, including those hesitant about the project, recognise the gains to their respective economies from investment opportunities for local firms in China, from preferential access to the China market and to Chinese investment, as well as access to lower priced final products and intermediate inputs from China. For the present, however, there remains some ambivalence about this project as regional leaders recognise the competitive elements of an China–ASEAN FTA.

China has, however, displayed considerable sensitivity to ASEAN concerns over the potential adverse consequences of liberalising trade with such a powerful competitor. Among others, China has offered an 'early harvest' programme under the China–ASEAN FTA. Under this programme, China has offered ASEAN countries a quick reduction of tariffs on a number of goods, including liberalisation of selected agricultural commodities to zero per cent by 2005 to be followed by full agricultural liberalisation by 2010. China has also agreed to extend MFN status to ASEAN's newest members, namely Vietnam, Laos, Cambodia and Myanmar while according them special and differential treatment in trade liberalisation, effectively opening up the China market to their exports far earlier than Chinese products will gain access to the markets of these countries. The sum total of these and other accommodating gestures from China towards ASEAN is that ASEAN has become much more assured that China intends to be a 'long-term' friend (Ba, 2003).

While there remain a number of security-related issues that might undermine the China–ASEAN relationship, notably over territorial claims in the South China Sea, even here, China is displaying a remarkable accommodation with ASEAN. Moreover, China is potentially a significant market and source of investment for Southeast Asia, and full realisation of the China–ASEAN FTA could well see the emergence of a region relatively less dependent on the US market. Both China and ASEAN also share similar approaches to development. Despite considerable economic liberalisation undertaken in both ASEAN and China, and their emphasis on market governance and private sector-led growth, both parties retain a role for the state in the economy. Such convergence of ideas and practices in economic governance can only help reinforce China's growing role in the regional order, while potentially laying the initial groundwork for an East Asian regionalism.

ASEAN+3 AND EAST ASIAN REGIONALISM

The 1997–98 Asian financial crisis not only led to advances in ASEAN regionalism, it also catalysed a wider East Asian regionalism that is aimed at helping regional states cope with problems stemming from global financial integration that present governance mechanisms at the global or regional levels either do not address or do so in a limited way (Ba, 2005). The regional response to the crisis started with the Japanese suggestion for an Asian Monetary Fund (AMF), a proposal that Washington roundly criticised and which Tokyo soon withdrew as a result. Initially capitalised at US$100 billion, the AMF had been expected to provide emergency support to regional countries struck by the crisis in a manner that was more flexible and indeed with fewer stringent conditionalities than the IMF (Altbach, 1997, 8–9). The US was, unsurprisingly, hostile to the AMF idea, which it saw as likely to undermine any chances for reforming East Asian developmental states through the tough conditionalities imposed by the International Monetary Fund (IMF), while the AMF was also seen as a direct threat to US strategic interests and influence in East Asia (Higgott, 2000b, 269). Despite these developments, interest grew amongst the ten Southeast Asian states and the three Northeast Asian states of Japan, South Korea and China for an East Asian mechanism to help avert future crises (Stubbs, 2002, 449). ASEAN also realised that it needed the Northeast Asian states with their considerably larger financial resources if it wished to develop a credible regional liquidity mechanism that could offer insurance against future crises. The coming together of East Asian states at this time also reflected shared resentment against the US for the way it responded (or not) to the crisis. The East Asian countries thus began to institutionalise annual leaders' summits and ministerial dialogues through the ASEAN+3 framework during and since the financial crisis.

The most notable, and to date, the most concrete project of the ASEAN+3 is the Chiang Mai Initiative (CMI) adopted in May 2000 with the aim of providing emergency foreign currency liquidity support in the event of a future financial crisis. The CMI comprises a series of bilateral swap arrangements negotiated among East Asian states plus an expanded ASEAN Swap Arrangement (ASA).[14] By February 2003, total funds potentially available under the CMI totalled US$32.5 billion, although each country is only able to draw on the amount it has negotiated bilaterally. The CMI is also able to draw on funds from the 1998 Miyazawa Initiative, under which Tokyo provided financial assistance to Asian countries hit by the crisis. Although the CMI has yet to be tested, it is said to provide a potentially substantial source of funds in the event a crisis does strike (Hamilton-Hart, 2003). A second track to the CMI is the agreement to exchange information on short-term capital movements in East Asia and to institute an early warning system to alert governments of potential danger points in their respective economies (Stubbs, 2002, 450). Although the ASEAN+3 process does go beyond the financial/monetary agenda to include broader cooperation in a range of areas such as small and medium-scale industry development, food security, human resource development, agriculture, tourism, and information technology development, it is clear that the financial/monetary agenda remains the most significant.

The ASEAN+3 regional project is best regarded as an insurance mechanism that will help East Asian states to remain engaged with the global economy by providing a buffer between individual national economies and the vagaries of the global financial system (Ba, 2005). Although the ASEAN+3 may have emerged out of deep concern about the malign effects of a largely unsupervised global financial system, and shared resentment against the US, in fact, it enhances the present system of neoliberal global governance. This is reflected in the fact that the CMI retains an official link to the IMF, and constitutes in reality, a *supplementary* financial facility to the IMF in the event of a crisis (Hamilton-Hart, 2003). For many regional leaders, the IMF link protects the credibility of the CMI in the eyes of global investors. It is for this reason that a proposal to multilateralise the CMI by unifying existing bilateral swap arrangements has no plan for delinking the CMI from the IMF.[15] The ASEAN+3, in short, helps facilitate the advance of the globalisation project by providing an alternative regional arrangement to mitigate against future financial crises that might otherwise retard or derail globalisation.

CONCLUSION

This chapter puts forward the argument that the various regional projects in the Asia-Pacific represent the responses of regional states, particularly the Southeast Asian states, to a set of external pressures that may be conveniently subsumed under the rubric of globalisation. In responding to globalisation, the Southeast Asian governments were driven by deep concern over their potential marginalisation in the world economy, particularly from global investment capital. However, these states were equally concerned by their potential domination in the international system, either by a dominant power, the US in particular, and/or by global capital, whether MNCs or financial capital, especially speculative capital. The precise form taken by these regional arrangements in terms of their respective agenda and modalities of cooperation, consequently, reflects the interplay between these twin concerns of marginalisation and domination.

Thus, the various regional projects adopted at the ASEAN level (AFTA and the AEC) are prompted by fears that global investment capital will bypass Southeast Asia. The ASEAN+3 project is best regarded as an insurance mechanism for its participants against future financial crises. By performing an insurance role, albeit untested as yet, the ASEAN+3 facilitates the continued engagement of its members with the global economy. Both ASEAN economic regionalism and the ASEAN+3 framework, consequently, reinforce the prevailing neoliberal version of global governance. The ASEAN+3 potentially consolidates an East Asian regionalism in which China could eventually become the dominant player. However, East Asian regionalism is unlikely to overshadow Southeast Asian regionalism in the near to medium term, as both assume complementary roles. Moreover, for the small Southeast Asian states, ASEAN undertakes a wide range of roles and functions that remain salient to the Southeast Asian region.

In addition, the range of bilateral FTAs negotiated by regional states[16] further reinforces the neoliberal norms, ideas and practices of global governance. These FTAs often go beyond current WTO liberalisation agreements, especially in their coverage of services and investment liberalisation, competition policy and government procurement arrangements, areas in which WTO negotiations have yet to progress. The bilateral FTAs are essentially instruments adopted by governments fearful of their economic marginalisation to secure access to export markets and to investment capital. They often fulfil national security agendas as well. While these arrangements raise a whole set of problems for market players by increasing economic fragmentation and raising the costs of doing business,[17] their strongly neoliberal features generally reinforce neoliberal globalisation.[18]

The nature of Asia-Pacific regionalism analysed in this chapter suggests that it does not threaten the prevailing norms and practices of global governance nor the present US-centred world order. Although many Southeast Asian states remain concerned about domination by a single power, currently the US, their equally pronounced preoccupation with maintaining their participation in global investment, production and trading networks, as reflected in their regional projects, means that both

Southeast Asian and broader East Asian regionalism is unlikely to challenge the neoliberal approaches to global governance preferred by Washington. To the extent that these states contemplate developmental approaches to regionalism or supplements to global governance, these regional projects will, in fact, enhance the capacity of regional states to engage in global economic processes. Moreover, APEC's shift to a security role centred on fighting terrorism in line with Washington's national security agenda further reinforces the US-centric world order. In addition, Washington's Enterprise for ASEAN Initiative by which the US negotiates FTAs with individual ASEAN states consolidates US centrality by entrenching it as the economic hub in this region (with the spokes represented by individual ASEAN states), and is likely to further embed neoliberal approaches to economic governance.

It is unclear at this point whether China's growing role in the region, reinforced by the China–ASEAN FTA and by Chinese participation in the ASEAN+3 framework, will undermine or provide an alternative to a US-centred *regional* order. Where Japan has clearly demonstrated that it does not wish to act against US interests in the region, as exemplified by its behaviour over the AMF issue, China may see no problem with taking on a regional leadership role, or in opposing US policies if these run counter to Chinese (or regional) interests. To the extent that China ends up as a significant market for regional economies and a significant source of investment, this could see a recalibration of interdependence in the region in that East Asian states reduce their current overwhelming dependence on the US market while increasing their economic links with China. Regional states are, however, likely to wish to continue their economic relationship with the US. In the end, whatever the specific contours of regionalism in the Asia-Pacific, it is unlikely to be a site for resistance to global governance for so long as regional governments tie their fortunes with engagement with the global economy. To put it another way, Asia-Pacific regionalism in all its diversity reinforces prevailing global governance arrangements, although it may not exactly reproduce its neoliberal characteristics.

NOTES

1. The Asia-Pacific region is defined in this chapter to include states bordering both the western and eastern rims of the Pacific Ocean, coinciding effectively with the membership of APEC.
2. ASEAN is the Association of Southeast Asian Nations, the region's most enduring intergovernmental organisation established in 1967 by Indonesia, Malaysia, the Philippines, Singapore, and Thailand. Brunei joined the grouping in 1984 on its independence from Britain. Vietnam joined in 1995, Laos and Myanmar in 1997, and Cambodia in April 1999, bringing ASEAN's total membership to ten. ASEAN is a multipurpose regional

organisation for the Southeast Asian region, and addresses a range of issue areas in the political, security, socio-cultural and economic domains.

3. The embedded liberal world order that emerged after the Second World War and lasted until around the middle of the 1980s was one that privileged domestic socio-economic priorities, notably employment and domestic social stability, while progressively reducing border barriers to international trade and investment. In the present AWC-based world order, the market is not as deeply embedded in society. Hence, I refer to a *quasi*-embedded liberal order. The term 'embedded liberalism' comes from Ruggie (1998).

4. The AWC approach to global governance has also been complemented by moves to democratise the international financial institutions, namely the World Bank, the World Trade Organisation (WTO) and the International Monetary Fund (IMF) by first, improving their transparency and accountability, and second, by allowing for greater interactions with civil society groups (Scholte, 2002).

5. The founding members of APEC in 1989 were the then six member states of ASEAN (Brunei, Indonesia, Malaysia, the Philippines, Singapore and Thailand), Australia, Canada, Japan, New Zealand, South Korea and the United States. In 1991, the 'three Chinas' were admitted to the grouping – the Peoples' Republic of China, Hong Kong and Taiwan. Papua New Guinea became a member in 1993, Chile in 1994 and Peru, Russia and Vietnam formally joined APEC in 1998. Since then, a moratorium has been placed on APEC membership.

6. The Southeast Asian states had also been concerned that APEC would overshadow ASEAN (Ravenhill, 2002, 231).

7. Open regionalism was originally defined as an approach to regional trade liberalisation based on unilateral offers by APEC members, which may be extended to non-APEC members on a most-favoured-nation basis, *without the need for reciprocity from the other party, whether or not an APEC member* (Drysdale and Garnaut, 1993, 187–8). The term is now used in a more general sense to characterise regionalist schemes that are fundamentally about engaging with globalisation and the global market (Gamble and Payne, 1996, 251).

8. *The Straits Times*, 'APEC out of touch, say businessmen', 22 October 2003.

9. These measures are outlined in APEC (2003).

10. Agricultural items follow a delayed schedule, while Malaysian automobile tariffs are currently exempted from AFTA disciplines until 2005.

11. Although tariff barriers were employed to shield domestic industries during the financial crisis, many of these import restrictions were temporary, and were part of a set of short-term fiscal measures designed to reduce immediate pressure on countries' external accounts through restricting big-ticket and luxury items (Shimizu, 2000, 83).

12. These responses are detailed in *Business Times (Singapore)*, 'All eyes on China push for FTA', 24 November 2000.

13. Confidential interview with a Malaysian trade official, December 2001.

14. The ASA, which has been in place since 1977, was enlarged from its original US$200 million to US$1 billion from November 2000.

15. *Far Eastern Economic Review*, 'Asian financial union: thinking the unthinkable', 8 April 2004.

16. For a listing, see Scollay and Gilbert (2001) and Lim (2004).

17. Discussed in detail in Scollay and Gilbert (2001, 16–18).

18. In some instances, however, bilateral arrangements allow the parties concerned to exempt politically sensitive sectors from liberalisation, as Japan did with cut flowers and goldfish in its FTA with Singapore. See Nesadurai (2004, 165–7).

11
The Global Politics of Regionalism: Africa

Daniel Bach

The African region offers a yardstick for measuring the extent to which globalisation and multilateralism can fail to alleviate poverty and promote a more equitable international order. Within the past two decades, Africa has become commonly described as a continent that 'has receded to the margins of most global markets' (Lewis, 2000, 22). This is especially the case in Sub-Saharan Africa where 37 out of the 48 states are Low Income Countries with a per capita income below $785. The whole of Africa accounted in 2000 for 2.3 per cent of world trade – Sub-Saharan African states scored then a mere 1.5 per cent. Foreign direct investment towards Sub-Saharan Africa did not fare any better with 0.5 per cent of world inflows and 2.6 per cent of flows into developing countries, mostly to Nigeria. Since then, a new strategic significance has emerged with the continent's new deep offshore oil resources and exports, but the overall implications for the continent and its people are shrouded with uncertainty.[1] Current US and Western concerns at diversifying oil supplies away from the Middle East are yet to bring an end to the 'predicament' that, with the exception of Botswana, has kept turning mineral resources into a development trap (Bach, 2005). Western scenarios on the continent's future continue to convey grim prospects, shaped by the persistence of 'soft' states and the empowerment of 'international organisations and non-state actors of all types: transnational religious institutions; international non-profit organisations, international crime syndicates and drug traffickers; foreign mercenaries; and international terrorists seeking safe heavens' (Bach, 2005, 74). There is little need to add that this vision of Africa's future has a renewed significance since 11 September 2001: in November that same year, the former US Assistant Secretary of State for African Affairs, Suzan Rice, characteristically challenged the 'conventional wisdom' that fighting terrorism should mean for Africa 'fewer resources and zero attention'. Sub-Saharan Africa, she argued, ought to be viewed as the 'world's soft underbelly for global terrorism', since its 'porous borders, weak law enforcement and security services, and nascent judicial institutions' could be easily taken advantage of (US Congress, 2001, 6–7). The national security strategy subsequently presented by President George W. Bush to Congress in September 2002, endorsed this vision of Africa as a soft interface for terrorism (Herbst and Mills, 2003). Depictions of Africa still convey this pervasive vision of a continent where the combination of weak states and porous borders offers an ideal backyard for terrorism. More generally, ever since the end of the Cold War, debates on the global 'reach' of Africa have come to contrast the continent's peripheral significance in the global economy with its alleged global nuisance capacity if this trend were to remain unchecked. Emphasis has been successively laid on the explosion of migrations targeting the European Union (EU), the continent's transformation into a global base for illicit-drug trafficking, state capture by criminal networks and, most recently, terrorist activity. Not surprisingly, these representations also loom large in discussions of what African regionalism entails.

In the non-Africanist literature, African regionalism is rarely mentioned. The assumption seems to be that there is little value in monitoring the global reach of a continent that is peripheral in the global economy and commonly features as an 'adjustment variable' in international politics. Indeed, Africa's international empowerment still primarily relates to its voting power in such international organisations as the United Nations (UN) or World Trade Organisation (WTO). The integration of its polities within cohesive regional economic or political agreements remains of limited consequence despite the multiplicity of intergovernmental organisations (IGOs) and agreements claiming to do so. Whenever lip service is being paid to the discussion of African regionalism, this tends to be associated with extensive reliance on rhetorical statements and stated ambitions; the gap between institution-building and policy implementation is usually acknowledged, but it is treated as a temporary dysfunction. This nurtures what may be described as an 'inching towards implementation' assessment of the failure of IGOs to achieve the priorities encased in their mandates. The fact that programmes have been going on for several decades with deadlines that keep being regularly 'updated', is completely overlooked.

Monitoring regionalism in Africa often involves focusing on its politics due to the coexistence of a dozen Regional (or sub-regional) Economic Communities (RECs) with overlapping mandates and memberships. In addition to these, about a hundred smaller, sectoral IGOs perform functions that have often little to do with their stated mandates and programmes. African regionalism has yet to overcome memories of the drama that often surrounded the dissolution of all colonial federations but one (Nigeria) into multiple sovereign states between the late 1950s and mid-1960s (Hazlewood, 1967). Today, the ideals of 'aggregative' regionalism are often caught between state concern at sovereignty enhancement and domestic demands for political fragmentation. Since the late 1980s, the discredit cast on the nation-state ethos due to its capture by parochial interests, the return to multiparty systems and the ongoing crisis of neo-patrimonial governance have fuelled a 'growing tendency towards regional assertion and autonomy seeking' on the part of sub-national groups (Bach, 1999; Forrest, 2004). The revival of regionalism, in Africa perhaps more than in any other continent, cannot be readily interpreted as integration through aggregation.

The distinction between regionalism and regionalisation enables to overcome a number of the limitations associated with emphasis on institutions and agreements. The notion of regionalism, for the purpose of this chapter will refer specifically to ideas or ideologies, programmes, policies and goals that seek to transform an identified social space into a regional project. Regionalism therefore involves the *construction* of an identity as opposed to its *formation*. It postulates the implementation of a programme and the definition of a strategy and is therefore often associated with institution-building or the conclusion of formal arrangements. By contrast, regionalisation refers to processes and outcomes: it can encapsulate inter-state or sub-national projects that achieve their stated objectives; regionalisation can also encapsulate a much broader range of situations where 'regionness' grows independently from identified regionalist strategies or aspirations. In such circumstances, regionalisation is simply an outcome of the behaviour of agents (diasporas, trade or religious networks, multinational corporations) whose activities contribute *de facto* to the formation of regional spaces although they are not motivated by a regionalist project. Emphasis is laid on transactions and interactions as opposed to cognitive representations and formal arrangements. Depending on time, location and circumstances, regionalisation can be associated with transactions that are licit or illicit, formal or informal, locally banned but internationally acceptable or conversely, locally condoned but highly criminalised abroad. As increasingly the case in Africa, regionalisation can also be underscored by networks with a global reach. When these combine characteristics traditionally associated with transnational and international relations, they can be referred to as trans-state interactions. Trans-state interactions relate to social, ethnic or religious bonds that challenge state sovereignty through their capacity to avoid, penetrate or permeate state structures. In Africa, trans-state networks thrive whenever they are embedded in neo-patrimonial states where institutional policies and territorial control are weakened by the privatisation of public functions.

The distinction between regionalism as a cognitive or state-centric project, and regionalisation as a *de facto* process or an *ex post* outcome is essential. It becomes of key significance when it facilitates the analysis beyond the description of (sometimes) purely formal agreements, or exclusive emphasis on the politics of summitry and verbal diplomacy. This is particularly the case whenever, as observed in Africa, regionalisation draws much of its flavour and stamina from the permeation of state and corporate policies by socio-ethnic or religious networks that straddle norms, institutions and boundary-lines.

The following pages do not seek to offer an exhaustive survey of Africa's regional integration schemes. I will first address the recent revitalisation of pan-Africanism, then describe what may be termed as Africa's recent 'scramble' for regional institution-building, before addressing the asymbiotic nature of interactions between formal arrangements and *de facto* regionalisation.

THE REVITALISATION OF PAN-AFRICANIST IDEALS

The pan-African movement was launched in the US and West Indies at the turn of the twentieth century. From the Second World War onwards, its objectives became more Africa-centred and focused increasingly on denouncing colonialism and white domination. As decolonisation suddenly gathered stamina in the early 1960s, pan-Africanist ideals were adjusted to the lack of any collective willingness to dissolve newly acquired state sovereignties into regional or continental schemes. In 1963, the adoption of the Addis Ababa charter established the Organisation of African Unity (OAU) which set the basis for a bifurcated approach to African unity. All independent states were invited to belong to the OAU and rally around the 'freedom from colonialism and apartheid' mandates of previous pan-African conferences – this was indeed to be pursued with unquestionable effectiveness thanks to the voting power of OAU member states in the UN. The OAU also sketched the contours of an African region that was in all respects an 'imagined' community. The OAU, which took its inspiration from the Organisation of American States, was primarily a multilateral forum where the pan-African ideals of sovereignty pooling subsided under more immediate concerns related to sovereignty enhancement, non-interference in domestic affairs and mutual respect for colonial boundaries. Accordingly, during annual OAU heads of state and government summits, the stigmatisation of arbitrary boundaries inherited from colonialism went along with equally stringent support for the preservation of these boundaries whenever their legitimacy came to be challenged.

As the Cold War came to an end in Africa, there were anticipations that it would trigger a vast movement of territorial and boundary adjustments, but these did not materialise: a decade and a half later, violence and insecurity on the continent are still rarely fuelled by irredentist claims. Inter-state conflicts sometimes involve direct military control over parts of another state but, as observed in the case of the Rwandan and Ugandan military presence in Eastern Congo, states still stop short of translating territorial control into formal territorial claims. Morocco's incorporation of Western Sahara on grounds of its alleged pre-colonial allegiance to the Cherifian kingdom is the only instance where international boundary-lines inherited from the colonial period were explicitly, albeit unilaterally, redrawn (Marfaing and Wippel, 2004).[2] Elsewhere, demands for boundary adjustments still remain focused on the endorsement or reinstatement of international or regional/ provincial boundary-lines inherited from the colonial period (viz the conflict between Cameroon and Nigeria over ownership of the Bakassi peninsula). Eritrea's noted accession to international sovereignty in 1993 is no exception to this insofar as it brought an end to a protracted liberation war through the reinstatement of the partition line that existed between the colony of Eritrea and the independent Ethiopian empire until the latter's invasion by Italy in 1936. In neighbouring Somalia, the *de facto* claim of Somaliland to independence similarly meant a reinstatement of the colonial boundary-line that separated Italian and British Somalia.

For the OAU, the 1990s created new challenges with respect to its mission and performance. Within international institutions, the voting power of African states was eroded by the admission of new states from Eastern and Central Europe. The decolonisation of Namibia (1991) and South Africa's transition to majority rule (1994) also meant the successful completion of a key aspect to the OAU's mandate. Meanwhile, the OAU's strict adherence to non-intervention in the internal affairs of member states kept preventing it from addressing new sources of conflict across the continent. Guarantees designed to preserve state sovereignty and ensure stability on the continent also appeared to provide impunity to authoritarian leaders and rogue regimes.

These challenges contributed to the adoption of a series of initiatives and reforms designed to instil new substance to the notion of African unity. A first set of initiatives endorsed a broadening of the notion of African unity. As early as 1980, heads of states had adopted what became known as the Lagos Plan of Action, superseded a decade later by the Abuja Treaty towards an African Economic Community (AEC) of 53 states.[3] After a succession of stages that are expected to unfold until 2025, the AEC should involve the free movement of peoples and factors of production, the creation of a single domestic market, an economic and monetary union, a central bank, a single African currency and a Pan-African Parliament. The original treaty stipulated that AEC is to rely on the emergence of regional building-blocs. Seven RECs are currently listed as such by the African Union (AU): the Arab Maghreb Union (AMU), the Economic Community of West African States (ECOWAS), the Economic Community of Central African States (ECCAS), the Common Market for East and Southern Africa (COMESA), the Southern Africa Development Community (SADC), the Intergovernmental Authority on Development (IGAD) and the Community of Sahelian-Saharan States (CEN-SAD). This list does not augur well for the project's future: ECCAS and AMU have been in existence since the 1980s, but are dormant due to conflicts among member states; CEN-SAD and IGAD function as mere 'talk-shops'. In East and Southern Africa overlapping membership between SADC, COMESA, the East African Community, IGAD and the Southern African Customs Union (SACU) is a source of complex politico-bureaucratic and normative hurdles. Simultaneously, the track record of the three African RECs within which transfers of sovereignty and common monetary and customs policies are a reality, is overlooked (see below). Ten years after it was launched, the AEC record says more about its politics than economic achievements. Nonetheless, commitment to AEC has been fully reasserted as a central component in the transformation of the OAU into an African Union (AU).

The decision to dissolve the OAU and rebuilt it as a *union* was adopted in Sirte, Libya, on 9 September 1999, at the close of the extraordinary OAU summit convened by Muammar Gaddafi of Libya. Within less than two years a new Constitutive Act was adopted and, on 9 August 2002, the AU was formally inaugurated in Durban. The Constitutive Act that provides for the transformation of the OAU into the AU reinstates it at the apex of all regional and sub-regional institutions. The mandate of the AU goes beyond political union and covers issues that were ignored or, in the case of economic integration, delegated to the UN Economic Commission for Africa prior to the Abuja Treaty. New emphasis is laid on the security, economic development and stability of the continent. A number of dispositions present a clear departure from the past. The AU's much noted change of abbreviation goes along with the assertion of new political ambitions through the renaming of pre-existing organs and the announcement of plans towards the creation of a multiplicity of new ones. The secretariat of the OAU is now to be known as the 'Commission'; the Council of Ministers is renamed 'Executive Council' and the Assembly of heads of states and government is referred to as 'the Assembly'. The overhaul of the (O)AU has been followed by the creation of two new key organs: the African Court on Human and Peoples' Rights, launched in January 2004, and the Pan-African Parliament, which convened for its inaugural meeting in March 2004. The transformation of the Bureau of the OAU into a Peace and Security Council (PSC) also reflects on the importance attached to the restoration of peace and stability on the continent. Related concern at the establishment of more effective mechanisms of mediation in the continent's numerous violent conflicts accounts for the adoption of exemptions to the principle of non-interference in the domestic affairs of member states. Limitations include: the Union's right to intervene in a member state 'pursuant to a decision of the Assembly' in 'grave circumstances' such as 'war crimes, genocide and crimes against humanity' (art. 4 section h); the signatories also assert their 'condemnation and rejection of impunity and political assassination, acts of terrorism and subversive activities' (art. 4, section o); and their 'rejection of unconstitutional changes of governments' (art. 4, section p). Article 30 also states explicitly that the Union reserves the right to suspend the membership of any government that comes to power through illegal means.[4]

During the 1960s, pan-African debates on the future of the continent polarised on the pros and cons of working towards merger into a 'United States' of Africa. Four decades later, the AU invites a number of parallels with two other models, namely the EU and (in the case of the PSC) the UN Security Council. In both cases, however, the new organs of the AU have had their powers severely capped. The Assembly of heads of state remains the 'supreme organ of the union' and its decisions are adopted by consensus or through a two-thirds majority. The powers of the subsequently established Pan-African Parliament are also limited: they are impaired by its composition and mode of recruitment,[5] an unclear agenda and no decisional power (Van Walraven, 2004). The Pan-African Parliament is therefore devoid of the democratic base and supranational functions associated with the European Parliament: it is presently more appropriate to compare its future role to that of regional assemblies in Latin America (Malamud and de Sousa, 2004, 16).[6] Within the AU, the PSC, also formally launched in 2004, also faces severe constraints. Truly, the PSC is entitled to decide on peace support operations when these have been agreed upon by the states concerned. But, unlike its UN (quasi) eponym, the PSC does not have the power to decide unilaterally on military operations. For these, the Peace and Security Council depends upon the endorsement of its recommendations by the AU Assembly. The AU also plans to set up an 'African standby force' made up of five regional brigades (15,000 soldiers) by 2010.

The new organs of the AU are only beginning to operate. It is therefore too early to conclude that the Union's enlarged agenda, restated ideals and reformed politico-bureaucratic structures have managed to overcome a legacy of instititional capacity devoid of much practical impact. Meeting the cost of the AU's enlarged institutional architecture still represents a serious challenge. The AU postulates enhanced budgetary contributions as much as a new culture of financial discipline on the part of its member states. Donor-constrained operational capacity, emphasis on rhetorical statements and dependency on summit diplomacy continue to dominate the picture. In spite of this, the amount of about $12 million that was collected in 2003 was largely insufficient to cover the budget of $43 million.

In stark contrast with traditional representations of pan-African unity as a state-centric and inward-driven process, the New Partnership for Africa's Development (NEPAD) represents an endorsement of the normative tenets of new regionalism. NEPAD was brought under the umbrella of the (O)AU in 2001. Its inception bore the imprint of South African president Thabo Mbeki's claim to transform the old pan-African notion of 'African renaissance' into a strategic notion; this concern acted as a catalyst in the collective impulse that eventually led to the merger of various competing drafts into an ambitious strategy designed to reverse Africa's peripheralisation (Maloka and Le Roux, 2000). In contrast with the Abuja Treaty, NEPAD staunchly commits all African states to international trade liberalisation and investment-friendly strategies. NEPAD thus hopes to achieve a sustained 7 per cent rate of annual economic growth for Africa through the diversification of production, the enticement of new investment and aid equal to US$64 billion a year. Another key innovation of NEPAD is the commitment of its signatories to the promotion of 'good governance' through their voluntary participation in an African Peer Review Mechanism. By September 2004, 23 out of Africa's 53 states had voluntary agreed to subject themselves to the assessment of their standards of democracy, human rights, governance and economic management; but none of the assessments had yet been completed. Active lobbying and this radical departure from past pan-African policy prescriptions contributed to the decision of the Genoa and Kananaskis G-8 summits to sponsor an 'Action Plan for Africa'. Today, NEPAD's unqualified endorsement by bilateral and multilateral donors makes it look as the most comprehensive scheme ever launched within and towards the continent. How much substance is to be instilled into pledges on recovery and partnership still remains unclear. On such key issues as agricultural subsidies, industrialised countries have shown little willingness to break new ground. The African states' readiness to undertake stated reforms and commitments has yet to be confirmed (Kappel et al., 2003, 24; Taylor, 2003). To be more specific, the peer review process is slated to become a litmus test for the credibility of the AU as a regional agency of restraint. If it fails to establish the credibility of its own ratings, the AU will have to pay the price, namely the ongoing primacy of extra-continental agencies in the assessment of risks incurred by potential lenders, investors, and business ventures.

INSTITUTIONAL EXPANSION VERSUS POLICY IMPLEMENTATION

Economic marginalisation and the regionalisation of international economic relations have prompted a significant overhaul of existing intergovernmental organisations in Africa during the early 1990s. Acronyms were updated, founding charters refurbished, mandates attuned to new ambitions; more recently, pressure for greater transparency has prompted the development of websites, with the result being a new capacity to circulate information on decisions, programmes and ambitions. In West Africa, ECOWAS member states undertook a revision of the Lagos charter that resulted in the adoption of the Treaty of Cotonou in 1993. In francophone Africa, it was the devaluation of the CFA (Communauté Financière Africaine) franc in January 1994 that sealed the dissolution of the Communauté Economique de l'Afrique de l'ouest (CEAO) and triggered its revival as the Union Economique et Monétaire de l'Ouest africain (UEMOA); similarly, in central Africa, the Union Douanière des Etats d'Afrique Centrale was transformed into a Communauté Economique et Monétaire d'Afrique Centrale (CEMAC). In Southern Africa, the SADCC decided to adhere to the more ambitious objective of promoting a Southern African Development Community (SADC) with its adoption of the revised Windhoek Treaty of 1992. In East Africa too, ratification of the treaty transforming the preferential trade area into COMESA, meant that ambitions to promote a free trade area (FTA) were superseded by a programme towards the establishment of a 'common market' in 1994. Pressure for change was of a different kind in the case of SACU, Africa's oldest customs agreement, which underwent a lengthy renegotiation process as a result of South Africa's democratic transition. A new treaty that 'democratised' the agreement and took into account South Africa's membership in WTO, was signed in 2002.

The global revival of regionalisation has prompted a spectacular broadening of the institutional agendas and strategies assigned to both pan-African and sub-regional institutions. These no longer confine their stated competencies to financial or socio-economic integration and cooperation objectives. The revised treaties include explicitly asserted social and politico-strategic concerns, including with respect to the security of states and their citizens. Such issues as the violence unleashed by regimes on their citizens or disregard for political opposition and the rule of law, are no longer taboo subjects either. They are acknowledged as preconditions to the implementation of the developmental objectives assigned to regional integration. They are also offering to institutions that have failed to fulfil their economic mandates, opportunities for re-legitimating themselves through new functions. This pattern is perhaps best exemplified by the changing mandate of the Intergovernmental Authority on Drought and Development (IGADD) since its initial establishment in 1986. During the following decade, IGADD failed to monitor any substantive progress towards its stated mandate of promoting food security and environmental protection due to tensions in the Horn and among its seven member states.[7] In 1996, member states decided to transform IGADD into an IGAD with a broader mandate so as to include conflict prevention, management, and resolution. Since then, IGAD has developed a more realistic record as a regional forum and an interface for AU, UN, EU and US initiatives towards a *pax africana* in the Horn and the Sudan.

Concern at promoting regional security is equally central to larger sub-regional organisations like ECOWAS or SADC. The involvement of

ECOWAS into peacekeeping and enforcement set the pace in the 1990s through the establishment of the ECOWAS Monitoring Group (ECOMOG). Prior emphasis of ECOWAS treaties on respect for sovereignty and non-intervention in domestic conflicts was blown into pieces with the military and diplomatic interventions of ECOMOG in Liberia (1990–97), Sierra Leone (1997–99) and Guinea-Bissau (1998–99). The shift was initiated on an *ad hoc* basis under the leadership of Nigeria[8] and it was only in 1999 that the signature of the Protocol relating to the Mechanism for Conflict Prevention, Management, Resolution, Peacekeeping and Security, established a permanent legal framework; since then this has stimulated a spectacular expansion of institution-building[9] and a renewal of regional peacekeeping, this time in close coordination with the UN and extra-African powers. In southern Africa too, SADC planned for the establishment of the Organ for Defence, Politics and Security Cooperation in 1996. Deep divisions over the role of the Organ meant that it could not function as a collective mechanism; nor did the Organ have any legal base until the adoption, in 2001, of the Protocol that provides for its establishment within the Secretariat of SADC. In an attempt to reduce tensions within the sub-region, a Mutual Defence Pact was also signed in 2003. In July 2004, a SADC Charter on democratic elections was also adopted by heads of states at their annual summit in Mauritius. Whether this pledge is to impact on the behaviour of authoritarian regimes in the sub-region is doubtful since no enforcement mechanism has been planned.

New security agendas and the establishment of organs designed to promote peacekeeping convey new patterns of interaction and 'resource capture'. Converging expectations among Western powers that African conflicts should be resolved by Africans and in a sub-regional context have opened new opportunities for security forces and agencies. In a similar fashion, the establishment of sub-regional parliaments or sub-regional courts of justice has contributed to a process of institutional expansion that appears largely disconnected from the poor record of these organs within member states.[10] Shifting concern at security also encourages a scramble towards institutional expansion and bloc building, a pattern that instils new blood into IGOs confronted with the failure of their developmental mandates.

As the ECOWAS treaty was being redrafted in the early 1990s, its executive secretary watered down expectations that this would be enough to revive integration: 'the slow pace of regional integration in West Africa has almost nothing to do with the insufficiencies noted in the 1975 ECOWAS Treaty. The adoption of an ideal treaty is of little importance if member states do not decide to consider regional integration as an important national enterprise ....' A decade later, one of his successors vented again his frustration when assessing the progress accomplished since 1976:

'An analysis of the West Africa experience of integration within the context of ECOWAS shows a poor record with regard to the execution of the Community programmes. The provisions of the revised Treaty instituting the principle of supranationality are not being applied. Several protocols are contravened, particularly those pertaining to free movement of goods and persons.' (ECOWAS, 2000; Bach, 2004, 69–92)

The discrepancy between institution-building agendas and implementation ambitions did not seem about to be reconciled as the Council of ECOWAS Ministers met in July 2004. The programme towards a common external tariff, regularly postponed since 1976, was now billed for 2005; the establishment of an autonomous ECOWAS monetary policy through the creation of a single monetary zone was still being envisaged for 2005, although this revised deadline was widely held to be unrealistic (Debrun, Mason and Pattillo, 2002; Uche, 2001). Similarly, in East and Southern Africa, COMESA and SADC plans towards the establishment of a common market have been regularly postponed.[11]

Regionalisation through hegemonic control by a single state still provides the only instances where regionalism involves transfers of sovereignty that are both legally endorsed and effectively implemented. In all cases, integration is institutionally guaranteed by a core state as opposed to a supranational institution. The guarantees are also and most significantly formally endorsed by decision-making structures. Integration through a core state refers accordingly to a pattern of *de facto* interactions as much as to a *de jure* status. Sovereignty pooling also proceeds in all these cases from the survival of patterns of domination and regulation inherited from the colonial period. In Southern Africa, integration within the SACU/Common Monetary Area is organised around a customs union and a *de facto* common currency (McCarthy, 1999). South Africa's interactions with SACU features as the core of its deeply asymmetrical interactions with the southern African sub-region.[12] The infusion of elements of supranational governance in the revised SACU agreement should not drastically change South Africa's interactions with the other SACU member states: Botswana, Lesotho, Swaziland, Namibia (BLSN). Interactions will continue to remain closer to patterns of hub-spoke regionalisation. Asymmetrical, quasi-organic, bilateral interactions link South Africa to the BLSN group but also, though less formally, to other states in the region. South Africa's controversial interactions with Southern Africa through the promotion of corridors and triangles of growth are evocative of such a pattern. The investment strategies pursued by South Africa's big conglomerates in Southern Africa also illustrate an unusual phenomenon in Africa, namely the congruence of regionalism with regionalisation.

In West and Central Africa, the CFA zone provides the other working instances of integration, this time through common currency arrangements that underscore UEMOA and CEMAC (Stasavage, 2004). Within UEMOA and CEMAC, monetary union may be described as the founding stone and the cement of regional integration. Both groupings belong to the CFA Franc Zone, a monetary union of 14 member states plus the Comoros (the latter has its own Central bank and currency), originally established before the Second World War, and reorganised after independence, in 1972–73. Intra-regional monetary integration is ensured through two regional central banks, the Banque centrale des Etats de l'Afrique de l'Ouest (BCEAO) and the Banque des Etats d'Afrique Centrale (BEAC). These operate on a parallel basis and issue their separate currencies, which are freely convertible on a one-to-one basis through the inter-banking system. The overall unity of the CFA Franc Zone, its stability and convertibility result from the role played by France: the CFA was pegged to the franc at a fixed parity and its convertibility was guaranteed by the French Treasury. Reserves of BCEAO and BEAC member states are kept there in operation accounts, which may incur overdrafts. Integration within UEMOA appears totally dependent on the future of the CFA zone, now pegged, through the guarantee of the French Treasury, to the euro.[13] In recent years, the civil war in Côte d'Ivoire, has stressed the limitations to integration when a key player fails to maintain its commitment – Côte d'Ivoire accounted for 40 per cent of UEMOA's total gross domestic product (GDP) until 2002. Internal instability in Côte d'Ivoire has severely undermined the fabric of the union: the flow of migrants, a key component of interactions between coastal and Sahelian member states has become considerably restrained by xenophobia and the split between north and south; with the decline of the economy of Côte d'Ivoire, the process of macroeconomic convergence and the programme towards a common external tariff have been severely hampered. Most importantly, rumours of a possible devaluation of the CFA have been spreading, along with the fear that, unlike in 1994, it might, this time, mean a break-up of UEMOA's monetary base. Were it not for the French Treasury's ongoing guarantees, the CFA's international convertibility, its credibility and the immediate future of UEMOA would be even bleaker.[14]

BLOC-BUILDING AND RESOURCE CAPTURE

In March 2002, the executive Secretary of the UN Economic Commission for Africa complained that only five Sub-Saharan African states belonged to a single regional agreement, while 27 were members of two, and 18 belonged to three or more.[15] Overlapping membership of IGOs and Regional Agreements with competing objectives reflects on the politics of bloc-building as much as on the scramble for resource capture and international patronage. Concomitant membership of several groupings often appears of little practical consequence since policies are episodically implemented and financial contributions irregularly paid. Far from being an inextricable source of conflicts, overlapping membership can be negotiated and translates into additional opportunities for the pursuit of conference diplomacy, participation in externally funded ventures or support from regional or extra-regional powers. Resource-driven regionalism was best epitomised by the huge success of SADCC's annual fund-raising conferences until donors suddenly reappraised their commitment in 1990–91 (Anglin, 1991).[16] Allegiance to regional or extra-regional powers has historically been a key aspect in the uneasy interactions between the francophone member states of CEAO/UEMOA and what they saw as a Nigeria-dominated ECOWAS. Similarly, during the 1958–70 period, membership of the Council of Entente made sense due to its members' acknowledgement of the leadership of Côte d'Ivoire president Félix Houphouët-Boigny – he used the Council and its compensation fund as a *machine de guerre* against Senegalese president Senghor's advocacy of federalism in Francophone West Africa or, later, Nigerian aspirations to regional influence (Bach, 1981).[17]

Institutional expansion and overlapping membership of RECs also reflects on the transfer of competing norms and models from Europe and the US. Thus, in 1994, the treaties establishing UEMOA and CEMAC were patterned on the Maastricht Treaty and its convergence criteria (Claeys and Sindzingre, 2004); earlier, the establishment of CEAO had involved its adoption of plans for a common agricultural policy inspired from the (then) European Economic Community, while, in the 1980s, the definition of SADCC's attempt to reduce dependency on South Africa claimed to emulate the low-key functional approach adopted in the early days of European construction. In December 1999, five ECOWAS member states who did not belong to UEMOA's common currency zone committed themselves to emulate the post-Maastricht macroeconomic convergence model so as to launch a second West African Monetary Zone. Recently too, the emulation of Europe's model of trans-frontier cooperation through a replication of its 'euro-regions' has become the object of extensive discussions in West Africa (Dahou, 2004).

The role of Europe as a model, a regulator and a key historical player on the African continent shows no sign of abating in so far as RECs are concerned. Their formal endorsement of European models is naturally inspired by the achievements of European construction. In addition to this, normative transfers are nurtured by the inter-regional dimension of European development policies. In this respect, it may be predicted that the ratification of the EU–ACPs Cotonou Agreement will unleash an unprecedented 'market' for normative and institutional transfers across the continent: the Agreement plans for the negotiation of (Regional) Economic Partnership Agreements and this will require substantial adjustments on the part of all RECs. Similarly, the US-inspired Africa Growth and

Opportunity Act and the hub-spoke model of interactions that it conveys seek to instil their own transfers of norms and regionalisation patterns. The endorsement and entrenchment of (technical, health or environmental) standards and procedures within inter-regional agreements has become of strategic significance in the conduct of multilateral negotiations by the EU and US. In Africa and in other world regions, this is not the least significant dimension to the current scramble for institutional expansion and bloc-building.

CONCLUSION: REGIONALISATION WITHOUT INTEGRATION

The notion of regionalism and its distinction from that of regionalisation helps to bridge a previous gap between the discussion of European 'construction' and the understanding of processes that, as observed in Africa, combine the formal preservation of territorial *status quo* with weak territorial control. Students of European integration conventionally assume the pre-eminence of aggregative interactions to assess the build-up of 'regionness'; conversely, in Africa, regionalist projects are commonly disconnected from patterns of regionalisation; in addition, regionalisation tends to proceed through state failure or its unwillingness to assert territorial control. The formal stability of boundary-lines and the deeply fragmented political map of the continent reflect on the weakness of regional integration and regionalism as supranational or transnational projects. Integration proceeds exclusively from the continuation of arrangements underscored by hegemonic domination and inherited from the colonial period. Elsewhere, the revival of regionalism is most commonly associated with sub-national strategies; these enhance the contrast between the day-to-day realities of fragmentary territorial control and cognitive representations of regionalism as a grand pan-African ideal.

In stark contrast with the reified landscape of African regionalism, a multiplicity of trans-frontier networks carve *de facto* regional spaces that operate through cognitive bonds and remain largely independent from territorial affiliations. With the exception of hub-spoke regional arrangements and transactions around South Africa, regionalisation relates to processes, which do not proceed from transfers of sovereignty nor result from the dynamism of multinational or transnational corporations. Regionalisation in Africa reflects primarily on the expansive dynamics of trans-state and trans-frontier networks which, depending on time and circumstances are associated with strategies ranging from survival to accumulation and, not least, state capture. Whereas trans-frontier interactions simply involve crossing boundary-lines, trans-state interactions combine this capacity with the ability to penetrate state institutions – controls assigned to state authorities are nullified through negotiation or avoided through complicities.

Trans-state networks simultaneously challenge the institutionalisation of the state and its territorial control. They promote regionalisation through their exploitation of the opportunities offered by the (customs, fiscal, normative or monetary) disparities that materialise along boundary-lines. For this very reason trans-state networks and lobbies have no interest in the harmonisation of policies under the aegis of formal regional institutions. Trans-state regional lobbies share a strong interest in the preservation of good relations between neighbouring states, but have little to gain from the implementation of sub-regional programmes towards the liberalisation of customs and tariff barriers: these are indeed a direct challenge to the rent-seeking opportunities associated with the preservation of (fiscal or tariff) barriers and/or the establishment of (formal or informal) checkpoints (Bach, 1997).

The reluctance of most African governments towards effective transfers of sovereignty and their inability to enforce commonly agreed policies stimulate debilitating patterns of regionalisation. Their stringent adherence to the preservation of national sovereignty and territorial *status quo* nurtures the formation of trans-boundary spaces in a context also marked by the dilution of inter-state relations into socio-ethnic and religious networks. Trans-state regionalisation mirrors the dynamics of deterritorialisation and deinstitutionalisation that are at work within most states. In Africa, regionalisation proceeds first and foremost from a recomposition of state–society interactions that negates the aggregative ambitions assigned to regionalism. In order to be meaningful, regional institution-building demands capacity-building.

NOTES

1. Africa is sometimes presented as the world's latest 'energy frontier'. Deep-water drilling technology has favoured a stream of new discoveries in Nigeria, Guinea-Bissau, Sao Tome and Principe, Chad, the Sudan and Mauritania.
2. Moroccan claims over Western Sahara illustrate the price to be paid for formally claiming sovereignty over an adjacent territory. Morocco has kept away from OAU meetings since 1984 and, despite an ongoing UN mediation, the international status of Western Sahara is still in limbo.
3. See the text of the treaty on <www.africa-union.org> (accessed 15 September 2004).
4. See the Constitutive Act of the AU on <www.africa-union.org> (accessed 20 September 2004).
5. Members of the Pan-African Parliament are elected or nominated by their national assemblies. National representation is based on strict equity (five seats per country), with the result that Nigeria (137 million inhabitants) and Sao Tome and Principe (181,000 inhabitants) have the same numbers of seats.
6. The intergovernmental nature and scarce competencies of regional assemblies in Latin America cannot be dissociated from a context where 'the election, authority and survival of the governments are independent from parliamentary will' (Malamoud and de Souza, 2004, 16).

7. Current member states are Djibouti, Ethiopia, Kenya, Somalia, Sudan, Uganda and (since 1993) Eritrea.

8. It is at the instigation of the Nigerian president Ibrahim Babangida that, in May 1990, ECOWAS heads of states resolved to form a Standing Mediation Committee (SMC); Nigeria's role was equally preeminent when the SMC agreed to form, in August 1990 a Cease-Fire Monitoring Group (ECOMOG) with the mission of ordering a cease-fire in Liberia, establishing an interim government and holding a general election within a year. Seven years later this objective was (partly and temporarily) achieved.

9. The new ECOWAS organs are the Mediation and Security Council, the Defence and Security Commission and the Council of Elders. The Protocol also calls for the establishment of a standard force of specially trained and equipped forces (a battalion) drawn from all 15 ECOWAS states.

10. The SADC parliamentary forum, an autonomous institution within SADC, has shown a notable commitment to human rights and democratic norms and standards, perhaps because it is open to parliamentarians from all member states.

11. In August 2004, COMESA announced that plans for launching its FTA by December 2004 (the original deadline of October 2002 was only met by nine states) were being postponed until December 2005. Within SADC, a FTA is not scheduled to begin operating before 2012.

12. South Africa's economy alone accounts for some 72 per cent of the GDP of the 14 member states of the SADC. South Africa also accounts for about 75 per cent of its total exports, 84 per of its exports. It also produces nearly 84 per cent of the electricity consumed in Southern Africa and hosts 60 per cent of the sub-region's railway network.

13. The European Council agreed on 28 November 1998 that the existing Franc Zone monetary arrangements could continue, but the decision established patterns and procedures amounting to a *de facto* empowerment of the EU as an agency of restraint. France continues to guarantee the stability of CFA, and retains control over the management of the operating account hosted within the French Ministry of Finance (Direction du Trésor). France is also required to inform the European Central Bank (ECB) and the EU Financial and Economic Committee about any adjustment of the euro/CFA parity. Reforms likely to affect the nature, scope and membership of the CFA zone now require prior approval by the European Council (after advice from the ECB and the European Commission).

14. In September 2004, BCEAO launched the conversion of 600 million banknotes into new ones within a relatively short period of time (15 September–1 December 2004), with the hope that this should undercut the circulation of 'dirty' money originating from the looting of BCEAO agencies in Côte d'Ivoire; *Le Monde*, 5–6 September 2004.

15. See <www.uneca.org/eca_resources/> (accessed 24 September 2004).

16. By 1990, external funding accounted for 90 per cent of the US$8 billion spent on 600 projects sponsored by SADC since its establishment in 1981.

17. The Council of Entente (Côte d'Ivoire, Burkina Faso, Bénin, Niger and, after 1966, Togo) was originally founded by Houphouët-Boigny, in 1958, to counter federalist ambitions of Senegal and (present-day) Mali; the Council remained a privileged instrument for the conduct of the West African diplomacy of Côte d'Ivoire until Houphouët-Boigny's support to the Biafran secessionist attempt (1967–70) became a source of sharp disagreements.

12
The Middle East:
Regional Instability and Fragmentation

Helena Lindholm Schulz and Michael Schulz

When the Declaration of Principle between Israel and the Palestine Liberation Organisation (PLO) was signed, in September 1993, hopes for change towards closer cooperation in the Middle East ensued. Regionalisation was gradually seen as an embryonic, but developing process. A decade later, Israelis and Palestinians are bitterly engulfed in a vicious cycle of violence. The US–UK led coalition war against Iraq and the following occupation have had far-reaching repercussions in the region at large. Middle East regionalisation seems to be an illusion with no real basis. The question is why the Middle East has such difficulties to build a regional project in a globalising world where many other regional systems are making strides forward.

Recent studies on regional cooperation, regional integration and regionalism (Miller, 2003; Schulz et al., 2001) often leave the Middle East out, or point to the bleak experiences so far of regional cooperation in the region. In fact, in 2004, the Middle East as a region appeared as far as ever from regionalisation, and as the exception to the rule. The Middle East as a region is today heavily influenced by US politics and interests defined in the new US doctrine toward the Middle East and most visible in its war and subsequent rule of Iraq. Also, the American administration under George W. Bush has applied staunch support for Israel, further diminishing prospects for resumed peace talks. However, it is also clear that the American policy faces difficulties. The current chaos in Iraq is a sign, if not yet evidence, that an imposed American regime is interpreted as imperialism to be fought.

Despite the preoccupations with the role of American rule and state-centred interests, regionalist discussions have not left the Middle East completely untouched.

One potential explanation to the lack of Middle East regionalisation is given by Miller who argues that: 'despite the post-Cold War expectations for a "New Middle East", which will engage the region in peaceful cooperation, the ME is still unstable and prone to conflict. My argument is that the underlying source of these dangers is the high extent of the state-to-nation imbalance in the region as compared to most other regions' (Miller, 2003, 153).

Challenges against state-structures are strong in the Middle East. In addition, several states in the region have pursued territorial claims outside existing state-boundaries. This logic, coined as *Westphalian*, places the region more in the corner of violent conflict. During the 1990s, we witnessed a process of conflict reduction (that is negative peace), although not genuine conflict resolution. There was a shift, however, from the Cold War logic when states in the region were acting more in the role of puppets to the superpowers (Miller, 2003, 157). Today's logic appears much more unpredictable and thus perhaps more dangerous. Although US ambitions belong to the most intriguing aspects of the contemporary geopolitical landscape, it is clear that it is not possible for the US to simply dictate its power in the Middle East. In fact, the lesson from the US intervention in Iraq ought to be that US interference causes further fragmentation rather than stability. Thus, although the Middle East is heavily influenced by American interests and ambitions, the interests of states as well as non-state actors in the region challenge American interests and underline the difficulties of the one remaining superpower in imposing its will. Uncertain state structures at odds with the American quest for global power including a strong foothold in the Middle East implies that 'regionalisation' appears to be a utopian project at best. However, there have been projects aiming to greater regional cooperation and it therefore appears appropriate to investigate these ambitions.

This chapter, therefore, aims to investigate historical as well as contemporary attempts, institutions and processes in the Middle East that aimed to or aim to further regional cooperation or regionalisation. We will do so through scrutinising existing regimes of regional cooperation as well as contemporary debates and proposals on greater regional integration.

ARABISM AS REGIONALISATION?

Attempts at regional cooperation and regionalisation have in fact flourished in the Arab world, although these attempts have not implied the establishment of a climate of functioning regional cooperation or exchange. Most attempts were, until the 1990s, produced on the lines of ideological pan-Arabism,[1] rather than on pragmatic politico-economic interest, or visions of trade as peace-promoting.

The ideological foundation of pan-Arabism has been to merge the 'artificially divided' Arab states. According to the various brands of Arabism, there exists a common Arab nation, based on the Arabic language, independent of state borders. The Arab League, founded in Alexandria in 1945, was the first initiative of a concrete organisation aiming at realising the ideas of Arab nationalism. The Arab League was also the first attempt at regional cooperation in the region. The prime item on the agenda of the Arab League was to 'liberate Palestine'. During those years, the Palestine question was a focus of Arabism and Arab politics and served as a factor that ideologically and politically united the Arab world. Although the Palestine question has remained top priority for the Arab states, it is also a fact that the Arab states soon came to practise their own politics vis-à-vis the issue of the liberation of Palestine.

Contradictions between state-building and Arabism soon came to the fore, however. Serious divisions emerged between the Arab states, on what kind of unitary state that would be the goal. The only concrete confederative state to be established was the United Arab Republic consisting of Egypt and Syria, declared in 1958 and brought to an abrupt end in 1961.

Under the umbrella of the Arab League, several institutions and organisations have been formed and several agreements on cooperation have been signed, on security as well as economic matters.

Economic integration

When it comes to economic exchange, the Middle East is extremely 'unintegrated'. The bulk of Arab trade is with Organisation for Economic Cooperation and Development countries, and primarily the European Union (EU). In world trade, the Middle East has, despite the oil factor, been a rather marginal region. The extent of Middle Eastern trade in the world amounts to only 4 per cent (cf. Çarkoglu et al., 1998, 86). In 2003, a strong price of oil contributed to rising prospects for Middle East economies at large. In addition, the war in Iraq appears to have contributed to stronger Middle East (and particular Gulf) economies, as oil revenues have been stronger than anticipated. Growth is however diversified and it is the oil economies that have benefited from recent upward trends and greater integration into the world economy.

In 1995, Arab exports of commodities to other Arab countries were a mere 4.2 per cent of their local trade and intra-Arab imports stood at 5.9 per cent (*MEED*, 4 July 1997). During the 1990s, Arab economies have opened up, but the pattern of low intra-regional trade remains at the same level (Euro-Med Partnership, 2002). If trade in services is included, the picture changes somewhat since particularly the remittances and to some extent tourism and aid have become important entries in the current balances for several Arab countries. For Israel, the US and the North American Free Trade Agreement region are important trading partners. Also the East Asian economies have become of larger importance to Israel (cf. Padoan, 1997, 187).

Of larger importance than trade when it comes to integration was the oil boom that resulted in *de facto* economic integration and more pragmatic relationships between the Arab states (see Richards and Waterbury, 1996; Owen, 1992). The Organisation of Petroleum Exporting Countries and primarily Saudi Arabia played an important role through the massive transfer of resources to the poorer Arab states (Padoan, 1997, 192; cf. Fischer, 1993; Çarkoglu et al., 1998). The redistribution of oil money, or the 'recycling of the petrodollar' meant a new form of economic integration and deepened interdependence. At the same time, however, international aid flows have by far superseded any intra-Arab aid politics. The relations became more 'normal', that is diplomacy, negotiations, treaties and agreements were made by sovereign states and not as part of Arabism. Thus, although oil flows in a way fostered regional integration, they also confirmed the state structure at the cost of ideological Arabism.

Labour migration implied another form of integration, demonstrating how people and population flows need to be taken into account when assessing for integration prospects (cf. Choucri, 1997, 96; cf. Fischer, 1993; Çarkoglu et al., 1998). Egypt, Jordan, then North Yemen and the Palestinians sent labour to the smaller oil states. For the sending countries, remittances were an important source of foreign exchange until the Gulf War in the early 1990s. For Egypt and Yemen, the worth of what was sent home by workers abroad exceeded the worth of any export commodity. Migration also contributed to the reduction of unemployment in home countries, but on the other hand created labour shortages and could undermine export-led development strategies (for example Richards and Waterbury, 1996).

The recession of the oil economies during the 1990s led to a reduction of the number of guestworkers in the Gulf. In connection to the Gulf War of 1990–91, this trend was reinforced, as the Gulf states tended to favour Asian labour rather than Arab workers. The Gulf states expelled Palestinian, Jordanian and Yemenite guestworkers as a punishment for Jordan, Yemen and PLO positions in the Gulf War. Thus, migration patterns are to an increasing extent globalised rather than regional, and one important prerequisite for regional integration appears to have reached a limit.

One reason often put forward as a factor, which has effectively hindered regional cooperation, is the lack of economic restructuring (cf. Fischer, 1993, 431ff.; Çarkoglu et al., 1998). In addition, the economic performance of the region as a whole was rather dim during the 1980s and 1990s. Average annual growth over the 1990s was largely negative. In the early 2000s, the crisis appears to have withered as stronger growth (although highly differentiated between the countries) is the case. However, the economic crisis that hit the Middle East in the 1990s resulted in a process of economic liberalisation of the Arab world. Gradually, Arab states have abandoned economic nationalism and import substitution strategies for neoliberal attempts and privatisation. In several cases, the International Monetary Fund (IMF) is the author of structural adjustment programmes, as for example in the cases of Egypt and Jordan.[2] Still, however, Arab economies are heavily protected. In addition, the gradual liberalisation strategies and integration into the world market occur at highly differentiated levels between the Arab countries. As part of this strategy, initiatives to promote joint ventures and private investment have been taken.

Thus, pan-Arabism between 1945 and 1970 in a sense provided one form of political regional identity, which served as a basis for regional organisations and cooperative projects. However, this worked more on the level of ideology and discourse than on the level of practical consequences. State-building projects necessitated state nationalisms and the promotion of state interests. Most of the cooperation that did take place under the umbrella of pan-Arabism was therefore based more on state-to-state cooperation. In the 1970s, this trend was reinforced. Now one form of integration emerged as the result of the oil boom, with cooperation enhanced in terms of redistribution of aid and labour migration.

Political integration

Neither has there been any coherent political integration. However, in relation to the conflict with Israel, the Arab League has at times behaved as one actor, at least on the level of political statements. Shown in the wars between the Arab states and Israel, the common statements of Arab states and from the Arab League, the impediments for independent action determined by ideological unity, the boycott of Israeli products and of contact with Israel, there has been an idea of political unity.

Under the surface of pan-Arabism, however, there was always mistrust and a serious ideological polarisation between the so-called progressive leadership in the Arab republics and the Arab monarchies. In 1967 the war between Israel and the Arab states provided a serious blow to pan-Arabism. During the 1970s, rather than progress along the lines of pan-Arabism and rather than the formation of a regionally integrated entity, the state system was gradually consolidated (for example Luciani, 1990; Owen, 1992). State interests and state nationalism took a *de facto* lead over pan-Arabism, although Arabism continued to play an ideological role.

Other forms of regional integration have taken the form of formation of sub-regional blocs based on closer interests.

Sub-regional cooperation: the Gulf Cooperation Council

The establishment of the Gulf Cooperation Council (GCC) in 1981 was a response to the Iranian Revolution of 1978–79, which was seen as a threat in the Gulf region. The GCC (Bahrain, Kuwait, Oman, Qatar, Saudi Arabia and the United Arab Emirates) basically served as a security regime. Contrary to the Arab League that had Israel as its main enemy, the GCC was formed as a response to other, geographically closer threats.

Because of the common enemy, the fact that all states are sheikdoms with politics based on family projects, with small populations that are difficult to mobilise, and with enormous oil wealth, there is a common identity or political structure which has served to facilitate integration. Ideologically, the GCC has a conservative Arab-Islamic basis combined with regional traditions and tribal identification.

Despite this, the 'common security' has failed to materialise into a joint defence (cf. Joffé, 1998, 54). Instead, the Gulf region is still heavily internationally dependent for its security, a dependency that was augmented with the first Gulf War, when Kuwait and Saudi Arabia turned to the US for help. The failure of the 'Gulf + 2' organisation (the Gulf states plus Egypt and Syria) which was formed after the war, further pushed the Gulf states towards the West for military protection. The US was now permanently stationed in the Gulf. The increased international security dependence also triggered an arms race in the region (Marr, 1998, 94). Intra-Gulf disputes over the preferred security regime (that is, to continue to depend on the US or to opt for regional security through a pact with Iran) augmented regional tensions. Despite their dependency on American security, the Gulf states came out against the US intervention in Iraq in 2003.

There are also clear intentions of economic integration in the Gulf. One of the aims of the GCC is to create a free trade area (FTA), but 'national interests' serve as impediments. One of the challenges for the GCC is the relationship to the EU, since a large part of the GCC export is made up of oil and petrol-chemical products to the Union. In late 1997, the GCC decided to form a tariffs union. Another project of 'real integration' is the United Arab Emirates-sponsored initiative to create a cross-border energy grid in the southern parts of the Gulf.

The EU represents about 25 per cent of Gulf trade. Japan is another major trading partner, representing 18 per cent (Aliboni, 1997, 218; Salamé, 1998, 36).

Sub-regional cooperation: the Arab Maghreb Union (AMU)

The North African countries are in a somewhat specific position, given their particular interests in relations with the EU, which are in part a result of the legacy of French colonial rule. There is also the issue of proximity and sharing the Mediterranean with countries of southern Europe. The North African states, including Egypt, are members of Arab, Islamic as well as African regional organisations.[3]

The AMU was established in 1989 with the aim to create a customs union along the same lines as the European Community. The West Sahara conflict was left outside the framework and member states were to respect each other's territorial integrity (Zartman, 1997, 216). The AMU was meant to be an area with open borders for free movement of goods, services, capital and persons, as well as cultural cooperation. The AMU attempts to stimulate trade between the member states, to increase the non-traditional export and reduce imports.[4] AMU members trade primarily with Western Europe, which constitutes 65 per cent of the total AMU trade (Aliboni, 1997, 218). Intra-Maghreb trade has been limited.

Relations with Europe also include the migration from the Northern African states to Europe. This is one reason behind the scepticism in some EU countries towards European cooperation with the AMU. Contemporary EU debates on refugee camps must be seen as part of EU–North African relations. Integration has also been hindered by political crises, such as different views on Morocco's relations to Western Sahara.

One further difficulty concerning Magrebi integration is differences between the countries. Whereas Morocco and Tunisia have by and large successfully completed their IMF-sponsored structural adjustment programme, Algeria still declines an IMF programme. Morocco and Tunisia have also diversified their production structures. Such differences are one of the reasons behind the fact that the AMU countries do not bargain with the EU as a collective actor. Given the political turmoil in Algeria, Morocco has proceeded as the major bilateral partner for the EU, and discussions have been held about a FTA between Morocco and the EU to be followed by the other Maghreb countries (Salamé, 1998, 37; Joffé, 1998). The Euro-Mediterranean Partnership Initiative (see below) is an extension of this agreement.

A dialogue between Southern European and North African countries has been envisaged in the 'five plus five' dialogue – Algeria, Libya, Mauritania, Morocco and Tunisia on the one hand and France, Italy, Portugal, Spain and Malta on the other. However, there are also Southern European anxieties concerning competition with North African agricultural products on the European market (Salamé, 1998, 38). Morocco and Tunisia have already suffered from the full integration of Spain and Portugal into the EU, which has meant a reduction of agricultural export from Morocco and Tunisia to the EU (Joffé, 1998, 64; Marr, 1998, 95).

To summarise, although sub-regional initiatives have been more concrete than cooperation under the heading of pan-Arabism, all kinds of integration schemes in the Arab world have remained low-level. In terms of integration, little has been achieved as part of regional organisations. Political conflicts, colliding power ambitions and tensions related to issues of regional hegemony have impeded Arab integration, as has heavy state control over economies. Also, the ideological tensions between radicalist one-party regimes and conservative monarchies, as well as disputes related to the unequal distribution of resources has served as constraints against deeper forms of integration.

Aarts mentions the following explanations for the lack of successful regional cooperation in the Middle East: the trade pattern largely consists of agriculture and raw materials, implying a lack of complementarity; there are different economic interests between the Arab states; there is great variation in terms of financial structures; protectionism and state-controlled economies; the lack of attention to economic factors in Arab nationalism (Aarts, 1997, 8ff.). Paradoxically, despite the calls for Arab unity, Arab nationalism has in itself provided an impediment for such unity (ibid., 10). Arab nationalism as a visionary option has further reduced its potential since the 1967 war. In addition, the rentier economies[5] (see Beblewi and Luciani, 1987) have hindered *de facto* integration (Aarts, 1997, 13).

THE PEACE PROCESS AND DIFFERENT VISIONS OF A NEW MIDDLE EAST

A turning point in discussions of regionalisation/regional cooperation in the Middle East was the peace process and the kind of relations that it brought. Through the Declaration of Principles in 1993 and the mutual recognition, optimism followed and new schemes of cooperation on banking, water, tourism, security, highway infrastructure, railways, electricity grids, and so on, were envisioned. Israel's diplomatic standing in the world and in the region improved considerably. The Gulf states supported the abolishment of the secondary and tertiary boycott of Israeli products. Different 'regionalist discourses' related to the peace process all included Israel as a partner to the Arab states.

One of the visionaries behind the ideas of what was called the New Middle East was Shimon Peres, then Israel's Foreign Minister. His ideas were grandiose and envisioned an integrated region with open borders, trade and cooperation that would be of benefit for all. To a large extent, however, the idea was built on Israel's strategic advantages in terms of economic size, comparative advantages in terms of levels of industrialisation, and so on. Therefore, the idea of 'a New Middle East' was met with as much scepticism as it was of enthusiasm. Shimon Peres was not alone in his visions, however. Also the international community favoured different strategies for regional integration. Some of these thoughts came to the fore in the highly profiled economic summits with governmental representatives and business elite. These were part of the multilateral part of the peace process.

The Middle East and North Africa idea

One of the 'regional projects' very much connected to the peace process was the one born in relation to the multilateral working groups, initiated at the Madrid conference in 1991. In addition to the bilateral negotiations[6] set up under the Madrid formula, five multilateral working groups were set up in which issues of regional character were discussed; environmental issues, water, arms control, refugees, and regional development (for details see Peters, 1996). Participants were Egypt, Jordan, Israel, the Palestinians, the Gulf states and the Maghreb countries minus Libya. The US and Russia were co-sponsors of the peace process, and the EU and Japan were observers. Syria and Lebanon were invited but never participated; Syria's position was that there should first be a comprehensive peace, and Lebanon followed the Syrian line. The large-scale and much talked about Middle East summits were part of the multilateral track. When relations turned more frosty from 1996 onwards, the multilateral talks in effect ceased to function. The halted multilateral talks were planned to be resumed in 2000, but this never happened.

Linked to this is the US-sponsored Middle East and North Africa (MENA) concept. This project has also given rise to the idea of 'Middle Easternism'. The heart of the matter was whether Israel would become a fully integrated member of the Middle East or not. Apart from the political text of this discourse there were also different economic motives and interests. For many Arab parties, the incentive would be to attract foreign capital and investments rather than to promote a FTA. A Middle East FTA, was seen as a road to Israeli hegemony (cf. Abdel-Fadil, 1997, 130). By Arab critiques, this project was seen as a US and Israeli aim to consolidate Israel's position in the Middle East from an economic point of view. That is, Israel would become part of the Middle East, which would, according to Arab critiques allow for an Israeli hegemonic position. An inclusion of Israel into the region and a shift towards a Middle Eastern rather than an Arab definition of the region would, according to this perspective threaten the Arabness of the Arab world. From this point of view, the peace process represented not 'integration' but rather 'fragmentation' of the Arab world.[7] According to this perspective, 'normalisation' of relations should be a result of the peace process and not precede final peace agreements. Sceptics on the Israeli side argued that there is much less for Israel in the 'regional integration paradigm' than conventionally argued (cf. Korany, 1997, 138).

From the perspective of Israelis (and Arabs) advocating this project, 'the New Middle East' rather represented a vision of a region characterised by mutually beneficial cooperation in order to foster peace and development. Behind this concept lies the conviction in interdependence theory, as well as the idea of pooling resources in order to achieve economies of scale beyond the nation-state borders (Korany, 1997, 137).

The multilateral working group on economic development is the one which resulted in the most visible attention through the much talked about large-scale regional conferences in Casablanca (1994), Amman (1995), Cairo (1996) and Doha (1997). The MENA Summit process aimed to encourage private-sector-led regional cooperation, to institutionalise cooperation and to integrate Israel into the Middle Eastern region. A Monitoring Committee was established in 1994 to identify priorities and develop projects. The Core Parties (Egypt, Israel, Jordan and the Palestinian Authority) were given a crucial role in this process. Until the spring of 1996, the Monitoring Committee promoted a high number of activities. Among the projects within the working group on economic development was the Middle East Development Bank (MEDB), decided upon in practice in Amman 1995, the Middle East–Mediterranean Travel and Tourist Association, the establishment of projects in the realms of transport, energy, and so on. Since 1996 and the gradual deterioration of Israeli–Palestinian relations, the work of the Committee has become more difficult and most of the initiatives were brought to a halt.

Israel, Egypt, Jordan and the Palestinians are defined as the regional partners in the MEDB, controlling 4 per cent each of the bank's equity. The United States was to be the largest shareholder, followed by Japan and Russia. The process of realising the institution, however, was difficult. The US saw the bank as an equivalent of the European Bank of Reconstruction and Development and as an important platform for fostering more 'normal' relations, and from there on stability and peace in the region. Despite American enthusiasm, the Americans never fulfilled their financial commitments. The Europeans were much more sceptical from early on. As the relations between the parties deteriorated, the Bank has not been fully realised.

The third MENA Economic Conference in Cairo in November 1996 clearly had a different setting since the increasing political tensions within the region and in particular the halting Palestinian–Israeli peace process marked the atmosphere before and during the meeting.[8] The fourth regional conference in Doha in 1997 was downgraded from a summit to a conference. Israeli politics under Benyamin Netanyahu had returned a climate of animosity and enmity, meaning that several Arab countries decided to stay away from the Doha conference, despite American pressure.

Economic integration momentarily exhibits a number of problems apart from political. Most Middle Eastern states choose their trading partners from outside the region. A potential complementarity pattern would consist of highly value added agricultural and capital-intensive light manufacturing products as well as technology from Israel, while the Arab side would concentrate on food products, oil, and labour-intensive manufacturing goods. There is a low level of complementarity (cf. Fischer et al., 1993; Çarkoglu, 1998, 128) between the Arab countries, and when Israel is brought into the equation, the differences in technology and economy are so vast that there is a risk that they create structures of dominance rather than mutual benefit.

Under the umbrella of multilateralism, progress was made also in changing perceptions of security. In October 1994, it was decided that a regional crisis resolution centre was to be established in one of the countries in the region. This idea was followed in 1995, when the multilateral working group on arms control decided to establish a regional security centre in Amman. However, the years since 1996 and particularly since the outbreak of the *al-aqsa intifada* in 2000, implied a step back towards more 'normal Middle East politics'.

Reaction: revival of Arabism

The impasse of the peace process led to a crisis of the embryonic Middle Eastern cooperation. At the Arab League meeting in Cairo in 1997, member states decided to freeze the process of normalisation with Israel. At the same time, the primary boycott was reinforced and all negotiations within the multilateral track were suspended (Shtayyeh, 1998, 28).

According to this view, Arab integration should be revitalised as an alternative to Middle Easternism or the MENA concept.[9] The prime mover in the talks calling for the establishment of an Arab common market has been Egypt, underlining Egypt's ambitions to play a significant role in different integration schemes (cf. Guazzone, 1997, 249). Eighteen Arab countries have endorsed the programme. The Arab Economic Unity Council and the Arab League Economic and Social Council have declared the goal of establishing an Arab common market, the Greater Arab FTA, within ten years starting from 1998. Through a cut by 10 per cent per annum of customs tariffs and the tariff-like charges, free trade is to be implemented by the year 2007.

Europe and the Middle East

In early 2001, Chris Patten, the External Relations Commissioner of the EU, stated that: 'The Mediterranean is our "near abroad" on our Southern flank. Thus, it should enjoy a special place in our external relations' (Patten, 2001). European relations with the Middle East have however proven highly fragmented, both vis-à-vis the Palestinian–Israeli conflict and vis-à-vis Iraq, as Great Britain has sided with the US, with other major EU states rather emphasising the role of the international community and the United Nations.

Compared to the US, in terms of security Europe has since the 1950s always had a backbench role vis-à-vis the Middle East. As a trading partner, Europe by far outweighs the United States.

The Euro-Mediterranean Partnership Initiative or the Barcelona process[10] was created to transform relations between Europe and the Middle East/ North Africa and to integrate the Mediterranean countries in a European framework. The Barcelona Declaration signed in 1995 called for the establishment of a common area of peace and stability, economic and financial partnership, as well as partnership in social, cultural and human affairs. A Euro-Mediterranean FTA is to be established by the year of 2010[11] and about $6 billion for the years 1995–99 in EU aid for the developing countries of the area was to be injected. Free trade is to be implemented through a network of bilateral free trade agreements. Such agreements have been signed between the EU on the one hand, and Tunisia, Israel,

Morocco, Jordan and the PLO on the other. The last mentioned is an interim agreement and it has been in force since July 1997. The bilateral agreement between the EU and Tunisia has been in force since March 1998. With Israel an interim agreement is applied until the ratification process of the real one is finalised (cf. Joffé, 1998). In January 2004, a trade agreement was signed between Syria and the EU (*MEED*, 2–8 January 2004).

The Barcelona conference established a three-tier *partnership*: a political and security partnership, an economic and financial partnership, and a social and cultural partnership. The economic and financial aspects include the gradual establishment of a FTA. Structural adjustment will be followed by attempts to alleviate negative social consequences. Political and security partnership includes enhancement of stability, fostering of democratic institutions, preventive diplomacy, confidence- and security-building measures, and joint efforts against transnational threats, such as terrorism. The third tier, social and cultural partnership, takes into account the encouragement of inter-cultural dialogue, civil society development, and learning about and fostering 'Mediterranean cultural heritage'. The Euro-Mediterranean formula explicitly includes issues of human rights, civil society and culture, and thus differ from the MENA concept. This might also be seen as the institutionalisation of a Western discourse advocating 'democracy', 'good governance', and so on.

At the Malta conference in April 1997, voices were heard from the southern Mediterranean countries that European commitment might not be whole-hearted, given EU barriers to agricultural import, immigration restrictions and reluctance to involve itself in the peace process (*MEED*, 11 April 1997). One of the reasons for EU involvement is its interest in keeping migration from the southern Mediterranean region at bay. In other regards, the Middle East was seen as a threat from a EU perspective and particularly as a security threat (Salamé, 1998, 38). In this sense, the Partnership Initiative is directly contradicted by the Schengen Agreements, the Trevi Accords and the Dublin Agreement, all of which served to severely restrict the free movement of non-EU citizens.

The Euro-Med Partnership Initiative is built upon an older idea, a proposal pushed forward by Spain and Italy in 1990 called the Conference on Security and Cooperation in the Mediterranean, to include all the countries bordering the Mediterranean (cf. Joffé, 1998, 57). The main instrument used in the Euro-Med Partnership is bilateral free trade agreements between individual states and entities and the EU. The objective is that those association agreements will enhance possibilities for further integration.

In February 2004, a free trade agreement, the Agadir Agreement, was signed by Jordan, Egypt, Tunisia and Morocco. This agreement was seen by Commissioner Patten as a step toward the realisation of a Euro-Med FTA.

REGIONAL INSTABILITY AND US INTERVENTIONISM

In the summer of 2000, the peace process between Israelis and Palestinians was brought to a halt, as the Camp David negotiations collapsed. The outbreak of the *al-aqsa intifada* and escalating violence brought the parties back to hardened positions, fear and insecurity. In January 2001, renewed attempts were made to continue the process, but these were to no avail. With a new Israeli government headed by Likud leader Ariel Sharon, Israel's policy vis-à-vis Palestinian violence was harsh military repression. Suicide attacks committed by Hamas as well as Fatah-related groups reached unprecedented levels. The Palestinian leader Yasir Arafat found himself virtually under house arrest in his compound in Ramallah and the Palestinian Authority, although pressed by the international community to reform its political structure, became incapacitated. The international community pushed for a Roadmap for Peace, but violence continued. This is not the place to reiterate various stages of the conflict, suffice it to say that the flawed peace process means that regional initiatives that include Israel are far-fetched at the moment. The ongoing Israeli occupation of the West Bank and Gaza combined with American (temporary) rule of Iraq, leaving the Arab states with a glaring feeling of neo-colonialism.

One current trend is therefore an inward-looking Arab region, searching for 'internal' solutions to political and economic problems, combined with growing instability and violence. There is a great deal of frustration because of external interference, of which the chaos in Iraq throughout 2004 was a sign. American ambitions in the region are seen as a threat and as a continuation of age-old imperialism and foreign control. However, the Arab states remain exceedingly fragmented, as shown by the abrupt cancellation of the Arab League summit held in Tunisia in April 2004.

Part of the US Middle East strategy is however a reinvention of regional initiatives. The US in December 2002 launched a Middle East Partnership Initiative (MEPI), ultimately aiming to reform the Middle East. The components of MEPI are economic reform, good governance, free press, democratisation, education and women's rights. Education, knowledge and gender equality were also stressed in the UNDP *Arab Human Development Report* (UNDP, 2002). The economic part includes, liberalisation, privatisation and regionalisation (*MEED*, 19 September 2003). In the aftermath of the war in Iraq, the US initiated the idea of a US–Middle East FTA. Free trade and economic liberalisation were seen as key factors through which to reform and transform the region.

An even larger initiative is what is called the Greater Middle East Initiative, proposed by the US prior to the G-8 meeting in June 2004, but played down at the meeting due to rapidly decreasing American credibility in its Iraq involvement. The basic ideas are to remedy the shortcomings in education, gender equality and democracy outlined in the *Arab Human Development Report*. The reaction in the Arab world has been hesitant or outright negative. The initiative is seen as yet another sign of American desires for hegemony and control, based in the neo-conservative ideology of American interests in the Middle East.

CONCLUSION

The Middle East of 2004 was a region of ambivalence and instability. Since the end of the Cold War, the US has become the dominant player in the region. The US is heavily criticised, but at the same time is seen as the only actor that can make a difference. Ill-concealed US attempts at control imply that the most probable short-term scenario is that all international initiatives of free trade, regional integration and promotion of democracy will backlash. In the Arab world, there is a growing sense of American neo-imperialism, and of an American–Israeli alliance. Thus, the Arab states may see further divisions between themselves as well as between them and the international community. Arab states are caught between American hegemony and popular discontent, which is a dangerous combination. US action can be seen as interference in the region, thus creating further instability, fragmentation and, in fact, global insecurity. At the same time, it is difficult to foresee a solution to either the Israeli–Palestinian conflict or the Iraqi predicament without a strong US commitment.

Schemes of regional cooperation have existed as regional initiatives primarily through the Arab League and the assumed notions of a common Arab cultural heritage. In terms of concrete regional integration, however, the record of the Arab League is bleak, and attempts at regional cooperation or integration have all stumbled. Despite this, the Arab League represses the broadest form of regional cooperation in the region. The Arab League is also a form of state-driven regional cooperation. It does not however represent a deep form of economic or political integration. Regional cooperation under the guidance of the Arab League is thin, although a number of institutions and arrangements exist.

Of somewhat more success have been the sub-regional cooperation schemes of AMU and the GCC. The GCC and AMU are also cases of state-driven regional cooperation, rather than market-initiated regionalisation. In the case of the AMU, regional cooperation is a response to development issues and represents strategies to attract global capital and to negotiate better terms of trade with the EU. Security issues on the other hand primarily motivate the GCC, although economic development and economic integration have become further underlined. The GCC and the AMU are also inspired by or pushed by the EU as an example. However, those do not provide for a thorough programme of regionalisation. When it comes to the Arab plus Israel schemes, those flourished for some years during the 1990s and in relation to the peace process. On the discursive or programmatic level, those discussions meant that new ground was broken. However, they did not allow for greater actual integration. Processes that promised greater leeway for regional openings were hampered by the impasse of the peace process.

What also emerged during the peace process were American and European initiatives aiming to create greater regional cooperation. The latest of these is the Greater Middle East Initiative. During the period post-1995, we can talk of an abundance of regional initiatives and the entrance of a new discourse on regional cooperation. The MENA idea, which flourished during the peace process, the Euro-Med initiative and the most recent deliberations on a Greater Middle East Initiative are all cases of regional cooperation initiated outside of the region. Rather than representing an internal process based on the interests, motives and concerns of regional actors, they are attempts at global governance. Regional cooperation is seen as an instrument for peace, democracy and stability and thus as an instrument to rule. Therefore, those initiatives will remain 'thin'. When states believe that participation will enhance economic opportunities, regimes will probably engage in regional arrangements for particular purposes but disregard the rest.

NOTES

1. Both politically and academically, Arab nationalism is a hotly debated issue. For a constructivist re-thinking of Arab nationalism, Gershoni and Jankowski (1997) is highly useful.
2. The oil-producing Gulf states have so far not been subject to IMF programmes.
3. Morocco, however, left the Organisation of African Union (OAU) in 1984, when Polisario/SADR became a member. Egypt is also a member of the OAU.
4. AMU includes Algeria, Liberia, Mauritania, Morocco, Tunisia and since 1994 Egypt.
5. Rentier economies imply that the main source of revenue comes from external sources, such as oil income, or aid, rather than being internally generated via the taxation system.
6. Four sets of bilateral negotiation tracks were established, between Israel and Jordan, the Palestinians, Syria and Lebanon respectively. Initially, Jordanians and Palestinians formed a common negotiation team.
7. On the fragmentation of the Middle East, see Guazzone, 1997 and Joffé, 1998.
8. In September 1996, there was an outbreak of violent clashes between the Israeli Defence Forces and Palestinian protesters and police. The outbreak of violence occurred in relation to the provocative action by Israel's Prime Minister Netanyahu to open another tunnel to the Hasmoean tunnel in Jerusalem's Old City.
9. Arab integration could also be seen as a stepwise approach to regional cooperation on a wider basis, that is Arab integration 'first', 'then' a broader Middle Eastern appraoch (cf. Abdel-Fadil, 1997; Korany, 1997).
10. The Barcelona process, was initiated in 1995 when the EU met together with twelve Middle East/North African partners. The Barcelona process works around a slightly different definition of the region, taking the Mediterranean as a basic principle. The Barcelona process is independent from the peace process, but nevertheless related in both timing and objectives.
11. Agricultural products will be excluded from agreements until 2005 because of internal European differences on the Agricultural Policy of the EU (Joffé, 1998, 60).

13
North America and the Americas: Integration among Unequal Partners

Robert A. Pastor

On the first day of January of 1994, the North American Free Trade Agreement (NAFTA) came into effect. If one judges a free trade area by the size of its product and territory, North America became the largest in the world, larger than the European Union (EU). Yet that fact escaped all but a few analysts. It is widely known that the United States has the world's largest economy, but North America also includes the eighth (Canada) and ninth (Mexico) largest economies as well. Within a decade, trade and investment among the three countries had nearly tripled, and North America had achieved a level of integration (defined as intra-regional trade as a percentage of world trade) that approached Europe's – 57.6 per cent as compared to 61 per cent. In other words, North America had become a formidable and integrated region, comparable in some respects to the EU.

Why then is North America not seen as a region? Or rather why do people tend to consider the 'Americas' as a whole – the entire Western Hemisphere – more of a region than the three countries of North America? There are two answers to these questions. First, there is no clear and agreed definition as to what constitutes a 'region'. Geography is the usual point of departure for thinking about regions, but that begs the question as to *which* geographical unit constitutes a region. Europe has a 'Committee of Regions' (CoR), but each is a sub-national unit. The fact that decision-authority is not given to the CoR, but rather to the Council of Ministers implies that the smallest unit should be the state. That criterion, however, does not help in deciding whether the region should be 'North America' composed of three states, or the Americas, composed of 35 states. We shall address that question in the next section.

A second answer to the question as to why 'North America' is not viewed as a coherent region, particularly as compared to the Americas, is because one of its members – the United States – accounts for more than 85 per cent of the gross product of the region, and the other two members have credible reputations as being independent of – indeed, resistant to – the United States. Mexico has long been considered a leader in Latin America, and its leaders have often been critical of US policies in international forums. Canada, while not as eager to be as defiant as Mexico, nonetheless, is widely regarded for its independent foreign policy – whether in United Nations (UN) peacekeeping efforts or its leadership in negotiating agreements on landmines or the International Criminal Court, despite US opposition to these initiatives. If we define a region in terms of a unified foreign policy, then North America would not qualify. But if it were defined in terms of economic and social integration and a network of bonds of governance – at all levels (national, state, local) and as including both formal and governmental and informal and non-governmental connections – then North America would qualify before the Americas.

North America is such a new entity that few recognise it as such. In contrast, the Americas have a long history even before the Europeans discovered it. Let us therefore proceed first by describing the wider region. Then, we will describe and analyse the evolution of the relationship among the three states and the emergence of North America as a region. Third, we will endeavour to judge whether a common identity is emerging from within the region, and finally, we will define the peculiar 'model' of North America as contrasted with the two other formidable and coherent regions, Europe and East Asia.

THE AMERICAS AS A REGION

Geography defines a region as much, if not more, by its external than by its internal boundaries. The Americas are therefore defined by the two oceans that separate it from Europe and Asia. Those oceans allowed the region's inhabitants to develop independent of Europe and Asia. Columbus punctured that isolation, and from the fifteenth to eighteenth centuries, the 'new world' was redefined by a collision between its past and the background and policies of the colonial powers.

The three main European colonisers – Spain, Great Britain, and France – were very different in the way they approached their colonies, and those differences were accentuated by the kind of native peoples with whom they interacted. The Spanish encountered the two great civilisations of the Americas – the Aztecs and the offspring of the Mayas in Mexico and Central America, and the Incas in the Andean highlands. By and large, the Spanish decapitated and replaced the native monarchs, leaving the vast majority of native peoples in a subservient state. The result was a very stratified and unequal society and an unstable and authoritarian polity. The British encountered sparse nomadic tribes in North America, and the 'Indians' went or were pushed west, leaving the new arrivals free to create their own communities, largely by themselves. Moreover, most of the British, who came to the new world, were not sent by the government to colonise, but rather they sought economic opportunity on their own, or they fled their home country for religious reasons. The result was a much more independent, socially equal, and autonomous region that insisted on self-determination. The French occupied a large expanse in the north of North America. They were mostly hunters, determined to live in their own enclave.

The result of these three distinct strains of colonialism was somewhat paradoxical. The Spanish colonies were the wealthiest and most advanced initially, but that wealth was based on extractive minerals and virtual slavery for the vast majority of the population, and so by the time that the area began to define itself as nations and sought independence, they were more unstable and less advanced than the British colonies, who were democratic and commercial. The French, having lost a war against the British in 1763, were the most insular and defensive (DePalma, 2001).

The first statement about the region as a whole came from a US President in a message to Congress in December 1823. The British government proposed to the United States that together, they should warn France and Spain not to consider re-colonising Latin America. President James Monroe prefe.red to declare unilaterally that the Americas were different and better than the old states of Europe, and that the United States would not accept re-colonisation. The 'Monroe Doctrine' was initially welcomed by Latin America, which feared re-colonisation. Simon Bolivar, 'the great liberator' even called for a Congress in Panama to develop a collective system of defence. That Congress made little progress, in part because the United States showed little interest in it and had neither the capability nor the will to enforce it.

The US war against Mexico (1846–48) led many in Latin America to fear that the United States might replace Spanish imperialism, but internal division within the United States between slave and free states precluded any further international ventures until the turn of the century. By that time, the gap in power between the United States and the rest of Latin America had become chasmic, and the ease with which the United States dislodged Spain from its two remaining colonies – Cuba and Puerto Rico – in 1898 was a terrifying reminder of that gap.

The Spanish-American War (1898) was a turning point for the Americas and for US relations in the hemisphere and the world. The United States was divided as to whether to go to war against Spain, and President William McKinley was granted the authority to do so only after he accepted the Teller Amendment, which declared the independence of Cuba as one of the US goals. That amendment represented the antithesis of imperialism, although only Queen Victoria recognised it at the time. Instead of joining the club of imperialists, the United States was impugning it (Pastor, 1999).

The war extracted the United States from its isolationist cocoon and changed fundamentally the nature of the foreign policy debate in the United States. Up until the war, the isolationists largely prevailed over those who would like for the United States to become imperialist. In the twentieth century, the debate would divide those who wanted to exercise US power unilaterally and those who believed the US had a higher calling – to devise international institutions that would end war and further trade. With the notable exception of President Woodrow Wilson's vision and efforts, the first unilateral approach largely defined US policy until 1934. Latin America sought every diplomatic means to contain US power by seeking support for the principle of 'non-intervention' at inter-American conferences under the Pan American Union.

President Franklin Roosevelt took the lead in establishing the UN and inviting Latin America to play a key role in the organisation. Many of the region's leaders also wanted a regional organisation, and in Bogotá in 1948, the states of the Americas established the Organisation of American States (OAS). Unlike the UN, the OAS did not have vetoes; the United States accepted a system in which its voice and vote were juridically equal to the other members. That did not mean that US power was irrelevant; it meant that the United States had to find other ways to influence the organisation's policies. Over time, that proved more difficult to accomplish. The 'inter-American system' spawned many other organisations. The Inter-American Development Bank, established in 1959, became the most prominent development institution. In the legal area, the Inter-American Court and Commission on Human Rights have been very effective vehicles for defending human rights. In addition, there are many sub-regional organisations such as the Central American Common Market (CACM), the Caribbean Community (CARICOM), and the Andean Pact, whose purpose was to foster trade.

Several events occurred which together changed the character of regionalism in the hemisphere. First, the Cold War ended, eliminating one excuse for authoritarianism and violent change. Secondly, the debt crisis in the early 1980s compelled governments to privatise state corporations and reduce trade and investment barriers, facilitating greater integration within new and more dynamic trading regimes. Third, the region moved toward democracy (Pastor, 2001).

These three changes combined to permit the Americas to strengthen the bonds connecting them. First, the 1960s trade agreements – CACM, the Andean Pact, CARICOM – were reinvigorated, and two new agreements – Mercosur and NAFTA – were founded. Secondly, Latin America's new democracies reassessed their governments' historical support for the principle of 'non-intervention'. Recognising that the same principle had been used by military governments to prevent democracy, Latin America joined with the United States in a series of initiatives that established a collective safety net and defence of democracy. Beginning at the OAS General Assembly in Santiago, Chile in 1991 and culminating in the Inter-American Democratic Charter, signed in Lima, Peru in September 2001, the governments of the region pledged to defend each others' democracies and isolate any military regimes.[1] Based on the movement toward freer trade and the strengthening of democracy, 34 governments of the Americas met in Miami in December 1994 and declared their intention to establish a Free Trade of the Americas (FTAA) in a decade.

These various initiatives gave rise to the idea that the Americas had finally arrived as an integrated region. And yet the talks for the FTAA moved very slowly, and the governments only kept them alive by agreeing to limit their scope. Moreover, by the end of the century, Mercosur, one of the most promising of the agreements, was foundering as its two main members, Brazil and Argentina, took steps to impede trade between them. Intra-regional trade among Mercosur countries climbed from 14.3 per cent in 1992 to 25 per cent in 1998, but then it fell back to 11.4 per cent in 2002 (IADB, 2003).

Moreover, the gulf between North and South America, always wide, seemed to grow even wider. The instability in the Andean countries, the self-preoccupation of Brazil and Argentina, combined with the focus, nearing obsession, in the United States on the war against terrorism after 11 September 2001 – all these were signs that the continents were drifting apart. That division was sharpened by the increasing economic and social integration of North America. Since NAFTA, Canada and Mexico became major trading powers. In 1980, Mexico and Brazil each exported about $25 billion of goods and services, accounting for roughly 25 per cent of their gross domestic product (GDP). In 2002, Mexico exported more than $185 billion – more than twice that of Brazil – and its trade accounted for 62 per cent of its GDP, also almost twice that of Brazil. Indeed, Mexico's trading power was roughly equal to that of the rest of Latin America, but 90 per cent of that trade was with North America. (See Table 13.1.)

The two continents had become distinct as well as distant. The three countries of North America had a combined population of 420 million people, which exceeded that of all the other countries in the hemisphere. Their combined North American GDP of $11.7 trillion accounted for a total of 97 per cent of all that of the Americas. The combined exports and imports of North America amounted to $3.6 trillion, which compared to less than $400 billion for the rest of the Americas.

The Americas had always been divided by language, culture, politics, and level of economic development. The main groups remained the Andean countries, Mercosur, Central America, the Caribbean, and North America. The inter-American institutions – the OAS, the IDB, the human rights commissions – all provided a thin, but sometimes meaningful, bond on political and economic matters. In trade, the conclusion of a FTAA might further integration, but intra-regional trade among the Latin American countries as a percentage of their world trade rose from 17 per cent in 1992 to nearly 20 per cent in 1998, before declining to 14.5 per cent in 2002. (See Table 13.2.) Perhaps as much as any other indicator, the fact that the nations

Table 13.1 Basic indicators for the Americas, 1980–2002

Group or Country	Population, 2002 (millions)	GDP (billions of dollars) 1980	GDP 2002	Exports (billions of dollars) 1980	Exports 2002	Imports (billions of dollars) 1980	Imports 2002	Trade[a] as % of GDP 1980	Trade[a] as % of GDP 2002
North America	**420.6**	**3,198.5**	**11,734.6**	**410.5**	**1,476.3**	**432.4**	**2,133.4**	**26.4**	**30.8**
US	288.4	2,709.0	10,383.1	301.8	965.7	314.8	1,611.4	22.8	24.8
Canada	31.4	266.0	714.3	82.0	324.9	828	311.4	61.9	89.1
Mexico	100.8	223.5	637.2	26.8	185.6	348	210.7	27.6	62.2
Mercosur	**219.4**	**356.9**	**571.6**	**36.9**	**114.8**	**48.4**	**100.0**	**23.9**	**37.6**
Brazil	174.0	234.9	452.0	23.5	78.1	33.8	76.9	24.4	34.3
Argentina	36.5	77.0	102.0	10.9	315	11.1	17.7	28.6	48.2
Paraguay	5.5	4.6	5.5	0.6	2.0	0.9	2.3	33.9	76.6
Uruguay	3.4	10.1	12.1	2.0	3.4	2.5	3.2	44.6	54.3
Andean Community	**117.1**	**138.0**	**263.8**	**36.6**	**61.1**	**36.2**	**62.6**	**52.7**	**46.9**
Venezuela	25.1	69.4	94.3	20.5	26.4	20.2	19.4	58.8	48.5
Colombia	43.7	33.4	80.9	6.5	15.6	7.0	19.2	40.5	43.0
Peru	26.7	20.6	56.5	5.2	10.5	4.2	12.2	45.9	40.3
Ecuador	12.8	11.7	24.3	3.2	6.9	3.6	9.4	57.7	67.2
Bolivia	8.8	2.8	7.8	1.1	1.7	1.1	2.3	80.1	51.4
Caricom[b]	**10.9**	**4.1**	**11.3**	**2.1**	**2.9**	**2.4**	**8.8**	**111.0**	**103.4**
Haiti	8.3	1.5	3.4	0.4	0.6	0.6	2.0	68.5	76.2
Jamaica	2.6	2.6	7.9	1.7	2.3	1.8	6.7	135.4	115.1
CACM	**34.4**	**21.0**	**65.0**	**5.9**	**21.1**	**8.5**	**31.3**	**68.9**	**80.8**
Guatemala	12.0	7.9	23.3	1.9	4.3	2.5	8.1	55.5	53.2
El Salvador	6.4	3.6	14.3	1.2	4.5	1.5	7.1	74.4	81.1
Costa Rica	3.9	4.8	16.8	1.4	9.0	2.1	9.6	72.3	110.3
Honduras	6.8	2.6	6.6	1.0	2.2	1.3	4.2	89.5	97.4
Nicaragua	5.3	2.1	4.0	0.5	1.1	1.1	2.4	76.4	89.0
The Americas	**802.3**	**3,726.1**	**12,074.7**	**492.1**	**1,676.3**	**527.9**	**2,336.1**	**27.38**	**33.2**

CACM = Central American Common Market
Caricom = Caribbean Common Market
a Trade is defined as Exports + Imports
b Export and import data included only for Haiti and Jamaica

Sources: import and export data taken from World Trade Organisation, Statistics Database <www.wto.org>; population and GDP data taken from World Bank, Data Query <www.worldbank.org>.

Table 13.2 Western Hemisphere: Total and Intra-Regional Exports, 1992–2002 (millions of US dollars and percentages)

	1992	1993	1994	1995	1996	1997	1998	1999	2000	2001	2002	AAGR 1992–2002[d]
Western Hemisphere[abc]												
Total Exports	698,047	727,050	858,436	994,328	1,071,955	1,179,833	1461,673	1,216,398	1,308,489	1,234,953	1,191,144	
% growth	6.1	4.2	18.1	13.8	7.8	10.1	-1.5	4.7	7.6	-5.6	-3.5	5.5
Extra-hemispheric exports	346,544	340,002	392,278	471,910	496,479	521,552	484,536	488,397	508,778	478,327	458,495	
% growth	0.4	-1.9	15.4	20.3	5.2	5.1	-7.1	0.8	4.2	-6.0	-4.1	2.8
Intra-hemispheric exports	351,504	387,048	456,178	522,419	375,475	658,280	677,138	728,001	799,711	756,626	732,649	
% growth	12.4	10.1	20.4	12.1	10.2	14.4	2.9	7.5	9.9	-5.4	-3.2	7.6
Intra/Total	50.4	53.2	54.3	52.5	53.7	55.8	58.3	59.8	61.1	613	61.5	
Lain America and the Caribbean (LAC)[bc]												
Total Exports	145,173	154,529	182,545	220,411	249,332	276,962	268,849	287,680	346,324	334,441	326,702	
% growth	7.3	6.4	18.1	20.7	13.1	11.1	-2.9	7.0	20.4	-3.4	n.a.	8.4
Extra-LAC exports	120,352	125,081	147,584	178,629	203,074	223,454	215,609	242,330	290,255	275,638	279,383	
% growth	4.0	3.9	18.0	21.0	13.7	10.0	-3.5	12.4	19.8	-5.0	n.a.	8.8
Intra-LAC exports	24,821	29,448	34,961	41,782	45,257	53,498	53,240	45,349	56,069	38,803	47,320	
% growth	26.7	18.6	18.7	19.5	10.7	15.7	-0.5	-14.8	23.6	4.9	n.a	6.7
Intra/Total	17.1	19.1	19.2	19.0	18.6	19.3	19.8	15.8	16.2	17.6	14.5	
Andean Community												
Total Exports	28,107	29,137	34,243	38,259	45,687	47,655	38,742	43,207	57,236	50,837	48,955	
% growth	-3.8	3.7	17.5	11.7	19.4	4.3	-18.7	11.5	32.5	-11.2	-3.7	5.7
Extra-Andean exports	25,888	26,276	30,816	33,524	40,996	42,028	33,402	39,268	52,045	45,181	43,766	
% growth	-5.7	1.5	17.3	8.8	22.3	2.5	-20.5	17.6	32.5	-13.2	-3.1	5.4
Intra-Andean exports	2,219	2,861	3,427	4,735	4,691	5,627	5,341	3,939	5,191	5,656	5,189	
% growth	25.6	28.9	19.8	38.2	-0.9	19.9	-5.1	-26.2	31.8	9.0	-8.3	8.9
Intra/Total	7.9	9.8	10.0	12.4	10.3	11.8	13.8	9.1	9.1	11.1	10.6	
CARICOM[c]												
Total Exports	3,970	3,215	5,069	5,531	5,439	6,008	5,543	5,933	7,754	8,393	—	
% growth	-4.1	-19.0	57.7	9.1	-1.7	10.4	-7.7	7.0	30.7	8.3	—	8.7
Extra-CARICOM exports	3,537	2,665	4,376	4,649	4,568	5,082	4,473	4,871	6,349	6,929	—	
% growth	-4.2	-24.7	64.2	6.2	-1.8	11.3	-12.0	8.9	30.3	9.1	—	7.8
Intra-CARICOM exports	433	550	693	882	872	925	1,070	1,062	1,404	1,464	—	
% growth	-3.2	26.9	26.0	27.2	-1.1	6.1	15.6	-0.7	32.2	4.3	—	14.5
Intra/Total	10.9	17.1	13.7	15.9	16.0	15.4	19.3	17.9	18.1	17.4	—	

CACM

												AAGR
Total Exports	4,674	4,899	5,509	6,864	7,778	8,242	10,313	11,175	12,765	10,510	10,008	
% growth	9.2	4.8	12.4	24.6	13.3	6.0	25.1	8.4	14.2	−17.7	4.8	7.9
Extra-CASM exports	3,615	3,797	4,280	5,408	6,192	6,417	8,125	8,886	10,194	7,693	7,198	
% growth	3.5	5.0	12.7	26.4	14.5	3.6	26.6	9.4	14.7	−24.5	−6.4	7.1
Intra-CACM exports	1,059	1,102	1,229	1,456	1,586	1,826	2,188	2,289	2,571	2,817	2,810	
% growth	34.7	4.1	11.5	18.5	8.9	15.1	19.9	4.6	12.3	9.6	−0.2	10.3
Intra/Total	22.7	22.5	22.3	21.2	20.4	22.1	21.2	20.5	20.1	26.8	28.1	

Mercosur

												AAGR
Total Exports	50,463	54,122	62,113	70,402	74998	82,342	81,323	74,320	84,659	87,876	88,880	
% growth	10.0	7.3	14.8	13.3	6.5	9.8	−1.2	−8.6	13.9	3.8	1.1	5.8
Extra-Mercosur exports	43,246	44,095	50,157	56,019	57,960	62,289	60,972	59,158	66,961	72,725	78,714	
% growth	6.0	2.0	13.7	11.7	3.5	7.5	−2.1	−3.0	13.2	8.6	8.2	6.2
Intra-Mercosur exports	7,216	10,026	11,957	14,384	17,038	20,053	20,351	15,163	17,698	15,151	10,166	
% growth	41.4	38.9	19.3	20.3	18.5	17.7	1.5	−25.5	16.7	−14.4	−32.9	3.5
Intra/Total	14.3	18.5	19.2	20.4	22.7	24.4	25.0	20.4	20.9	17.2	11.4	

Mercosur+Chile+Bolivia (MCB)

												AAGR
Total Exports	60,872	63,927	74,790	87,977	91,700	100,632	97,197	91,355	104,120	106,839	107,675	
% growth	10.0	5.0	17.0	17.6	4.2	9.7	−3.4	−6.0	14.0	2.6	0.8	5.9
Extra-MCB exports	50,231	50,056	58,333	67,903	68,732	73,874	70,615	70,664	79,581	84,668	90,720	
% growth	6.0	−0.3	16.5	16.4	1.2	7.5	−4.4	0.1	12.6	6.4	7.1	6.1
Intra-MCB exports	10,641	13,871	16,458	20,074	22,968	26,758	26,582	20,691	24,539	22,171	16,955	
% growth	33.6	30.4	18.6	22.0	14.4	16.5	−0.7	−22.2	18.6	−9.6	−23.5	4.8
Intra/Total	17.5	21.7	22.0	22.8	25.0	26.6	27.3	22.6	23.6	20.8	15.7	

NAFTA

												AAGR
Total Exports	599,027	624,352	737,888	853,694	918,077	1,013,108	1012,114	1,071,355	1,134,834	1,061,548	1,021,497	
% growth	6.0	4.2	18.2	15.7	7.5	10.4	−0.1	5.9	5.9	−6.5	−3.8	5.5
Extra-NAFTA exports	335,184	332,960	383,349	460,581	485,698	517,457	490,885	486,296	491,695	464,133	432,856	
% growth	2.1	−0.7	15.1	20.1	5.5	6.5	−5.1	−0.9	1.1	−5.6	−6.7	2.6
Intra-NAFTA exports	263,843	291,392	334,539	393,113	432,379	495,651	521,229	585,059	643,140	597,415	588,541	
% growth	11.3	10.4	21.7	10.9	10.0	14.6	5.2	12.2	9.9	−7.1	−1.5	8.4
Intra/Total	44.0	46.7	48.0	46.0	47.1	48.9	51.5	54.6	56.7	56.3	57.6	

Source: DDB, Integration and Regional Programs Department, based on data from DataIntal, Hemispheric Database, Comtrade and official country data.
[a] Western Hemisphere includes Latin America, Canada, and the United States. There are gap in some years for some Caribbean countries.
[b] Latin America and the Caribbean include Argentina, Bolivia, Brazil, Chile, Colombia, Costa Rica, Dominican Republic (except 1998–2002), Ecuador, El Salvador, Guatemala, Honduras, Mexico, Nicaragua, Panama (except 1994), Paraguay, Peru, Uruguay, Venezuela and CARICOM (see note c for exceptions). CARICOM data for 2002 is not available, for which reason the growth rates for LAC exports for 2002 are not calculated for this year.
[c] CARICOM includes Bahamas, Barbados, Belize, Dominica, Grenada, Guyana, Jamaica, St Lucia, St Kitts and Nevis, St Vincent and the Grenadines, Suriname, and Trinidad and Tobago, because of the unavailability of data for the other CARICOM member states. Totals exclude Bahamas (1992–96), Dominica (1992), Grenada (1993), Guyana (1992–97), St Kitts and Nevis (1992, 1996), St Vincent and the Grenadines (1992) and Suriname (1993).
[d] AAGR: Average Annual Growth Rate. Calculated using the formula $[(Y(t)/Y(s))^{(1/n)}-1]*100$, where $Y(t)$ and $Y(s)$ are the values in years 't' and 's', respectively, where $t>s$ and $n=t-s$. For CARICOM the formula is based on the 1992–2001 period.

in the region conduct less than 15 per cent of their world trade with each other suggests that they are connected more to nations outside than within the Americas.

Despite the Rio Pact, the 1947 collective security agreement signed by the United States and most Latin American governments, few would call the region a 'security community', a region in which there were no expectations of conflict. The emergence of democracy had dampened the likelihood of war but, in part because many of the democracies were fragile, there were still conflicts.[2] The Americas, in brief, constitutes a region in which there are other sub-regions and in which the bonds connecting the various sub-regions are more symbolic than substantial.

North America, like all of the Americas, is characterised by the strikingly unequal power of its members, but it has already achieved an impressive degree of economic and social integration, almost as advanced as Europe's. Unlike Europe, however, North America's model relies more on the market than institutions.

THE EVOLUTION, EMERGENCE, AND CHARACTERISTICS
OF NORTH AMERICA

In 1990, when Mexico's President Carlos Salinas proposed a free trade agreement with the United States, the US GDP was about twenty times larger than Mexico's and ten times larger than Canada's. Asymmetry, whether in size of the economy or power of the military, is the defining characteristic of the relationship of North America's three states, and history has reinforced this imbalance. In contrast to Europe where its catastrophic wars propelled its post-Second World War leaders to unify, North America has been divided by its history and, more precisely, by its memory of nineteenth-century conflicts.

'Americans do not know, but Canadians cannot forget,' writes Seymour Martin Lipset, 'that two nations, not one, came out of the American Revolution.' America emerged confident and proud of its revolution, and Canada defined itself to a considerable extent as 'that part of British North America that did not support the [American] Revolution' (Lipset, 1991). In 1812, the United States tried, but failed, to annex Canada, and the fear that the formidable Union army in 1865 might trek north to try again to expel the British was the principal reason why Canadians sought independence, and why the British accepted it in the form of Dominion in 1867 within the British Empire. Both judged correctly that the United States was less likely to make war against an independent Canada (Howlett et al., 1999).

Canadians remained wary of a close relationship with the United States. In 1911, the Canadian Prime Minister lost an election for concluding a free trade agreement with the United States. Thirty-seven years later,

Prime Minister William Lyon McKenzie King refused, at the last minute, to approve a freer trade agreement with the United States, evidently fearing a similar political result.

Having lost its war and one-third of its territory in the nineteenth century and having suffered several military interventions in the early twentieth century, Mexico's distrust of the United States was deeper than Canada's. Because it has been less stable, prosperous, and democratic, Mexico also bears a heavier sense of inferiority. For this reason, any proposal from the United States to reduce trade or investment barriers was usually met with a curt rejection when officials deigned to respond.[3]

The rationale for a more distant relationship with the United States was most clearly articulated by a young intellectual in the 1980s. 'In the case of two nations as disparate in size, power, and wealth as Mexico and the United States,' wrote Jorge G. Castañeda, 'the weight of economic superiority can be crushing and can lead to a permanent loss of significant attributes of sovereignty and cultural identity.' Castañeda, who would become Mexico's Foreign Minister during the first two years of the Vicente Fox Administration (2000–02), then felt that integration could lead to 'political subservience in foreign policy and domestic affairs, as well as a progressive fading of the country's heretofore vigorous cultural personality'. Mexico, he feared, could become 'less Mexican', and so the best foreign policy was to keep Washington at arm's length (Pastor and Castañeda, 1988).

Given the history and the imbalance in power, perhaps the only way to have reached a North American free trade agreement was for America's neighbours to lead. And, of course, that is what occurred, starting in the mid-1980s by Canada. In the 1970s, the Liberal Party under Pierre Trudeau had given Canadian nationalism an edge that made many Canadians proud, and others very uneasy. New laws promoted by Trudeau discouraged foreign investment and raised tensions with the United States, and when a deep recession struck Canada in 1982, businesses realised that the Canadian market was not large enough to permit them to grow. Michael Hart, a Canadian scholar and trade negotiator, wrote: 'They [Canadian businessmen] wanted to become more export-oriented, but were reluctant to make the necessary investment in the face of continued trouble in the Canada-U.S. relationship' (Hart, 1998, 168). In 1984, a national election brought the Progressive Conservative Party under Brian Mulroney to power with a large majority. Although his party had also opposed free trade with the United States, Mulroney recognised a change in the public mood in favour of experimenting with more open trade with the United States. President Ronald Reagan responded positively, and both governments negotiated and signed a free trade agreement in 1988 (Wonnacott, 1987; Schott and Smith, 1988). In the same year, Mulroney called an election, and the free trade agreement was heatedly debated with the Liberals strongly opposed.

Mulroney won re-election but by a narrower margin. The reversal on free trade by Mexico and its president Carlos Salinas was even more startling than Mulroney's. Mexico had a history of defensive nationalism, particularly aimed at its neighbour, that was always more strident than Canada's. In the mid-1970s and the early 1980s, Mexico sharply restricted foreign investment and increased the state's role in the economy. When the debt crisis threatened to bankrupt the country in 1982, its leaders reassessed their development strategy and embarked on an export-oriented policy. The government imposed fiscal discipline, sharply reduced tariffs and limitations on foreign investment, and privatised state corporations.

When Salinas took office in December 1988, he understood that the success of the Mexican economy depended on whether it could attract large sums of private investment. He went first to Western Europe, but found the governments focused on helping Eastern Europe after the end of the Cold War. He went next to Japan, but found them very cautious about challenging the United States in its neighbourhood. He pondered his next step, realising that the opening of Mexico's economy in the previous five years had left it vulnerable to arbitrary acts of protectionism by the United States, and that the Canadian Free Trade Agreement, which had just been concluded, had addressed that concern. He therefore turned to Washington for a free trade agreement and for the key that would presumably unlock the door to foreign investment.[4]

NAFTA became the first draft of a constitution of North America, but it was defined in very narrow and business-like terms. It aimed to eliminate all trade and investment barriers and level the playing field on procurement, telecommunications, banking, services and other sectors (Pastor, 1993; Hufbauer and Schott, 1993). To secure the market, the three governments created a state-of-the-art dispute-settlement mechanism. Instead of trying to establish an institution for negotiating the reduction or harmonisation of policies, as the EU did, NAFTA selected a few sectors and harmonised the policies. The agreement was a minimum one that reflected the Canadian and Mexican fear of being dominated by the United States and the US antipathy toward bureaucracy and supranational organisations. It was an 'invisible hand', classical liberal framework whose principal shared goal was the elimination of impediments to trade.

There is a vast literature on the consequences of NAFTA which reflects to a certain extent the debate that preceded it (Pastor, 2001b; Hufbauer and Schott, 1993; Grayson, 1995; Orme, 1996). In an astute review of the debate on NAFTA, Sidney Weintraub shows that many of the arguments of both advocates and opponents use similar criteria – related to the balance of payments or the gain and loss of jobs. Weintraub argues persuasively that these criteria are misleading and that a more useful assessment of NAFTA's progress would be based on its effect on total trade, productivity, intra-industry specialisation, industrial competitiveness, environmental effects, and institution-building (Weintraub, 1997, chapter 2).

With regard to NAFTA's principal goals on trade and investment, the agreement has been a resounding success. In 1993, Mexican tariffs averaged about 10 per cent, 2.5 times those of the United States. By 1999, Mexican tariffs fell to 2 per cent while import licensing and other non-tariff barriers were eliminated. Today, nearly all goods traded between the United States, Mexico and Canada now enter duty-free. Agricultural products are the most sensitive and thus freer trade in this area is delayed until 2008.

As barriers declined, trade and investment soared in all three directions. US exports to Mexico increased fourfold, from $28 billion to $111 billion, and exports to Canada more than doubled, from $84 billion to $179 billion. Annual flows of US direct investment to Mexico, went from $1.3 billion in 1992 to $15 billion in 2001. US investment in Canada increased from $2 billion in 1994 to $16 billion in 2000, while Canadian investment flows to the United States grew from $4.6 billion to $27 billion over the same period. More than 36 per cent of the total energy imports of the United States now come from its two neighbours. Travel and immigration among the three countries also increased dramatically. In 2000 alone, people crossed the two borders 500 million times. But the most profound impact came from those people who crossed and stayed. The 2000 census estimated that there were 22 million people of Mexican origin living in the United States. Nearly two-thirds of them have arrived in the last two decades. As many as 600,000 Americans living in Canada were eligible to vote in the 2004 US election – more than those voting in six US states (Brautigam, 2004).

Intra-regional exports as a percentage of total exports – an index of integration – climbed from around 30 per cent in 1982 to 58 per cent in 2002. As in the auto industry – which makes up nearly 40 per cent of North American trade – much of this exchange is either intra-industry or intra-firm – two other indicators of an increasingly integrated economy. Many industries and firms have become truly North American.

There are still other signs of an increasingly integrated community. After 75 years of single party rule in Mexico, in the year 2000 a highly professional electoral service, trained in part by Canadian election officials, conducted an election that was very closely contested. The result was an unprecedented acceptance of the process and outcome by all Mexican parties and the international community and a peaceful transfer of power. Indeed, the Mexican elections was much more effectively administered than the one in the United States in the same year (Pastor, 2004a).

The signatories of NAFTA deliberately wanted to avoid establishing any bureaucratic or supranational institutions. The core of the agreement was therefore self-executing or designed to be implemented by *each* government. With regard to the dispute-settlement mechanism, William Davey, a

Canadian scholar, concluded that it 'worked reasonably well ... the basic goal of trade dispute settlement ... is to enforce the agreed-upon rules. By and large, these dispute settlement mechanisms have done that' (Davey, 1996, 288–9).

Both the Commission for Labour Cooperation and the Commission for Environmental Cooperation provide citizens, corporations, unions, and non-governmental organisations an avenue for presenting their complaints. In the case of the labour agreement, since 1994, the Commission received 23 complaints – 14 were directed against Mexico, seven against the United States, and two against Canada.[5] Both Commissions have done some useful work, and non-governmental organisations from the United States and Canada have helped their counterparts in Mexico to develop and pursue complaints. Both Commissions reflect the caution of their governments. No one has criticised them for being too aggressive or trying to forge common responses on difficult questions such as pollution on the border or labour rights in the apparel industry. Nonetheless, Mexico's environmental standards and capacity has actually improved faster than the United States' or Canada's, not surprising giving the initial level, but encouraging nonetheless.

Another institution established under NAFTA was the North American Development Bank (NADBank), which has channelled funds into the border area to improve the environment. On a parallel track, the United States and Mexico negotiated the establishment of a Border Environment Cooperation Commission (BECC) to assist border states and local communities to design and coordinate environmental infrastructure projects. The BECC, based in Ciudad Juarez, Chihuahua, involves local communities in the development of projects and then seeks financing from the private sector and NADBank, which is based in San Antonio, Texas. Mexico and the United States have each contributed $225 million of paid-in capital, which gives the bank a lending capacity of $2 billion. The combination of chronic poverty and rapid urbanisation and industrialisation on the border have created a multiplicity of health problems, involving water and waste treatment, solid and toxic wastes, and air pollution. The two institutions were very slow in getting organised, but by 2000, 29 projects had begun or been completed.

During the past decade, Mexico changed from an oil-dependent economy to an urban one based on manufactured exports. The impact on Canada was also quite pronounced. NAFTA deepened Canada's dependence on the US market, but it also helped diversify and internationalise its economy. Canada's trade as a percentage of its GDP expanded from 52.4 per cent in 1990 to 74.2 per cent in 1999 – making it the most trade-oriented country in the G-7/8 (Department of Foreign Affairs and International Trade of Canada, 1999).

As for the United States, its total trade as a percentage of GDP increased by 25 per cent during the 1990s. Given the size of the US economy and the rapid growth of jobs in the 1990s, those who predicted substantial job loss were wrong. While Mexico and Canada grew more dependent on the United States – up to 90 per cent of its trade and with exports accounting for 35 per cent of its GDP – the United States also grew more dependent on its two neighbours. More than one-third of the total trade of the United States is now with its two neighbours. More broadly, many firms became continental and more competitive.

An evaluation of NAFTA should not be confined just to trade and investment criteria or the side agreements. One needs to view NAFTA as the centre of a unique social and economic integration process and of an effort to redefine the relationship between advanced countries and a developing one.

The flow of people, cultures, food, music, and sports across the two borders has accelerated even more than the trade in goods and services. In 1996, the first destination for most American tourists abroad was Mexico; 20 million Americans went. The second most popular destination for American tourists was Canada; 13 million travelled there. In 2003, the same pattern held, although fewer Americans travelled abroad – only 15.8 million to Mexico. Of the millions of tourists who visit the United States each year, the vast majority (20 million) come from Canada (Fry, 1992, 78). The second source is Mexico with 7.5 million in 1996 and 10 million in 2003 (Crosette, 1998).

The increase in numbers of immigrants understates their social impact. While the overall population of the United States grew by 13.2 per cent in the last decade of the twentieth century, the Hispanic population increased 57.9 per cent (from 22.4 million to 35.3 million) and of Mexicans, by 52.9 per cent (from 13.5 million to 20.6 million). About 30 per cent of the immigrants living in the United States today are from Mexico (Martin and Midgley, 2003). While half of all Hispanics live in California and Texas, during the past decade, the Hispanic population in Oregon doubled; in Minnesota, tripled; in Georgia, quadrupled; and in North Carolina, quintupled (Guzman, 2001).

Remittances have played an increasingly important role in the relationship between Mexicans in the United States and their relatives. The most recent Mexican government report estimates that Mexican workers send their families about $17 million a day, and in 2000, that amounted to $6.2 billion – in the last decade, $45 billion ('Remesas de Migrantes Equivalen a 83per cent de la Inversion de EU en Mexico', *La Jornada*, 30 October 2000). A recent survey found that 61 per cent of Mexicans had relatives living outside the country, mostly in the United States, and 21 per cent received remittances from family members working in the United States (Edgar et al., 2004).

The outlines of a new North America are now visible, and one sign is the growing literature on the future agenda for the region – aimed more on what NAFTA omitted than what it contained. President Vicente Fox has pressed that agenda most vigorously at the governmental level, but the Canadian Parliament and think tanks and many American scholars have raised issues and made specific proposals on where North America should go from here (Fry, 2003; Goldfarb, 2003; House of Commons of Canada, 2002; Pastor, 2004).

A NORTH AMERICAN IDENTITY

The most vigorous and eloquent voices in Mexico and Canada have emphasised the sharp differences between their countries and the United States. In Mexico, Carlos Fuentes has been one of a legion of intellectuals, who have criticised the United States for its imperialist pretensions and asserted that Mexico would prefer to be a distant than a close neighbour. In Canada, Stephen Clarkson and Michael Adams have made the parallel case that Canada is different and needs to fortify itself from the inevitable efforts by the United States to control its destiny. Karl Deutsch offered a contrasting view, believing that as states become integrated, they begin to develop a sense of 'community', which he defined as an assurance 'that they will settle their differences short of war'. In a volume edited by Emanuel Adler and Michael Barnett (1998) testing this thesis, Guadalupe Gonzales and Stephan Haggard concluded that the US–Mexican relationship falls short because of a lack of trust and common identity. Sean Shore concludes, in the same volume, that the United States and Canada had become a 'community', and the main reason was that the long (5,000 miles) border was not defended. Of course, the US–Mexican border has been demilitarised almost as long as the US–Canadian border, so other factors must explain the difference, if there is one. Unfortunately, these studies and others that emphasise cultural differences omit one key variable, public opinion, and when these are included, one can discern the outline of an emerging North American identity and community.

Convergence of values

Under the direction of Ronald Inglehart of the University of Michigan, scholars conducted surveys evaluating the values and attitudes of people in about 44 countries. Miguel Basanez of Mexico and Neil Nevitte of Canada joined Inglehart to survey the three countries of North America in 1981, 1990, and 2000. Instead of documenting cultural differences, they found a convergence of values among the people in the three countries in twelve of 16 key domains. For example, people in all three countries increasingly emphasise independence and imagination in child rearing; there is less support for state ownership of industry, and national pride is waning; church attendance rates are falling; respect for authority is declining. This last point is particularly significant because Canadians had long been viewed as having a 'culture of deference' (Lipset, 1991).[6] In the last two decades, the traditionally restrained debates in Canada became heated on critical issues like the Constitution, the independence of Quebec, the environment, and social issues like gay rights and equality for women. Mexico's long-standing political authoritarianism had led many scholars to describe a corrupt political culture, but Mexico moved to democracy in the last decade (Cornelius, 2000; Pastor, 2000).

Indeed, there was not just a convergence in North America toward similar values, but also toward basic public policies. In all three countries, there was movement toward political liberalisation, a market-based, regulatory economic policy, and more respect for the rights of minorities and indigenous peoples. The larger point is that civic culture and the policies converged not toward an American average but toward a different point. 'North Americans', Inglehart, Nevitte and Basanez (1996) concluded, 'have become significantly more alike.'

Trinational perceptions

Despite the suspicions that each country was said to have harboured toward one another, public opinion surveys found that the three peoples of North America have very positive views of each other. The Chicago Council on Foreign Relations has been doing public opinion surveys on American views of the world every four years since 1974. One of the questions measures 'favourability' – the warmth that Americans feel toward other countries. During the past 25 years, Americans have consistently given Canada the highest 'favourability' rating among all nations. The US view of Mexico is also very positive, just below that of Canada and Great Britain and on roughly the same level as leading countries in Europe (Italy, Germany and France).

Roughly three-quarters of all Mexicans hold a positive view of the United States (almost the same percentage of Americans with a positive view of Mexico). More than 80 per cent of Mexicans believe that the United States exercises the most influence on their country, but rather surprisingly, 67 per cent of Mexicans view US influence as positive, a marked difference from the way that the elite had long portrayed the Mexican public's views.

Canadians also have warm feelings about the United States, although not quite as warm as Americans have towards them. For example, in a 1999 survey in Canada, 49 per cent of Canadians viewed Americans as similar to themselves, whereas 71 per cent of Americans viewed Canada as similar.[7] Many Canadians feel that Americans take them for granted or are arrogant, but the more telling point is that 26 per cent of the Canadian public would become US citizens if they could, and 25 per cent of the American public expressed a similar preference for Canadian citizenship.

So, in brief, not only are the three countries of North America more alike today than ever before, but their people like each other more than before or than most other countries. In addition, the percentage of the public that identified themselves as 'North American' doubled during the 1980s, although that was only from 2 to 4 per cent.[8] One possible explanation for the shift is the arrival of a more cosmopolitan generation.

Views of NAFTA

Public attitudes towards NAFTA in the three countries in the past decade have changed, but today, there is a modest net support in all three countries. There is also a neat consensus: each nation agrees that the other signatories have benefited more than it has.

A North American identity?

In the 1990 world values survey, about a quarter of the Canadian and Mexican population were in favour of erasing the border with the United States, and nearly half (46 per cent) of Americans favoured eliminating the border with Canada (Nevitte and Basanez, 1998, 139). In 2000, a survey of American attitudes found Americans still evenly divided about doing away with the Mexican border. The Mexicans agree with the Americans on this issue. Fifty-five per cent of Mexicans oppose doing away with the border with the United States, and only 36 per cent favour it (Inglehart and Basanez, 2000).

When Mexicans, Canadians, or Americans are asked whether they are prepared to give up their cultural identity in order to form one state or a union, all overwhelmingly reject the proposition. *But when the question is asked whether they would be prepared to form a single country if that would mean a higher quality of life for their country, a majority of the people in all three countries answer affirmatively.*

Forty-three per cent of Canadians think it 'would be a *good thing* to be part of a North American Union in ten years', and only 27 per cent think it would be a bad thing. Moreover, *nearly one-half (49 per cent) think North American Union is likely to happen.* As with the Mexicans, Canadians are much more willing to contemplate a union in a new North American entity than to be part of the United States. A majority (57 per cent) would oppose joining the United States while only 23 per cent would consider it.[9] When asked whether Canada and the United States should have a common currency, the Canadian public split – 45 per cent in favour, and 44 per cent opposed.[10] This suggests that Canadians are much further along than their leaders in thinking about some of the practical, but sensitive, questions of integration.

For the American public, a relatively higher percentage favour continental political union than is true of Mexicans and Canadians. Support for union soars when the contingency options – e.g., if that would mean a better quality of life, etc. – are included. *In 1990, 81 per cent of Americans said they would favour forming one country with Canada if it meant a better quality of life, and 79 per cent agreed if it meant the environment would get better* (Inglehart and Basanez, 2000). These numbers declined a bit in 2000 but remained relatively high – 63 per cent approved of forming one country if it would improve the quality of life, and 48 per cent if the environment would get better. When one disaggregates the data, younger and wealthier Americans are readier to contemplate political union than older or poorer citizens.

What should one conclude from this data? *First, the majority of the people in all three countries are prepared to contemplate a reconfiguration of the North American political system provided they can be convinced that it will produce a higher quality of life and handle problems – like the environment – more effectively than if these are done by each country. Second, the principal motive is economic, the approach is pragmatic,* and the main drawback is the fear of its effect on culture and identity. To the extent that people perceive their cultures at risk, they resist integration. Third, younger people are more connected and ready to experiment with new political forms and so the prospects for future integration are likely to get better. Fourth, as Karl Deutsch predicted a half century ago, more contact and trust among peoples can facilitate integration, which, in turn, can increase trust. In disaggregating the data on a regional basis, one finds greater support for integration among those regions that have the most commerce – i.e., the southwest of the United States and the northern part of Mexico and on the Canadian border (Nevitte and Basanez, 1998, 139).

The underlying basis of a community exists. Provided people are not threatened by a loss of culture or identity, and incentives for productivity and improvements for standard of living are evident, the three peoples of North America are ready to listen to ideas, including political union, on how to accomplish those ends.

CONCLUSION: THE MODEL OF NORTH AMERICA

Each of the three main regional groups – the EU, East Asia and North America – offer distinct models that are a composite of other factors: the origin and timing of the regional agreement, its objectives, its policies on internal disparities, the composition of its membership, the security foundation on which it rests, the nature of its governing authority, and the philosophy that defines its distinctive vision.

The EU is the most integrated of the regional trading regimes, and is the only common market that permits the free movement of goods, services, capital and labour among its 25 members. It was born from two devastating wars and a compelling dread. In the Treaty of Rome establishing the *European Economic Community*, the six nations of Europe declared that they were 'determined to lay the foundations of an ever closer union among the peoples of Europe' (Nelsen and Stubb, 1998, 113–15).

Asia has not resolved the first question as to which organisation represents its interests and the absence of a security foundation, particularly joining China and Japan, defines the limits of integration in East Asia.

NAFTA was born of different soil, and until Vicente Fox was inaugurated President of Mexico on 1 December 2000, it aspired to be nothing more than a free trade area in which goods, services, and capital should be traded freely, but labour's movements should be restricted. Fox was the first to propose a common market; no other leader in the three countries had even broached a preliminary step – a customs union with a common external tariff. NAFTA is also silent on an issue – internal disparities – in which the EU is preoccupied, though the income and employment gaps are far wider in North America than in Europe.

The origin of NAFTA was the growing fear in Canada and Mexico that a resurgence of US protectionism could devastate their economies. The only way to make the US market secure and stable was to negotiate a free trade area. Having long sought freer trade, the United States could not reject the idea when its neighbours finally proposed it. The goals of NAFTA, as specified in the preamble, speak of strengthening 'the special bonds of friendship and cooperation among their nations' – not their peoples; of expanding and securing markets; of establishing rules consistent with the General Agreement on Tariffs and Trade; and of preserving each nation's 'flexibility to safeguard the public welfare' (NAFTA, 1992). The two-volume treaty aims to reduce trade and investment barriers and to establish a framework for resolving disputes, but not to create a community of people of North America or to promote the well-being of all the people.

After his inauguration in January 1993, President Bill Clinton added two side agreements on labour and the environment and establishing Commissions, whose purpose was to encourage each government to fulfil its promises in each area. These side agreements are fully consistent with the theme of the treaty – to respect the sovereignty of each nation and avoid any supranational authority. The philosophy is to liberalise the continental market, but to insist that each state should address on its own any transnational problems. NAFTA includes a state-of-the-art dispute settlement mechanism, but the courts are *ad hoc* and therefore cannot accumulate an historical memory. *The style of NAFTA's governance is laissez-faire, reactive, and legalistic: problems are defined by plaintiffs and settled by litigation. There is no mechanism for defining problems in a proactive way or addressing them from a continental perspective.*

The three governments of North America have devoted so much of their history to stressing their differences that the idea of 'North America' – an entity to which they all belong – has not had time to take root. Nonetheless, as we saw from the public opinion surveys, there is a growing recognition on the part of the people for a new approach to neighbours and to continental problems – one that looked to commonalities rather than differences. That is the challenge for North America's second decade – to sketch an alternative future for the entire continent that the people will embrace and the politicians will feel obligated to accept.

NOTES

1. See the entire issue of *Canadian Foreign Policy*, Vol. 10, No. 3 (Spring 2003) for an excellent discussion of the strengths and limitations of the Charter and the prospects for strengthening a democratic regime in the Americas.
2. The concept of 'security community' was first developed by Karl Deutsch in the mid-1950s, but a more recent study by Emanuel Adler and Michael Barnett (1998) operationalised the idea and applied it to different regions.
3. In the 1970s, the Carter administration proposed a number of possible agreements to minimise trade disputes, and Ronald Reagan, during his campaign and his administration, also proposed a 'North American Accord', a free trade agreement.
4. This summary of Carlos Salinas' views on trade is derived from numerous interviews that the author had with Salinas from 1979 through 1994 and particularly during the period 1989–92, when his views on NAFTA took shape.
5. For the submissions, see <www.dol.gov/dol/ilab/public/programmes/nao>; also see <www.naalc.org>.
6. In his important book, Neil Nevitte (1996) offers a persuasive critique of the interpretation of Canadians as historically and culturally different, if not opposite, from Americans – a view most effectively developed by S. Lipset (1991).
7. Cited in A. Phillips, 'Benign Neglect', *Maclean's*, 20 December 1999, 25.
8. Nevitte and Basanez (1998, 158–60). They surveyed attitudes in the three countries in 1981 and 1990 as to the principal geographical unit with which people identified: town, region, nation, North America, and world, and they found 'a consistent pattern: in all three countries, there was a substantial shift from emphasis on the town … toward the broader geographical units'. One shouldn't exaggerate. Even though, for example, the number of Americans who identified with 'North America' doubled in that period, that only went from 2 to 4 per cent. Still, the shift toward 'nation' was impressive in all three countries – from 20 to 30 per cent in the United States, 30 to 40 per cent in Canada, and 18 to 28 per cent in Mexico.
9. Ekos Resesarch, Canada, 'Shifting Perceptions of Globalisation and the New Economy', 21 September 2000. Ekos prepared a compilation of surveys. The ones cited were in 1999. [This information is available on the web – <www.ekos.com>]
10. *Maclean's*, '17th Annual Poll', 25 December 2000. The 1999 poll by *Maclean's* was consistent with that survey, showing 44 per cent of Canadians believing Canada would benefit from a common currency, and 42 per cent believing it would be very costly.

14
Regional Integration in Europe

Brigid Gavin

Regional integration has brought about a multifaceted process of political, economic and societal transformation in Europe over the past half century. This process of 'Europeanisation' has transformed national political practices in line with modern European values and norms; it has brought about objective changes in national economic structures making them more open and integrated; and it has brought about subjective changes in the beliefs, expectations and identity of citizens who are gradually assuming more multiple-layered identities – from ethnic/religious to national/regional to, most recently, European. As the European Union (EU)[1] has expanded to include the countries from the former Eastern Bloc, Europeanisation has acted as a powerful mechanism for the modernisation and democratisation of those countries emerging from decades of communist dictatorship.

The process of Europeanisation is not, of course, a smooth linear process, and it is far from non-controversial. Viewed as a foundation for peace and prosperity by the advocates of integration, Europeanisation is viewed as a threat to the fundamental cultural diversity of Europe by its adversaries. Their attachment to national sovereignty coupled with ideological distrust of continental integration is still deeply entrenched. They view with dismay the nation-state losing its political powers as competences are increasingly transferred to the EU.

But the notion of the nation-state based on absolute autonomy belongs to the past in Europe. By working together through peaceful means, European states have demonstrated that it is possible to replace the rule of force by the rule of law. The evolution of previously hostile nation-states away from the Westphalian war system towards the Kantian ideal of perpetual peace, gives hope that the emerging new European polity will endure as a democratic, non-hegemonic, multinational, multicultural, inclusive and integrative society.

There is no one single theory that can explain the multidimensional process of European integration. A single theory is neither feasible nor desirable. What has evolved is a state of healthy competition between various paradigms focusing on different dimensions and approaches. Classical integration theories of neo-functionalism and intergovernmentalism were concerned with the question of whether the EU would evolve into a European super-state or whether it would just devolve into an ordinary international organisation (Haas, 1958; Hoffman, 1966, 862–91). Neither has happened in fact. While economic integration has advanced significantly the EU has not taken on the attributes of nationhood. The EU has developed into a *sui generis* system of transnational governance that has adopted some characteristics of statehood.[2] The political deficiencies of this system of governance have triggered the debate about how to improve the democratic legitimacy of the Union through institutional reform.[3] The governance debate has led to increasing cross-fertilisation with political and legal studies of modern constitutionalism and the extent to which its principles could be applied towards achieving democratic governance beyond the nation-state (Weiler, 1999; Meny, 2003, 1–13).

The old dichotomy between the neo-functionalists and the intergovernmentalists has been revived since the 1990s with the new dichotomy that has emerged between the rationalist approach typified by the work of Moravcsik (1993) and the social constructivist approach reflected in Christiansen, Jorgensen and Wiener (1999, 528–44). While the former school emphasises the primacy of state-led schemes of regional integration, the latter stresses the deeper cognitive and sociological forces at work in integration processes as well as the growing role of non-state actors in the process.[4] The constructivist approach has been strengthened by the development of 'new regionalism' which emphasises the multidimensional process of integration in the context of globalisation. The new forms of regionalism emerging in the 1990s have been characterised by a multitude of actors and shaped by exogenous formative factors in the post-Cold War security setting and rapid economic globalisation. This author believes that the two approaches are complementary and that dichotomy, where it exists, is in the eye of the beholder.

This chapter will not go into theorising about European integration. Rather, my objective is to present and assess the major 'concrete achievements' of the EU.[5] The chapter will be separated along three tracks: first, the economic track that was the primary activity of the EU during the first four decades; second, I will analyse the pillar of political integration that has been slowly taking operational form since 1993; third, I will explore the next big step in European integration – the wider Europe and the new neighbourhood policy. My conclusions will dwell on the role of Europe in the world.

ECONOMIC INTEGRATION – WIDENING AND DEEPENING

Starting from the Treaty of Rome, which was the cornerstone of the European Union, up to the most recent enlargement in 2004, the primary activity of European integration can be analysed through the matrix of widening and deepening. The Community expanded from the relatively homogeneous group of its six founding states to become a much more heterogeneous and diverse union of 25 members. In parallel to this gradual widening, there has been a simultaneous deepening of integration, the essence of which can be captured in the matrix (Table 14.1) presented below.

Table 14.1 The Matrix of Widening and Deepening

Widening →	EC-6 1957				EU-25 2004
Deepening ↓	Zero tariffs	Common external tariff	The four freedoms & harmonisation of standards	Adoption of the euro	Adoption of Constitutional treaty
Free trade area	1967				
Customs union		1967			
Internal market			1992		
Monetary union				2002	
Political union					2004

The top horizontal vector reflects widening through successive enlargements of the Union from its origin to the 'historic' expansion of 2004 when eight new countries from the former communist bloc were 'reunited' with Europe, together with Cyprus and Malta. The policy vectors correspond to the stages of regional integration that have marked the deepening of integration in the EU. Although the boundaries are not always so clear cut in practice, these stages of integration, represent the hierarchy of integration regimes that the EU itself has relied on and they are still relevant today in how the Union manages its external relations with its new neighbours.

From the very beginning, European integration went beyond the idea of a free trade area. The key objective of the Treaty of Rome was to establish a common market that is now referred to as the internal market providing for the four freedoms – free movement of goods, services, people and capital. But the treaty mandated not only market freedom, it also stipulated that the market should be subject to the rule of law. Therefore, rules and regulations that were deemed necessary for the proper functioning of the internal market would have to be developed.

The internal market was only completed in 1992. Why did it take so long? Because it was a vast legislative programme that required extensive rewriting of national legislation. Many of the member countries were still steeped in protectionist practices and state monopolies were prevalent in many service sectors. Lessons from the 1960s had shown that the required change would not be possible without a massive shift away from unanimity to majority voting. This was done in the Single European Act of 1986, which paved the way for one of the most dynamic integration periods in the history of European integration.

The internal market programme was not a static, one-off liberalisation event, which is typical in tariff reduction.[6] It went much further than border restrictions and had much more far-reaching effects in that it acted as a powerful driver of domestic economic (political) reform in the member states.[7] It reduced state intervention in the economy, created new institutional incentives for private enterprise and generally oriented economies towards more free market practices. By using the competition rules, the Commission further triggered the privatisation of telecommunications, broadcasting, banking and transport. What followed was a clear trend towards the Europeanisation of business that undermined the hitherto popular practice of governments supporting their 'national champions'.

The equity provisions provided for under the instrument of the so-called 'structural funds' and more recently the 'cohesion fund' counterbalanced the efficiency considerations of the internal market. Gaping divergence between rich and poor regions of a country, which national governments took responsibility for, were mirrored in the divergence between rich and poor countries in the EU. Financial assistance for infrastructure development and modernisation of their economies was channelled to the countries on the periphery – Ireland, Spain, Portugal and Greece. This has resulted in remarkable economic success with Ireland providing the most dramatic example (O'Toole, 2003).

The need for a single currency to complement the single market was argued – in economic terms – as the need for macroeconomic stability to underpin the intensive trade integration of the internal market (Padoa-Schioppa, 2004). Of course, the elimination of national currencies and their substitution by a single European currency, was an event of major political significance (Dodd, 2001). The national currency is a powerful symbol of sovereignty as it is the confidence in the government that makes it possible to use money for economic transactions. Historically, the creation of a national currency was associated with the emergence of nation-states in Europe. Currency union preceded political union in the case of Germany and Italy. European monetary union (EMU) was also driven by political forces. The primary concern was about the position of Germany in European integration. Following reunification, there was the need to bind this large, new, potentially destabilising, German nation into the integration process and to consolidate European integration.

Although the goal of monetary union was not explicit in the Treaty of Rome, advocates of European integration always considered it as an essential element of the integration process. The first policy steps were submerged in the macroeconomic activism of the 1970s. The excesses of Keynesian policies for priming economies, which resulted in higher inflation and higher unemployment in the 1980s, opened up the debate on the need for rules and constraints rather than political discretion. The Delors report of 1989 provided the path to monetary union, which was formally accepted in the Maastricht Treaty of 1993. The plan gradually took on concrete operational form during the 1990s leading to a remarkably smooth introduction of the euro in 2002.

Economists never fully endorsed EMU arguing that the Eurozone would not fulfil the necessary conditions for optimal currency union. Critical economists argued that a single market does not need a single currency.[8] They predicted that a single currency would put the EU at a competitive disadvantage, that it would lead to less intra-EU trade and more macroeconomic fluctuations as member states lost control over monetary policy and the ability to determine their exchange rates. However, economists on the opposite side pointed to the advantages that the euro would bring including lower transaction costs, increased trade, increased competition and economies of scale, all of which were likely to boost economic growth and compensate for the disadvantages argued by the critics of the euro.

The great concern about the convergence criteria (set out in the Maastricht Treaty) on the part of policy makers and political leaders was, perhaps, an over-reaction to the scepticism of economists. The Commission argued there was need not only for convergence of macroeconomic policy performance, but also convergence of policy preferences in terms of common objectives and choice of instruments. The common goal of price stability was not considered sufficient to lead to full convergence. Therefore, it needed to be underpinned by other ground rules that were set out in the Stability and Growth Pact.[9] The Maastricht Convergence criteria formed a restrictive set of rules that effectively acted as the eligibility criteria for monetary union and formed the core of the EU macroeconomic constitution.

The criteria were:

- The ratio of government deficit to gross domestic product should not exceed 3 per cent;
- The ratio of government debt to gross domestic product should not exceed 60 per cent;
- There must be a sustainable degree of price stability and an average inflation rate, observed over a period of one year before the examination, which does not exceed by more than one and a half percentage points that of the three best performing member states in terms of price stability;
- There must be a long-term nominal interest rate which does not exceed by more than two percentage points that of the three best performing member states in terms of price stability;

- The normal fluctuation margins provided for by the exchange rate mechanism on the European monetary system must have been respected without severe tensions for at least the last two years before the examination.

The financial architecture of EMU is a complex system based on the principle of subsidiary. The European Central Bank (ECB) was modelled on the German Bundesbank and independence is the key. The ECB has not replaced national banks. It has taken over some of the functions previously performed by national central banks, but policy implementation is at the national level. Political accountability lies with the governor of the ECB who has to report annually to the plenary session of the European Parliament. The eleven central bankers on the governing council are national appointees and are accountable to national governments.

The European macroeconomic constitution has so far achieved impressive macroeconomic stability. In addition, EMU has led to growing convergence between poor regions and core countries, so much so that the cohesion countries have grown faster than the large economies at the centre. But it has not delivered on economic performance and the greatest weakness is that the overall economic growth rate of the Eurozone is too sluggish to cope with enlargement and the absorption of ten new countries, a situation aggravated by an ageing population.

Many, including the President of the Commission, have argued that the Stability and Growth Pact needs to be made more flexible. Fiscal policy should be more active in an economic downturn. The United States and Britain had much more pro-active fiscal policy in 2003, which resulted in stronger economic growth while keeping inflation low. Reformers argue that the 3 per cent ceiling need not be abolished but there could be stricter budgetary surveillance combined with a more flexible interpretation of the rules. In any case these rules need to be revised as, in practice, they are being flouted by the larger countries – France and Germany.

STARTING THE PROCESS OF POLITICAL UNION

The construction of the internal market and the single currency extended European activity way beyond the economic field into environment, health and consumer protection, social and labour market policy, education, culture, and immigration. The EU began to encroach more and more on the symbols of national sovereignty. 'Europe without frontiers' – the slogan of the internal market sacrificed the powerful symbol of territorial autonomy. 'Europe in your hand', the slogan of monetary union, led to the disappearance of the cherished symbol of national currencies. The Maastricht Treaty of 1993, which changed the name from Economic Community to the more overtly political European Union, gave a strong signal that political integration would be moving up the agenda from then on.

The Maastricht Treaty was a defining moment in European integration. It provoked a strong public reaction and a public debate about Europe. It brought the citizens into the European debate for the first time and challenged the legitimacy on which the EU was based. The social backlash against Maastricht was triggered by fears that the newfound freedoms of business in the internal market would trample on the fundamental rights of citizens. Many of the new economic rights acquired by corporations in the internal market reduced their responsibilities to labour, to the environment and to communities and governments that provided the infrastructure necessary for those corporations to be profitable.[10]

But Maastricht was really only the tip of the iceberg in the sense that profound constitutional change had already taken place.[11] The European Court of Justice (ECJ) had already spoken of the EU treaties as a 'constitutional charter' of EC law.[12] Lawyers spoke about the constitutionalisation of the treaties. The supremacy of European over national law had been recognised as far back as 1964 so European law was a constitutionally higher law with direct effect at national level so far as it related to the Community sphere of activities. But no public debate had ever taken place about this constitutional change. European integration had always been the preserve of elites and conducted in a top down fashion. That changed dramatically in the 1990s when Europe became a citizens' issue (Gavin, 2003).

Although the internal market guaranteed the free movement of persons – which is the freedom of most immediate concern to citizens – it is still the most underdeveloped of all. The Maastricht Treaty, which introduced a new policy of citizenship, did little to change that. Although the policy broke important new ground (Wiener, 1999), it met with scathing criticism and was castigated as 'bread and circus politics' of EU governments by Weiler (1999). Citizens' groups were not much more positive. So what was intended to bring Europe closer to its citizens only further alienated them.

European citizenship, which is complementary to national citizenship, has major gaps. It is only granted to national citizens, while the 15.5 million persons who are legally resident in the EU have no right to European citizenship – although they live, work and pay their taxes in a member state. The rights conferred by European citizenship are very limited and emanate from the four freedoms of the internal market (free movement of goods, services, capital and people):

- The right to travel, live and work in another country of the Union – but this is incomplete;
- The right to vote in municipal elections and in elections to the European Parliament;

- The right to diplomatic protection by the authorities of the host country;
- The right to submit petitions to the European Parliament;
- The right to refer to the European ombudsman.

Beyond this short list there are a number of rights that are not presented as attributes of European citizenship but which are derived from national citizenship, for example, non-discriminatory treatment for non-nationals, laws extended to family members and the social security laws relating to migrant workers.

European citizenship applies mainly to nationals living outside of their own country, although some aspects of European citizenship are applied irrespective of migration, for example, equality between men and women, environmental rights and consumer protection. Overall, the scope of European citizenship is very narrow as it only relates to the 5.5 million people who work or live in another member state. And even in this area there are still many unanswered questions like what happens to a worker when she loses her job in a foreign country? How to look for a job in another country? Are qualifications recognised? What is the health insurance? Free movement of citizens is still the least developed of the four freedoms.

The need to flesh out the skeletal structure of European citizenship led to the proposal to draw up a charter of citizens' rights. The goal of increasing citizens' rights, which was considered as an essential element for consolidating the legitimacy and identity of the EU, was spearheaded by the German government. The Charter of Fundamental Rights, which resulted from the German political impulse, has been incorporated into the new Constitutional Treaty thereby elevating it to the highest political status in the EU and making it legally binding.

By putting human rights at the heart of a new European constitution, it is hoped to reach out to citizens and provide connectivity with the European institutions. The Charter will increase the 'visibility' of human rights in the EU and provide a clear list to citizens of the rights upheld by the Union. Furthermore, the EU will become party to the European Convention on Human Rights, and can therefore be held accountable for violation of the rights of its citizens. If European citizens can gain redress against EU institutions, it will increase the standing of human rights in Community courts. The Charter will bring benefits not only to citizens by giving them a sense of ownership of the institutions but also to the Union by conferring legitimacy and increased accountability.

The success of the Charter will ultimately depend on how it is used. Engel (2001, 151–70) predicts that the Charter will open up a new window of political opportunity that can be used by all actors. Citizens will ultimately be empowered to bring complaints before the ECJ. Without this the EU would only provide a regime of diplomatic protection similar to that under international public law. The power of citizens to take legal action against EU institutions, with the backing of the ECJ, would give them power to influence the agenda. It would also influence relations between the member states. The Charter could be used by one country to block a new directive or regulation, for example on environmental standards, or social policy.

Others see the incorporation of the Charter into a future constitution as an exercise in spin rather than substance. There is no real need for the Charter as there is no deficit of human rights protection in Europe. So the only goal is to achieve visibility of human rights in the EU. Although human rights are in the EU treaty, they are scattered all over and not very easy for citizens to find. So visibility will improve this. But by this exercise, the EU is avoiding the hard choice of establishing a true human rights policy (Weiler, 2002, 563–81). What is really needed is to establish a Commissioner for Human Rights with a full Directorate equipped with powers to investigate human rights abuses, in a manner analogous to what the Competition Directorate does in monitoring the behaviour of companies.

Moreover, the Charter is incomplete in one key area of importance for meaningful participation of citizens in European policy-making. European Citizens Action Service (ECAS) which is the civil society body representing citizens in Brussels considers 'the right to information' as an essential element of EU democracy and they have formulated the following demand: *All citizens of the EU (plus natural and legal persons) should have a right to be informed of the activities of the EU institutions and their rights and duties derived from the Treaties.* The dearth of information has been blamed for citizens' apathy towards the EU institutions and, in particular, the declining participation of citizens in the elections for the European Parliament – which is the institution closest to the citizens. It is also one of the biggest barriers to labour mobility within the Union.

The right to information would force the EU institutions to be more transparent. At present, information is scattered across several different directorates of the Commission. The right to information would require the Commission to publish a document explaining who does what. Furthermore, ECAS argues that the EU needs to have a bigger programme for citizens and to have a bigger budget. At present it spends .01 per cent of its budget on citizenship policies, which represents four euros per person per year!

Although European integration has been constructed by the democratically elected leaders of its member states, there is no direct European democratic process. Fundamental principles of constitutional democracy such as majoritarian voting, and a direct linkage between the executive and the legislature through a popular vote, as well as a clear separation of powers have not been fully implemented in the Union. The EU has been characterised by a technocratic style of governance with only indirect legitimacy.

To remedy this situation, the political process of drawing up a constitution for Europe was launched by European leaders in 2001.[13] Three key areas of reform were identified: one, how to make the EU more citizen-friendly and especially to bring the EU closer to young people; two, how to make decision-making more efficient as the Union expands to more than 30 members in the foreseeable future; and third, to give the Union capacity to evolve into a more powerful player on the global stage so that it can act as a stabilising factor in a new multipolar world. The political strategy to address those issues was based on four key elements: clarification, simplification, democracy and a constitution. It was necessary to clarify 'who does what' in the EU and to draw a clear demarcation line between the increasingly overlapping competences of the Union and its member states. Next, simplify the plethora of policy instruments that had increased and multiplied in the Union over the years. This, it was believed, would greatly help to make the EU more comprehensible to its citizens. Tackling the democratic deficit would have to make the Union more democratic, transparent and efficient.

Although the language on a possible constitution for Europe was hesitant, the decision to explore institutional reform though a constitution changed the parameters of the debate in important ways (Wallace, 2003). It shifted the focus of discussion away from incremental change to more systemic design of a new institutional architecture. Governance is a rather fuzzy concept. The concept of constitution is much more precise and substantive in a legal sense. A constitution creates the legal framework for government. Thus, the possibility of a constitution raised expectations that the fundamental ambiguities inherent in the Union since the beginning of the Community could be clarified or even eliminated (Gavin, 2003).

The Constitutional Treaty that was adopted in June 2003 is not a constitution for the 'United States of Europe' – reminiscent of the 1789 Constitution of Philadelphia. But it is a federative constitution in the philosophical meaning of the term, that is, a constitutional system in which several states share a common government to pursue common interests. In the language of contemporary political science it is a decentralised system of multilevel governance based on the principle of subsidiarity. This ensures that there is no one-way movement of power from national to European level. On the contrary, power devolves to lower levels of government according to the particular needs of policy sectors.[14]

The Constitutional Treaty contains a number of features derived from modern constitutional experience and recent advances in political and legal theory.[15]

- Values of the Union: it enshrines the political, social and ethical values of the Union.

- Clearly written rules: it clearly sets out the powers of each institution of the Union and, in addition, how the institutions interact with each other.
- Separation of powers: vertically, power is separated between the member states and the union; horizontally, power is separated between the major institutional branches of the Union – the executive, the legislative and the judiciary.
- Equality of citizens and states: it contains a bill of rights for politically equal citizens. It also provides for equality of states and mutual respect between them.
- Primacy of constitutional law: it provides for judicial procedures to interpret and enforce the Constitution and establish the primacy of European law over national law in case of conflict between the two.
- Democratic legitimacy: the laws and policies adopted within the constitutional framework will be accepted and maintained with the rational consent of citizens.
- Stability: the constitution will provide long-term stability for the Union. It provides the necessary balance between stability and flexibility so that the Union will be able to adapt to changing political, economic and social conditions in the future.

The fact that it is called a Constitutional Treaty means that political union still remains incomplete, and the two traditional models of decision-making in the Union will continue in the future. The so-called community method used in certain policy areas (principally economic issues) will coexist with the intergovernmentalist method, which allows member states to retain their power of veto in the field of foreign and security policy. Thus, political integration still lags behind economic integration.

The Constitutional Treaty strengthens and consolidates the checks and balances for policy-making under the community method. The Commission's prerogative, and exclusive power, to propose legislation in the general European interest has been maintained. Decision-making will be shared between the two chambers of the legislature – composed of the Council of Ministers, which represents governments, and the European Parliament, which represents citizens. The co-decision procedure, which will become the general standard for enacting legislation, provides a good balance for law making in the Union. In addition, the ECJ has the power to review the legality of all legislative acts under the community method.

Policy-making under the intergovernmental method reflects a much shallower constitutional process. The right to propose policy resides with the Council of Ministers. All decision-making is centred in the Council working up though the hierarchy from the first stage of working group to the ambassadorial level to the ministerial level in the Council. Voting is either on the basis of unanimity or qualified majority voting at each stage of decision-making. The European Parliament – the voice of the people – is almost completely absent from the process. The Council of Ministers is only obliged to consult the Parliament and there is no obligation to follow its recommendations. The Commission participates in Council meetings but it has no voting rights. In summary, the Council of Ministers, which represents the interests of governments, has the sole power to propose and enact laws thereby combining executive and legislative powers in a virtually uncurtailed manner.

AFTER ENLARGEMENT – THE WIDER EUROPE

Successful enlargement in May 2004 was a major foreign policy success for the EU. Fifteen years after the fall of the Berlin Wall, the former communist countries have made monumental progress towards rebuilding their nations in the mould of free market economies and pluralist democracies. This is the triumph of Europe's 'soft power', defined as the power to attract and persuade other countries without relying on the 'hard power' of military coercion (Nye, 2003). The EU has used its soft power effectively in shaping and moulding the new members' policies and institutions over the last ten years in preparing them for enlargement.

Enlargement has not only closed the door on Yalta and the Cold War, it has also redrawn the map of Europe. The expansion of the Union eastwards will extend its borders to Russia and the Western Newly Independent States and on the southern Mediterranean shores its new borders will stretch from Morocco to Syria. The EU now proposes enhanced integration to create 'a ring of friends' with its new neighbours. They include the southern Mediterranean countries of Algeria, Egypt, Israel, Jordan, Lebanon, Morocco, Palestinian Authority, Syria, Tunisia, and the Eastern countries of Russia, Ukraine, Moldova and Belarus.

The EU does not plan to continue enlarging over the next decade – that would be unsustainable.[16] Instead, the Commission (2003) proposes a new neighbourhood policy to extend the benefits of enlargement to neighbouring countries but without actually offering them the prospect of membership.[17] To achieve this post-enlargement goal the EU is developing a two-pronged strategy: to work together on a broad horizontal programme of economic, political and institutional reforms with all neighbouring countries and, simultaneously, to create a vertical framework of bilateral trade agreements with each country. The aim is to create a Pan-Euro-Mediterranean market along the lines of the existing European Economic Area, which is a model for those European countries that wish to cooperate closely with the EU but do not want to become members, such as Switzerland and Norway.

The security dimension of the new neighbourhood policy will be central as the most important security threats to the Union, which are perceived by citizens to be international terrorism, weapons of mass destruction and organised crime, are all sourced in neighbourhood countries. Therefore, the EU is now building up a more activist external policy to enhance both economic and security integration. Terrorism is frequently harboured in poor countries and, inversely, economic prosperity is a powerful factor for conflict prevention. One of the EU's most important assets for conflict prevention is regional economic integration, which has provided the basis for its own peace and prosperity over the past 50 years. It now wants to share this experience with the Wider Europe in order to build security and stability as well as economic integration in the region.

EU policy for the Wider Europe can be differentiated into two culturally separate regions (Emerson, 2004). The Wider Europe refers to those countries that identify with European values, history and culture. In practice, they correspond to Council of Europe membership, which is the European organisation explicitly committed to democracy and human rights. Europeanisation is generally accepted in this region without overtones. The EU's 'new neighbourhood' which extends from North Africa to the Greater Middle East, is a region – with the exception of Israel – composed of Arab–Muslim countries characterised by Islamic civilisation where political organisation and the daily lives of citizens are dominated by Islamic values.

Despite our 'common Mediterranean civilisation', there are fundamental divisions and fractures between Europe and the Middle East. The Arab–Muslim world has not accepted secularisation of values and attitudes in the twentieth century although it has accepted some formal and material secularisation such as Western legal codes, and some modern institutions. In the sphere of values, the status of the individual and the position of women have not changed much. Most Arab–Muslim countries have authoritarian governments that do not allow much popular voice and civil society remains weak. This situation is compounded by widespread economic underdevelopment coupled with high population growth. The discourse on Europeanisation does have overtones of cultural imperialism in this region, where 'the weight of the past' still hangs heavy.

Against this background, the EU has proposed a broad multilateral framework for a set of common policy spaces to be achieved over the next 10–20 years.

- The EU will work together with the Council of Europe to construct a common European space of democracy and human rights.
- A European space of education and research will be built on opening of EU research programmes and much fuller funding than the existing technical assistance programmes.

- The EU proposes a pan-European free trade area together with a modular approach for individual countries to achieve deeper integration.
- A European macroeconomic and monetary area will lead to increasing use of the euro as the main trading currency in the Wider Europe.
- Pan-European networks in transport, energy (oil, natural gas pipelines, and electricity grids) and telecommunications will be developed with synchronised financial support from European institutions.
- A common space of freedom, security and justice will be constructed which will offer increased possibility for free movement of persons (visas and immigration) in exchange for improved border controls and law and order at home.
- A space of cooperation in the field of external security will be developed for conflict resolution and peacekeeping (European Commission, 2003).

CONCLUSIONS

This chapter has outlined the economic development of the EU into a large single market with a single currency as it has expanded from a community of six to 25 members. And the next logical step will be integration of the Wider Europe. As the ultimate goal of the Union is peace, it is characterised as a community of shared values based on democracy, human rights and the rule of law. As such, the EU is considered a normatively attractive entity in international relations but it is not yet a cohesive, compact actor in the global arena. The major challenge ahead for the EU now is how to consolidate its political union so that it can be not only a model of democratic governance in the world, but also play an influential role in the *EU* reform of global governance. *long term goal*

NOTES

1. Throughout this chapter I will use the term European Union to provide consistency for readers and will not refer to the title of European Economic Community that was used prior to 1993.
2. There is a very large and varied literature on governance in the EU. An excellent synthesis is provided by Jachtenfuchs (2001, 245–64).
3. There is also voluminous literature on the democratic deficit of the EU and a very good overview of the issues and the debates can be found in Karlsson (2001).
4. Pollack (2001, 221–44) gives a good overview of the debates between the rationalist and constructivist schools.
5. Robert Schuman said in his declaration of 9 May 1950 said: 'Europe will not be made all at once or according to a single plan. It will be built through concrete achievements.' Cited in Devuyst (2002).

6. The internal market programme included liberalisation of non-tariff barriers, the harmonisation of regulatory standards and de-regulation of service industries, that had both an internal and external dimension (Gavin, 2001).

7. For a discussion of liberalisation of 'behind the border barriers', which economists call deep integration, see Lawrence (1995).

8. American economists were most critical of EMU. Martin Feldstein writing in *The Economist*, 13–19 June 1992, argued that the single currency would put the EU at a competitive disadvantage. A similar argument was made by Robert Barro writing in *The Wall Street Journal*, 14–15 August 1992. And 60 German economists signed a manifesto in the *Frankfurter Allgemeine Zeitung*, 11 July 1992, supporting these views.

9. The economics of convergence played no role in the theory of optimal currency but they played a major role in the practice of monetary integration in the EU. See Nigel Dodd (2001, 45–51), 'The Hidden Side of the Euro'.

10. By the 1990s, the member states had completely sacrificed sovereignty in the areas of trade, agriculture and monetary policy. They had partially sacrificed sovereignty in environment, social policy, consumer protection, etc. But governments had voluntarily paid the 'cost' of sovereignty in return for the 'benefit' of greater economic prosperity.

11. There is a vast academic literature on constitutionalism in the EU. For an overview of the issues see Craig (2001, 125–50). Weiler (1999) brings together his collection of essays on various aspects of constitutionalism in Europe.

12. European Court of Justice, Opinion 1/91.

13. The European Council of December 2001 produced the Laeken Declaration which called for the establishment of a European Convention to prepare the ground for the next Intergovernmental Conference dealing with institutional reform.

14. The principle of subsidiarity, which was introduced into the EU by the Maastricht Treaty, states that action at the EU level is only possible when national action cannot achieve the desired result. Therefore, it is a mechanism for preventing excessive centralisation.

15. See Yves Meny (2003) for an analysis of modern constitutionalism in the light of American history and experience of twentieth-century history in Europe. Dahl (2002) provides a critique of the American constitution in light of modern scholarship.

16. EU membership is governed by Article 49 of the Treaty on European Union. Any European state may apply for membership but it must meet the criteria of democracy, the rule of law, human rights, respect for minorities, a functioning market economy, and the capacity to cope with competitive pressures and the ability to take on the obligations of membership.

17. Communication from the Commission to the Council and the European Parliament. *Wider Europe – Neighbourhood: A New Framework for Relations with out Eastern and Southern Neighbours.* The Communication responds to the request of the European Council at Copenhagen (December 2002) which decided on the first round of enlargement to include ten countries in 2004, two further countries, Romania and Bulgaria, in 2007, and the possibility of starting negotiations for accession with Turkey in 2004. The European Council also decided on separate treatment for the western Balkan countries by providing a special regime of 'Stabilisation and Association Process' that puts them on the track for accession.

15
China: Towards Regional Actor and World Player

Tie Jun Zhang

INTRODUCTION

In the reform era since the late 1970s, China has experienced an almost unprecedented rate of economic growth unparalleled by any other countries of the world and unknown in China's own recent history. The country sustained average annual growth rates of some 10 per cent within the last two decades and escaped the Asian financial crisis of 1997–98. In 2002, with its 1.28 billion people and a GDP of just $4,600 per capita, China was the second largest economy in the world after the US, measured on a purchasing power parity basis (CIA, 2002).

With this increasing power, China has been redefining its global and regional roles. In this chapter, I argue first of all that the Chinese leadership and its intellectual followers have reconstructed the country's self-identity in a dualist form, that is a developing country in the era of globalisation and a potential responsible world power on the international arena. I indicate that this dual identity in fact reveals the deeply embedded mentality in the Chinese mind-set, that is, the strong-weak power mentality, which is reflected both by Deng Xiaoping's statement in the initial period of the reform era and the domestic and international strategies of the present Chinese leadership. In accordance with the Chinese identity as a potential responsible world power, Chinese elites perceive the emergence of a multipolar world in which China, will be one of the poles, alongside the other four powers of the US, the European Union (EU), Japan and Russia. I argue that the biggest challenge China faces in creating a multipolar world is properly dealing with the US as the latter seems intent on 'preserving the unipolar moment'. On the inter-regional level, China has actively participated in inter-regional economic and security cooperation schemes as part of its desire for modernisation as well as to enhance its international influence and to promote the multipolarity of Sino-ASEAN–Japan trilateral relations, and especially various aspects of Sino-Japanese hegemonic competition in East Asia. The conclusion will identify the major challenges China faces in securing the dual identity and enhancing the country's global and regional roles.

CHINA'S SELF-IDENTITY AND ROLE PERCEPTION

In this section, the dual identity of the present China is seen as officially constructed. On the one hand, the Chinese leadership and its intellectual followers conceive the country as a developing country in the globalisation era; and on the other, they also perceive that the country is a potential world power in the international arena.

One side of the dual identity, China as a developing country in the globalisation era, highlights the weaknesses that continue to exist within the economy and the urgent necessity for economic development, an interest which China shares with many other developing countries.

National leaders have on many occasions emphasised the weaknesses China has as a developing country. Former president Jiang Zemin, in an interview with reporters from the *Washington Post*, admitted that 'China has a large population and weak economic basis, and its economic development level is still not high and thus it is still a developing country.'[1] The weaknesses of the country are further highlighted by the processes of globalisation, which leaders regard as a 'double-edged sword' for all the developing countries including China. For most developing countries, globalisation means more challenges and pressures than opportunities.[2]

Identifying the country as a developing country endowed with weaknesses, Chinese leadership has repeatedly indicated that economic development and modernisation are the highest priority for China. Deng Xiaoping, the initiator of China's economic reforms after the Cultural Revolution, proposed his argument of 'development as the hard fact' (*fazhan shi yingdaoli*) and claimed that virtually all the problems China faced would be solved with economic development (Li Baojun, 2001, 146–7).

While stressing the centrality of economic development at home under the guise of its identity as a developing country, the Chinese leadership has also been emphasising the common interests it shares with many developing countries in opposing Western criticisms on human rights, environmental and various other problems, exemplified, for instance, by objection to Western (especially the US) proposals of criticising the human rights records of China in the annual United Nations (UN) Conference on Human Rights. With many developing countries backing the Chinese position, these proposals have never been passed in the conferences.

The other side of the dual identity is China as a potential responsible world power. National leaders' frequent assertions of China as the largest developing country are framed alongside unabashed calls to the US (as the largest developed country) to recognise China's increasing international influence, exemplified by its permanent seat on the UN Security Council, the most populous country of the globe, and a nuclear power. While the Chinese leadership has never openly claimed to become a world power,

China's strong appeal for creating a multipolar world order where it would constitute one pole, the country's determination to oppose hegemony, and especially its mission to become a 'medium developed' country by the mid-twenty-first century, all suggest a vision among the Chinese elites to make the country a world power in the future. Considering its sheer size and large population, it would mean that China would be among the largest economies in the world.

In recent years, there have been basically two positions within the country concerning the role of China in the international arena. One position favours China as a 'world power', supporting multipolarity (Xia, 2001). The other position is that China should be a 'responsible country'.

According to the first position, China has not yet become a 'world power' but is on its way towards such an end. China's intention of becoming a world power, it is so claimed, refers to the willingness of the country to play a larger role in international society (both at the regional and global levels), and to realise the rejuvenation of the Chinese nation in the twenty-first century by becoming rich and strong. Then, how should we understand this rejuvenation? Since China was historically a world power, the grand rejuvenation of the Chinese nation would naturally mean a return to its former status as a 'world power', according to this position.

Concerning the view that China would be a 'responsible country', the wish is that China needs to be 'connected to the international track' (*yu guoji jiegui*). Under the 'connection to the international track' thesis, China should develop as other countries do according to prevailing international norms, and to improve the international image and position of the country gradually.

The above two positions both make sense on the surface. But when we examine them against the international and domestic environment, both of the arguments are insufficient. The first position combines the realism of international relations with cultural particularism, while the second reflects a mixture of liberalism and universalism. The extreme form of the first position would certainly not be desirable for the international society, since it would possibly imply a return to the central kingdom status in the ancient sense while using the modern Western *realpolitik* to strengthen its power. The reaction from the West and China's neighbours would work against China's own interests, since in such a scenario both the West and China's neighbours would most likely adopt a policy of containment against China, the last thing China would like to see. The second position, while closely conforming to the demands from the West, would present problems on the domestic front, and likely generate much resistance.

In the official construction of China's self-identity, a potential 'responsible world power' is the most desirable. On the way towards such an end, Chinese policy and behaviour would most likely contain the following features: firstly, the necessity of economic development would still be emphasised, very much in line with the logic of Deng Xiaoping's assertion of 'development as the hard fact'. Any actions provoking hostile international responses would be avoided unless there is an issue of highest concern to Chinese sovereignty. Secondly, China would still adhere to the sovereign rights central to its national interests, such as territorial integrity. Lastly, the country would gradually move towards conformity to international norms and institutions and in the process attain normality and responsibility.

The dual identity lies in China's self-image as a strong-weak power, something which is deeply embedded in the Chinese mind-set. Both Deng Xiaoping's arguments in the initial period of the reform era and the proposals of the present Chinese leadership on China's domestic and international strategies reflect this mentality.

Deng argued in the mid-1980s that 'China is a great power but also a small power at the same time' and the country needed to follow a diplomatic strategy in line with the strong-weak power mentality, this is 'concealing one's strength' (*taoguangyanghui*) and 'taking some effective actions' (*youshuozhuowei*) in dealing with other major powers.[3] This strategy in fact can best be described as the one applied specifically in the process of China's march towards a potential responsible world power.

Towards the end of 2003, the Chinese leadership poposed the national strategies of 'rising in a peaceful way' (*hepingjueqi*) and 'developing in a scientific way' (*kexuefazhan*). While the former indicates the determination of the Chinese leadership to secure the self-identity of a potential responsible world power and the consequent attainment of that position peacefully and responsibly, the latter reveals a clear understanding of the country's weaknesses and the need for development to be linked to scientific and technological progress.

CHINA AND THE WORLD MULTIPOLARITY

Chinese perspective on the world multipolarity

In the post-Cold War era, foreign policies have focused upon creating a regional and international environment conducive to the goals of national modernisation and economic reforms. More specifically, national leaders looked upon the external environment through the prism of the officially constructed identity of China as a potential responsible world power and an emergent multipolar world order.

Chinese commentators conceive the present stage of international relations as a transition era leading towards multipolarity, in line with the official view on the issue. It should be noted, however, that Chinese official and academic views differed between the period before the Kosovo War and that after it. Below, I will analyse the perspectives of the Chinese leadership and its intellectual followers on the supposedly emergent multipolar world order before and after the Kosovo War.

At the end of the Cold War, China expected the global pattern of power to gradually shift from US–Soviet bipolarity to a multipolar world in which China would play a much larger role. After the collapse of the Soviet Union, Chinese experts estimated that the global order based upon the United States as the sole superpower was a temporary one, to last perhaps one or two decades and then to be replaced by a pattern of many powers or power centres, including China, Japan, Europe, and Russia, rising as independent 'poles' to challenge American power and ambition.

There are basically two reasons behind the Chinese expectations of a rapid transition to a multipolar world order: the desirability of a multipolar world and the feasibility of such an order.

The desirability of a multipolar world order is conspicuous since such an order would definitely include China as one of the poles. In a speech delivered at Harvard University in 1998, General Xiong Guangkai, Deputy Chief of the General Staff of the People's Liberation Army, asserted, 'Any efforts towards seeking hegemony and world dominance can only result in accumulating contradictions and fermenting war', and 'Only by facing up to and promoting such a trend as the co-existence of multipolarity can we bring about peace and prosperity' (Xiong, 1998). Concerning the feasibility of multipolarity, Chinese commentators referred mainly to the decline of the US and the rise of other major powers, especially the EU. Many Chinese commentators considered that the US decline was both inevitable and potentially far-reaching (Chen, 1996). While assuming a big role for Europe in the emergent multipolar world, the rapprochement of a powerful Europe and Asia through the Asia–Europe Meeting (ASEM) process is also considered by some Chinese authors as presaging further decline in US global influences.[4]

After the Kosovo War and the NATO (North Atlantic Treaty Organisation) bombing of the Chinese Embassy in Belgrade, a growing number of Chinese analysts and officials concluded that the transition period toward multipolarity would take longer than previously envisaged, with the US remaining at the apex as the sole, unchallenged superpower. In August 1999, the then Chinese President Jiang Zemin admitted, 'The process towards multipolarisation would be marked by zigzags and be complicated' while at the same time claming that the trend is irresistible.[5]

On the reasons why the time frame for the transition had to be extended, Chinese commentators referred foremost to the fact that the US was *objectively* still powerful. This powerful position of the US, as perceived by some, was not only sustainable for a reasonable period of time, but would even be strengthened. The second reason Chinese commentators cited for the delay of a multipolar world order was that the US *subjectively* or intentionally attempts to strengthen its 'leadership' around the globe. The third argument made by Chinese commentators in explaining the delay of multipolarisation was that the other major powers, including the EU, were still not capable of confronting the US.

While acknowledging that the speed of the multipolarisation has decreased, and predicting future growth in the US power, Chinese analysts stress that the present situation does not necessarily mean that the US will be able to create a unipolar world. The current trend is only considered as a temporary setback in the transition to a new world structure.

Implications of the world multipolarity for China

In an international system characterised by anarchy, a multipolar world order is conceived by the Chinese elites as the best possible structure in which Chinese national interests can be safeguarded. As such, it is the preferred external environment through which China could have a bigger role to play as one of the poles. For the Chinese elites, a multipolar world would have several implications for the country.

Firstly, it suggests a favourable *power structure* for China, since it would ensure, in the minds of Chinese elites, China's position as a responsible world power. It should be indicated, however, that this position does not mean that China would seek to restore its historical status as the hegemon of its known world (East Asia), but to be one among the relatively equal poles of the world. Even in the region of East Asia, most Chinese writings conceive that Japan would certainly be included as one of the poles, alongside China. Secondly, it would result in a new international *decision-making framework* in which China as a pole would have greater influence. Chinese leaders such as the former president Jiang Zemin and the present president Hu Jintao[6] have in recent years repeatedly argued for the democratisation of the world. One of the rationales is that while the West and especially the US pressure for the democratisation of Chinese domestic politics, the Chinese, as a counter measure, argue for the democratisation of world politics. A similar argument can also be found in China's emphasis on the superiority of sovereignty to human rights. However, when the Chinese leaders argue for the democratisation of the world, the direct international consequences, instead of just as a counter measure, are certainly of greater concern.

Lastly, a multipolar world should also, according to the Chinese elites, give rise to new *policy efforts* concerning creating and promoting a 'just and righteous new international political and economic order (NIPEO)'. Chinese president Hu Jintao, in his first overseas visit, made to Moscow in March 2003, urged 'people of all countries in the world' to make joint efforts to promote the establishment of the NIPEO.[7] This proposed NIPEO should be understood as the Chinese-perceived norms for an emergent multipolar world.

Referring back to the Chinese dual identity, a multipolar world order and the new international decision-making framework fit China's identity as a potential responsible world power, while the new international political and economic order, especially the economic one, satisfies China's identity as a developing country in the globalisation era.

CHINA AND INTER-REGIONALISM

The Chinese dual identity is not only reflected in China's foreign strategy on the global level, but equally exemplified by China's participation in the inter-regional arrangements of the following: the Asia-Pacific Economic Cooperation Forum (APEC), the ASEAN Regional Forum (ARF), the ASEM, and the Shanghai Cooperation Organisation (SCO).

China and Asia-Pacific inter-regionalism

China has so far participated in both the APEC (an organisational forum for Asia-Pacific economic inter-regionalism) and ARF (an organisational forum for Asia-Pacific security inter-regionalism) cooperation.

APEC, which came to exist in 1989, is based upon regionalism, consultation and is non-binding with respect to its major principles. China, as the largest developing member in APEC, shares common interests with other developing members in a number of areas, including: the speed of trade and investment liberalisation, especially in certain strategic and infant sectors; the need of economic and technological cooperation within the forum, or more plainly the necessity for economic and technological assistance from developed members to developing ones; and the 'Asian Way' of cooperation (consultation and non-binding decision-making mechanism), and so on. Ever since the Informal Leaders' Meeting in 1993 when different timetables for developing and developed members in the areas of trade and investment liberalisation were formulated, China has been aligning with developing members in safeguarding these common interests.

Participation in the APEC cooperation serves China's identity needs as a developing country in the era of globalisation. As APEC is the first significant international cooperation mechanism with Chinese involvement, it is an important 'platform' through which to launch the internationalisation of the Chinese economy. It is also a significant forum in which Chinese voices can be heard, and a site where Chinese interests can be promoted or at least not be sacrificed.

The rationale for participation in the APEC cooperation is to a large extent also reflected in China's involvement in Asia-Pacific security inter-regionalism, where the ARF is so far the most comprehensive organisational framework. China joined the ARF in 1994 when it was formally established, attracted by cooperative and consensual principles upon which the organisation operated. While ASEAN countries saw that bringing China into the forum would enhance its own bargaining position, the Chinese intention of participating in the ARF cooperation lies in the following two areas: firstly, to reduce regional apprehension about the rise of China and to persuade ASEAN members that China was committed to a 'peaceful' rising; and secondly, to prevent the ARF from being too heavily influenced by the US and/or Japan at the expense of China.

Within the ARF framework, the Chinese hope is to actively play a role in shaping the regional security arrangement in the ASEAN Way, stressing consultation and dialogue as the preferred mode of regional diplomacy on how to interact. Obviously, China would be unwilling to participate in any regional security arrangements that are initiated and dominated by the US and/or Japan. The ARF also serves as a learning platform for the country in a multilateral framework, an opportunity for socialising with regional elites, and a site for China to express its own concrete concerns regarding regional security.

China and Asia-Europe inter-regionalism

While participation in the APEC largely secures China's identity needs as a developing country in the globalisation era, Chinese involvement in the ASEM process is more or less a reflection of both sides of the dual identity.

It is conspicuous that the Chinese participation in the ASEM process helps China enhance its economic contacts with EU members, promoting bilateral trade and European investment into China, thus aiding China in its modernisation and development programme. In the Chinese conception, the ASEM also promotes the emergence of a multipolar world on two levels: the Asia–Europe level and the China–EU level. On the one hand, it provides the Eurasian inter-regionalisation with an organisational forum, and a framework in which the Asian and European members express their concerns over global and inter-regional issues without the involvement of the only superpower (the US) and beyond the mass territory of Russia (one of the potential poles in the Chinese anticipated emergent multipolar world). With such an arrangement, world multipolarity is promoted precisely because the position of Europe and East Asia as independent world players is enhanced, with no interference from the US. Writing for the *People's Daily*, Huang Qing argued that 'the creation and strengthening of the connecting line between Asia and Europe would promote the multipolarity of international relations' (*People's Daily*, 9 April 1998).

On the other hand, of more strategic importance for China is that the ASEM framework provides China with a regular format with which China can cooperate with EU members, and therefore promote multipolarity of the world. In the Chinese conceived emergent multipolar world power structure, there are three entities within the ASEM framework (the EU, China and Japan) and two outside it (the US and Russia). Commenting on the Asia–Europe Meeting in 1998, Yu Fen, a senior researcher from China Institute of Contemporary International Relations stated that 'the EU urgently needs to promote its relations with the "rising" China so as to strengthen the European position in the world' (Yu, 1998, 49).

While the first level of Asia–Europe cooperation promotes inter-regionalisation between the 'hard' regionalised Europe and 'soft' regionalised East Asia, in the Chinese understanding, the second level of China–EU cooperation is conducive to the promotion of world multipolarity in the traditional sense of providing a balance of power. For China, of similar relevance in the latter prospect is the creation and evolution of the SCO.

China and the SCO

The SCO was established in June 2001 in Shanghai with the involvement of six members: China, Russia and four central Asian countries (Kazakhstan, Kyrgyzstan, Tajikistan and Uzbekistan). The SCO is an outgrowth of the 'Shanghai Five' mechanism set up in 1996 that involved China, Russia, Kazakhstan, Kyrgyzstan and Tajikistan. Members of the Shanghai Five and the SCO have been engaged in cooperation in areas of demilitarisation and confidence-building measures in border regions, anti-terrorism and economic cooperation.[8]

For China, the importance of the SCO lies in the following domains: a framework for the country to tackle the problem of Muslim independent forces and terrorists; a vehicle for China to gain cooperation from Russia and Central Asian countries in importing oil and natural gas; and most importantly an instrument with which to promote the formation of a multipolar world, with the trilateral relations between China, Russia and the US taken into account.

Concerning the last aspect, Wang Jinchun of the Institute of World Economics and Politics argued, 'The Shanghai Spirit itself is a great appeal against hegemony and power politics. … Besides, the establishment and evolution of the SCO would further promote the deepening of the strategic cooperative partnership between China and Russia. Opposing hegemony and power politics, promoting world multipolarity, creating a just international political and economic order, and promoting world peace, are in turn the most important political factors putting China and Russia closely together' (Wang, 2001, 80–1).

The SCO is so far mainly a security cooperation organisation, and in this case, it is in many aspects comparable to the ARF as far as China's involvement in international multilateralism is concerned. The SCO and the ARF both serve China's vital security interests. Both are frameworks for cooperative security, and share consensual characteristics. However, different Chinese security interests are served in the two arrangements. In the SCO, China has gained more realist benefits in areas such as border issues and internal stability, while in the ARF China has gained experience of cooperating in a more liberal multilateral setting with different kinds of states (from friends to potential adversaries) and at the same time highlighting China's responsibility for regional peace and stability, thus convincing regional states of China's peaceful intention in its security policy conduct. It should be indicated that while the ASEAN does not want the ARF to replace the regional balance of power structure centred on the US military presence and alliance with regional countries, China does strongly declare that alignment patterns in the region are obsolete and should be replaced by cooperative security. Meanwhile, it needs also to be emphasised that the SCO process is a more preferred form of cooperation for China precisely because it is a Chinese initiative and China (together with Russia) sets the agenda for the organisation. Referring back to Chinese identity as a potential responsible world power, the SCO serves more in the 'world power' part while the ARF more in the 'responsible' part.

CHINA AND EAST ASIAN REGIONALISM

In December 1997, the first informal leaders' meeting of the ASEAN states with China, South Korea and Japan was held in Kuala Lumpur to later develop into the ASEAN, with China, Japan and South Korea (ASEAN+3) mechanism. For the first time in history, Asian leaders sit together to discuss regional issues of common concern, to set an agenda for regional cooperation and tackle a number of related issues, without the involvement of the sole superpower. Two years later, in November 1999, the third ASEAN+3 meeting was held in Manila in which leaders of the 13 countries issued a 'Joint Declaration of East Asian Cooperation'.

The initial rationale for ASEAN states to have this mechanism was their realisation of the inadequacy of the existing ASEAN framework to deal with the financial crisis, and the need for Northeast Asian countries (especially Japan and China) to handle the problem. Japan had long been the leading goose in the Asian 'flying geese' mode of economic development, which can be seen as an informal regionalism based on division of international labour. In this role, Japan was a major source of investment in, and one of the most important destinations of commodities from the rest of East Asia. China's significance for ASEAN states in the financial crisis was of a different nature to that of Japan. Two issues have contributed to the upgrading of China's image among Southeast Asian countries. The first was China's promise (and evident commitment) of not devaluating the Chinese currency (renminbi), and thus not taking advantage of the worsening export competitiveness of ASEAN countries. The second was China's non-interference policy during the conflict against ethnic Chinese in Indonesia in 1998, a stance in sharp contrast to the position taken in the late 1960s. The 'China threat', though not losing its appeal totally among ASEAN countries, has decreased significantly. Increasingly, the ASEAN members have seen the rise of China more as an opportunity and less as a threat to them. Under this circumstance, ASEAN members accepted the Chinese proposal in 2000 to establish the China–ASEAN Free Trade Area (CAFTA). In November 2002, the then Chinese Prime Minister Zhu Rongji and his ASEAN counterparts signed the 'Framework Agreement of Comprehensive Economic Cooperation between China and ASEAN Members', in which the two sides agreed to establish the CAFTA (*People's Daily*, 8 November 2002).

The improvement of Sino-ASEAN relations and particularly the anticipated establishment of the CAFTA exert great pressures on the Japanese. Given the present troublesome relationship between Japan and China, the increasing influence of China over Southeast Asia is a source of irritation for the Japanese. The founding of the CAFTA would embarrass Japan greatly, if Japan does not have a similar arrangement with the ASEAN. China would become the dominant force in East Asian organised economic regionalism, without Japan's involvement. Since Japan has long seen Southeast Asia as its economic 'backyard', it has a great deal to worry about with that prospect. Therefore, immediately after the agreement between China and ASEAN on establishing the CAFTA, the Japanese Prime Minister Kuizumi visited Southeast Asia to attempt to mend relations with ASEAN members. But, due to the Japanese insistence on the protection of its agricultural goods, Kuizumi's visit was basically unsuccessful, with the only result being the signing of a bilateral free trade agreement between Japan and Singapore.

The Japanese quick reaction to the improved Sino-ASEAN relations and the anticipated establishment of the CAFTA should be understood in the wider background of hegemonic competition between Japan and China in East Asia. This competition can be interpreted in the following three aspects: a competition between a continental power (China) and a maritime power (Japan); that between Japan's becoming a normal country and China's rising to a world power; and the deep distrust between the two countries.

Concerning the first aspect, the sheer size and rich natural resources of China contrast with those of Japan. Geopolitically speaking, China, with its geographical centrality in East Asia, is obviously in an advantageous position in the Sino-Japanese hegemonic competition in East Asia. That is also one of the reasons why Japan chooses to strengthen its alliance with the US in the post-Cold War era.

The second aspect lies at the core of the Sino-Japanese hegemonic competition, and is the source for the Sino-Japanese security dilemma. The Chinese worry that 'normalisation' of Japan would imply remilitarisation, threatening China and other regional countries. A primary cause of such

Chinese worry is Japan's unwillingness to face its own history of invading neighbouring countries, including China.[9] Japan is apprehensive that China's rise would pose a threat to Japan and to the region. In the past two decades, the Japanese have formulated two versions of the 'China threat'. In the early 1980s, some Japanese portrayed a prospect of the 'Chinese military threat'. After two decades of high economic growth in Japan ended in the 1990s, the Japanese described China as the 'world factory' and put forward the thesis of the 'Chinese economic threat'. Here, we observe that both countries see each other as either a threat or potential threat.

As for the third aspect, although there are essential mutual needs in promoting bilateral economic cooperation,[10] deep distrust exists between the two countries. The distrust between China and Japan lies in the fact that there is not only insufficient understanding between the two governments, but to some extent, hatred between the two peoples. While the distrust in the bilateral relations have been documented and studied substantially by both Asian and Western analysts, a new development has thus far not attracted enough attention from the outside world. Since the end of 2002 when an editor of the *People's Daily* wrote an article for the Beijing-based influential journal of *Strategy and Management*, there has been a debate on the so-called 'Chinese New Conception on its relations with Japan'. Several Chinese researchers in the debate argued that China needed to have a new conception of its relations with Japan. They based their argument on the assumption of the worsening Chinese strategic environment in which the US is more and more demanding towards China. Primarily for this reason, they proposed that China needed to improve its relations with Japan by enhancing mutual trust, and they argued that China should not stick persistently to the historical concerns. The initial academic analysis immediately resulted in a nation-wide online debate among Chinese researchers and the general public. Some of the analysts who proposed the new conception were named in the discussions as 'traitor scholars'. This is just one incident that shows how deep the distrust and hatred are among the Chinese towards the Japanese. Similar patterns can also be found in the speeches of right-wing Japanese politicians, in some of the Japanese media, and online discussions among the ordinary Japanese people. This kind of mutual distrust makes the hegemonic competition between Japan and China all the more severe, long lasting and difficult to resolve.

CONCLUSION

In the proceeding discussion, I analysed the dual identity of China as a developing country in the globalisation era and a potential responsible world power on the international arena. This dual identity, in turn, has determined that the primary goals for China in the early twenty-first century are to make the country rich and strong, and to promote the emergence of a multipolar world in which China would be one pole. The two sides of the dual identity are not in contradiction with each other, since the status as a developing country is a description of the present situation and that of responsible world power is a future vision.

For securing the dual identity, on the global level the biggest challenge for China is how to deal with the US as the sole superpower. Both China and the US now face a dilemma in their bilateral relations. For China, one of the primary objectives in its current phase of nation- building is to make China a pole in the (Chinese perceived) emergent multipolar world. The most important means to such an end is the modernisation of the country, and to reach this goal, China badly needs economic cooperation with the US. Then again, the Chinese objective of becoming a pole in the emergent multipolar world is in severe conflict with the US vital interests in 'preserving the unipolar moment'. US economic interests depend upon the potential large Chinese market and thus the necessity of deepening economic cooperation with China. However, this cooperation would promote China's rise to becoming a pole in a US-dominated, reluctant multipolar world. The Chinese proposal of 'peaceful rising' national strategy is, to a large extent, a response to such a dilemma.

As indicated in the first section, Chinese leadership proposed a national strategy of 'peaceful rising'. With the above-mentioned dilemma in Sino-US relations taken into account, the question now is: if we assume that the Chinese leadership is sincere on such an approach, what would be the reaction from the US side towards this Chinese 'peaceful rising'? The fact is that the US primary purpose of foreign policy now is to 'preserve the unipolar moment', and the goal of China's 'peaceful rising' is to become a world power or a pole in the Chinese perceived multipolar world. Under such a circumstance, whether the Chinese rise is peaceful or not it would be in conflict with the US, and the US would take certain actions considered to be necessary to slow down the process of China's rising.

On the inter-regional level, the ASEM (especially with regard to Sino-EU cooperation) and the SCO (particularly Sino-Russian cooperation) frameworks serve China's goal of promoting world multipolarity, but they are not without problems in this regard. The Russians are not only weak and declining but they (just like China) also need good ties with the US despite their grumbling about NATO expansion and their disappointment over the paltry economic support that has been provided by the US (and Western Europe) to underpin their democratic experiment. Europe is not united enough to say 'no' to the US and there are also a host of differences between China and Western European countries in terms of human rights, Taiwan and Tibetan issues. Therefore, it is problematic, if not totally impossible, for China to make a coalition of states (or groups of states) seeking to counter US power.

In order to become a world power, China has to first of all develop as a regional power. To act as a responsible world power, China ought to begin with behaving as a responsible regional power. In the genuine East Asian regionalisation, China could build such an image, just as it has been attempting to do recently, particularly during and after the East Asian financial crisis. The building of such an image, in turn, is conducive largely to creating a peaceful regional environment for China's modernisation programme. ASEAN+3, the existing pan-East Asian regional arrangement, is now at best the miniature of APEC plus ARF. It is to a great extent because of this that the US has not shown its opposition to it. To change the present situation of the ASEAN+3, a miniature of the slowly progressing APEC and the mere 'talk shop' ARF, reconciliation between China and Japan and coordination in promoting regional integration by the two countries are crucial. Without these, East Asian regionalisation will be at most a loosely organised regional arrangement with no core, and world multipolarisation by means of inter-regional arrangements will still be rhetoric and there will be no significant role for East Asia in it. So far, there is no sign that such reconciliation and coordination will come any time soon. As discussed earlier, the reverse is more of a reality. Therefore, while China makes great efforts (though presently less in words) on creating a multipolar world, Japan as a regional concern for China would divert substantially the Chinese energy that could otherwise be used in its goals on the global and inter-regional levels.

NOTES

1. <www.fmprc.gov.cn./chn/9535.html>.
2. Tang Jiaxuan (former Chinese foreign minister), 'Speech at the ASEAN-Dialog Countries Meeting', <www.fmprc.gov.cn/chn/2493.html>.
3. For this section, the following source has been useful: Centre for Study of Establishing Socialism with Chinese Characteristics, 'Deng Xiaoping guoji zhanlue sixiang yanjiu' (A Study on Deng Xiaoping's International Strategic Thoughts), Guofang daxue chubanshe (National Defense University Press), Beijing, 1997, 224.
4. Chen Feng of the China Institute of International Strategic Studies indicated that the ASEM revealed that for the first time the US, as the only superpower in the world, was unable to take part in such a significant international conference. Chen Feng, '1997 nian de guoji zhanjue xingshi' (The Strategic Situation in 1997), *Guoji zhanlue yanjiu* (International Strategic Studies), Vol. 47, No. 1 (January 1998), 12.
5. For the rest of the speech, see Jiang Zemin, 'Speech Delivered in the "Shanghai Five" Leaders' Meeting', 25 August 1999, Website of Chinese Ministry of Foreign Affairs, <www.fmprc.gov.cn/chn/11855.html>.
6. In Hu Jintao's speech on the five principles of the new international political and economic order, the first one is 'to promote the democratisation of international relations'. Hu

Jintao, 'Speech Delivered in Moscow College of International Relations', <http://news.
sina.com.cn/c/2003-05-28/1519165028s.shtml>.

7. Ibid.

8. The last one has so far been very limited, primarily since Russia and the Central Asian
members have little to offer to China for its economic modernisation programme as
compared with the West and Japan.

9. Recent Chinese online discussion indicates the worry among Chinese people that Japan's
unwillingness to admit its history of invading neighbouring countries makes the younger
generation of Japanese unaware of or misunderstanding that period of dark history.
Under such circumstance, a remilitarised Japan would face little domestic opposition.
<www.sina.com.cn>.

10. While Japan has long been the largest trading partner of China, in recent years, Japanese
investment in China has also been increased to a great extent, and at present Japan
is the second largest source of foreign direct investment for mainland China (after
Hong Kong).

16
Regionalism in the Indian Ocean Region

S. D. Muni

It may sound odd to talk of an ocean as a region. The concept of Ocean Region may be understood in terms of a regional identity among the countries located on the rim of the ocean. Conceptually, it is like talking of the Persian Gulf region or regionalism in the Persian Gulf. There again we include the countries that are located on the rim of the Gulf. On the same lines, some scholars have also talked about the Bay of Bengal region and cooperation among the countries constituting its periphery, such as India, Bangladesh, Sri Lanka, Myanmar and Thailand. In fact the idea of BIMSTEC (Bangladesh, India, Myanmar, Sri Lanka and Thailand Economic Cooperation) emerged from such a definition of a region.[1] This idea is also reflected in concepts like 'Pacific Rim', 'Atlantic Community', 'North Sea nations', and so on. In the case of the Indian Ocean, the idea of cooperation in this region was initiated in 1993 and the institutionalisation of this concept took place in 1997, with the establishment of the Indian Ocean Rim Association for Regional Cooperation (IOC-ARC). This chapter is not confined to the IOC-ARC only, but will also look at various other regional groupings that are in operation involving the countries located on the rim of the Indian Ocean.

The Indian Ocean is spread over a vast area of about 75 million square kilometres, covering almost the whole of Asia and also washing the shores of West and South Africa. There is a debate about the boundaries of the Indian Ocean Rim, but if we follow the 1974 United Nations definition, then between 45 and 47 countries are covered, of which nearly 40 are littoral countries (Muni, 1996a). Regionalism in this vast region has naturally evolved in different stages, and continues to redefine and enrich itself to be in rhythm with the unfolding economic and strategic contexts of global and regional changes. There is a tendency among scholars and policy-makers to assume that what happens in the developed regions of Europe and America may replicate or be followed in Asia and Africa. This is a debatable assumption, though several scholars have tried to underline the experiences of Europe as an exemplar for a successful and effective regional grouping in the developing world, and indeed there are important inspirations and lessons to be drawn from the experiences of the developed countries in Europe that took the lead in building institutions of regional cooperation.

This assumption is perhaps driven by the fact that world developments have been shaped and decisively influenced by the developed world, particularly during the colonial period and after the Second World War. Accordingly, as Europe has demonstrated its push towards greater economic and political integration, or as the American continent has witnessed the process of the US economy integrating with smaller and more vulnerable neighbouring economies, the countries of Asia and Africa will also follow the same course; perhaps with a time lag in a manner similar to embarking on the course of economic development with a time lag. Even Nehru, while projecting his vision of Asian resurgence, seemed inspired by the Western world's experience in regional cooperation. He told a gathering of Asian countries in 1949:

The Americans have already recognised a certain community of interests and have created machinery for the protection and promotion of common interests. A similar movement is in progress in Europe. Is it not natural that free countries of Asia should begin to think of some permanent arrangement than this conference for effective mutual consultation and concerted effort in the pursuit of common aims.[2]

Nehru was thinking of a broader grouping, which could also focus on regional economic issues. There is a point in the assumption that what happens in the developed world may be taken as an example to consider in shaping relations in Asia and the developing world. The experiences of the developed world present themselves as ideals and role models for the developing world to emulate. Also, the developed world wants the developing world to shape itself within the framework of what is considered desirable by the former. The developed world also provides incentives and punishments to get the developing world to follow the path already charted. What is ignored in pursuing these assumptions is that development is not conditioned by external stimulation and injections *alone*. The inherent strengths, assets and shortfalls are equally, if not more powerful components in the developmental process. One of the most articulate leaders of contemporary Asia, Dr Mahathir bin Mohammad of Malaysia, reflecting in 2000 on the contrast between Europe and Asia in the context of developmental paths, said:

Asia is most unlike Europe. The Europeans are of three major ethnic groups, the Slavs in the East, the Germanic race in the north and the Latin in the South. All these races are very acquisitive, especially of the territories of the neighbours. As a result, over the past two millennia there has not been a year when there was not a war between their states. In the process they got rather mixed and developed more or less along the same line culturally and economically. Since they are prone to fighting, they developed greater skills in devising and producing even more efficient killing instruments. This skill spilled over into other commercial activities so that they became industrialised very early. It is not so in Asia. The area is so vast that delineation of boundaries was not easy. Though there are distinct ethnic groups, most Asians are subdivided into tribes, which off and on come together under strong tribal leaders. Thus the Seljuks, the Ottomans, the Mongols and the Manchus. The Asians built empires mostly in Asia but these empires were not durable. The death of a powerful leader invariably led to a break-up into numerous little empires or states. By the beginning of the twentieth century all the Asian countries had come under the rule of various European powers, including the European Russians who subjugated the Central Asians. Almost without exception the Asian countries under European domination remained backward and poor. The only country which managed to remain independent and to industrialise along the European pattern was Japan. This then is the historical and cultural background against which we must consider the present and future of Asia.[3]

The contrast between Asia and Europe is clearly evident in the diversity of regionalism as well. Besides the cultural, historical and geographical differences underlined in the above speech, the regionalism experience in Europe benefited from the fact that it had external support without any pressure or restraint. The post-Second World War economic reconstruction pursued by the US under the Point Four agreement helped stimulate regional cooperation in Europe. In contrast to this, in Asia there has been little contribution from the developed economies to the process of development, and politically the great powers have always been suspicious regarding any moves towards regionalism that did not appear compatible with the broader Western interests and strategic perspective. No wonder then that while Europe has forged itself into a Union with formidable economic and political integration, there are no such signs in Asia, even in a sub-region like Southeast or East Asia where regionalism has been relatively more successful. Regionalism has been an important phenomenon in the post-Second World War world, evolving in different patterns and at different speeds.

EVOLUTION OF REGIONALISM

Soon after the end of the Second World War, global activity was marked by two tendencies: namely, the structuring of the Cold War by the great power rivalry, and the reconstruction of the war-torn economies in Europe and Japan. The influence of these two activities was reflected in the first generation regionalism moves made in Europe, the Americas and Asia. On the one hand, there were predominantly military-oriented regional groupings, formed from collaboration between a superpower and a group of countries in a given region. Organisations like the Rio Pact, Organisation of American States, North Atlantic Treaty Organisation (NATO), Central Treaty Organisation, and Southeast Asian Treaty Organisation (SEATO), may be mentioned here. Then there were organisations with an economic purpose but strategically oriented to serve specific interests of the great powers that were promoting these organisations. Organisations like the Regional Cooperation for Development, Association of Southeast Asia, and its successor the Association of Southeast Asian Nations (ASEAN), Southern African Development Coordination Conference (SADCC), and the Gulf Cooperation Council (GCC), may be mentioned in the developing regions. In Europe, the Treaty of Rome of 1957 that established the European Economic Community (EEC), and the Organisation of Economic Cooperation and Development (OECD) were also established for the purpose of economic cooperation.

Sometimes it is argued that regional groupings like the EEC, ASEAN and SADCC emerged independently to promote regional cooperation. This may be true in some respects, but the powerful strategic backup and stimulation from the great power behind these organisations should not be lost sight of. The US concern in Southeast Asia arising out of its deteriorating military efforts in the Vietnam War were a major stimulating factor in the forging of ASEAN. Perhaps, the idea was to save dominos from falling, in the case of defeat in the war against Vietnam as indeed happened. Why else were only non-communist states brought together under ASEAN and how could this organisation not hold its first summit until 1976, that is, after the US withdrawal from Vietnam? Similarly, the EEC and the OECD could not have come up without the security umbrella created by NATO. As for SADCC, the support and encouragement from the former European colonial powers to ensure greater independence of the regional economy from that of the South African economy was a strong motivating impulse behind this organisation (Holland, 1995; Mehrota, 1991; Thompson, 1992).

These early regional cooperation initiatives may therefore be considered as examples of *hegemonic regionalism*, as compared to those that followed in the 1980s, which were more autonomous in their motivations and manifestations and can be called examples of *autonomous regionalism*.[4] The creation of the South Asian Association for Regional Cooperation (SAARC) in 1985, following an initiative taken in 1980, and the Economic Cooperation Organisation (ECO) established in 1985, may be taken as examples of *autonomous* regionalism. They had no supportive impetus from any of the great powers, though for SAARC, the US was initially interested in getting its goals and broad objectives defined in the context of the Afghanistan crisis precipitated by the Soviet military intervention in December 1979 (Muni, 1984). The *hegemonic* regionalism emerged during the conditions of intense Cold War, which led to the division of regional entities so as to suit the strategic interests of the sponsoring or supporting superpower. Norman D. Palmer, commenting on this has observed:

The regional structure that emerged as a result of the conflictual state of Soviet–American relations, was a system of rival alliances. That system sharply divided the Asia-Pacific region along communist–non-communist lines and greatly added to the tensions and divisions in a region where conditions already existed to an alarming degree. In each set of alliances, the initiative was taken not by indigenous powers but by the contending super powers. (Palmer, 1991, 64)

The next stage of regionalism started unfolding as the end of the Cold War approached. In the post-Cold War order, global hegemony acquired a new meaning and structure. Now there was no pressing need for competitive, military and strategic grouping to be created and nursed. Accordingly, old regional groupings started experiencing internal transformations, including expansion. One of the most illustrative examples of this has been ASEAN, where the communist/non-communist divisions got blurred and all those countries originally excluded from the regional organisation, like Vietnam, Laos, Cambodia and Myanmar, were now made members between 1995 and 1999. In fact, the ASEAN countries did not succumb to Western pressures and persuasions to delay granting membership to Myanmar despite the latter being subjected to economic sanctions and political pressures on account of its suppression of democracy by the military regime since 1990. Such pressures continue even today. There was delay in the entry of Cambodia into ASEAN but that was more due to internal ASEAN preferences for democracy and stability, in view of ASEAN's long-standing position on the Cambodian conflict.

This 'new regionalism' in the post-Cold War world has some striking characteristics. To begin with, it is an open regionalism, both in terms of the composition of the region and also in its agenda on economic cooperation. The geographical definition of a region chosen for cooperative engagement has become flexible and less decisive. This is clearly evident in IOC-ARC where countries spanning Australia to South Africa have come together. Similarly, the arrangement of Asia–Europe Meeting (ASEM) also spans continents and it avoids following the geographical definition of Asia since the Asian component is represented only by ASEAN. ASEAN's innovation of ASEAN+3 and ASEAN+1 summits also reflects a flexible geographical framework. There are examples of geographically overlapping and converging regional grouping like BIMST-EC (now BIMSTEC, see endnote 1), Greater Mekong Sub-region (GMS: including ASEAN countries and China), and the Mekong–Ganga Cooperation Initiative (MGC: launched in November 2000, between India and the Mekong basin countries). Sub-regional groupings are also encouraged and accepted to expedite cooperative activity, like the South Asia Growth Quadrangle (SAGQ) within SAARC and growth triangles within ASEAN. In fact the latter, which emerged earlier, inspired the former in 1997.

In terms of its agenda for economic cooperation, the 'new regionalism' has invariably been driven by economic liberalisation and globalisation. As a result, it is open ended in its structure. In fact open regionalism that first asserted itself in the form of Asia-Pacific Economic Cooperation (APEC) was a reaction to the protectionist tendencies evident in the North American Free Trade Association, General Agreement on Tariffs and Trade and even moves towards European union, the latter of which being seen by many as a step towards 'fortress Europe'. Accordingly, a protective and restrictive tendency is becoming visible in a number of attempts at establishing free trade agreements within already established regional economic groupings like ASEAN, SAARC, and so on. But here again, the free trade agreements go beyond the generally understood geographical confines of a given regional grouping. Thus we see that not all regional groupings have followed an integrationist approach in the regional sense of the term. There is also the issue of compatibility with the new WTO (World Trade Organisation) framework, within which only such trading preferences that do not conflict with the WTO regime can be practised. The driving consideration seems to be to maximise economic gains in whatever manner is considered feasible rather than being conditioned by the goal of economic integration in a geographically defined region.

Yet another noticeable aspect of new regionalism is the greater sensitivity towards regional security concerns and initiatives. This has been reflected in the attempts either to introduce a security dimension in existing regional groupings or to evolve new and additional institutional arrangements. ASEAN, for example, decided to set up new security forum in the name of ASEAN Regional Forum (ARF) in 1995. SADCC and the GCC also laid stress on regional security aspects when they were initially conceived in 1980 and 1992 respectively. In the post-11 September 2001 context, regional groupings are adopting anti-terrorism mechanisms and forging agreements to join the 'war against global terrorism', led by the US. SAARC had a convention on 'Suppression of Terrorism', which is being revamped. ASEAN has also entered into specific commitment with the US to facilitate the fight against global terrorism. The Shanghai Five group has been expanded and renamed as the Security Cooperation Organisation in view of the fundamentalist threat posed to the member countries. A notable dimension of the security consciousness in 'new regionalism' is the use of the instrumentalities of economic cooperation like trade and investments to create mutual stakes and build security. ASEAN always had a strong bias in favour of the economic route to security. China has made use of such economic instrumentalities in building a stable, cooperative and secure neighbourhood. Strategic undercurrents were an important aspect of the Indian Ocean Rim cooperation initiative launched in 1993.

REGIONAL GROUPINGS IN THE INDIAN OCEAN REGION

If the Asian and African countries having projections into and access to the Indian Ocean are taken into account, they are members of a number of regional groupings operating in the Indian Ocean region. These groupings can be divided into three categories, namely: those that are security related, those that focus primarily on economic cooperation, and those that are broad based, taking into consideration both economic cooperation and strategic aspects of the given region. Let us identify these categories.

In the security-related category, there is only one regional organisation that needs mention and that is the ARF. After the winding down of the Cold War-related military alliances like the SEATO, there were bilateral and multilateral security agreements and arrangements, such as the US military presence in Japan, Korea, Thailand, the Philippines and Australia. The ARF was conceived as a broad-based forum, not even a type of military alliance to discuss security issues in order to find ways and means to enhance regional security in the Asia-Pacific region. It was established in 1995, as a result of the concern for regional security in the aftermath of the Cold War and the expected prospects of the withdrawal or reduction of a US security presence from the region. The lurking reality of the rise of China as a major economic and military power in the region was also taken into consideration. The ARF is, in other words, a security extension of the ASEAN and has the membership and presence of almost all the major powers of the region such as the US, Russia, China, Japan, the European Union and India. Since we are concerned more with economic regionalism, we need not go into the details of ARF and its dynamics in this chapter (Ball and Acharya, 1999). It may however be kept in mind that the security role of ARF is supplementary and complementary to the economic and developmental role being played by the parent organisation, ASEAN.

A large number of regional groupings may be included in the category of economic cooperation organisations. The names, the year of establishment and the membership may be mentioned as follows:

1. The Colombo Plan (1950–51); the members include Afghanistan, Australia, Bangladesh, Bhutan, Fiji Islands, India, Indonesia, Iran, Japan, Republic of Korea, Laos, Malaysia, the Maldives, Mongolia, Myanmar, Nepal, New Zealand, Pakistan, Papua New Guinea, the Philippines, Singapore, Sri Lanka, Thailand, the US and Vietnam.
2. APEC (1989) includes all the ASEAN members and China, Hong Kong and Taiwan, US and Canada, as well as Australia, Japan, New Zealand and South Korea. India tried to become a member during the early 1990s, but did not succeed, in part because some of the APEC countries had reservations about its membership. In practice, India was itself a reluctant

applicant since there was some ambivalence regarding the benefits as well as the difficulties that membership might bring to the country.

3. GMS (1992) comprises Cambodia, Laos, Malaysia, Myanmar, Singapore, Thailand and Vietnam. China has also associated itself with this economic cooperation programme, which is being supported by the Asian Development Bank.

4. BIMSTEC (1996) includes Bangladesh, India, Myanmar, Sri Lanka and Thailand. Nepal and Bhutan have recently joined this grouping, but the current political dynamics across the region give rise to caution about further expansion. If China and Pakistan seek to join the organisation, some existing members may not be in support of their membership – particularly India and Thailand. In addition, Thailand may also have reservations regarding countries like Singapore and Malaysia seeking membership since its initial support for the BIMSTEC initiative was prompted by the government's 'look West' policy in search of alternative economic options to the ASEAN grouping.

5. IOC-ARC (1997) has a membership which includes Australia, India, Indonesia, Kenya, Madagascar, Malaysia, Mauritius, Mozambique, Oman, Singapore, South Africa, Sri Lanka, Tanzania and Yemen. This grouping was expanded in March 1999, by admitting five more members, namely: Bangladesh, Iran, Seychelles, Thailand and United Arab Emirates.

6. MGC (2000) brings together Cambodia, India, Laos, Myanmar, Thailand and Vietnam.

In addition to these groupings, sub-regional groupings have also emerged. Significant innovation has been made by ASEAN since 1992, through the development of growth triangles. Such triangles not only involve member countries but also their specified territories that can mutually increase each other's productivity depending on geographical proximity and production complementarities. As noted earlier, ASEAN has also developed another mechanism for expanding the scope of regional cooperation, through establishing summit structures with non-member countries and other regions. ASEAN's 'plus' summits (+3 with China, Japan and South Korea, +1 with India) and summit meetings with ASEM may be mentioned here. SAARC also got inspiration from this idea and established a growth quadrangle involving Bangladesh, Nepal, Bhutan and India. These four countries can together harness the Brahmaputra River basin, covering the north-eastern part of the South Asian region, as is being done in the case of the Mekong or other ASEAN growth triangles. BIMSTEC, on the other hand, may be seen as yet another example of inter-regionalism, or rather inter-sub-regionalism where members of ASEAN and SAARC have joined hands in pursuance of their developmental objectives.

The regional groupings falling into the third category, of broad-based organisations, are as follows:

1. ASEAN (1967) with Indonesia, Malaysia, the Philippines, Singapore and Thailand as early members. Brunei joined in 1984 and Vietnam became a member in 1995, Laos and Myanmar in 1997, and Cambodia joined in 1999. East-Timor may join ASEAN soon. ASEAN has a number of other countries as dialogue partners and observers.
2. GCC (1981) has as members Bahrain, Kuwait, Oman, Qatar and Saudi Arabia and the United Arab Emirates. (The absence of two major Gulf powers, Iran and Iraq, may be noted here, as both of them were locked in a war at that time.)
3. SAARC (1985) includes Bangladesh, Bhutan, India, the Maldives, Nepal, Pakistan and Sri Lanka. Attempts to include Afghanistan in this grouping have not succeeded so far.
4. ECO (1985) originated with Iran, Pakistan and Turkey as the founding members. In February 1992, this organisation was expanded to include newly emerged Central Asian countries, and now has a total of eight members.
5. South African Development Community (SADC) (1992) is represented by Angola, Botswana, Lesotho, Malawi, Mozambique, South Africa, Swaziland, Tanzania, Zambia and Zimbabwe. This was the enlarged version of its predecessor SADCC established in 1980, without South Africa which was then under the apartheid rule.

All these regional groupings are focused on economic cooperation for development. However, they are open to cooperation in some security and political areas. For instance, ASEAN gave birth to the Zone of Freedom, Peace and Neutrality (ZOFPAN) in 1971, under which specific assurances were sought from dialogue partners and all other great powers operating in the ASEAN region that they would keep the region free from conflict and mutual rivalry. The ZOFPAN idea has been extended in the nuclear field by the declaration of a Southeast Asia Nuclear Weapons Free Zone (SEANWFZ). Accordingly, ASEAN disapproves of ferrying and deployment of nuclear weapons in the region. ASEAN as a group strongly disapproved of the Indian and Pakistani nuclear tests in May 1998. In recent years, ASEAN has also sought to intervene in situations of internal political crisis, like in Indonesia. The initiative for this was taken by Thailand under the concept of constructive engagement and as a response to emerging problems of political instability in the region.

The concept of Troika has emerged in this respect. But to make it compatible with the initial ASEAN principle of non-interference in internal affairs, under the 1976 Treaty of Amity and Cooperation, the acceptance of the Troika mechanism is subject to voluntary option of the affected member country. However, ASEAN is not immune to external influences and has to take account of diverse factors, especially in the broad area of security (Acharya, 2001). We have noted earlier that ASEAN also agreed to cooperate with the US in its war against global terrorism.

The dimensions of security aspect reinforced are also evident in SAARC, GCC and SADC. SAARC has taken positions on global disarmament issues and there is a SAARC convention on 'Suppression of Terrorism', which is currently in the process of being revamped and reinforced in the context of post-11 September developments (Rahman, 2001). The GCC, having emerged in the context of Iran–Iraq War, underlined the members' 'determination to defend their independence and territorial integrity', within the framework of the Arab League (Sandwick, 1987). It would be an unnecessary digression here to go into the security aspects of these organisations, though we may recall, as mentioned above, that economic cooperation has the potential of building mutual confidence and security stakes as reflected in the 'new regionalism'.

REGIONAL GROUPINGS AND ECONOMIC INTEGRATION

Of the regional groupings functioning in the Indian Ocean region, ASEAN is the only one that stands out for its performance on building economic cooperation. It has maintained a reasonably high level of intra-regional trade (ranging between 20 per cent and 25 per cent during the past decade) and the growth triangle concept is integrating economically compatible parts of the region. The process of integration through trade is a strong point of ASEAN. It decided to establish the ASEAN Free Trade Area (AFTA) in 1992 and set the target of 15 years to do so. In 1994, the deadline for AFTA was reduced to ten years and the scope was expanded to include even unprocessed agricultural products in addition to manufactured and processed agricultural products as agreed in 1993. Since the expansion of ASEAN through the inclusion of Laos, Myanmar and Vietnam in 1997 and Cambodia in 1999, it was realised that the new members would not be ready for the AFTA deadline in 2004. A deferred time scale has, therefore, been agreed to facilitate the poorer and weaker members to join later, by 2007 or 2008.

The ASEAN has also stepped up economic regionalism by establishing institutional mechanisms of +3 and +1 as well as ASEM. ASEM may be seen as an example of inter-regionalism between one and another continent. This is expanding the regional economic framework and adding dynamism to development and integration processes. Such expansion was also necessitated by the economic downturn that gripped ASEAN from 1997. Recovery is still the main goal of the region, but the whole process is linked with the global trends in growth and economic recovery. To rebuild its economic dynamism, ASEAN has for the past few years been forging free trade agreements with powerful economies in the region such as China, Japan and the US. India also decided to have a free trade agreement with ASEAN.

Intra-ASEAN investments have generally followed economic logic of productivity and profits. No strong evidence of investments on the basis of regional considerations is available. During the late 1970s and early 1980s, attempts to set up a regional industrial fund through requests for contributions amounting to 1 per cent of gross domestic product from every member state did not make much headway. In recent years, the relocation of some industries is taking place within ASEAN from one country to another as well as from those outside the region, such as Japan. This is motivated by labour costs, raw material availability and profit margins. China is also investing in some of the poorer ASEAN countries like Laos, Myanmar and Cambodia to link them with its own economy and help develop its far flung and less developed regions like Yunnan. The ASEAN+3 arrangement with China, Korea and Japan is also geared to encouraging investments in and closer trade relations with the ASEAN region.

In comparison to ASEAN, other regional groupings in the Indian Ocean have made only limited progress towards advancing economic integration in the region. In South Asia, impressive expansion of bilateral trade has taken place between India on the one hand and Nepal, Sri Lanka and Bangladesh on the other, but this happened not within the regional framework or through SAARC. There also exists a free trade agreement between India and Sri Lanka since 1998, and a similar agreement is being envisaged between India and Bangladesh. A virtual free trade regime operates in practice between India and Nepal, and India and Bhutan. With all this, the regional trade in the SAARC region stands at a paltry 4 per cent of its global trade. This percentage may be slightly higher if we also include the sizeable informal bilateral trade in the region. A decade or more earlier, formal SAARC regional trade was 1.5–2.0 per cent of its total global trade. The regional economic scene is vitiated by the India–Pakistan divide, where the latter refuses to have even normal trade relations with India on the basis of Most Favoured Nation status. This is the reason that the projects establishing a South Asian Preferential Trading Arrangement (SAPTA) and a South Asian Free Trade Agreement (SAFTA) in the region under the SAARC umbrella have not got off the ground effectively until recently (Bhattacharya and Katti, 1996).

There are signs of change in the dynamics within the SAARC region since the Islamabad SAARC summit held in January 2004. The Indo-Pakistani conflict had cast a shadow even on the possibility of this summit being held, because India was insisting on a complete stoppage of cross-border terrorism from the Pakistani side in Kashmir before any meaningful bilateral and regional cooperative activity could be promoted. In Islamabad, on the sidelines of a SAARC summit, India and Pakistan, following a meeting between Pakistan's General Musharraf and India's Prime Minister Atal Behari Vajpayee agreed to restart bilateral dialogue on confidence-building measures and cooperation between them. The benign impact of this understanding was clearly reflected on SAARC when Pakistan agreed to the SAFTA and to the adoption of the SAARC Social Charter. The Indo-Pakistani dialogue has been carried forward by the new United Progressive Alliance of Dr Manmohan Singh and the prospects of a positive turn in Indian–Pakistan relations have been strengthened, including cooperation in the field of energy between the two countries.

There are two sets of pressures behind this positive turn in South Asia. One obvious pressure is coming from the people in India and Pakistan, and other neighbouring countries who are sick of persisting regional discord and conflict and are gradually asserting their support for regional cooperation. Then there are international pressures, particularly from the US, which does not want discord between India and Pakistan, particularly in the context of the continuing 'global war on terrorism' being fought by the American and Pakistani troops along the Pakistan–Afghanistan frontier. The US, at the highest levels, has repeatedly made it known that it wants an amicable India–Pakistan relationship, and for that is even willing to play the role of a mediator or a facilitator. The Pakistan army's collaboration with the US in this war has also alienated extremist *jihadi* Islamic forces in Pakistan and they are venting their anger against General Musharraf. A positive spin-off of this internal schism within Pakistan is that General Musharraf is realising the inherent dangers of encouraging terrorism against India and is keen to show that he wants an amicable relationship with the eastern neighbour. Accordingly SAARC is looking more hopeful now than at any time in its past.

SAARC has also encouraged sub-regional cooperation in the form of a Growth Quadrangle involving four countries, namely: Bangladesh, Bhutan, India and Nepal. The primary basis for this approach was to harness potential natural resources like water, timber, oil and natural gas, and minerals. The geographical proximity of the participating countries and the easy approach of this Quadrangle area with the dynamic ASEAN region were additional considerations. It was also thought that this sub-regional approach would perhaps reduce the obstacles from the political conflict between India and Pakistan that has not allowed SAARC to achieve its true potential. Though the concept is viable and the promise is attractive, the SAGQ has not been able to make much progress. The factors responsible are both economic and political. Economically, the region has poor infrastructure and the huge investments required to launch major developmental projects have been shy in forthcoming, including from international and regional multilateral financial institutions like the World Bank and the Asian Development Bank. Politically, mutual suspicions and fear continue to haunt the participating countries from realising their objectives (Dubey et al., 1999).

The Indian Ocean Rim countries have also recorded increased trade with each other since the late 1980s. This was one of the important factors that led to the IOC-ARC initiative. It was also thought that the force of big and growing economies would be able to pull up the smaller and developing economies. The performance of the IOC-ARC, while being positive both on trade and investment counts, remains far below expectations and real potential. Difficulties have been created in this respect by the tariff and non-tariff barriers, as well as investment restrictions and lack of robust financial infrastructure. Not all the member countries have completed their economic reforms in any meaningful manner and responded to the positive implications of globalisation. There are also varying levels and approaches in respective member countries to the issues of economic development and cooperation (Kerr and Thrope, 2000; Wadhva, 2003).

The performance of GCC and SADC in terms of economic cooperation is also mixed. While trade is increasing among the member countries, the potential of trade creation is not being realised fully. Similarly, there are also impediments to the flow of investments as diversification of economies has not taken place adequately. In SADC, the South African economy continues to dominate regional economic activity. In the GCC, oil trade underlines most of the economic thrust.

CONCLUSION

Thus we find that within the regional groupings that are active in the field of economic cooperation in the Indian Ocean region, by far the best performers have been the ASEAN and APEC organisations. In SADC and SAARC, the core and biggest economies of South Africa and India respectively, have moved towards integrating the smaller economies of their respective regions, but mostly through bilateral activities rather than as a part of building regional integration. Though this pattern has led to economic integration, it has not occurred without complaints from the smaller countries. There are possibilities of inter-regional cooperation particularly between ASEAN and the SAARC members, and that cooperation is growing significantly (Kelegama, 2002, 80–110). The prospects of such horizontal cooperative linkages between other groupings are not very encouraging. The only exception in this regard is in terms of the prospects for the larger and more diversified economies of the region, like Australia, Singapore, Malaysia,

India and South Africa, to gradually strengthen their mutual cooperative linkages. Mention may also be made here of the Chinese economy fast expanding its engagement with the regional groupings in Indian Ocean and other areas.

The problems that have come in the way of greater economic integration in the region are many and varied. To begin with, not all regional economic groupings are focused on the objective of economic integration. They started as structures of open regionalism and continue to see advantage in that framework. Secondly, there are still sharp political differences among the member countries that continue to hinder faster and firmer moves towards integration. Differences between India and Pakistan in South Asia are the most illustrative in this regard. This is reinforced by the fact that economic size and levels of development are unequal. As a result the gains of greater economic activity and integration steps are also unequally distributed leading to further political difficulties between cooperating partners. And lastly, the impact of globalisation and liberalisation has been divergent among the countries of the Indian Ocean region. This has affected their performance in generating regional trade and attracting foreign direct investment.

In a recent commentary on the value of regional cooperation, the Asian Development Bank said:

> Many nations across the globe are struggling to respond to formidable challenges while accepting the principle of globalisation. The challenges extend from economic adjustment and restructuring to overhauling institutional frameworks and rebalancing governance systems. Also, globalisation has increased constraints on the sovereign authority of nation states in managing economic affairs. Likewise, new information and communication technology has further reduced operational independence at national as well as international levels of governance. It has also constrained those with limited control over the rules of competition, including such issues as brand names and patent rights. Many developing nations are not well equipped to respond effectively on their own. (ADB, 2002)

Under the thrust of these developments, economic integration has acquired new meaning and dynamics. In the developing region of the Indian Ocean, with countries of vast inequalities of resources, levels of development and capacities to cope with globalisation dynamics, the challenge of achieving economic integration will continue to be complex and formidable. An important aspect of such integration is that the economies of developing countries are also becoming closely linked with those of the developed world under the thrust of globalisation. The patterns of economic integration that seem viable are therefore mixed ones, and not defined either along the

South–South linkages of the 1970s and 1980s or within regional and sub-regional geographical contexts alone.

NOTES

1. BIMSTEC has since been renamed, at the first summit of this grouping held in Thailand in July 2004, where after the inclusion of Nepal and Bhutan, the new name given to the organisation remains BIMSTEC but it is now called 'Bay of Bengal Initiative for Multi-Sectoral Technological and Economic Cooperation' – BIMSTEC-EC.
2. Text of Nehru's speech at the Conference on Indonesia, New Delhi, January 1949 – see Jawaharlal Nehru, Speeches, vol. I, 1946–49, 325–30, Publications Division, Government of India.
3. Mahathir bin Mohammad's speech at the Asia Society, Hong Kong Centre, 28 October 2000 <www.asiasociety.org/speeches>.
4. I have discussed the theoretical aspects of 'hegemonic' and 'autonomous' regionalism in details elsewhere, in Muni (1996b).

Part Four

Conclusion

17
Regionalism and World Order

Björn Hettne

INTRODUCTION

This book has shown that a major trend after the Cold War has been global regionalisation: a new, genuinely world-wide economic and political phenomenon having a significant impact on various issue areas. Not only does it emerge all over the world but, as described in many of the chapters (for instance S.D. Muni's discussion of the Indian Ocean region, and in the overview by Louise Fawcett in Chapter 2), regional formations increasingly interact, overlap and transform, thus creating a new global political landscape which is significantly different from the Westphalian international system. Since most chapters have focused on individual regions this new landscape may not have come out clearly enough. This last chapter therefore deals with the issue of regionalism and world order. My purpose is to consider the regional dimension of alternative world orders, in the context of 'the war on international terrorism'. This recent geopolitical change has enforced one particular world order alternative: a US-driven project to change the world in accordance with its perceived 'national interest', a project that would be incompatible with regionalism, pursued above all by the European Union (EU). To understand the future world order is thus to consider the relative strength of these two competing world order projects. This is not a question of power balance in the traditional Westphalian sense. Both projects go beyond power balance and aim to restructure the world in accordance with a certain set of values; they are transformative but resting on incompatible principles: neo-imperialism and 'hard' power of the sole superpower versus inter-regionalism and 'soft' or 'civilian' power of a regional formation. The chapter starts with a discussion of regionalism and agency, then moves into the question of alternative world orders, to end up with contrasting the inter-regionalist project pursued by the EU to the unilateralism of the current US administration.

REGIONALISM AND AGENCY

Regions are not simply geographical or administrative objects, but should be conceived of as subjects in the making (or un-making); their internal cohesion as well as their boundaries are shifting, and so is their capacity

269

as actors. When different processes of regionalisation in various fields and at various levels intensify and converge within the same geographical area, the cohesiveness and thereby the distinctiveness of the region in the making increases. This process of regionalisation can in general terms be described in terms of levels of 'regionness' – i.e. successive orders of regional space, system, society, community and institutionalised polity. Increasing regionness implies that a geographical area is transformed from a passive object to an active subject – an actor – increasingly capable of articulating the transnational interests of the emerging region.

The concept of regionness thus defines the position of a particular region in terms of its cohesion; this can be seen as a long-term endogenous historical process, changing over time from coercion, the building of empires and nations in history, to voluntary cooperation: the current logic of regionalisation. The political ambition of establishing regional cohesion and identity has been of primary importance in the ideology of the regionalist project. As Robert A. Pastor shows in Chapter 13 with regard to the North American Free Trade Agreement (NAFTA) a convergence of values may happen even if this is not the explicit purpose. The approach of seeing region as process implies an evolution of deepening regionalism, not necessarily following the idealised stage model presented here, that mainly serves a heuristic purpose. Since regionalism is a political project, created by human actors, it may, assuming that it gets off the ground in the first place, not only move in different directions but, just like a nation-state project, fail. In this perspective decline would mean decreasing regionness. As pointed out by Fredrik Söderbaum (Chapter 6) processes of increasing (or decreasing) regionness may occur on the different interrelated levels (macro–micro) of the regional system.

Actorness, usually referring to external behaviour, implies a larger scope of action and room for manoeuvre, in some cases even a legal personality. The concept of actorness (with respect to the EU's external policies) was developed by Bretherton and Vogler (1999). Capacity to act is of course relevant internally as well, for instance what I have referred to as security regionalism, development regionalism and environmental regionalism, three areas where increased regional cooperation may make a difference (Hettne, 2001). Actorness is closely related to regionness, the latter implying an endogenous process of increasing cohesiveness, the former a growing capacity to act that follows from the strengthened 'presence' of the regional unit in different contexts, as well as the actions that follow from the interaction between the actor and its external environment. Actorness is thus not only a function of regionness but an outcome of a dialectic process between endogenous and exogenous forces.

ALTERNATIVE WORLD ORDERS

The rarely defined concept of 'world order' is commonly used both positively and normatively, that is to say it can describe the actually existing order or desirable models/utopian projects. After the First World War, Europe believed in the power of collective security through the League of Nations. Hitler and Mussolini were soon to smash that dream and throw Europe into another war. After the Second World War, the United Nations (UN) constituted mankind's new hope of a stable and just world order in which war as a method to solve conflicts was outlawed. The Cold War undermined that type of world order. Later, in the 1970s, there was discussion of 'a new international economic order' which would accord justice to the poor countries of the Third World. Instead there was established a new hegemonic discourse of development, according to which the poor countries were blamed for their own misery. More recently, after the first Gulf War in 1991, President George Bush coined the concept 'a new world order', once again with the meaning that international society in the future would resolutely take action against tyrants and terrorists. The order envisaged did not become reality either. But the interventionist movement started from here and continued throughout the 1990s. It was based on multilateralism and international law, until then upheld through US hegemony. Significantly, George Bush did not change the regime in Baghdad after the first Gulf War, which gives an indication of his respect for the old multilateral world order, since then demolished by the Bush 2 administration.

Let me propose a non-normative definition of world order as constituted by three dimensions: *structure, mode of governance,* and *form of legitimacy.* Structure is the way the units of the system are related. Mode of governance refers to avenues of influence on decision-making and policy-making. Legitimacy is the basis on which the system is made acceptable (legitimisation) to the constituent units.

On the structural dimension a distinction is made between unipolar, bipolar, and multipolar; in the area of governance between unilateral, plurilateral, and multilateral. In terms of legitimisation, there is a declining scale from the universally accepted rule of international law, over hegemony exercised by one great power (which means 'acceptable dominance') to dominance, legitimised by the national interest and relying on coercion and preemption.

With the help of this framework, comparative analysis can be made between alternative models, as well as changes in models, and of world orders over time. The distinction between *plurilateral* and *multilateral* is important. A plurilateral grouping of actors is exclusive, whereas multilateral by definition implies inclusion, provided the rules of the game are accepted by all parties. Multilateralism is therefore often seen as preferable, but for many purposes, *regionalism* (the form of plurilateralism defined by geographical proximity) is useful. In contrast, unilateralism undermines collective arrangements and may be a path towards imperialism.

Theoretically there are of course various options of world order. For the present purpose we are more concerned with ideal types than hybrid forms (which of course are more realistic and may constitute political projects). The liberal view of globalisation, which still enjoys a hegemonic position, stresses the homogenising influence of market forces towards the open society of Hayek. Liberals normally take a minimalist view on political authority and are sceptical of regionalism. The original historical background for this argument was mercantilist regulation (seen as an obstacle for economic development), but subsequently the 'negative other' took the form of planning (or other non-market forms of economic and social organisation). Today neoliberalism is described by some as a form of fundamentalism, a terminology which is questionable in view of the strong belief in individualism characteristic of this ideology.

However, to the extent that 'liberty' is imposed on others as a collective duty (similar to the 'proletarian consciousness' in communism) one could usefully compare with religious fundamentalism. This contradictory ideology has appeared in the US in the form of 'neo-conservatism', which perhaps more appropriately should be called 'militant libertarianism'. To interventionist thinkers on the left, wanting to politicise the global, the liberal project is not realistic; these critics tend to see the unregulated market system as analogous to political anarchy, giving rise to demands for political control of the market (Polanyi, 1957). Many of the classical theorists (whether conservative or radical) held that the liberal ideology of ever expanding and deepening markets lacked ethical content. Similarly, the morality of the market system can, according to contemporary critics of 'hyperglobalisation', only be safeguarded by some kind of organised purposeful will, manifested in a return of 'the political', or 'reinvention of politics' (Beck, 1996), for instance in the form of a 'new multilateralism' and new social movements (Cox, 1997; 1999, 3–28).

The return of 'the political', may appear in various forms of governance. One possible form, assuming a continuous role for state authority, is a reformed 'neo-Westphalian order' ('the rescue of the nation-state'), governed either by a reconstituted UN system that can be called *assertive multilateralism*, or by a more loosely organised 'concert' of dominant powers, assuming the privilege of governance (including intervention) by reference to their shared value system focused on stability and order. This we can call *militant plurilateralism*. The first is preferable in terms of legitimacy but, judging from several unsuccessful attempts at reform, hard to achieve; the second is more realistic but dangerously similar to old power balance politics (the Concert of Europe). This model, unsurprisingly suggested by Henry

Kissinger, seems compatible with the current foreign policy of multipolarism of relevant great powers other than the US.

Even if the UN is the only legitimate world actor in security crises, there are many flaws due to its anachronistic structure dating from the Second World War. The Westphalian logic makes it non-operative in a post-Westphalian context in spite of attempts at strengthening it. The multilateral model in a more 'assertive' form would be based on radical reforms in order to upgrade the UN as a world order model. For instance, the Security Council should be made more representative, and the General Assembly should have representatives also from global civil society. A strengthened Economic and Social Council should take primary responsibility for global development. These suggestions were made by the International Commission on Global Governance in 1995. The proposed reforms were intended to increase the efficiency and the legitimacy of the global institution. Instead it entered its worst crisis ever, after the unilateral attack on Iraq in 2003. After that a new high-level panel of prominent persons was established to rethink collective security, to save the organisation which would celebrate its 60th anniversary in 2005.

A more appropriate form for the return of 'the political' in today's globalised world would be a post-Westphalian order, where the locus of power moves up the ladder to the transnational level by the voluntary pooling of state sovereignties. The state can be replaced or complemented by a regionalised order, as suggested by the *New Regionalism* or by a strengthened global civil society supported by a new 'normative architecture' of world order values (Falk, 2002, 147–83). *Global cosmopolitanism* thus emphasises the role of community on the global level as well as the formation of global norms. However, from a realist perspective it needs institutionalisation. The most likely candidate for such a role, although it does not appear to be imminent, is the inter-regional organisation pursued by the EU, facilitating multi-regional governance as the major alternative to unilateralism. There is also the possibility of moving down the ladder, which implies a decentralised, 'neo-medieval', world. Transnational forms of government are meant to prevent such a 'decline of world order' and 'pathological anarchy' (Falk, 2004).

9/11 AND WORLD ORDER

Since the atrocities of 11 September 2001, generally referred to as 9/11, the world is waging 'global war' against 'terrorism'. Is it a war? What makes it global? The unique scale of the terrorist attack (probably more massive than intended) against political, military and commercial centres in the US moved the Security Council to assert the applicability of the principle of self-defence in this case; the North Atlantic Treaty Organisation (NATO) subsequently enforced this legalistic position by confirming that the principle of collective self-defence was valid.

Because of the criminal side of international terrorism, to work against it is a self-evident objective for all democratic states and respectable regimes. If we moreover consider its political side, the effort must relate to forming a world order in which terrorism is not automatically generated. This suggests a long-term political counter strategy: to combat terrorist methods without losing the political perspective. Reliance on violence alone simply engenders new violence. Here the EU approach differs from the US position, a difference usually described in terms of 'civil' or 'soft' power.

War accelerates the pace of change in society and usually signals a new political order. By relying on unilateral decision-making, which means prioritising the 'national interest' over collective security, structural anarchy is promoted, as long as no single power is able to impose its will on the international society. In that case the structural result, to the extent that such a policy ultimately succeeds, will be unipolarity.

A well functioning multilateral world order requires a certain degree of institutionalisation which counters unilateral action, limited bilateral solutions, or ill-considered political or military reactions which aggravate a sensitive security situation. The degree of order within a region or in the international system can vary; different security theories speak of regional security complexes, anarchies, anarchic societies, regional security communities, and so on. As discussed in Elzbieta Stadtmüller's chapter, the security agenda has broadened which makes regional approaches to security more relevant.

Regional approaches to security are fully compatible with, and even necessitate, multilateralism. After 11 September there existed, to an even greater degree than in connection with the first Gulf War, the possibility of an institutionalised multilateralism, an international regime based on the premises of international law and extensive participation by states and other transnational actors. Multilateralism can, however, take different forms. By 'false multilateralism' is meant political and military actions that take place in the guise of multilateralism but which in reality are an expression of more limited interests: *plurilateralism* if it is a matter of a group of major powers; *regionalism* if it is a geographically united bloc; or *unilateralism* if a superpower or regional major power is in reality acting alone. A certain kind of regionalism (inter-regionalism) may, however, be supportive to multilateral principles (regional multilateralism, or multi-regionalism). But this is a long-term perspective and will depend on the strength of the political project of taking regionalism as the crucial element in reorganising world order. At present this project faces a great challenge.

THE UNIPOLAR MOMENT

In the period since the Second World War no politician has been given greater room for manoeuvre as regards the ability to influence the shape of the world order than President George W. Bush. The tendency could go in two main directions, ranging from genuine multilateralism, implying that the international society of states decides in common, to unilateralism, implying that a powerful state assumes leadership of the rest of the world and dictates the rules: 'either you are with us or with the terrorists'. A unilateral attitude of this kind implies a privilege for the hegemon also to determine what is meant by 'terrorism', 'war', 'prisoner of war' and so on. Before 9/11 one could still discuss several alternative world orders (Hettne and Odén, 2002). After the terrorist action there seem to be fewer alternatives; a trend towards one distinct world order model can be discerned. This order in embryo appears for the present to be unilateral rather than multilateral or regional, and unipolar rather than multipolar. However we do not know how stable and durable a new order will be. Unilateralism is particularly provocative and, arguably, therefore inherently unstable.

Regionalism, implying a multipolar world order structure, as preferred by the EU, is unacceptable to the United States, which, furthermore, has made it very clear that multilateralism, although desirable, has its limitations set by the United States' own security interests. This is wholly in line with the traditional realist security doctrine and therefore not new. However, the current policy of the US goes beyond classical realism (type Kissinger or Brzezinski) towards reinforcing what the neo-conservative thinktank, the Project for the New American Century, describes as 'a policy of military strength and moral clarity' (inspired by Ronald Reagan). This formulation captures the essence of neo-conservatism: military strength and willingness to use it, and a moral mission to change the world in accordance with American values, first of all liberty. The opportunity, 'the unipolar moment', came after the end of the Cold War and this thinking is thus older than 9/11. The concept was coined by the American publicist Charles Krauthammer (1991–92, 23–33) and stands for the US policy of taking advantage of its military superiority by shaping the world order in accordance with the US national interest. This is a project rather than a fact. To my mind it is wrong to call the present world order 'unipolar', since the remaining superpower has to fill the power vacuum created by the collapse of the other. As shown in Iraq there is no automaticity involved.

To name this ideological structure 'neo-conservatism' is hardly an appropriate description of what seems rather to be a militant revolutionary doctrine, rejecting the multilateral world order model and the role of the UN as the protector of this order. Neo-conservatism, or 'militant libertarianism', and isolationism, however different these typically American doctrines may seem, are both sceptical about subsuming national interests to international cooperation and collective security and constitute different expressions of the specificity (exceptionalism) of the US as a 'chosen people'.

Before 9/11 the unipolar moment was just one ideological current in the US, fostered by ideological thinktanks like American Enterprise Institute and the Project for the New American Century, as well as a number of individual publicists and politicians. From the US point of view, the question of multilateralism was a realistic balancing between legality and effectiveness, and priority was always given to the latter. For a long time they did not clash in a too conspicuous way. International law was maintained, although there were many flaws. The UN was of course, in accordance with its Charter, conceived as a multilateral organisation, but its most important organ, the Security Council, is still dominated by a plurilateral group of major powers, the victors in the Second World War. The Security Council decided to put the struggle against terrorism on its agenda, but there are still no legal possibilities for sanctions against the host nations of terrorism, because it is in the UN context still unclear what should be meant by terrorism. NATO and the EU immediately declared themselves ready to participate in the US struggle against terrorism, which in its first phase was defined as a defensive war – and therefore legal.

Unilateralism has since gained the upper hand, and the gigantic multilateral coalition fell apart, instead to become a 'coalition of the willing', where the motives for participation were quite mixed. Certain countries supported the US because of common values and solidarity. Others offered their support in exchange for the dismantling of sanctions, arms purchases, relaxation of trade restrictions, debt re-scheduling and aid. A number of states supported the US in order to be able, under the legitimising umbrella of fighting international terrorism, to deal, undisturbed, with their own domestic 'terrorists'. Similar circumstances, characterised by uninhibited repression, could be observed in Russia in Chechnya, in China in the Muslim Xinjiang province, in some of the neo-Stalinist former Soviet Republics in Central Asia, in the Philippines in its southern Muslim island region, and in India in Kashmir. The government of Nepal termed the ongoing Maoist uprising as terrorism. Robert Mugabe described the political opposition in Zimbabwe as terrorism. Arab countries such as Algeria, Egypt and Saudi Arabia have never made any distinction between internal opposition and terrorism. Russia declared that it also had the right to preemptive warfare in order to fight terrorism in the 'near abroad'. Even regionalism was seen as a means to control the spread of terrorist networks (as pointed out in this volume by J.D. Muni).

The 'war' against terrorism thus came in a number of cases to mean legitimised state terrorism and a strengthening of the state and the military. The violent polarisation between regimes that, from a democratic viewpoint, are dubious, and their more or less fundamentalist opponents, created the premises for a further proliferation of terrorism. The multilateralist world order, in distinction to what might be expected of a loose and temporary alliance, must grapple with these structural conditions in a more systematic way. It must also be built on political pluralism, a coexistence between civilisations instead of 'the clash of civilisations'. To achieve this will require much time, patience and resources. The alternative is a repressive world order which breeds terrorism with different faces in different regions. This will also impact on the role of regional institutions.

A WORLD OF REGIONS

Andrew Hurrell (Chapter 3) makes the point that the most important 'lesson' of Europe is that there are so few grounds for believing that Europe is the future of other regions. Regionalisation as a world-wide process is giving shape to a number of different regionalisms which can be categorised in different ways. Taking a global, structuralist view, a distinction can be made between three different types of regions: *core regions, peripheral regions* and, between them, *intermediate regions.* An advanced structural position is here defined in terms of economic dynamics and political stability, and regions move between different positions as these conditions change for better or worse.

The core, consisting of Europe, North America and East Asia (also called the Triad), make up the larger part of the world economy. To the extent that they organise they do so for the sake of being better able to control and to get access to the rest of the world, one important means of control being to achieve ideological hegemony, since they represent different traditions in terms of economic ideology. Europe has become the paradigm of regionalisation, but represents a highly legalistic form, difficult to achieve elsewhere; the other two are far less institutionalised as regions and so far lack a regional political order. On the North American continent the core is constituted by the US, Canada and Mexico, organised in the NAFTA. East Asia is marked by a rather low level of institutional regionness, particularly in the field of security, although this is compensated for by a dense transnational economic network. East Asian regionalism is therefore often described as *de facto* regionalism, whereas regionalisation in Europe takes place *de jure.*

Examples of intermediate regions are Southeast Asia (Association of Southeast Asian Nations, or ASEAN) and the Cone of Latin America (Mercosur), and of peripheral regions Africa, South Asia (South Asian Association for Regional Cooperation) and the Middle East. South Asia now seems to prove to be a case of a peripheral region moving into intermediate status, due to successful application of security regionalism and development regionalism. In Africa, Southern African Development Coordination could be a similar success story provided South Africa is willing to take on responsibility as a constructive regional hegemon. Structural positions are not fixed, but can be changed by some form of agency, acting in some concrete field where regional cooperation can make a difference. Thus increased regionness strengthens actorness, but more joint action also has a positive impact on regionness.

There are areas of the world where regional cooperation has a very uncertain role to play. The complex post-Soviet area is now in the process of being reintegrated by Russia in the form of the Commonwealth of Independent States (CIS). The CIS may perhaps lay the ground for a future core region but this is, at least in the short run, a very uncertain prospect. This large area is very weak in terms of regionness. The historical Soviet Union can best be seen as an empire, an enlargement of the old Russian empire; and as has been the case with declining empires, the constituent parts, belonging to different natural regions, move in different directions: European, Caucasian and Central Asian.

A convergence of economic policies and political regimes was defined above as a high degree of regionness, but there is no exact correlation between structural position and regionness, as shown in the case of East Asia with an advanced structural position and a low level of regionness, if we look at, for instance, institutionalised regional collaboration. Only the EU has an explicit regionalist ideology and strategy, not only for the region of Europe but also as a model of world order, to be discussed below. As the EU coherence and actorness strengthens, this model will have stronger influence on world order.

The EU is, in terms of regionness, so far the only example of 'an institutionalised regional polity', at present lingering between intergovernmentalism and supranational governance, but with an uncertain future, due to a new wave of Euroscepticism and the decreased coherence and consistency following the inflow of new members. The initial failure to agree a European Constitution in December 2003 even gave rise to speculations about a possible break-up of the Union. On the other hand there was on this occasion an agreement on a common European security policy, marking a significant disassociation from the US and the NATO framework. The stress was here on prevention rather than preemption, thus holding on to 'civil power', at the same time as the transatlantic relationship was cautiously referred to as 'irreplaceable'. The UN Charter is described in this document, however, as 'the fundamental framework' for international relations and international action. Thus the EU muddles through, familiar as it is to reacting in crisis situations. In June 2004, the new Constitution was thus accepted by all governments. What now remains is consent from the peoples of Europe.

The predominant economic philosophy in the Core is neoliberalism, which therefore also, with varying and perhaps declining degrees of conviction, is preached throughout the world. The stronger economies demand access to the less developed in the name of free trade; regionalisation (open regionalism) may be a push in that direction. We can thus speak of 'neoliberal regionalism', although the concept may sound as a contradiction in terms. This is the 'stepping stone', rather than 'stumbling block', interpretation of regionalism with respect to its relation to market-led globalisation. There are, however, different emphases among the three core regions due to their contrasting economic-historical traditions, differences that may become more important, depending on which of the current types of capitalism turns out to be more viable in the longer run. At present, neoliberal globalisation faces many counterforces and may be in decline.

Regionalisation has structural consequences also beyond the particular region in which it takes place. Its importance for a specific regional order as well as for order between regions should be taken into consideration (Fawcett and Hurrell, 1995, 310). *Trans-regionalism* refers to institutions and organisations mediating between regions; if in a formalised way between the regions as such we speak of *inter-regionalism*; and if constituting a form of world order through the criss-crossing multitude of such relations (a sort of 'regional multilateralism'), we can speak of *multi-regionalism*. Inter-regionalism, which is a formal relation, can encourage informal trans-regionalism, and there are also hybrid forms of the three varieties.

Inter-regionalism can be seen as one of the more regulated forms that globalisation may be taking. As compared to market-led globalisation in a Westphalian world of nation-states, it is more rooted in territory; and in contrast to traditional multilateralism, it is a more exclusive relationship, since access to regional formations is limited by the principle of geographical proximity. Inter-regionalism, not to speak of multi-regionalism, is a long-term, non-linear and uncertain trend which certainly will include setbacks and the outcome of which we cannot know. Below, an attempt is made to present an overview of current inter-regionalist trends.

TOWARDS INTER-REGIONALISM?

Looking at the existing patchwork of trans- and inter-regional agreements there is, in terms of structural outcome, so far no clear picture on the horizon. Trans-regional arrangements are voluntary and cooperative. They are also very diverse and difficult to categorise. Few are inter-regional in the proper sense of the word, some relations are trans-regional, some bilateral (hybrid relations between a regional organisation and a great power). To get some order in this emerging cobweb of relations between regions, one can relate to the three above-mentioned structural levels: core regions, intermediate regions and peripheral regions. That the EU constitutes the hub of these arrangements is in full accordance with its regionalist ideology, encompassing not only trade and foreign investment but also political dialogue and cultural relations between the regions. The EU ambition is also to formalise the relations (now called 'partnerships') as being between two regional bodies rather than bilateral contacts between countries, but for pragmatic reasons, the forms of agreement show a bewildering variety. The EU's relations with the various geographical areas are furthermore influenced by the 'pillared approach' in the EU's internal decision-making (Holland, 2002, 7), creating artificial divisions between foreign policy and development policy. The development of the pattern has also been influenced over time by shifting bilateral concerns among additional members.

Intra-core relations: a question of power

The first level of the inter-regional complex contains triangular relations within the Triad, that is between the three core regions: the US, the EU and East Asia. East Asia is dominated by the two great powers China and Japan, with which both the US and the EU have bilateral relations as well. Trans-regional links within the Triad are constituted by Asia-Pacific Economic Cooperation (APEC), and Asia–Europe Meeting (ASEM) and various transatlantic agreements between the US and Europe. In spite of massive contacts on the level of civil society, the formal inter-regional transatlantic links (EU–NAFTA) are institutionally weak or non-existent, the reason being that the US in principle prefers bilateralism to regionalism. As explained by Pastor (Chapter 13), NAFTA is for various reasons not seen as a coherent region.

Unsurprisingly, the intra-Core relations are sometimes rather tense, due to power balance concerns, trade competition that risks degenerating into trade wars, and the somewhat different economic ideologies in the three regions. Between the US and Europe, the close relationship manifested in NATO has grown increasingly strained. Joint operations are difficult to agree on and when implemented can leave a lingering bitterness. NATO itself has therefore been marginalised. I return to the complexity of US–EU relations in the final section.

Southeast Asia and East Asia are more and more merging into one region: East Asia. In East Asia there are, as mentioned above, competing trans-regional institutions: APEC where the US is the driver, and the ASEM process, involving the EU and ASEAN plus China, Japan and South Korea (but so far excluding Myanmar). Behind the latter is the need felt by European and Asian partners to relate to and perhaps try to balance the US dominance. ASEM has been seen as 'the missing link' in the Triad, since Europe had been excluded from APEC.

ASEAN+3 is now emerging as a new regional formation covering both Southeast and East Asia, and actually socially constructed in the process of maintaining an inter-regional relationship between Asia and Europe (Gilson, 2002), at the same time as being a response to various urgent needs in the regions, such as maintaining or restoring financial stability and controlling communicable diseases.

As Helen E.S. Nesadurai indicates in Chapter 10, the Asian financial crisis of 1997–98 underlined the interdependence within the larger region of Southeast and East Asia. It also 'exposed the weakness of existing regional institutional economic arrangements' and led to a crisis for both ASEAN and APEC, the two competing regional organisations (Higgott, 2002). The affected countries were frustrated over the lack of remedies on the global level, as well as the lack of concern for the problems and interests of the South. The opportunity was instead taken to impose neoliberal policies in a region known for, and criticised for, its interventionism. Before the Asian crisis happened, there was little discussion about regional approaches to the management of financial stability outside Europe. Regarding the cure, a regional approach in the form of an Asian Monetary Fund was proposed by Japan but received little support and was resisted by the International Monetary Fund, the US and the EU. This, however, seems to have undermined the confidence in the 'soft institutionalism' of the 'ASEAN way' and underscored the need for deeper institutionalisation and stronger commitments from the countries. In May 2002 there was a meeting by the ASEAN+3 countries in Chiang Mai about regional cooperation (monetary regionalism) in combating financial crises at the regional level.

Neighbourhood relations: a question of security

Going beyond the Core triangle it is necessary to make a distinction between the EU's relations with the countries in the 'near abroad' (taking geography rather than structure as the point of departure) and those countries beyond; since the former category (including first of all Central and Eastern Europe, the Balkans and the Mediterranean, secondly bilateral relations with Russia and Turkey) plays a central role in the EU's security strategy (Charillon, 2004). The frontier between 'Europe', as organised by the EU, and surrounding areas is unclear, some of these areas (or countries in them) being new members or applicants, others defined (through a political discourse) as being 'non-Europe' (but 'near abroad'). The area in question is large and includes much of the post-Soviet area where Russia of course has its interests as a re-emerging great power. Since the CIS has not (so far) taken off, EU has also to deal with Ukraine, Belarus and Moldova (the European part of the post-Soviet area) independently.

Relations between the EU and Russia are rather similar to the ones between the EU and the US, in the sense that Russia also prefers bilateralism, although the EU has a Partnership and Cooperation Agreement with Russia which covers human rights, the economy, trade, security and justice issues (*Financial Times*, 11 February 2004). Russia at one stage rejected automatic extension of this agreement to the new member states, thereby threatening the entire platform for EU–Russia relations. An understanding was subsequently reached. In the rest of the post-Soviet area, that is the European part (except of course the Baltic sub-region now part of the EU) and Caucasus/Central Asia, the EU presence is weak (Dannreuther, 2004). The idea of a strategic partnership between the EU and Russia (where EU membership is a non-issue) implies a substantive geopolitical room for manoeuvre from the latter.

The Barcelona process (see Chapter 12) is a strategy of cooperation between the EU and its Mediterranean neighbours, where peace is the first priority, in accordance with the basic concern for stability. The Mediterranean 'region' has no formal existence, it is a social construction shaped by EU security concerns. North Africa is linked to France through colonial legacy, Cyprus and Malta are now members, and Turkey is an applicant. Regarding the countries involved in the former peace process (Israel and the eastern Arab countries) the US influence is what counts, and the EU has consequently taken a low profile.

The major European security problem is the Balkans. Few observers would consider the EU response to the Balkan crises (Bosnia, Kosovo and Macedonia) an unqualified success. The record has rather underlined the persistent power vacuum in a Europe searching for a viable security order, with institutional responses lagging behind the events. It provides a dilemma for the new Europe, since the sub-region must be seen as forming part of Europe rather than constituting its permanent 'near abroad'. The dividing line between what is 'Europe' and a 'non-Europe' close enough to constitute the 'near abroad' is ultimately a political issue. To define the Balkans out of Europe might be tempting but politically incorrect and also dangerous. Therefore it will also be included in the EU in the future. At present, Bosnia is under the military protection of the EU.

Thus the general method involved in the foreign policy towards the near abroad is a soft form of imperialism, an asymmetric partnership based on conditionalities, the price ranging from assistance to full membership. The success story is the transformation and integration of Central and Eastern Europe, which in fact implied a large number of resolved and prevented conflicts. For countries that are not being considered for EU membership, the policy is a rather weak way of influencing the external world. Thus, actorness shifts from one context to another.

Relations with intermediate regions: a question of partnership

ASEAN has already been dealt with above. Europe's relations with Latin America were intensified in the 1990s after a long period of neglect. The

EU–Mercosur relationship, on the level of the core/intermediate relation, is another clear example of inter-regionalism, since there exists an agreement between two regional organisations (the EU–Mercosur Inter-regional Framework Cooperation Agreement, 1995), which also is built on three pillars: a political dialogue, substantive financial support to Mercosur's institutional development, and economic and commercial cooperation. Relations between the EU and South Asia have been rather weak, but are now becoming more important as the region stabilises politically and becomes successful in terms of economic dynamics, that is, it moves into an intermediate position. India is now often seen as a future great power.

Relations with peripheral regions: a question of development

Turning to the peripheral level, EU relations with the Countries of Africa, Caribbean and the Pacific (ACP) are rooted in colonial and neo-colonial associations, and are now, as for instance in the Cotonou agreement (June 2000), described in more symmetric terms as 'partnerships'. The background to this is the gradual abandoning of the 'pyramid of privilege' implied in the Yaoundé–Lomé framework that since the mid-1960s defined the relationship between the EU and peripheral regions, originally selectively favoured in accordance with former colonial interests. The ACP is not a regional organisation, therefore the EU is trying to encourage cooperation within the three constituent regions, stressing as an article of faith that regional integration is the best development strategy. Over the years, the ACP countries have been marginalised in the European-led inter-regional system, but interestingly they have made efforts to act as a collective unit, while the EU makes efforts to regionalise and differentiate the group, the first principle based on territorial, the other on developmental criteria (less developed countries, landlocked countries, island countries, etc). To this confusing picture is added the fact that the meaning of development has not remained the same from Yaoundé to Cotonou.

To sum up, it cannot be said that the EU external policy has developed in a coherent and consistent way, revealing a firm purpose. On the contrary, different policies have been applied in different contexts and at different points in time by different combinations of actors. This gives some credibility to the intergovernmentalist theory of integration, but the reality is far more complex: 'narrow training, rationalist rule application and the employment of overly "scientific" procedure that rests on the illusion of ethical neutrality in social enquiry are not the most appropriate methodological blueprints for enriching out understanding of European integration' (Chryssochoou, 2001, 8).

The European interests are not hidden, though. According to a statement from the Commission (quoted in Bretherton and Vogler, 1999, 129): 'the EU can commit itself to supporting only economic and social organisation models which contribute to the objectives of its cooperation policy and which comply with the political and social values which it means to promote'. Some would call this a kind of imperialism as well. It is rather obvious that the policies have failed to instil confidence in the partners, whether those have been Arabs, Indians, Latin Americans or Africans. However, the outcome is, in spite of all contradictions, a pattern of governance with its own distinctive characteristics and the potential of becoming a world order. This world order could be called 'multi-regionalism'. The question is to what extent this potential is realised by European politicians and other decision-makers, as well as the sceptical European public. This is a question of future European regionness and actorness. The element of competition with the US is particularly obvious in the cases of Asia and Latin America, where the European presence has increased substantially.

REGIONAL AND GLOBAL FUTURES

What will the future world order look like? I will not discuss here the scenario of further fragmentation and disorder but I will focus on more positive political options, where regionalism may play a role. The alternative world orders discussed above will of course not appear in their pure 'ideal' form, but in various hybrid forms of combination. From a moderately conservative perspective one form of world order could be a 'neo-Westphalian order', governed either by a reconstituted UN system, in which preferably the major regions or, perhaps more likely, the major powers of the world have a strong influence; another alternative would be a more loosely organised global 'concert' of great powers. The relevant powers in both models will be the regional powers of the world. In the latter case, regionalism will suffer from imposed or hegemonic regionalism, and the regions as such will be far from the ideal of security communities. It will thus be a multipolar world, but the concert model will be lacking in multilateralism and legitimacy.

Regionalism would, however, put its mark on a future post-Westphalian governance pattern. In such a world order the locus of power would move irreversibly to the transnational level. The states system would be replaced or complemented by a regionalised world order, and by a strengthened global civil society supported by a 'normative architecture' of world order values: multiculturalism and multilateralism. Here the emphasis on inter-regionalism by the EU may in the longer run prove to be important in the reconstruction of a multilateral world order, perhaps in a regionalised form here called multi-regionalism. In the shorter run, this development is now challenged by the unipolar project.

The terminology of war in the struggle against terrorism underlines that the new threat image, which reflects the globalised situation, is being handled on the basis of conventional thinking about security, in which the importance of the state, the military and the security service is reinforced and the scope for new post-sovereignty initiatives is diminished. There is polarisation between the standpoints of the US and most of Europe, particularly as regards that aspect of the struggle against terrorism which relates to Iraq.

International terrorism constitutes part of a global security complex in which security must be defined in ways radically differing from the nation-state idea of security with its emphasis on national security and military defence. The war against terrorism, as manifested in Afghanistan and Iraq has, as is usually the result of war, reinforced the power of the state and the military apparatus, and for that reason a neo-Westphalian type of world order with a continuous strong role for the nation-states appears, at any rate in the relatively short term, to be more likely than a post-Westphalian experiment with transnational forms of governance. That applies particularly to the unilateral superpower which ever more explicitly disdains multilateral forms of global governance. That was the US attitude even before 9/11 and hopes that the anti-terrorist consensus which arose after this terrible event would strengthen multilateralism rapidly came to nought.

The struggle against terrorism was more and more subordinated to the US geopolitical strategy characterised by the right to carry out pre-emptive strikes. The supposed sources of terrorist threat were extended to include unpopular states that seem to have very little to do with al-Qaeda. The US has consistently applied a *realist* security policy by forming pragmatic alliances with 'the enemy of the enemy'. The global alliance was after the occupation of Iraq exposed to major strains and reduced to a 'coalition' of a handful of states which in many cases got involved without much popular support. The exit of Spain from this group after 3/11 ('Europe's 9/11') was a major blow and changed the balance between the models. The second exit seems to be Poland's. The withdrawal by the Philippines from Iraq also put a strain on the alliance. A NATO meeting in Turkey in July 2004 showed an increasing isolation of the unilateral power. The rift is widening between the US and Europe; the EU to a greater extent stands for 'civil power', that is to say, for the achievement of security through sustainable social development rather than through the elimination of enemies.

Both the US and the EU protect their security interests by projecting their values and political models on the rest of the world. There are three major differences between the EU and the US as regards these values. The first is the EU preference for long-term multidimensional, horizontal, institutional arrangements, whereas the US prefers more temporary 'coalitions of the willing' under its own leadership. While the US acts from a perceived national interest, the EU is in itself an international arrangement, an institutionalised regional polity, based on compromise and dialogue.

The second difference can be related to contrasting ideas in political philosophy, as was recently pointed out by Robert Kagan (2004). According to him, Europeans (from Venus) live in the ideal world of 'permanent peace' of Immanuel Kant, which, according to Kagan, is the natural choice of the weak, whereas the Americans (from Mars) live in the real world of Thomas Hobbes, which shows the responsibility and mission of the strong in dealing with evil forces.

A third dimension of this European–American contrast in political culture is what Javier Solana, the EU spokesman in foreign affairs, occasionally refers to as the US religious approach to foreign policy, whereas the European approach is supposed to be rationalist and secular. Thus the US tends to see political conflict as a struggle between good and evil, or God and the Devil. This makes the US a revolutionary power (Kagan, 2004, 120). Europe, on the other hand, has supposedly a tradition of making a political analysis of conflict, pragmatically looking for compromises.

The future of regionalism, and ultimately multi-regionalism, depends very much on the outcome of the struggle between these two contrasting world order models. It is important to note that the differences do not express varieties of national mentality – Europe versus America – but constitute contrasting world order principles held by political groupings in both areas. It is, as was pointed out by Louise Fawcett (Chapter 2), also reasonable to expect coexistence, uneasy or not, and hybrids between competing world order models.

Even in the absence of a thoroughly regionalised world (multi-regionalism), the process of regionalisation is, in one way or the other, bound to have an impact on the future world order. The current ideology of globalism argues in favour of a particular form of globalisation, namely neoliberal economic globalisation. It is a simplification, however, to identify globalisation with neoliberalism. Other political contents should in principle be possible. There is an emerging struggle for the political content of globalisation. Regionalism can influence the nature of globalisation. Stronger regions would, for example, shape the form and content of the global order in different ways, depending on the political trends in the respective regions, trends that may shift direction, thus altering the preconditions for constructing world order. Still, changes in the US are by far the most important. Against unilateralism there is in the US in spite of the re-election of president Bush for a second term a call for a return to multilateralism. This would bring Europe and the US closer, but there would nevertheless be a difference between the models of multi-regionalism and a global concert of regional powers; between a genuine post-Westphalian and a neo-Westphalian world order.

Bibliography

Aarts, P. *The Middle East: A Region without Regionalism or the End of Execeptionalism?*, Draft text for workshop on 'The Political Economy of Regionalisation', University of Amsterdam (18–19 December 1997).

Abdel-Fadil, M. 'Macroeconomic Tendencies and Policy Options in the Arab Region' in Guazzone, L. (ed.) *The Middle East in Global Change: The Politics and Economics of Interdependencey versus Fragmentation* (New York: St Martin's Press, 1997).

Acharya, A. *The Quest for Identity: International Relations of Southeast Asia* (Singapore: Oxford University Press, 2000).

Acharya, A. *Constructing a Security Community in Southeast Asia: ASEAN and the Problem of Regional Order* (London and New York: Routledge, 2001).

Adebajo, A. *Building Peace in West Africa; Liberia, Sierra Leone and Guinea-Bissau* (Boulder, CO: Lynne Rienner, 2002).

Adler, E. and Barnett, M. (eds) *Security Communities* (Cambridge: Cambridge University Press, 1998).

Agbeyegbe, T. 'On the Feasibility of Monetary Union in the Southern African Development Community', *Department of Economics Working Paper* (New York: City University, 2002).

Agnew, J. 'Political Power and Geographical Scale', paper for Third Pan-European IR Conference and Joint Meeting with ISA, Vienna, Austria (16–19 September 1998).

Alagappa, M. 'Regional Institutions, the UN and International Security: A Framework for Analysis', *Third World Quarterly*, 18:3 (1997).

Alesina, A. and Spolaore, E. *The Size of Nations* (Cambridge, MA: The MIT Press, 2003).

Aliboni, R. 'Change and Continuity in Western Policies Towards the Middle East' in Guazzone, L. (ed.) *The Middle East in Global Change: The Politics and Economics of Interdependencey versus Fragmentation* (New York: St Martin's Press, 1997).

Allen, V., Wilder, A. and Atkinson, M. 'Multiple Group Membership and Social Identity' in Sarbin, T. and Scheibe, K. (eds) *Studies in Social Identity* (New York: Springer, 1983).

Allison, R. 'Regionalism, Regional Structures and Security Management in Central Asia', *International Affairs*, 80:3 (2004)

Altbach, E. 'The Asian Monetary Fund Proposal: A Case Study in Japanese Regional Leadership', *Japan Economic Institute Report*, No. 47A: 8–8 (1997).

Anglin, D. 'Afrique du Sud: politique extérieure et rapports avec le continent', *Etudes internationales* (Québec), XXII, no. 2 (June 1991).

APEC Bangkok Declaration on Partnership for the Future, Bangkok, Thailand (21 October 2003).

ASEAN Declaration of ASEAN Concord II (Bali Concord II), Bali, Indonesia (7 October 2003).

Asian Development Bank (ADB), *Moving Regional Cooperation Forward* (October 2002).

Austin, J.L. *How to Do Things with Words* (Oxford: Clarendon Press, 1961).

Ba, A. 'Negotiating the Market and the Social: Complex Engagement in Sino-ASEAN Relations', paper delivered to the Inaugural Conference of the Asian Political and International Studies Association (APISA), Singapore (28 November–1 December 2003).

Ba, A. 'Contested Spaces: The Politics of Regional and Global Governance in Southeast Asia' in Hoffman, M.J. and Ba, A.D. (eds) *Coherence and Contestation: Contending Perspective in Global Governance* (London and New York: Routledge, 2005).

Bach, D. 'L'Insertion de la Côte d'Ivoire dans les rapports internationaux' in Médard, J.-F. and Fauré, Y.-A. (eds) *Etat en Bourgeoisie en Côte d'Ivoire* (Paris: Karthala, 1981).

Bach, D. 'Institutional Crisis and the Search for New Models' in Lavergne, R. (ed.) *Regional Integration and Cooperation in West-Africa: A Multidimensional Perspective* (Ottawa: IDRC and Trenton: Africa World Press, 1997).

Bach, D. (ed.) *Regionalisation in Africa: Integration and Disintegration* (Oxford: James Currey, 1999).

Bach, D. 'The Dilemmas of Regionalisation' in Adebajo, A. and Rashid, O. (eds) *West Africa's Security Challenges* (Boulder, CO: Lynne Rienner, 2004).

Bach, D. 'Inching Towards a Country Without a State: Prebendalism, Violence and State Betrayal in Nigeria' in Clapham, C., Herbst, J. and Mill, G. (eds) *Africa's Big States* (Johannesburg: Wits Press, 2005).

Balassa, B. *The Theory of Economic Integration* (Homewood, IL: Irwin, 1961).

Ball, D. and Acharya, A. (eds) *The Next Stage: Preventive Diplomacy and Security Cooperation in the Asia-Pacific Region* (Canberra: Australian National University, 1999).

Bamba, L. 'Analyse du processus de convergence dans la zone UEMOA', *WIDER Working Paper*, 18 (2004).

Barnett, M. 'Identity and Alliances in the Middle East' in Katzenstein, P. (ed.) *The Culture of National Security* (New York: Columbia University Press, 1996).

Barnett, M. and Adler, E. (eds) *Security Communities* (Cambridge: Cambridge University Press, 1998).

Barrett, M. 'English Children's Acquisition of a European Identity' in Breakwell, G. and Lyons, E. (eds) *Changing European Identities* (Oxford: Butterworth-Heinemann, 1996).

Barry, F. 'Economic Integration and Convergence Processes in the EU Cohesion Countries', *Journal of Common Market Studies*, 41:5 (2003).

Barry, F. and Begg, I. 'EMU and Cohesion: Introduction', *Journal of Common Market Studies*, 41:5 (2003).

Bawumia, M. 'The Feasibility of Monetary Union in West Africa', mimeo (Addis Ababa: UNECA, 2002).

Bayoumi, T. and Eichengreen, B. 'Shocking Aspects of European Monetary Unification', *CEPR Discussion Paper*, 968 (1992).

Bayoumi, T. and Eichengreen, B. 'Monetary and Exchange Rate Arrangements for NAFTA', *Journal of Development Economics*, 43:1 (1994).

Bayoumi, T. and Eichengreen, B. 'Exchange Rate Volatility and Intervention: Implications of the Theory of Optimum Currency Area', *Journal of International Economics*, 45 (1998).

Bayoumi, T. and Mauro, P. 'The Suitability of ASEAN for a Regional Currency Arrangement', *IMF Working Paper*, 162 (1999).

Beblawi, H. and Luciani, G. (eds) *The Rentier State* (London: Croom Helm: 1987).

Beck, U. *The Reinvention of Politics: Rethinking Modernity in the Global Social Order* (Cambridge: Polity Press, 1996).

Beck, U. *Was ist Globalisierung?* (Frankfurt: Suhrkamp, 3rd edition 1997).

Beck, U. *Was ist Globalisierung?* [What is Globalisation?], 2nd modern edn (Frankfurt am Main: Suhrkamp, 1998).

Beeson, M. 'ASEAN: The Challenges of Organisational Reinvention' in Beeson, M. (ed.) *Reconfiguring East Asia: Regional Institutions and Organisations After the Crisis* (London: Routledge Curzon, 2002).

Bénassy-Quéré, A. and Coupet, M. 'On the Adequacy of Monetary Arrangements in Sub-Saharan Africa', *THEMA Working Paper* (2003).

Berg, A., Borensztein, E. and Mauro, P. 'Monetary Regime Options for Latin America', *Finance and Development* (September 2003).

Bhattacharya, B. and Katti, V. *Regional Trade Enchancement: SAPTA and Beyond* (New Delhi: Indian Institute of Foreign Trade, 1996).

Billig, M. 'Nationalism as an International Ideology: Imagining the Nation, Others and the World of Nations' in Breakwell, G. and Lyons, E. (eds) *Changing European Identities* (Oxford: Butterworth-Heinemann, 1996).

Bleaney, M. and Fielding, D. 'Exchange Rate Regimes, Inflation and Output Volatility in Developing Countries', *Journal of Development Economics*, 68 (2002).

Boas, M., Marchand, M. and Shaw, T. 'The Weave-World: Regionalisms in the South in the New Millennium', *Third World Quarterly*, 20:5 (1999).

Bordo, M.D. 'Exchange Rate Regime Choice in Historical Perspective', *IMF Working Paper*, 160 (2003).

Bourne, A. 'Regional Europe' in Cini, M. (ed.) *European Union Politics* (Oxford: Oxford Univerity Press, 2003).

Boutros-Ghali, B. *Agenda for Peace* (New York: United Nations, 1992).

Boutros-Ghali, B. 'An Agenda for Democratisation' in Holden, B. (ed.) *Global Democracy, Key Debates* (London: Routledge, 2000).

Bowles, P. 'Regionalism and Development after (?) the Global Financial Crisis', *New Political Economy*, 5:3 (2000).

Braun, D. *The Indian Ocean: Region of Conflict or 'Zone of Peace'?* (London: C. Hurst and Co., 1983).

Brautigam, T. 'As Many as 600,000 Americans Living in Canada Eligible to Vote in U.S. Election', *Canadian Press*, Canada.Com News (18 October 2004).

Breakwell, G. and Lyons, E. (eds) *Changing European Identities* (Oxford: Butterworth-Heinemann, 1996).

Breslin, S. and Higgott, R. 'New Regionalism(s) in Historical Perspective', *Asia-Europe Journal*, 1:2 (May 2003).

Breslin, S. and Hook, G. (eds) *Microregionalism and World Order* (Basingstoke: Palgrave Macmillan, 2002).

Breslin, S., Hughes, C., Phillips, N. and Rosamond, B. *New Regionalisms in the Global Political Economy* (London: Routledge, 2002).

Bretherton, C. and Vogler, J. *The European Union as a Global Actor* (London: Routledge, 1999).

Bull, H. *The Anarchical Society: A Study of Order in World Politics* (London: Macmillan, 1977).

Burca, G. and Scott, J. (eds) *The EU and the WTO* (Oxford: Hart, 2003).

Buzan, B. and Waever, O. *Regions and Powers: The Structure of International Security* (Cambridge: Cambridge University Press, 2003).

Cameron, J. and Campbell, K. (eds) *Dispute Resolution in the WTO* (London: Cameron May, 1998).

Canela-Cacho, J.A. 'The Social Dimension of the Liberalisation of World Trade and Trade Labour Standards: Can Common Rules be Agreed' in Demaret, P., Bellis, J.-F. and Garcia Jeménez, G. (eds) *Regionalism and Multilateralism after the Uruguay Round* (Brussels: European Interuniversity Press, 1997).

Çarkoglu, A., Eder, M. and Kirisci, K. *The Political Economy of Regional Cooperation in the Middle East* (London and New York: Routledge, 1998).

Carlsnaes, W., Sjursen, H. and White, B. (eds) *Contemporary European Foreign Policy* (London: Sage, 2004).

CEDEAO, *Le progrès continu dépend d'un effort soutenu, rapport intérimaire du secrétaire exécutif M.A. Bundu*, mimeo (Lagos: Secrétariat exécutif, November 1992).

Central Intelligence Agency (CIA), 'The World Fact Book 2002: China', <www.odci.gov/cia/publications/factbook/geos/ch/html>.

Cerutti, F. and Enno, R. *A Soul for Europe: On the Political and Cultural Identity of the Europeans* (Virginia: Peeters, Weuven and Sterling, 2001).

Charillon, F. 'Sovereignty and Intervention: EU's Interventionism in its Near Abroad' in Carlsnaes, W., et al. (eds) *Contemporary European Foreign Policy* (London: Sage, 2004).

Chen, Q. 'Qianyan' [Introduction], in Chen Q. (ed.) *Kua shiji de shijie geju da zhuanhuan* [Major Changes in the International Structure at the Turn of the Century], (Shanghai jiaoyu chbanshe [Shanghai Education Press], 1996).

Chopra, H.S., Frank, R. and Schroder, J. *National Identity and Regional Cooperation: Experiences of European Integration and South Asian Perceptions* (Manohar Publishers, 1999).

Choucri, N. 'Demography, Migration and Security in the Middle East' in Guazzone, L. (ed.) *The Middle East in Global Change: The Politics and Economics of Interdependencey versus Fragmentation* (New York: St Martin's Press, 1997).

Christiansen, T., Jorgensen, K.E. and Wiener, A. 'The Social Construction of Europe', *Journal of European Public Policy*, 6:4 (1999).

Chronologies, *Maghreb Mashrek*, 162 (1998).

Chronology, *Middle East Journal*, 51:2 (1997).

Chryssochoou, D.N. *Theorising European Integration* (London: Sage, 2001).

Cinnirella, M. 'Social Identity Perspectives on European Integration' in Breakwell, G. and Lyons, E. (eds) *Changing European Identities* (Oxford: Butterworth-Heinemann, 1996).

Claeys, A.S. and Sindzingre, A. (eds) *Transfer of Rules and Superposition of Regional Groupings: The Interaction of WAEMU, ECOWAS and ACP Countries with the European Union*, The Hague: Fifth Pan-European Conference of the Standing Group on International Relations, 9–19 September 2004.

Cohen, B.J. *The Geography of Money* (Ithaca, NY: Cornell University Press, 1998).

Cohen, B.J. 'Are Monetary Unions Inevitable?' *International Studies Perspectives*, 4:3 (2003).

Coleman, S. 'An Aggregate View of Macroeconomic Shocks in Sub-Saharan Africa', *WIDER Research Paper*, 9 (2004).

Cornelius, W.A. 'Politics in Mexico' in Almond, G.A., Powell, B., et al. (eds) *Comparative Politics Today* (New York: Longman, 2000).

Cowell, A. and Halbfinger, D. 'A Plot Seen Behind Every Door: Conspiracy Theorists Take Global Viewpoint', *International Herald Tribune* (13 July 2004).

Cox, R.W. *The New Realism: Perspectives on Multilateralism and World Order* (Tokyo: United Nations University Press, 1997).

Cox, R.W. 'Civil Society at the Turn of the Millennium: Prospects for an Alternative World Order', *Review of International Studies*, 25:1 (1999).

Craig, P. 'Constitutions, Constitutionalism and the European Union', *European Law Journal*, 7:2 (2001).

Craig, P. and de Burca, G. *EU Law* (Oxford: Oxford University Press, 3rd edition, 2003).

Crosette, B. 'Surprises in the Global Tourist Boom', *New York Times* (12 April 1998).

Dahl, R. *How Democratic is the American Constitution?* (New Haven, CT: Yale University Press, 2002).

Dahou, K. *Coopération Transfrontalière: vers un Dialogue euro-africain* (Paris and Dakar: Club du Sahel et de l'Afrique de l'Ouest, WABI/DT/15/04, March 2004).

Dannreuther, R. (ed.) *European Union Foreign and Security Policy: Towards a Neighbourhood Strategy* (London: Routledge, 2004).

Davey, W. *Pine and Swine: Canada–United States Trade Dispute Settlement – the FTA Experience and NAFTA Prospects* (Ottawa: Centre for Trade Policy and Law, 1996).

DBSA, 'Maputo Development Corridor: Development Perspective', Development Bank of Southern Africa, <www.dbsa.org/Corridors/maputo/MaputoDevCorridor> (2001).

De Lombaerde, P. 'Optimum Currency Area Theory and Monetary Integration as a Gradual Process' in Meeusen, W. and Villaverde, J. (eds) *Convergence Issues in the European Union* (Cheltenham: Edward Elgar, 2002).

Debrun, X., Mason, P. and Pattillo, C. *Monetary Union in West Africa: Who Might Gain, Who Might Lose and Why?* (Washington, DC: IMF Working Paper, December 2002).

Delancey, M.W. and Mays, T.M. *Historical Dictionary of International Organisations in Sub-Saharan Africa* (Lanham, MD: Scarecrow Press, 2002).

Demaret, P., Bellis, J.-F. and Garcia Jeménez, G. (eds) *Regionalism and Multilateralism after the Uruguay Round* (Brussels: European University Press, 1997).

DePalma, A. *Here: A Biography of the New American Continent* (New York: Public Affairs, 2001).

Department of Foreign Affairs and International Trade of Canada, *Opening Doors to the World: Canada's Market Access Priorities, 1999* (Ottawa, 1999).

Deutsch, K.W. *The Analysis of International Relations*, 2nd edn (Englewood Cliffs, NJ: Prentice Hall, 1978).

Devarajan, S. and de Melo, J. 'Evaluating Participation in African Monetary Unions', *World Development*, 15 (1987).

Devuyst, Y. *The European Union at the Crossroads: An Introduction to the EU's Institutional Evolution* (Brussels: P.I.E. – Peter Lang, 2002).

Dodd, N. 'The Hidden Side of the Euro', *Finance and the Common Good*, 9 (2001).

Drysdale, P. and Garnaut, R. 'The Pacific: An Application of a General Theory of Economic Integration' in Bergsten, C.F. (ed.) *Pacific Dynamism and the International Economic System* (Washington, DC: Institute for International Economics, 1993).

Dubey, M., Baral, L.R. and Sobhan, R. (eds) *South Asian Growth Quadrangle: Framework for Multifaceted Cooperation* (Delhi: Macmillan, 1999).

Dworkin, R. *Law's Empire* (Cambridge, MA and London: Harvard University Press, 1986).

Dworkin, R. *Taking Rights Seriously* (Cambridge, MA: Harvard University Press, 1977).

ECOWAS, *Executive Secretary's Reports, 25th Anniversary Report* (Abuja: ECOWAS, 2000).

Edgar, J., Meissner, D. and Silva, A. 'Keeping the Promise: Immigration Proposals from the Heartland', Chicago Council on Foreign Relations, Report of an Independent Task Force (2004).

Eichengreen, B. 'A More Perfect Union? The Logic of Economic Integration' in *Essays in International Finance* (Princeton, NJ: Princeton University Press, 1996).

Eichengreen, B. and Bayoumi, T. 'Is Asia an Optimum Currency Area? Can It Become One? Regional, Global and Historical Perspectives on Asian Monetary Relations', *CIDER Paper*, 81 (1996).

Ellis, E. (ed.) *The Principle of Proportionality in the Laws of Europe* (Oxford/Portland: Hart Publishing, 1999).

El-Naggar, S. and El-Erian, M. 'The Economic Implications of a Comprehensive Peace in the Middle East' in Fischer, S., Rodrik, D. and Tuma E. (eds) *The Economics of Middle East Peace* (London: The MIT Press, 1993).

Emerson, M. *The Wider Europe Matrix* (Brussels: Centre for European Policy Studies, 2004).

Engel, C. 'The European Charter of Fundamental Rights: A Changed Political Opportunity Structure and its Normative Consequences', *European Law Journal*, 7:2 (2001).

Ethier, W.J. 'Regional Regionalism' in Lahiri, S. (ed.) *Regionalism and Globalisation: Theory and Practice* (London: Routledge, 2001).

European Citizen Action Service, 'The Convention on the Future of Europe and NGOs', *The European Citizen*, Special Edition (October 2002).

European Commission, Wider Europe – Neighbourhood: A Framework for Relations with our Eastern and Southern Neighbours. Brussels: COM(2003) 104 final (2003).

European Commission, 'Regional Policy, Inforegio', <http://europa.eu.int/comm/regional_policy/intro/working4_en.htm>, collected, 20040927, 2001 (2004).

European Convention, *Treaty Establishing a Constitution for Europe*, Brussels: CONV 850/03 (10 July 2003).

European Union, *Charter of Fundamental Rights of the European Union*. Brussels: European Commission (2000/C 364/01) (2000).

Falk, R. 'The Post-Westphalia Enigma' in Hettne, B. and Odén, B. *Global Governance in the 21st Century: Alternative Perspectives on World Order* (Stockholm: EGDI, 2002).

Falk, R. *The Declining World Order* (New York and London: Routledge, 2004).

Fawcett, L. 'Regionalism in Historical Perspective' in Fawcett, L. and Hurrell, A. (eds) *Regionalism in World Politics: Regional Organisation and World Order* (Oxford: Oxford University Press, 1995).

Fawcett, L. 'The Evolving Architecture of Regionalisation' in Pugh, M. and Sidhu, W.P.S. (eds) *The United Nations and Regional Security: Europe and Beyond* (Boulder, CO: Lynne Rienner, 2003).

Fawcett, L. 'Alliances, Cooperation and Regionalism in the Middle East' in Fawcett, L. (ed.) *The International Relations of the Middle East* (Oxford: Oxford University Press, 2004).

Fawcett, L. and Hurrell, A. (1995) *Regionalism in World Politics* (Oxford: Oxford University Press, 1995).

Fielding, D. and Shields, K. 'Modeling Macroeconomic Shocks in the CFA Franc Zone', *Journal of Development Economics*, 66 (2001).

Fielding, D. and Shields, K. 'The Impact of Monetary Union on Macroeconomic Integration: Evidence from West Africa', *WIDER Research Paper*, 17 (2004).

Fischer, S. 'Prospects for Regional Integration in the Middle East' in De Melo, J. and Panagariya, A. (eds) *New Dimensions in Regional Integration* (Cambridge: Cambridge University Press, 1993).

Fischer, S. Rodrik, D. and Tuma, E. (eds) *The Economics of Middle East Peace* (London: MIT Press, 1993).

Foqué, R. *De ruimte van het recht* (Arnhem: Gouda Quint, 1992).

Foqué, R. 'Legal Subjectivity and Legal Relation. Language and Conceptualisation in the Law' in Fleerackers, F., van Leeuwen, E. and van Roermund, B. (eds) *Law, Life and the Images of Man: Modes of Thought in Modern Legal Theory. Festschrift for Jan M. Broekman* (Berlin: Duncker & Humblot, 1996).

Forrest, J. *Subnationalism in Africa: Ethnicity, Alliances and Politics* (Boulder, CO and London: Lynne Rienner, 2004).

Fortmann, M., MacFarlane, S.N. and Roussel, S. (eds) *Multilateralism and Regional Security* (Toronto: The Canadian Peacekeeping Press, 1997).

Friedman, M. 'The Case for Flexible Exchange Rates' in *Essays in Positive Economics* (Chicago: University of Chicago Press, 1953).

Fry, E.H. *Canada's Unity Crisis: Implications for U.S.–Canadian Economic Relations* (New York: Twentieth Century Fund Press, 1992).

Fry, E.H. 'North American Economic Integration: Policy Options', *Policy Papers on the Americas*, Vol. XIV, Study 8 (Washington, DC: Center for Strategic and International Studies, July 2003).

Gamble, A. and Payne A. *Regionalism and World Order* (Basingstoke: Macmillan, 1996).

Gavin, B. *The European Union and Globalisation: Towards Global Democratic Governance* (Cheltenham (UK) and Northampton (US): Edward Elgar, 2001).

Gavin, B. 'From the Convention to the IGC: Visioning the Future of Europe', The Federal Trust, Online Paper 36/03 (2003).

Gershoni, I. and Jankowski, J. (eds) *Rethinking Nationalism in the Arab Middle East* (New York: Columbia University Press, 1997).

Gerven, W. 'Het evenredigheidsbeginsel: een beginsel met een groot verleden en een grote toekomst' in *In het nu, wat worden zal. Opstellen aangeboden aan Prof. Mr. H.C.F. Schoordijk* (Deventer: Kluwer 1991).

Giddens, A. *The Consequences of Modernity* (Stanford: Stanford University Press, 1990).

Giddens, A. *Modernity and Self-identity: Self and Society in the Late Modern Age* (Cambridge: Polity Press, 1991).

Gilson, J. *Asia Meets Europe* (Cheltenham (UK): Edward Elgar, 2002).

Goldfarb, D. 'Beyond Labels: Comparing Proposals for Closer Canada–US Economic Relations', *C.D. Howe Institute Backgrounder*, Toronto, <www.cdhowe.org> (October 2003).

Goto, J. 'Financial Cooperation in East Asia and Japan's Role', Paper presented at the *Euro 50 Group Roundtable*, Tokyo (11–12 June 2003).

Goto, M. 'Les performances économiques de l'union monétaire de l'Organisation des Pays de la Caraïbe de l'Est', *Région et Développment*, 14 (2001).

Grandes, M. 'South Africa's Monetary Area: An Optimum Currency Area: What Costs, Which Benefits?' *DELTA Working Paper* (2003).

Grayson, G. *The North American Free Trade Agreement: Regional Community and the New World Order* (Lanham, MD: University Press of America, 1995).

Gros, D. and Steinherr, A. 'Openness and the Cost of Fixing Exchange Rates in a Mundell-Fleming World' in Blejer, M., et al. (eds) *Optimum Currency Areas: New Analytical and Policy Developments* (Washington: IMF, 1997).

Guazzone, L. (ed.) *The Middle East in Global Change: The Politics and Economics of Interdependence versus Fragmentation* (London: MacMillan Press Ltd; New York: St Martin's Press, 1997).

Guazzone, L. 'A Map and Some Hypotheses for the Future of the Middle East' in Guazzone, L. (ed.) *The Middle East in Global Change: The Politics and Economics of Interdependencey versus Fragmentation* (New York: St Martin's Press, 1997).

Guzman, B., US Census Bureau, US Department of Commerce, 'The Hispanic Population: Census 2000 Brief', C2KBR/01–1 (May 2001).

Haas, E. *The Uniting of Europe: Political, Social and Economic Forces, 1950–57* (Stanford: Stanford University Press, 1958).

Habermas, J. 'Struggles for Recognition in the Democratic Constitutional State' in Gutmann, A. (ed.) *Multiculturalism: Examining the Politics of Recognition* (Princeton, NJ: Princeton University Press, 1994).

Habermas, J. *Between Facts and Norms: Contributions to a Discourse Theory of Law and Democracy* (Cambridge, MA: MIT Press, 1996).

Hamilton-Hart, N. 'The Origins and Launching of the Chiang Mai Initiative and the Prospects for Closer Monetary Integration in East Asia', paper presented to the INSEAD-ASEF Conference on Regional Integration in Europe and Asia: Pasts, Presents and Futures, Singapore (July 2003).

Hardt, M. and Negri, A. *Empire* (Cambridge, MA: Harvard University Press, 2000).

Hart M. *Fifty Years of Canadian Statecraft: Canada at the GATT, 1947–1997* (Ottawa, Canada: Centre for Trade Policy and Law, Carleton University, 1998).

Hazlewood, A. (ed.) *African Integration and Disintegration* (London: Oxford University Press, 1967).

Held, D. *Democracy and the Global Order: From the Modern State to Cosmopolitan Governance* (Cambridge: Polity Press, 1995).

Held, D., McGrew, A., Goldblatt, D. and Perraton, J. *Global Transformation* (Cambridge: Policy Press, 2003).

Herbst, J. And Mills, G. *The Future of Africa: A New Order in Sight?* (London: Oxford University Press and IISS, Adelphi Paper 361, 2003).

Herzig, E. 'Regionalism, Iran and Central Asia', *International Affairs* 80:3 (2004).

Hettne, B. *Development Theory and The Three Worlds* (London: Longman, 1995).

Hettne, B. 'Globalisation and the New Regionalism: The Second Great Transformation' in Hettne, B., Inotai, A. and Sunkel, O. (eds) *Globalism and the New Regionalism* (Basingstoke: Macmillan Press, 1999).

Hettne, B. 'The new regionalism: a prologue' in Hettne, B., Inotai, A. and Sunkel, O. (eds) *The New Regionalism and the Future of Security and Development* (London: Macmillan Press, 2000).

Hettne, B. 'Regionalism, Security and Development: A Comparative Perspective' in Hettne, B. et al., *Comparing Regionalisms: Implications for Global Development* (London: Palgrave Macmillan, 2001).

Hettne, B. 'The New Regionalism Revisited' in Söderbaum, F. and Shaw, T. (eds) *Theories of New Regionalisms: A Palgrave Reader* (Basingstoke: Palgrave Macmillan, 2003).

Hettne, B. and Odén, B. (eds) *Global Governance in the 21th Century: Alternative Perspectives on World Order* (Stockholm: EGDI, 2002).

Hettne, B. and Söderbaum, F. 'Towards Global Social Theory', *Journal of International Relations and Development*, 2:4 (1999).

Hettne, B. and Söderbaum, F. 'Theorising the Rise of Regionness', *New Political Economy* 5:3 (November 2000).

Hettne, B., Inotai, A. and Sunkel, O. (eds.) *Globalism and the New Regionalism* (Basingstoke: Macmillan Press, 1999).

Hettne, B., Inotai, A. and Sunkel, O. *Studies in New Regionalism*, Vols I–V (London: Macmillan, 1999–2001).

Hettne, B., Inotai, A. and Sunkel, O. (eds) *Comparing Regionalisms: Implications for Global Development* (Basingstoke: Palgrave Macmillan, 2001).

Higgott, R. 'Contested Globalisation: The Changing Context and Normative Challenges', *Review of International Studies*, 26 (2000a).

Higgott, R. 'The International Relations of the Asian Economic Crisis: A Study in the Politics of Resentment' in Robison, R., Beeson, M., Jayasuriya, K. and Hyuk-Rae, K. (eds) *Politics and Markets in the Wake of the Asian Crisis* (London and New York: Routledge, 2000b).

Higgott, R. 'From Trade-Led to Monetary-Led Regionalism: Why Asia in the 21st Century will be Different to Europe in the 20th Century', UNU/CRIS e-Working Papers 2002/1, Bruges: UNU-CRIS (2002).

Higgott, R. 'The Limits to Multilateral Economic Governance', paper presented to the Workshop on Economic Security in East Asia: Governance and Institutions, organised by the Institute of Defence and Strategic Studies, Singapore, 11–12 September 2003.

Hoffmaister, A., Roldos, J. and Wickham, P. 'Macroeconomic Fluctuations in Sub-Saharan Africa', *IMF Staff Papers*, 45 (1998).

Hoffman, S. 'Obstinate or Obsolete? The Fate of the Nation State in Western Europe', *Daedalus*, 95:3 (1966).

Hofman, J.E. 'Social Identity and Intergroup Conflict: An Israeli View' in Stroebe, W., Kruglanski, A., Bar-Tal, D. and Hewstone, M. (eds) *The Social Psychology of Intergroup Conflict* (New York: Springer, 1988).

Holland, M. 'South Africa, SADC, and the European Union: Matching Bilateral and Regional Policies', *Journal of Modern African Studies*, 33:2 (1995).

Holland, M. *The European Union and the Third World* (London and New York: Palgraven Macmillan, 2002).

Hooghe, L. and Marks, G. *Multi-level Governance and European Integration* (Boulder, CO: Rowman and Littlefield, 2001).

Hopkins, N. and Reicher, S. 'The Construction of Social Categories and Processes of Social Change: Arguing about National Identities' in Breakwell, G. and Lyons, E. (eds) *Changing European Identities* (Oxford: Butterworth-Heinemann, 1996).

Horenczyk, G. 'Migrant Identities in Conflict: Acculturation Attitudes and Perceived Acculturation Ideologies' in Breakwell, G. and Lyons, E. (eds) *Changing European Identities* (Oxford: Butterworth-Heinemann, 1996).

Horowitz, D. *Ethnic Groups in Conflict* (Berkeley, CA: University of California, 1985).

Horvath, J. 'Optimum Currency Area Theory: A Selective Review', *BOFIT Discussion Papers*, 15 (Helsinki: Bank of Finland, 2003).

House of Commons of Canada, *Partners in North America: Advancing Canada's Relations with the United States and Mexico: Report of the Standing Committee on Foreign Affairs and International Trade*, Ottawa, <www.parl.gc.ca> (December 2002).

Howlett, M., Netherton, A. and Ramesh, M. *The Political Economy of Canada: An Introduction* (New York: Oxford University Press, 2nd edition, 1999).

Hufbauer, G.C. and Schott, J.J. *NAFTA: An Assessment* (Washington, DC: Institute for International Economics, 1993, revised edition).

Hurrell, A. 'An Emerging Security Community in South America?' in Barnett, M. and Adler, E. (eds) *Security Communities* (Cambridge: Cambridge University Press, 1998).

Hurrell, A. 'Hegemony and Regional Governance' in Fawcett, L. and Serrano, M. (eds) *Regionalism and Governance in the Americas* (Basingstoke: Palgrave Macmillan, 2005).

Hveem, Helge 'Explaining the Regional Phenomenon in an Era of Globalisation' in Stubbs, R. and R.D. Underhill (eds) *Political Economy and the Changing Global Order* (Ontario: Oxford University Press, 2000).

IMF, *Annual Report 2000* (Washington, DC: IMF, 2000).

Inglehart, R. and Basanez, M. *World Values Survey: USA and Mexico*, 2000.

Inglehart, R., Nevitte, N. and Basanez, M. *The North American Trajectory: Cultural, Economic, and Political Ties Among the United States, Canada, and Mexico* (New York: Aldine de Gruyter, 1996).

Ingram, A. *A Political Theory of Rights* (Oxford: Clarendon Press, 1994).

Inter-American Development Bank, Integration and Regional Programmes Department, *Integration and Trade in the Americas: A Preliminary Estimate of 2003 Trade* (Washington, DC: Inter-American Development Bank, December 2003, periodic note).

International Peace Academy, 'The UN and Euro-Atlantic Organisations: Evolving Approaches to Peace Operations Beyond Europe', Report from the 14 November 2003/IPA Conference on 'The UN and European Security Organisations: Evolving Approaches to Crisis Management' (2004).

Jachtenfuchs, M. 'The Governance Approach to European Integration', *Journal of Common Market Studies*, 39:2 (2001).

Jaeger, W. *Paideia: The Ideals of Greek Culture* (New York/Oxford: Oxford University Press, 1967).

Jakobsen, P.V. 'The transformation of United Nations Peace Operations in the 1990s. Adding Globalisation to the Conventional "End of the Cold War explanation"', *Cooperation and Conflict: Journal of the Nordic International Studies Association*, 37:3 (2002).

Jenkins, C. and Thomas, L. 'Is South Africa Ready for Regional Monetary Integration?' in Peterson, L. (ed.) *Post-Apartheid South Africa: Economic Challenges and Policies for the Future* (London: Routledge, 1998).

Jessop, R. 'The Political Economy of Scale and the Construction of Cross-Border Micro-regions' in Söderbaum, F. and Shaw, T. (eds) *Theories of New Regionalisms: A Palgrave Reader* (Basingstoke: Palgrave Macmillan, 2003).

Joffé, G. 'Relations between the Middle East and the West: The View from the South' in Roberson, B.A. (ed.) *The Middle East and Europe: The Power of Deficit* (London and New York: Routledge, 1998).

Jönsson, C., Tägil, S. and Törnqvist, G. *Organising European Space* (London: Sage, 2000).

Kagan, R. *Paradise and Power: America and Europe in the New World* (New York: Atlantic Books, 2004).

Kappel, R., Mehler, A. and Melber, H. *Structural Stability in an African Context* (Uppsala: Nordiska Afrikainstitutet (Discussion Paper 24), 2003)

Karlsson, C. 'Democracy, Legitimacy and the European Union', PhD Thesis, Uppsala University (2001).

Keating, M. 'The Political Economy of Regionalism' in Keating, M. and Loughlin, J. (eds) *The Political Economy of Regionalism* (London: Frank Cass, 1997).

Keating, M. *The New Regionalism in Western Europe: Territorial Restructuring and Political Change* (Cheltenham: Edward Elgar, 1998).

Kelegama, S. 'South Asia and Other Regional Economic Groupings' in Bhargava, K.K. and Khatri, S.D. (eds) *South Asia 2010: Challenges and Opportunities* (New Delhi: Konark Publisher, 2002).

Kenen, P. 'The Theory of Optimum Currency Areas: An Eclectic View' in Mundell, R.A. and Swoboda, A.R. (eds) *Monetary Problems of the International Economy* (Chicago: University of Chicago Press, 1969).

Kenen, P.B. 'Currency Unions and Policy Domains' in Andrews, D.M., Henning, C.R. and Pauly, L.W. (eds) *Governing the World's Money* (Ithaca: Cornell University Press, 2002).

Kerr, I.A. and Thrope, M. 'Impediments to Trade and Investment in the Indian Ocean Region', *The Indian Ocean Review*, 13:2 (June 2000).

Kerr, M. *The Arab Cold War*, 2nd edition (London: Oxford University Press, 1997).

Khamfula, Y. and Huizinga, H. 'The Southern African Development Community: Suitable for a Monetary Union?' *Journal of Development Economics*, 73 (2004).

Knight, W.A. *A Changing United Nations: Multilateral Evolution and the Quest for Global Governance* (Basingstoke: Palgrave Macmillan, 2000).

Korany, B. 'The Old/New Middle East' in Guazzone, L. (ed.) *The Middle East in Global Change: The Politics and Economics of Interdependency versus Fragmentation* (New York: St Martin's Press, 1997).

Krasner S. (ed.) *International Regimes* (New York: Cornell University, 1983).

Krauthammer, C. 'The Unipolar Moment', *Foreign Affairs*, 70:1 (1991–92).

Krugman, P. 'Increasing Returns and Economic Geography', *Journal of Political Economy*, 99 (1991).

Lalonde, R. and St-Amant, P. 'Áreas de moneda óptima: el caso de México y de Estados Unidos', *Monetaria* (October–December 1995).

Laursen, F. *Comparative Regional Integration: Theoretical Perspectives* (Aldershot: Ashgate, 2003).

Lawrence, R. *Regionalism, Multilateralism and Deep Integration* (Washington, DC: Brookings Institution, 1995).

Leifer, M. 'The Paradox of ASEAN: A Security Organisation without the Structure of an Alliance', *The Round Table*, 271 (July 1978).

Lelart, M. 'The Franc Zone and European Monetary Integration' in Bach, D. (ed.) *Regionalisation in Africa: Integration and Disintegration* (Oxford: James Currey, 1999).

Lemke, D. 'African Lessons for International Relations Research', *World Politics*, 56 (2003).

Lepgold, J. 'Regionalism in the Post-Cold War Era' in Diehl, P.F. and Lepgold, J. (eds) *Regional Conflict Management* (Oxford: Rowman and Littlefield, 2003).

Lewis, P. 'US Economic Interests', CSIS, *A Review of US Africa Policy* (Washington, DC: Centre for Strategic and International Studies, December 2000).

Li Baojun, 'Dangdai zhongguo waijiao gailun' [Outline of Contemporary Chinese Diplomacy], Zhongguo Renmin Daxue Chubanshe [People's University of China Press] (2001).

Lim, I.S. *ASEAN Economic Community: Challenges and Prospects* (Unpublished) M.Sc. (International Relations) dissertation, Institute of Defence and Strategic Studies, Nanyang Technological University, Singapore (2004).

Lindstrom, G. (ed.) *Shift or Rift: Assessing US–EU Relations after Iraq* (Paris: Institute for Security Studies, 2003).

Lipset, S.M. *Continental Divide: The Values and Institutions of the United States and Canada* (New York: Routledge, 1991).

Lipsey, P. 'Japan's Asian Monetary Fund Proposal', *Stanford Journal of East Asian Affairs*, 3:1 (2003).

Lipsey, R.G. 'The Theory of Customs Unions: A General Survey', *Economic Journal*, 70 (1957).

Lipsey, R.G. 'Canada and the Mexico Free Trade Dance: Wallflower or Partner?' *Commentary*, 20 (Toronto: Howe Institute, 1990).

Lucas, R. 'On the Mechanics of Economic Development', *Journal of Monetary Economics*, XXII:1 (1988).

Luciani, G. (ed.) *The Arab State* (London: Routledge, 1990).

Lyons, E. (ed.) *Changing European Identities* (Oxford: Butterworth-Heinemann, 1996).

Maalouf, A. *In the Name of Identity* (London: Penguin Books, 2003).

McCarthy, C. 'SACU and the Rand Zone' in Bach, D. (ed.) *Regionalistion in Africa: Integration and Disintegration* (Oxford: James Currey, 1999).

MacCormick, N. *Questioning Sovereignty* (Oxford: Oxford University Press, 1999).

McKinnon, R.I. 'Optimum Currency Areas', *American Economic Review*, 53:4 (1963).

McKinnon, R.I. 'Comment' in Mundell, R.A. and Swoboda, A.R. (eds), *Monetary Problems of the International Economy* (Chicago: University of Chicago Press, 1969).

McMichael, P. 'Globalisation: Trend or Project?' in Palan, R. (ed.) *Global Political Economy: Contemporary Theories* (London and New York: Routledge, 2000).

Mahapatra, C. *American Role in the Origin and Growth of ASEAN* (New Delhi: ABC Publishers, 1990).

Malamud, A. and de Sousa, L. 'Regional Parliaments in Europe and Latin America : Between Empowerment and Irrelevance', Paper presented at the Fifth Pan-European International Relations Conference, mimeo (The Hague, September 2004).

Maloka, E. and Le Roux, E. (eds) *Problematising the African Renaissance*, Research Paper no. 62 (Pretoria: Africa Institute of South Africa, 2000).

Manioc, O. and Montauban, J.G. 'Is a Monetary Union in CARICOM Desirable?' *Conference Towards Regional Currency Areas*, CEPAL, Chile (26–27 March 2002).

Mansfield, E.D. and Milner, H. (eds) *The Political Economy of Regionalism* (Columbia: University Press, 1997).

Marfaing, L. and Wippel, S. (eds) *Les Relations transsahariennes à l'époque contemporaine* (Paris: Karthala, 2004).

Marr, P. 1998, 'The United States, Europe and the Middle East: Cooperation, Co-optation or Confrontation' in Roberson B.A. (ed.) *The Middle East and Europe: The Power of Deficit* (London and New York: Routledge, 1998).

Martin, P. and Midgley, E. 'Immigration: Shaping and Reshaping America', *Population Bulletin*, 58:2, Population Reference Bureau (June 2003).

Mattli, W. *The Logic of Regional Integration: Europe and Beyond* (Cambridge: Cambridge University Press, 1999).

Meade, J. *The Theory of Customs Unions* (Amsterdam: North Holland, 1955).

Meeusen, W. and Villaverde, J. (eds) *Convergence Issues in the European Union* (Cheltenham: Edward Elgar, 2002).

Mehrotra, S. 'South Africa Development Coordination Conference (SADCC): Evaluating Recent Trends in Regional Cooperation', *International Studies* (New Delhi), 28:4 (1991).

Meny, Y. 'De la démocratie en Europe: Old Concepts and New Challenges', *Journal of Common Market Studies*, 41:1 (2003).

Mertens de Wilmars, J., 'The Case Law of the Court of Justice in Relation to the Review of the Legality of Economic Policy in Mixed-Economy Systems', *Legal Issues of European Integration*, 1 (1983).

Mertens de Wilmars, J. and Steenbergen, J. 'The Court of Justice of the European Communities and Governance in an Economic Crisis', *Michigan Law Review*, 82 (1984).

Meyers, J. and Steenbergen, J. 'Deregulering, Europese eenmaking en bescherming van het nationaal belang' in *Sociaal-economische deregulering, Referaten 18e Vlaams Economisch Congres* (Antwerpen: VEV, 1987).

Miller, B. 'Explaining Variations in Regional Peace. Three Strategies for Peace-making', *Cooperation and Conflict*, 35:2 (2000).

Miller, B. 'Conflict Management in the Middle East: Between the "Old" and the "New"' in Diehl, F.P. and Lepgold, J. (eds) *Regional Conflict Management* (Lanham/Boulder/New York/Oxford: Rowman and Littlefield Publishers, Inc., 2003).

Mittelman, J.H. *The Globalisation Syndrome: Transformation and Resistance* (Princeton, NJ: Princeton University Press, 2000).

Mittelman, J.H. and Falk, R. 'Hegemony: The Relevance of Regionalism?' in Hettne, B. et al. (eds) *National Perspectives on New Regionalism in the North* (London: Macmillan, 1999).

Mongelli, F.P. 'New Views on the Optimum Currency Area Theory: What is EMU Telling Us?' *ECB Working Paper*, 138 (2002).

Moravcsik, A. 'Preferences and Power in the EC: A Liberal Intergovernmental Approach', *Journal of Common Market Studies*, 31:4 (1993).

Moravcsik, A. *The Choice for Europe: Social Purpose and State Power from Messina to Maastricht* (Ithaca: Cornell University Press, 1998).

Mundell, R. 'A Theory of Optimum Currency Areas', *American Economic Review*, 51 (1961).

Mundell, R.A. 'Uncommon Arguments for Common Currencies' in Johnson, H.G. and Swoboda, A.K. (eds), *The Economics of Common Currencies* (Allen and Unwin, 1973).

Mundell, R.A. 'Updating the Agenda for Monetary Union' in Blejer, M. et al. (eds) *Optimum Currency Areas: New Analytical and Policy Developments* (Washington, DC: IMF, 1997).

Mundell, R.A. 'What the Euro Means for the Dollar and the International Monetary System', *Atlantic Economic Journal*, 26:3 (1998).

Muni, S.D. 'Post-Cold War Regionalism in Asia', *VRF Series* No. 258 (Tokyo: Institute of Developing Economies, February 1996a).

Muni, S.D. *Prospects of the Emergence of Indian Ocean Community: The Security Dimension* (New Delhi, April 1996b).

Muni, S.D. and Muni, A. *Regional Cooperation in South Asia* (New Delhi: National Publishing House, 1984).

NAFTA, *The North American Free Trade Agreement between The Government of the United States, The Government of Canada, and the Government of the United Mexican States* (Washington, DC: Government Printing Office, 1992).

Nelsen, B.F. and Stubb, A.C.G (eds) *The European Union: Readings on the Theory and Practice of European Integration* (Boulder, CO: Lynne Rienner Publishers, 2nd edition, 1998).

Nesadurai, H.E.S. 'APEC: A US Tool for Regional Domination?' *The Pacific Review*, 9:1 (1996).

Nesadurai, H.E.S. *Globalisation, Domestic Politics and Regionalism: The ASEAN Free Trade Area* (London and New York: Routledge, 2003).

Nesadurai, H.E.S. 'Asia-Pacific Approaches to Regional Governance: The Globalisation–Domestic Politics Nexus' in Jayasuriya, K. (ed.) *Asian Regional Governance: Crisis and Change* (London and New York: Routledge, 2004).

Nevitte, N. *The Decline of Deference* (Ontario: Broadview Press, 1996).

Nevitte, N. and Basanez, M. 'Trinational Perceptions' in Pastor, R.A. and de Castro, R.F. (eds) *The Controversial Pivot: U.S. Congress and North America* (Washington, DC: Brookings Institution, 1998).

Ng, T.H. 'Should the Southeast Asian Countries Form a Currency Union?' *The Developing Economies*, 40:2 (2002).

Niemann, M. *A Spatial Approach to Regionalisms in the Global Economy* (Basingstoke: Macmillan, 2000).

Nussbaum, M. *Cultivating Humanity: A Classical Defense of Reform in Liberal Education* (Cambridge, MA and London: Harvard University Press, 1997).

Nye, J.S. *Peace in Parts: Integration and Conflict in Regional Organisation* (Boston: Little Brown, 1971).

Nye, J. 'Europe is Too Powerful to be Ignored', *International Herald Tribune* (10 March 2003).

Nye, J. *The Paradox of American Power* (New York: Oxford University Press, 2002).

O'Toole, F. *After the Ball* (Dublin: Tasc at New Island, 2003).

Oates, W.E. 'An Essay on Fiscal Federalism', *Journal of Economic Literature*, XXXVII (1999).

Ohmae, K. *The End of the Nation State: The Rise of Regional Economies* (London: Harper Collins, 1995).

Orend, B. 'Considering Globalism, Proposing Pluralism: Michael Walzer on International Justice', *Millennium: Journal of International Studies*, 29:2 (2000).

Orme, W.A. *Understanding NAFTA* (Austin: University of Texas Press, 1996).

Owen, R. *State, Power and Politics in the Making of the Modern Middle East* (London and New York: Routledge, 1992).

Padoan, P.C. 'The Political Economy of Regional Integration in the Middle East' in Guazzone, L. (ed.) *The Middle East in Global Change: The Politics and Economics of Interdependence versus Fragmentation* (New York: St Martin's Press, 1997).

Padoa-Schioppa, T. *Europe, A Civil Power* (London: Federal Trust for Education and Research, 2004).

Palmer, N.D. *The New Regionalism in Asia and the Pacific* (Lexington: Lexington Books, 1991).

Papaioannou, M.G. 'Determinants of the Choice of Exchange Rate Regimes in Six Central American Countries: An Empirical Analysis', *IMF Working Paper*, WP/03/59 (2003).

Pastor, R.A. *Integration with Mexico: Options for U.S. Policy* (Washington, DC: Twentieth Century Fund, 1993).

Pastor, R. 'The United States: Divided by a Revolutionary Vision' in Pastor, R. (ed.) *A Century's Journey: How the Great Powers Shape the World* (New York: Basic Books, 1999).

Pastor, R.A. 'Mexico's Victory: Exiting the Labyrinth', *Journal of Democracy*, 11:4 (October 2000).

Pastor, R.A. *Exiting the Whirlpool: U.S. Foreign Policy Toward Latin America and the Caribbean* (Boulder, CO: Westview Press, 2001a).

Pastor, R.A. *Toward a North American Community: Lessons from the Old World for the New* (Washington, DC: Institute for International Economics, 2001b).

Pastor, R.A. 'Democracy and Elections in North America: What Can We Learn From Our Neighbours?' *Election Law Journal*, 3:3 (2004a).

Pastor, R.A. 'North America's Second Decade', *Foreign Affairs*, 83:1 (January/February 2004b).

Pastor, R.A. and Castañeda, J.G. *Limits to Friendship: The United States and Mexico* (New York: Alfred A. Knopf, 1988).

Patten, C. 'Common Strategy for the Mediterranean and Reinvigorating the Barcelona Process', Speech by the Rt Hon. Chris Patten, Speech/01/49, European Parliament, Brussels (31 January 2001).

Peers, S. 'Fundamental Right or Political Whim: WTO Law and the European Court of Justice' in de Burca, G. and Scott, J. (eds) *The EU and the WTO* (Oxford: Hart, 2003).

Perkmann, M. and Sum, N. (eds) *Globalisation, Regionalisation and the Building of Cross-Border Regions* (Basingstoke: Palgrave Macmillan, 2002).

Peters, J. *Pathways to Peace: The Multilateral Arab–Israeli Peace Talks* (London: Royal Institute of International Affairs, 1996).

Petersmann, E.U. 'European and International Constitutional Law: Time for Promoting "Cosmopolitan Democracy" in the WTO' in de Burca, G. and Scott, J. (eds) *The EU and the WTO* (Oxford: Hart, 2003).

Pivetti, M. 'Monetary versus Political Unification in Europe. On Maastricht as an Exercise in "Vulgar" Political Economy', *Review of Political Economy*, 10:1 (1998).

Plane, P. 'Performances comparées en matière de croissance économique' in Guillaumont, P. and Guillaumont, S. (eds) *Strategies de Développement Comparées* (Paris: Economica, 1988).

Plummer, M. 'ASEAN and Institutional Nesting in the Asia-Pacific: Leading from Behind in APEC' in Aggarwal, V.K. and Morrison, C.E. (eds) *Asia-Pacific Crossroads: Regime Creation and the Future of APEC* (London: Macmillan, 1998).

Poiares Maduro, M. 'Is There Any Such Thing as Free or Fair Trade? A Constitutional Analysis of the Impact of International Trade on the European Social Model' in de Burca, G. and Scott, J. (eds) *The EU and the WTO* (Oxford: Hart, 2003).

Polanyi, K. *The Great Transformation* (Boston: Beacon Press, 1957, new edition 2001).

Pollack, M.A. 'International Relations Theory and European Integration', *Journal of Common Market Studies*, 39:2 (2001).

Pridham, G., Herring, E. and Sanford, G. (eds) *Building Democracy? The International Dimension of Democratisation in Eastern Europe* (London and Washington: Leicester University Press, 1997).

Pugh, M. and Sidhu, W.P.S. *The United Nations and Regional Security: Europe and Beyond* (Boulder, CO: Lynne Rienner, 2003)

Rahman, S.M. 'SAARC and the New Paradigm of Security', *Defence Journal*, Karachi (September 2001).

Rasmussen, M.V. 'A Parallel Globalisation of Terror': 9/11, Security and Globalisation, *Cooperation and Conflict: Journal of the Nordic International Studies Association*, 37:3 (2002).

Rasmussen, M.V. 'Reflexive Security: NATO and International Risk Society', *Millennium: Journal of International Studies*, 30:2 (2001).

Ravenhill, J. 'Institutional Evolution at the Trans-Regional Level: APEC and the Promotion of Liberalisation' in Beeson, M. (ed.) *Reconfiguring East Asia: Regional Institutions and Organisations After the Crisis* (London: Routledge Curzon, 2002).

Ravenhill, J. *APEC and the Construction of Pacific Rim Regionalism* (Cambridge: Cambridge University Press, 2001).

Rawls, J. *A Theory of Justice* (London/Oxford/New York: Oxford University Press, 1971).

Renner, K. *Die Nation: Mythos und Wirklichkeit*, Manuscript aus dem Nachlass [The Nation: Myth and Reality – Manuscript from the Posthumous Paper] (Vienna: Europa, 1964).

Richards, A. and Waterbury, J. *A Political Economy of the Middle East*, 2nd edition (Oxford: Westview Press, 1996).

Riley, J. 'Constitutional Democracy as a Two-Stage Game' in Ferefoin, J., Rakove, J. and Riley, J. (eds) *Constitutional Culture and Democratic Rule* (Cambridge: Cambridge University Press, 2001).

Rodan, G. 'Reconstructing Divisions of Labour: Singapore's New Regional Emphasis' in Higgott, R., Leaver, R. and Ravenhill, J. (eds) *Pacific Economic Relations in the 1990s: Cooperation or Conflict?* (Boulder, CO: Lynne Rienner Publishers, 1993).

Rodrik, Dani (2002) 'After Neoliberalism,What?' <http://ksghome.harvard.edu/~.drodrik>.

Romer, P. 'Endogenous Technological Change', *Journal of Political Economy*, 98:5 (1990).

Rosamond, B. *Theories of European Integration* (Basingstoke: Macmillan, 2000).

Rosenau, J.N. and Czempiel, E.O. *Governance without Government: Order and Change in World Politics* (Cambridge: Cambridge University Press, 1992).

Ruggie, J.G. 'Territoriality and Beyond: Problematising Modernity in International Relations', *International Organisation*, 46:1 (1993).

Ruggie, J.G. *Constructing the World Polity* (London: Routledge, 1998).

Sacerdoti, G. 'Standards of Treatment, Harmonisation and Mutual Recognition: A Comparison Between Regional Areas and the Global Trading System' in Demaret, P., Bellis, J.-F. and Garcia Jeménez, G. (eds) *Regionalism and Multilateralism after the Uruguay Round* (Brussels: European Interuniversity Press, 1997).

SADCC, *Annual Report 1990–01* (1991, mimeo).

Salamé, G. 'Torn between the Atlantic and the Mediterranean: Europe and the Middle East in the Post-Cold War Era' in Roberson B.A. (ed.) *The Middle East and Europe: The Power of Deficit* (London and New York: Routledge, 1998).

Sandholtz, W. and Stone Sweet, A. (eds) *European Integration and Supranational Governance* (Oxford: Oxford University Press, 1998).

Sandwick, J.A. *The Gulf Cooperation Council: Moderation and Stability in an Interdependent World* (Boulder, CO: Westview Press, 1987).

Saxena, S.C. 'India's Monetary Integration with the Rest of Asia: A Feasability Study', *Working Paper* (University of Pittsburgh, 2003).

Schmitter, P.C. 'Neo-neo-functionalism' in Wiener, A. and Diez, T. (eds) *European Integration Theory* (Oxford: Oxford University Press, 2003).

Scholte, J.A. 'Civil Society and Governance in the Global Polity' in Ougaard, M. and Higgott, R. (eds) *Towards a Global Polity* (London and New York: Routledge, 2002).

Scholte, J.A. 'Global Civil Society' in Woods, N. (ed.) *The Political Economy of Globalisation* (London: Macmillan, 2000).

Schott, J.J. and Smith, M.G. (eds) *The Canada–United States Free Trade Agreement: The Global Impact* (Washington, DC: Institute for International Economics, 1988).

Schulz, M. 'The Palestinian–Israeli Security Complex: Inconciliatory Positions or Regional Cooperation?' in Ohlsson, L. (ed.) *Case Studies of Regional Conflicts and Conflict Resolution*, Padrigu Papers (Göteborg, 1989).

Schulz, M., Söderbaum, F. and Öjendal, J. (eds) *Regionalisation in a Globalising World* (London: Zed Books Ltd, 2001).

Scollay, R. and Gilbert, J.P. *New Regional Trading Arrangements in the Asia Pacific?* (Washington, DC: Institute for International Economics, 2001).

Seidelmann, R. 'European Peace: From Vision to Reality' in Remacle, E., Seidelmann, R. (eds) *Pan-European Security Redefined* (Baden-Baden: Nomos Verlaggesellschaft, 1998).

Sen, A. 'Capability and Well Being' in Nussbaum, M. and Sen, A. (eds) *The Quality of Life* (Oxford: Clarendon Press, 1993).

Shaw, T. 'Beyond Post-Conflict Peace Building: What Links to Sustainable Development and Human Security?' *International Peacekeeping*, 3:2 (1996).

Shimizu, K. 'The Asian Economic Crisis and Intra-ASEAN Economic Cooperation', *Economic Journal of Hokkaido University*, 29 (2000).

Shore, S.M. 'No Fences Make Good Neighbours: The Development of the U.S.–Canadian Security Community, 1871–1940' in Adler, E. and Barnett, M. (eds) *Security Communities* (Cambridge: Cambridge University Press, 1998).

Shtayyeh, M. *Israel in the Region: Conflict, Hegemony or Cooperation?* (Jerusalem: Palestinian Economic Council for Development and Reconstruction, 1998).

Singh, B. *ZOFPAN and the New Security Order in Asia-Pacific* (Petaling Jaya: Pelanduk Publications, 1991).

Slaughter, A.-M. *A New World Order* (Princeton, NJ: Princeton University Press, 2004).

Slocum, N. 'Realising the Future: On Collaboration Between Policy-Makers and Social Scientists to Facilitate Social Change' in OECD Proceedings, *Social Sciences for Knowledge and Decision Making*, chapter 13 (2001).

Slocum, N. and Van Langenhove, L. 'Integration Speak: Introducing Positioning Theory in Regional Integration Studies' in Harré, R. and Moghaddam, F. (eds) *The Self and Others: Positioning Individuals and Groups in Personal, Political, and Cultural Contexts* (USA: Praeger/Greenwood, 2003).

Slocum, N. and Van Langenhove, L. 'The Meaning of Regional Integration: Introducing Positioning Theory to the Study of Regional Integration', *Journal of European Integration*, 26:3 (2004).

Smith, A.D. *The Ethnic Origins of Nations* (Oxford: Basil Blackwell, 1986).

Söderbaum, F. *Handbook of Regional Organisations in Africa* (Uppsala: Nordiska Afrikainstitutet, 1996).

Söderbaum, F. and Shaw, T. (eds) *Theories of New Regionalisms: A Palgrave Reader* (Basingstoke: Palgrave Macmillan, 2002).

Söderbaum, F. and Taylor, I. 'Transmission Belt for Transnational Capital or Facilitator for Development? Problematising the Role of the State in the Maputo Development Corridor', *Journal of Modern African studies*, XXXIX:4 (2001).

Söderbaum, F. and Taylor, I. (eds) *Regionalism and Uneven Development in Southern Africa: The Case of the Maputo Development Corridor* (Aldershot: Ashgate, 2003).

Solingen, E. *Regional Orders at Century's Dawn: Global and Domestic Influences on Grand Strategy* (Princeton, NJ: Princeton University Press, 1998).

Stadtmüller, E. 'Future Path to European Security' in Farrell, M., Fella, S. and Newman, M. (eds) *European Integration in the 21st Century, Unity in Diversity?* (London: Sage, 2002).

Stasavage, D. *The Political Economy of a Common Currency: The CFA Franc Zone since 1945* (Aldershot: Ashgate, 2004).

Steenbergen, J. 'The Contribution of the Court of Justice' in Norton, J.J. (ed.) *EEC Trade and Investment* (New York: Matthew Bender, 1986).

Steenbergen, J., De Clercq, G. and Foqué, R. *Change and Adjustment* (Deventer: Kluwer, 1983).

Sterner, J. and Skoog, W. *ASEAN – An Optimum Currency Area?* (Stockholm: Stockholm University, 2003).

Stiglitz, J. *Globalisation and Its Discontents* (London: Allen Lane (Pengiun Press), 2002).

Stubbs, R. 'ASEAN Plus Three: Emerging East Asian Regionalism?' *Asian Survey*, 42:3 (2002).

Stubbs, R. 'Performance Legitimacy and "Soft Authoritarianism"' in Acharya, A., Frolic, B.M. and Stubbs, R. (eds) *Democracy, Human Rights and Civil Society in Southeast Asia* (Toronto: Joint Centre for Asia Pacific Studies, York University, 2001).

Summers, R.S. 'Naïve Instrumentalism and the Law' in Hacker, P.M.S. and Raz, J. (eds) *Law, Morality and Society: Essays in Honour of H.L.A. Hart* (Oxford: Clarendon Press, 1977).

Taguieff, P.A. *L'illusion populiste* (Paris: Berg International, 2002).

Taylor, C. 'The Politics of Recognition' in Gutman, A. (ed.) *Multiculturalism: Examining the Politics of Recognition* (Princeton, NJ: Princeton University Press, 1994).

Taylor, I. *Poverty and Global Transformation: Does the New Partnership for Africa's Development Help or Hinder?* (Portland, OR: International Studies Association annual Convention, 26 February–1 March 2003, mimeo).

Teló, M. (ed.) European Union and New Regionalism. Regional Actors and Global Governance in a Post-hegemonic Era (Aldershot: Ashgate, 2001).

Teló, M. 'Introduction: Globalisation, New Regionalism and the Role of the European Union' in Teló, M. (ed.) *European Union and New Regionalism: Regional Actors and Global Governance in a Post-Hegemonic Era* (Aldershot: Ashgate, 2001).

Theurl, T. 'Linkages between Monetary Union and Political Union in the European Union' in Lang, F. and Ohr, R. (eds) *International Economic Integration* (Heidelberg: Physica-Verlag, 1995).

Thomas, C. *Global Governance, Development and Human Security* (London: Pluto, 2000).

Thompson, C.B. 'African Initiatives for Development: The Practice of Regional Economic Cooperation in Southern Africa', *Journal of International Affairs*, 46:1 (Summer 1992).

Torregrosa, J. 'Spanish International Orientations: Between Europe and Iberoamerica' in Breakwell, G. and Lyons, E. (eds), *Changing European Identities* (Oxford: Butterworth-Heinemann, 1996).

Trebilcock, A. 'Social Dimensions of International Trade Liberalisation' in Demaret, P., Bellis, J.F. and Garcia Jeménez, G. (eds) *Regionalism and Multilateralism after the Uruguay Round* (Brussels: European Interuniversity Press, 1997).

Trew, K. and Benson, D. 'Dimensions of Social Identity in Northern Ireland' in Breakwell, G. and Lyons, E. (eds) *Changing European Identities: Social-Psychogical Analyses of Social Change* (Oxford: Butterworth-Heinemann, 1996).

Trivisvanet, T. *Do East Asian Countries Constitute an Optimum Currency Area?* (Durham, NC: Duke University, 2001).

Uche, C.U. *The Policies of Monetary Sector Cooperation among the Economic Community of West African States* (Washington, DC: The World Bank Institute Policy Research Working Paper 2647, July 2001).

UNDP, *Arab Human Development Report 2002: Creating Opportunities for Future Generation* (2002).

UNDP, *Human Development Report* (Oxford: Oxford University Press, 1994).

UNDP, *Human Development Report*, <www.undp.org/hdr2003> (2003).

US Congress, House of Representatives, *Africa and the War on Global Terrorism, Hearing before the Subcommittee on Africa of the Committee on International Relations*, Serial No. 107–76 (Washington, DC: US Government Printing Office, 15 November 2001).

US President, *The National Security Strategy of the United States of America* (Washington, DC: The White House, 2002).

van Ginkel, H., Court, J. and Van Langenhove, L. (eds) *Integrating Africa: Perspectives on Regional Integration and Development* (New York: United Nations University and CRIS, 2002).

Van Walraven, K. 'From "Union of Tyrants" to "Power of the People"? The Significance of the Pan-African Parliament for the African Union', *Afrika Spectrum*, 39:1 (2004).

Vandaele, A. *International Labour Rights and the Social Clause: Friends or Foes*, Ph.D. thesis (Leuven: K.U. Leuven, 2003).

Verdun, A. 'An "Asymmetrical" Economic and Monetary Union in the EU: Perceptions of Monetary Authorities and Social Partners', *Journal of European Integration*, XX:1 (1996).

Viner, J. *The Customs Union Issue* (New York: Carnegie Endowment for International Peace, 1950).

von Bogdandy, A. and Makatsch, T. 'Collision, Co-existence or Co-operation? Prospects for the Relationship between WTO Law and European Law' in de Burca, G. and Scott, J. (eds) *The EU and the WTO* (Oxford: Hart, 2003).

Von Busekist, A. 'Uses and Misuses of the Concept of Identity', *Security Dialogue* 35:1 (2004).

Wadhva, C.D. *Trade Cooperation in the Indian Ocean Rim* (New Delhi: Sterling Publishers, 2003).

Walker, N. 'The EU and the WTO: Constitutionalism in a New Key' in de Burca, G. and Scott, J. (eds) *The EU and the WTO* (Oxford: Hart, 2003).

Wallace, B. 'What Makes a Canadian?' *Macleans* (20 December 1999).

Wallace, H. 'Designing Institutions for an Enlarging European Union' in De Witte, B. (ed.) *Ten Reflections on the Constitutional Treaty for Europe* (Florence: European University Institute, 2003).

Wang, J. 'Juyou lishi yiyi de kuayue' [A Historical Transition – From 'Shanghai Five' to Shanghai Cooperation Organisation], *Shijie jinji yu zhengzhi* [*World Economics and Politics*], 9 (September 2001).

Weiler, J.H.H. *The Constitution of Europe* (Cambridge: Cambridge University Press, 1999).

Weiler, J.H.H. 'A Constitution for Europe? Some Hard Choices', *Journal of Common Market Studies*, 40:4 (2002).

Weintraub, S. *NAFTA at Three: A Progress Report* (Washington, DC: Center for Strategic and International Studies, 1997).

Wet de, E. 'The Relationship between the Security Council and Regional Organisations during Enforcement Action under Chapter VII of the United Nations Charter', *Nordic Journal of International Law*, 71 (2002).

Whitehead, L. *The International Dimensions of Democratisation* (Oxford: Oxford University Press, 1996).

Wider Europe – Neighbourhood: Proposed New Framework for Relations with the EU's Eastern and Southern Neighbours, Communication from the European Commission to the Council and European Parliament (11 March 2003).

Wiener, A. 'Citizenship Policy in a Global Framework: The Case of the European Union' in Thomas, K.P. and Tetreault, M.A. (eds) *Racing to Regionalize* (London: Lynne Rienner, 1999).

Wolfowitz, P. *Building a Military for the 21st Century*, Statement for the House and Senate Armed Services Committees, 3–3 October (Washington, DC: United States Department of Defense, 2001).

Wonnacott, P. *The United States and Canada: The Quest for Free Trade* (Washington, DC: Institute for International Economics, 1987).

Wouters, J. and van Eeckhoutte, D. 'Giving Effect to Customary International Law through European Community Law' in Prinssen, J.M. and Schrauwen, A. (eds) *Direct Effect: Rethinking a Classic of EC Legal Doctrine* (Groningen: Europa Law Publishing, 2002).

Xia Liping, 'China: A Responsible Great Power', *Journal of Contemporary China*, 10:26 (2001).

Xiong G., 'Mianxiang 21 shiji de guiji anquan xingshi yu Zhongguo jundui jianshe' [Gearing towards the Global Security Situation and the Building of Chinese Armed Forces in the 21st Century], *Guoji zhanlue yanjiu* [*International Strategic Studies*], 48:2 (April 1998).

Yam, J. *The Asian Bond Fund* (Bangkok: Ministry of Foreign Affairs, 19 June 2003), <www.mfa.go.th/internet/ACD/asianbond/AsianBondFund.doc>

Yu, F. 'Lundun dierci Yaou shounao huixi pingshu' [On the Second Asia–Europe Meeting in London], *Fazhan luntan* [*Development Forum*], 6 (1998).

Yuen, H. *Is Asia an Optimum Currency Area? 'Shocking' Aspects of Output Fluctuations in East Asia* (Singapore: National University of Singapore, 2000).

Zahler, R. et al. *Política cambiaria en los países miembros del FLAR* (Bogotá: FLAR, 1997).

Zartman, W. 'The International Politics of Democracy in North Africa' in Entelis, J. (ed.) *Islam, Democracy, and the State in North Africa* (Bloomington, IN: Indiana University Press, 1997).

Zhang, Z., Sato, K. and McAleer, M. 'Is East Asia an Optimum Currency Area?' *Proceedings of iEMSs 2002. Integrated Assessment and Decision Support*, Lugano (24–27 June 2002).

Zoellick, R.C. 'Economics and Security in the Changing Asia-Pacific', *Survival*, 39:4, 1997/98.

Notes on Editors and Contributors

EDITORS

Mary Farrell is Senior Research Fellow at United Nations University – Comparative Regional Integration Studies, Bruges, Belgium. She has published on various aspects of regional integration, on European integration, and inter-regionalism. Her research interests also include international political economy, and African regionalism.

Björn Hettne is Professor at the Department of Peace and Development, Göteborg University, Sweden. He is the author of a number of books on development theory, international political economy, European integration and ethnic relations. He was programme director of the UNU-WIDER project on new regionalism, and co-edited the five-volume series, *Globalism and the New Regionalism* (1999–2001, Macmillan, UNU-WIDER).

Luk Van Langenhove is since 1 October 2001 Director of the Comparative Regional Integration Studies of the United Nations University (UNU-CRIS) in Bruges. He also teaches at the Vrije Universiteit Brussel (VUB) and the College of Europe. Recent publications include: H. Van Ginkel, J. Court, and L. Van Langenhove (eds), *Integrating Africa: Perspectives on Regional Integration and Development* (Tokyo: UNU Press, 2003); B. Gavin and L. Van Langenhove. 'Trade in a World of Regions' in G.P. Sampson and S. Woolcock (eds), *Regionalism, Multilateralism and Economic Integration: The Recent Experience* (Tokyo: UNU Press, 2003); L. Van Langenhove, 'Regional Integration and the Individualism/Collectivism Dichotomy', *Asia Europe Journal* (1), 1–13; N. Slocum and L. Van Langenhove. 'The Meaning of Regional Integration: Introducing Positioning Theory in Regional Integration Studies', *European Integration*, 26 (3), 227–52.

CONTRIBUTORS

Daniel Bach is a CNRS Director of Research (Centre d'Etude d'Afrique Noire of Bordeaux) and a professor at Institut d'Etudes Politiques, Bordeaux University. His research interests are in international relations and the politics of regional integration. He has extensively published on: Nigerian federalism; regional institutions and regionalisation processes in Africa; the interactions between regionalisation and the globalisation of the world economy; and relations between the European Union and Africa. His most recent publications include 'The Dilemmas of Regionalization' in Adekeye Adebajo and Rashid (eds), *Towards a Pax Africana: Building Peace in a Troubled Sub-Region*, (Boulder, CO: Lynne Rienner, 2004) and an edited volume on *Regionalisation in Africa: Integration and Distintegration* (Oxford and Bloomington: James Currey and Indiana University Press, 1999).

Ludo Cuyvers is Professor of international economics and trade policy and Chairman of the Department of International Economics, International Management and Diplomacy at the University of Antwerp (Belgium). He is also Director of the Centre for ASEAN Studies at the same university and Chairman of the European Institute for Asian Studies in Brussels. He is the author of numerous publications on the History of Economic Thought, International Economics, and Southeast Asia.

Philippe De Lombaerde is Research Fellow at the United Nations University – Comparative Regional Integration Studies (UNU-CRIS) in Bruges (Belgium). Previously he was an Associate

Professor of international economics at the Faculty of Economics of the Universidad Nacional de Colombia (Bogotá) and a Lecturer at the University of Antwerp. He has published on international economics, regional economic integration, the EU, ASEAN, Latin America.

Eric De Souza is Lecturer of macroeconomics and quantitative techniques at the European Economic Studies Department of the College of Europe in Bruges (Belgium). He is specialised in European macroeconomic policy.

Louise Fawcett is University Lecturer and the Wilfrid Knapp Fellow and Tutor in Politics at St Catherine's College, University of Oxford. Her recent research has focused on issues of comparative regionalism, with particular reference to developing countries. Publications include *The International Relations of the Middle East* (Oxford: Oxford University Press, 2004); *The Third World Beyond the Cold War*, co-edited with Yezid Sayigh (Oxford: Oxford University Press, 2000); and *Regionalism in World Politics*, co-edited with Andrew Hurrell (Oxford: Oxford University Press, 1995). A volume on *Regional Governance in the Americas* (with Monica Serrano) is forthcoming.

David Fielding is Professor of Economics at the University of Otago (New Zealand). Previously he was a Professor of Economics at the University of Leicester. He is also an External Fellow of the Centre for Research in Economic Development and International Trade at the University of Nottingham and a Research Associate of the Centre for the Study of African Economies at the University of Oxford. His main area of interest is macroeconomic policy in Africa.

René Foqué is Professor of Law at the University of Leuven and at the Erasmus University Rotterdam. He teaches philosophy of law, legal theory and European legal thinking. He is director of the Leuven Centre for the Study of the Foundations of Law, is regularly lecturing at the European Inter-University Centre for Human Rights and Democratisation in Venice and was lecturing at several European universities. He is a corresponding member of the Royal Dutch Academy of Sciences and is chairman of the jury of the International Spinoza Prize. He received the Diplôme d'Études Françaises from the Université de Lille, and his doctoral degree in law and his master's degree in philosophy from the University of Leuven. His many publications are in the field of legal and political philosophy, legal theory, European legal thinking, human rights and international relations.

Brigid Gavin is currently Research Fellow at the United Nations University – Comparative Regional Integration Studies (UNU-CRIS). Prior to that she was Lecturer in the economics of European Integration at the Europa Institute of the University of Basle, Switzerland. She has also been policy adviser for Greenpeace International on EU and international biosafety legislation. During the 1980s, she worked for the Permanent Delegation of the European Community to the International Organisations in Geneva specialising in multilateral trade negotiations. During the Uruguay Round of trade negotiations, which led to the establishment of the World Trade Organisation, she coordinated a series of seminars for trade negotiators at the Graduate Institute of International Studies, Geneva.

Andrew Hurrell is Director of the Centre for International Studies at Oxford University and a Fellow of Nuffield College. His research interests include theories of international relations, with particular reference to international law and institutions; theories of global governance; the history of thought on international relations and the history of international law; comparative regionalism; and the international relations of the Americas, with particular reference to Brazil. Publications include: co-editor with Louise Fawcett, *Regionalism in World Politics* (Oxford: Oxford University Press, 1995); co-editor with Ngaire Woods, *Inequality, Globalisation and*

World Politics (Oxford: Oxford University Press, 1999); co-editor with Rosemary Foot and John Gaddis, *Order and Justice in International Relations* (Oxford: Oxford University Press, 2003); co-author with Monica Hirst, *The United States and Brazil: A Long Road of Unmet Expectations* (New York: Routledge, 2004). He is currently completing *International Society and the Problem of World Order* to be published by Oxford University Press.

S.D. Muni is holder of the Appadorai Chair in International Politics and Area Studies at the School of International Studies, Jawaharlal Nehru University, New Delhi. He has 14 books and more than 60 research articles published. He was nominated to India's proposed National Security Advisory Board. His research interests include security and the foreign policies of Asia, with particular reference to South Asia.

Helen E.S. Nesadurai is Assistant Professor at the Institute of Defence and Strategic Studies, Nanyang Technological University, Singapore. She is also an External Associate of the Centre for the Study of Globalisation and Regionalisation (CSGR) at the University of Warwick, UK. Working within the field of international political economy, her current research focuses on how globalisation leads to new forms of regionalism in world politics, drawing on the Southeast Asian, East Asian and Asia-Pacific experiences. She has published on APEC, the ASEAN Free Trade Area (AFTA), institutional design and cooperation in ASEAN, Asian-Pacific approaches to regional governance, the Southeast Asian development model as well as the Malaysian political economy. Her book on *Globalisation, Domestic Politics and Regionalism: The ASEAN Free Trade Area was* published in 2003 by Routledge.

Robert A. Pastor is Vice-President of International Affairs, Professor of International Relations, and Director of a new Center for North American Studies at American University. From 1985 until September 2002, he was Professor at Emory University and from then until 1998, he was a Fellow at the Carter Center and the Founding Director of the Latin American and Caribbean Programme and the Democracy Programme. He served as National Security Advisor on Latin America (1977–81). Dr Pastor received his PhD in Political Science from Harvard University and is the author of 15 books, *including Toward a North American Community: Lessons from the Old World for the New* (Washington, DC: Institute for International Economics, 2001) and *Exiting the Whirlpool: U.S. Foreign Policy Toward Latin America and the Caribbean* (Boulder, CO: Westview, 2001).

Helena Lindholm Schulz is Associate Professor and Teacher at the Department of Peace and Development Research, Göteborg University. She is the author of *Reconstruction of Palestinian Nationalism*, published by Manchester University Press in 1999 and *The Palestinian Diaspora*, published by Routledge, 2003.

Michael Schulz is PhD and Teacher at the Department of Peace and Development Research, Göteborg University. He is co-editor of *Regionalisation in a Globalising World*, published by Zed Books in 2001.

Nikki Slocum is a Research Fellow at the United Nations University – Comparative Regional Integration Studies (UNU-CRIS). She has a PhD in psychology from Georgetown University. Her main research interests include peace and human security, the social-cultural aspects of regional integration and participatory and prospective methodologies. She has recently worked on teaching and facilitating 'Visioning' workshops, a method used to engage multiple stakeholders in designing shared visions and strategies to achieve them.

Fredrik Söderbaum is Associate Professor at the Department of Peace and Development Research (Padrigu) at Göteborg University and Associate Research Fellow at the United Nations University – Comparative Regional Integration Studies (UNU-CRIS). His main research interest is in international political economy, Africa and the regional phenomenon. Söderbaum's most recent books are *The Political Economy of Regionalism: The Case of Southern Africa* (Basingstoke: Palgrave Macmillan, 2004), *Theories of New Regionalism* (co-edited with Tim Shaw, Palgrave Macmillan, 2003), *The New Regionalism in Africa* (co-edited with Andrew Grant, Ashgate, 2003), and *Regionalism and Uneven Development in Southern Africa: The Case of the Maputo Development Corridor* (co-edited with Ian Taylor, Ashgate, 2003).

Elzbieta Stadtmüller is Professor of International Relations; Research Director of the Institute of International Studies and Head of European Studies Section at the University of Wroclaw, Poland. Main fields of present teaching and research activity are: political aspects of international relations focused on global problems and security, regional cooperation and governance, democratisation and democracy in international relations, foreign policy of the Central and Eastern European (CEE) countries. European integration, especially its role in processes of transformation in the CEE, Eastern enlargement, internal reforms from 1990s, Polish foreign policy towards NATO, the EU and neighbourhood. Publications in total – over 70, including 8 books, 7 edited books, 41 articles, 4 textbooks, and others. Last books: *Farewell Distrust? Enlargement of NATO and the EU and Polish-Russian Relations in the Security Context* (Wroclaw, 2003) (in Polish); *Dictionary of the EU* (ed. and co-author) (Wyd. Europa, Wroclaw 2003) (in Polish).

Jacques Steenbergen is a partner in the European Union practice group of the Brussels office of Allen & Overy LLP. He practises competition and European law. He teaches competition law at the University of Leuven, is a regular visiting professor at the University of Amsterdam and is chairman of the Board of Editors of the Belgian-Dutch law review *SEW*. He is an active member of various professional and scientific organisations. He has published extensively on European Community and economic law and international relations and lectures at seminars and universities in Europe, the United States and China. Jacques Steenbergen received his first degrees in law, philosophy and economics from the University of Antwerp (UFSIA), and his Masters and Doctoral degrees in law from the University of Leuven (KULeuven).

Tie Jun Zhang is Associate Research Professor and Deputy Director, Department of American Studies, Shanghai Institute, China. He received his PhD from the Department of Peace and Development Research, Göteborg University, Sweden. His areas of research lie in East Asian regionalism, Chinese foreign policies and Sino-US relations, and he has publications both in the West and in China. His recent publications include: *APEC and Open Regionalism* (Commercial Press of China, 2000), *Chinese Strategic Culture*, and *Self-Identity Construction of the Present China* (*Comparative Strategy*).

Index

Compiled by Sue Carlton